Best wishes
Ben Austin
Dec 1980

THE 40 YEAR CYCLE

Ben Austin

THE KILMARNOCK PRESS
South Pasadena, California
91030

The Kilmarnock Press
South Pasadena, California
91030

Printed in the United States of America by
The Kingsport Press, Inc., Kingsport, Tennessee

DEDICATED TO MY WIFE

PRISCILLA MOERDYKE AUSTIN

A graduate of Stanford and Smith, who,
after working with this manu-
script, has adopted
Vanderbilt as
her third
ALMA MATER

"Forty years ago, when I was an undergraduate at Oxford, voices were in the air there which haunt my memory still. Happy the man who in that susceptible season of youth hears such voices! They are a possession to him forever."*

Matthew Arnold

* Discourses in America, ed 1894. P. 138.

PROLOGUE

At brunch one Sunday at the Valley Hunt Club in Pasadena, California, Mrs. Corella Van Riper Carhartt told me that Father Hugh Robert Percy, quoted one of my Letters To The Editor in his sermon at The Church of the Angels, Episcopal church. I was curious to know which one was appropriate for use in a sermon so I called and asked. It was one that I had written several years ago and had almost completely forgotten. Upon re-reading it, however, I realized that it had pertinence to this book and I decided to include it as one of the frontispieces. Here it is:

>   *Just for the fun of it I will take issue with Max Morrison's fine article in Saturday's Star-News suggesting throwing away the useless keys of the past and he quotes the many authorities who say: "You can't go home again."*
>
>   *Physically I don't suppose you can, but I cringe when I hear a public figure state he is not interested in looking back. He is interested only in the future.*
>
>   *I suppose looking forward is associated with youth and therefore good. These are mere words though. How dull life would be if we could not look back.*
>
>   *Most present pleasures are based on past experience. We like good food because we have eaten good food before. Even when sex becomes commonplace, the memory of more exciting encounters can make them live again. In adversity a memory of better times provides an avenue of escape.*

The richness of life is not the future, or even the present, but the past. Fortunate is the man who never loses his vivid imagination; an instant recall of reveries.

When Browning wrote "Grow old along with me, the best is yet to be" I think he had in mind reaching the age when one can look back in pure joy on the good things that have happened to him during a lifetime. Memory strains out the bad and only the good remains. You can't do that with present pleasures.

What is life and experiences but feeding data into the computer of the mind and spirit? Without recall, both life and the computer are meaningless.

BEN RAGAN AUSTIN
South Pasadena

NOTE: Max Morrison, a famous minister and newspaper columnist on the west coast, is a younger brother of Ray Morrison, former football player and coach at Vanderbilt. Quarterback Morrison was for Vanderbilt in 1908 and 1909, what "The Gipper" was to Notre Dame, Ernie Nevers was to Stanford, or Albie Booth to Yale.

INTRODUCTION

How fortunate can a group of people be to have the opportunity to read about themselves through the eyes of history. Most history is written in retrospect, after the main subjects are dead. There is no way to challenge a statement or observation.

The good fortune of this book is that most of the people written about are still alive. They can react. There can be a give and take between the author and his subjects. What better way is there to get at truth!

A person can write to the author and say: "That is not the way it happened at all. What you didn't know was this or that." In this way we all become historians as well as actors on the scenes of history. We will both benefit, as well as future historians, from this dialogue.

Nashville, Tennessee is the general setting for this book, and in particular, the Vanderbilt University campus. The time frame is the beginning of the fall term in 1937 and it ends four hundred pages later with the graduation exercises in June 1940.

There are more radios in the United States today than there are people, but in 1940 the industry was not more than fifteen years away from the crystal sets that young boys experimented with. WSM in Nashville was one of the pioneers in radio and was awarded a clear-channel status.

There was no format of what would be sent over the airways so the people did what came naturally, they invited the country troubadours to perform. They were an instant success and have been going strong ever since. Uncle Dave Macon plunked his banjo and Roy Acuff played the fiddle and sang: "The Wabash Cannonball." The "Solemn Ole Judge," George Hay, did the announcing.

The "Grand Ole Opry," radio's first regularly scheduled program is almost as old as the medium itself. It started in the studios of WSM, November 28, 1925, moved to the Hillsboro Theatre, the Dixie Tabernacle, the War Memorial Building and eventually to the Ryman Auditorium, where it gained its greatest fame. A lot of the rustic charm of the "Satty Nite" program was lost when it moved to Opryland.

As somewhat of an outside observer of the Nashville scene I was always amused at the sophisticated set that tried for years to ignore the "Opry" out of existence, but it kept on growing until now the city itself is known all over the world as Music City U.S.A.

It has been said that most institutions are the lengthening shadow of one man. I am not sure that can be said of the growth of country music in Nashville, but if I were called on to pick a candidate for the title of Father I think I would go with the late C. A. Craig, who as a state insurance inspector, persuaded Messrs. Tyne, Fort, Clements and Wills to join him in buying the National Life and Accident Insurance Company. Mr. Craig may not have even liked country music, but he knew a good thing when he saw it and shepherded its development as an adjunct to his insurance business.

Vanderbilt University life was gay and carefree just before the United States became involved in World War II. The coeds wore loafers, bobby sox and skirts, almost as if they were a uniform, and the men wore slacks and sweaters, with or without sports letters emblazoned across the front. It was an era of candid cameras and convertibles on campus during the week and parties and football games on the weekend.

On the occasion of fraternity and sorority dances a transformation took place. The men appeared in formal suits or tuxedoes and the ladies in long flowing evening gowns. Big name bands played for the Proms and each coed had her own spot on the gym floor, where she ruled supreme. Long lines of stags awaited their turn to break on the good dancers. If a lady's escort danced with his date more than half a dozen times during an evening, he was lucky. There were about four men to every coed. The dances varied from swing and jitterbug to the slow dreamy waltzes.

Francis Craig, who wrote "Near You" and Vanderbilt's famous fight song "Dynamite," was a widely known orchestra leader who preferred to remain in one place, rather than to travel, so Vanderbilt, the Nashville country clubs and the Hermitage Hotel Grill had a built-in big time orchestra.

Minor league baseball was still a major attraction and Larry Gilbert's

"Volunteers" were drawing sizeable crowds to the old Sulphur Dell ball field. Fred Russell was reporting sports for the Nashville Banner and Raymond Johnson for the Tennessean. Both were contributing periodically to the national magazines.

The trend to decentralize the public school system, and to build in the suburbs had not gotten underway. Hume-Fogg High School, which looked like a medieval castle, located in the center of the city, at Eighth and Broad, drew over two thousand students. It was the end of an era and many of the teachers were elderly and wise. They had acquired a lifetime of rich and varied experiences and were one of the best conglomeration of high school teachers ever assembled under one roof. There was Miss Mary Louise Goodwin, who was acclaimed as great, even by her fellow teachers in the English department, and the brilliant Miss Ella Haiman; "Pop" Stetson and Miss Pope in Latin. Miss Dortch taught American History as an eyewitness reporter on many historical events. Mrs. Inez Bassett Alder gave many aspirants to theatre, such as Dinah Shore and Delbert Mann, their first taste of acting.

The days of our youth are always glorious, but I suspect that the late thirties will have a special significance in American history. It was in July 1975 that I took a cross-country train trip from Toronto to Vancouver, Canada. For reading material I brought several diaries, which I had written, but had not seen in thirty five years. I was utterly fascinated. They read like a novel. I resolved to publish them.

When I returned to my home in Atlanta, Georgia I made arrangements for Emory University to Xerox the diaries. Elizabeth Miller, Dale Hadley and Sherry Rampton, of the University of Southern California, typed the manuscripts. Eighty year old patriarch of the publishing industry, Gervaze Dawes, aided by Rich Jenkins of the Pasadena Star-News, took on the monumental task of proofreading. This was after my wife Priscilla Austin did the editing.

There will be items I wish I had included, and others I wish I had left out. Like every author, I'll cry bitter tears over the mistakes that slip through and are discovered too late for corrections, but there is one thing I'll never regret and that is doing this book. What a marvelous experience writing about people of a bygone era, most of whom have survived the tempestuous, last half century and have arrived, with me, at a point in life when we can look back in pure joy.

One of the most poignant statements that I encountered during the process of writing and publishing this book came, not from one but, from several secretaries. After encountering the marvelous simplicity of charting a life, said this: "Why I could have done this! Why didn't I?"

BEN AUSTIN

PREFACE

VOLUME II

Ben Austin enjoyed the best of two worlds in his early literary training. He revelled in a great romantic presentation of literature; the uncritical complete surrender to the lyrical beauty of the writings of an Edgar Allan Poe, or an Alfred Lord Tennyson, as presented by the late great professor of English Literature, Dr. Edwin Mims of Vanderbilt, while studying and associating with the likes of Randall Jarrell, proteges of, the dean of American poetry critics, John Crowe Ransom.

Later he was to study Creative Writing under such luminaries of the literary world as Helen Hull, Martha Foley, Jacques Barzun and Donald Clark of Columbia University in New York. It was at Vanderbilt, however, and even before that, at Hume-Fogg High School, which had a collection of teachers in the late thirties, which were just before retiring, and perhaps not surpassed anywhere, that his early writing interests were shaped. The fact that his college trained mother quoted poetry to him while cooking breakfast on a wood stove, on cold mornings, prepared his mind for the reception of learning from the great teachers he was to encounter in the above mentioned institutions.

George Herbert Palmer once said: "Never pass up an opportunity to express yourself in writing." Ben Austin applied this wisdom, not only to writing, but to public speaking. To prevent being embarrassed, in speaking to large student bodies, while participating extensively in extra-curricular activities, he had to learn to write, and to write well.

This led to keeping a diary, from the day he entered Vanderbilt University in 1935, and has extended throughout his life.

Austin had no mind for mathematics and therefore enrolled in Engineering at Vanderbilt, in order to strengthen this side of his character and personality. He spent the most miserable year of his life trying to accomodate to a swift pace of five hours per week of higher mathematics in the Engineering school. One of his professors, appreciating the nature of his struggle, mercifully said to him one day: "Austin, you don't have to be an Engineer. Get the heck out of this torment and get into something closer to your nature."

The next year was as if a veil had been lifted. He transferred to the academic school and was off and running. His entire outlook changed. He started doing again the things he liked and became a joy to himself and to his professors.

This change forced him to spend an extra year at the University, but during his last year, when the academic pressure was off, he experienced for the first time, a university life in its most idealistic form, in the tradition of Oxford and Cambridge.

Bill Jordan, possessing perhaps one of the truly great minds of his generation, became a constant challenger in intellectual discussions. William Simpson, a truly authentic scholar; Partee Fleming, a great hulk of a man, who could win national wrestling championships, but at the same time could hold his own in the arena of highest scholarship and common sense, were a few contemporaries, who shook the campus as no other group since the Agrarians, John Crowe Ransom, Allen Tate, Donald Davidson, Jesse Wills, Merrill Moore, Robert Penn Warren, Walter Clyde Curry, Myron Hirsch and others did a few years earlier.

Austin enrolled in the Engineering school of Vanderbilt University September 20, 1935. The first three years will be covered by Volume I, which will be published subsequently. The war years will be covered by Volume III and IV. We pick up the story of Volume II July 12, 1937, beginning his junior year.

FALL
1937

Tuesday, July 12, 1937 Lucia Bellinger was at that stage of life when a pretty girl is at her prettiest. There is a time, I suppose, in the life of every really pretty girl when beauty reaches a peak; for a fleeting instant the delicate blending of the color of her skin and eyes are breathtakingly beautiful. There is perhaps no sight on earth so devastating, so completely captivating, as that one instant when the young girl blossoms into womanhood and for a moment surpasses all other beauty that nature has created.

To view such spectacular beauty at any age is challenging, but to the youth of the opposite sex, who himself is just awakening to the glories of spring, the compulsion is overwhelming. With just a suggestion of perfume in the windblown golden hair and a shy quisical smile, nothing else in all the world is so enticing.

But add to that the warm, balmy atmosphere of a summer evening on Rabun Lake, high in the hills of north Georgia and a consistent picture begins to emerge. Persimmon Point juts out into the lake, surrounded by water on three sides. The grassy lawn leads to the water's edge and the only sound, other than the croak of night creatures, is the lapping of the water against the shore, and the sound of the motors as an occasional Criscraft thunders by.

It is the year 1937 and the big bands are sounding on car radios throughout the land. Deep throated vocalists are belting out "He used to like waltzes, so please don't play a waltz . . . Music Maestro, Please "

The moon is full and her mother and sister are in Atlanta and will not return until late. I had borrowed my brother's car and had slipped away from the boy's camp nearby to fill the date.

In order to listen to the radio and still be outside we sat in the car, parked in the driveway near the garage. I don't know why it is but a car radio always sounds better than any other. Guy Lombardo swings out with the "sweetest music this side of heaven," from the Roosevelt Grill in New York, Don Ricardo comes in from Santa Catalina in California and the strains of Jan Garber's violins come in from everywhere.

As I held her hand and sat close I noticed that the pupils in her eyes seemed large. I asked her to shut her eyes and then wait a few minutes before opening them, so I could see if there was any change while they were closed. I took advantage of her and planted a tender kiss upon her lips. She did not draw away rapidly, but sat peacefully for a few moments and then said: "You should not have done that. What will you think of me tomorrow?"

Hal Kemp, by this time, had finished his program and with the strains of "How I miss you when the summer is gone" fading into a commercial message, we got out of the car, walked down to the edge of the water, sat down on the lawn and watched the moon shine across the shimmering water.

This was our last date before returning to school in the fall. She would go to her winter home in Atlanta and finish her last year in high school and I would return for my junior year at Vanderbilt.

Wednesday, September 1, 1937 As I begin my junior year at Vanderbilt, my thoughts have travelled back to the summer of 1931, when, as a 13 year old, I first came to Nashville. I felt grown-up and wanted a summer job. My first job in Nashville was vending peanuts at the Vols baseball games. My mother's sister, Aunt Nell, with whom I was staying, came to a game one evening and observed the nature of the work, and the crowd with whom I was associated, and advised that summer school would be a more constructive activity. The next day I was enrolled in Clemmons Junior High School. It was fun, and when the autumn leaves began to turn I asked if I could stay on and attend high school in Nashville. It was just as well, because it was the depths of the depression and schools in Alabama did not have enough money to keep open a full year. My father was the only dentist in a small town, Stevenson, Alabama, and even though patients came from hundreds of miles up and down the Southern and N., C., & St. L. railroad tracks, to get good dental work, at small town prices, it was not easy to feed, clothe and educate a young family of five boys and two girls. Dad was an excellent dentist. In fact, he won the Founder's Medal for technical excellence when he graduated from the Vanderbilt Dental School in 1908. My mother was attending Peabody College, at the same time, and it was in his dental chair that they met. It was her beautiful teeth that first attracted the attention of my father. When my father first set up practice, his price for pulling a tooth was $1.00. If a whole mouthful of teeth had to be pulled he would give a discount; about two dollars for every three teeth. Thirty five years later his prices were approximately the same.

It was quite an adjustment for an adolescent boy, from a small town, with a population of less than 700, to be thrown into a large high school with more than two thousand enrollment. I did not know a soul at Hume-Fogg. Nashville is a "clannish" town; family means a great deal. I attended many of the prep school fraternity and sorority dances, often, at first, without formal invitations, and soon got to know a few people. Hume-Fogg was tough academically and I had a hard time keeping up with a much faster pace of study than I had been accustomed to. As soon as I got a little breathing room, however, I played varsity football, was a cadet Captain, commanding a "rookie" company in R.O.T.C., founded the school newspaper, the Fogg Horn, and when I was elected President of the Student Council, the largest city newspaper, The Nashville Tennessean carried a three column picture on the front page, proclaiming that I, and my Vice President and Secretary, were the "student bosses" at Hume-Fogg. Nevertheless, my good friend and supporter, Mr. C. T. Kirkpatrick, the principal, refused to let my name be considered for the Civitan Medal, in the class of 1935, because he was afraid I wouldn't graduate. It was nip and tuck to the very end. The fact that Miss Handly, my French teacher, and Mrs. Claire Graham, the teacher-sponsor for the Fogg Horn, did not have heart failure over my close call, is a tribute to their inner strength. They really suffered with me.

Thursday, September 2, 1937 I once wrote a story about my football exploits at Hume-Fogg. Here it is:

A FOOTBALL ENCOUNTER

I wasn't big enough to play right tackle on a large high school's football team, but I couldn't run fast enough to play in the backfield, so I had no choice. I could make up for lack of size much easier than I could bridge the gap of speed required for a back.

I was determined to make the team, however, and I figured I'd have to outsmart the opposition in order to have a chance. The regulars on Hume-Fogg's team had been going out for football for a couple of years and were known to the coaches. I had not started out until my senior year and was not even issued a complete uniform during the first week or so of practice. Vanderbilt University was in the same city, Nashville, Tennessee, and in those days did not have such a bad team. Dan McGugin, "Hurry Up" Fielding Yost's brother-in-law, who had starred at guard on the famous "point-a-minute" Michigan teams of 1901–02, and was assistant coach there, brought big time football to the South, and Vanderbilt stacked up with the best teams in the nation. When Dudley Stadium was dedicated in 1922, the Commodores' tied mighty Michigan, which went on to win the Big 10 championship. In the late '20's and '30's, they were still a team to be contended with nationally.

In 1934, in order to pick up some pointers that might help me make the Hume-Fogg team, I went to several Vanderbilt games. I noticed on kickoffs, the linemen dropped back and formed a wedge close to the ball carrier. The next time I lined up with the receiving team for a kickoff, I dropped back and attempted to block. We had not been taught this and our "loudmouthed" coach stopped the play and yelled: "Somebody's yeller!"

I knew who he was talking about, and it made me furious. "I'll show that S.O.B. whose yellow!" I declared to myself. On every play from that moment forward, just before the snap of the ball, I would remind myself of what the coach had said and it would make me mad all over again.

Soon I had worked up to the second team, and on a particularly pleasing afternoon, our first team ran a series of sweeps to the weak side of the line, where I was playing defensive right tackle. On the first play from scrimmage, I shifted far out towards the end, and their offensive end and tackle, being high school players too, didn't know whether to follow me out, or to stay put. They followed me just enough to leave a hole in the middle of the line. When the ball was snapped, I jumped back to my normal position, and tackled the ball carrier for a five yard loss.

On the next play I "submarined" and hit the ball carrier for another loss. On the third play I actually jumped over the low-squatting lineman and tackled the ball carrier for another loss. By this time the "loud-mouthed" coach was beside himself. His varsity couldn't get off any offensive plays, so again he stopped play and shouted: "If someone could take out that right tackle, we could make a thousand yards."

I had my revenge, but the making-myself-mad technique had worked so well that I kept it up all season, even in the games, after I had made the first team.

One day in late October, we were playing Knoxville Central. We played both ways in those days and every time we had the ball, our right guard would pull out and block, or run interference, and I would have to fill the hole that he left. The coach had taught us to run our heads into the hole. I did it for the entire first half and my head felt like it had been in a meat grinder. The opposing left guard would charge through the hole on each play, and I would ram my head into his "gut," and together we rolled into our backfield. He didn't get many tackles that afternoon, but he sure gave me a working over.

I remember crying to our coach at halftime: "I don't know who that left guard is, but he is a 'ringer' if I ever saw one."

My knees had hit the hard, cold ground so many times they were like quick-flesh. My head was throbbing from the continual pounding it was taking from the incredibly fast charging guard. I was praying for the game to be over.

In a last ditch desperation move, remembering the deceptive tactics I had used in practice, I decided to make one final all-out effort. I watched for a lineup that might indicate a sweep to the left side. I tipped off my right defensive half back that I was going to stunt and I moved to the outside, then jumped back, and found myself in the enviable position of being able to hit their ball carrier for a five yard loss. I spread my arms and started in for the kill. About that time something hit me from the left and my feet went straight up in the air. The ball carrier had to be tackled by my back up half back, but at least his interference blocker was gone and he was vulnerable to being tackled.

On the next play I "submarined" and rose up with the ball carrier practically in my arms. This time something like a freight train rolled over me.

Still not willing to give up, I was determined to try again. This time I jumped into the air, and when I came down, I was nearly off the playing field. I had sailed so far from the block, that their left guard had put on me, that my own team mates, after the game, crowded around to find out how I happened to sail through the air so gracefully on that particular play.

Somewhere the bands may be playing, and somewhere hearts may be light and gay, but I am sure the Mighty Casey, and nobody else in Mudville, or Nashville, or anywhere else, was more bruised or sadder than I was the day I played opposite Bob Suffridge, who later was named three time all-American at the University of Tennessee, and honored more recently, by being named to the All-Time team at guard. He deserved 'em all!

Friday, September 3, 1937 At Vanderbilt things were different, for awhile anyway. I had done well in extra-curricular activities at Hume-Fogg, but my grades were nothing to brag about. Maybe if I did nothing but study, things would be different. I did just that for a year. But another obstacle reared it's ugly head; Mathematics. My early teachers thought I was smart enough to skip the fifth grade, so they sent me directly from the fourth to the sixth. Unfortunately it is in the fifth grade that you learn about fractions and decimal points. I arrived at the sixth grade not even knowing the multiplication tables. I got behind and never caught up. I thought by taking Engineering at Vanderbilt, I could strengthen this obvious weakness in my educational background. The fast pace of Engineering math compounded the problem and added to the hopelessness. It is a tribute to my inner strength and stubborn character that I survived a year with Dean Lewis, Walter Graham, Albert Hutchinson, Mr. Coolidge and Mr. Castleman. They were all kindly and considerate, but I simply could not "cut the mustard."

Saturday, September 4, 1937 In the fall of 1936 the sun came from behind the clouds and I emerged into it's sunlight. A new day dawned. I transferred to the academic school and instead of phrases like "sine and cosine," which meant absolutely nothing to me, I entered the world in which a poet wrote: "A thing of beauty is a joy forever." That I could understand and appreciate. I even knew why it was better than the way he first wrote it. "A thing of beauty is a lasting joy." I could feel it and sense the improvement. I started working on the college newspaper staff and even began to notice girls again. It was like becoming alive after a siege in purgatory. At no time in life is living more interesting than college days.

Sunday, September 5, 1937 I read a good article in The Saturday Evening Post, by Carey Ford, entitled: "After They Have Seen Paree." Clarence K. "Flip" Timberlake has invited me to Decatur, Alabama on the 11th for the German Club dance. Probably I can't go, but I enjoyed seeing Ozzie Nelson and Harriet Hilliard at that dance a few years ago. I have interviewed three families interested in swapping my board for free rent of my dad's property at 912 Villa Place. This property is what is left from his $25,000.00 plunge into Florida real estate during the "boom" of 1925. As I approach the opening days of school, I keep thinking what a romantic time of life this is. The mere mention of student life on the left bank of Paris, for example, or the beer cellars of Heidelberg, set off flights of fancy, and yet there is no time filled with more stresses. The frantic rush to do everything, and to get everything done, is maddening. Lack of sleep, lack of money and routine uncertainty take their toll. College life is perhaps best in reverie. I went up to the Albemarle apartments and spent the afternoon with the janitor, Howell Delk, in his basement apartment. Over the years tenants have moved and have given him the excessive books from their personal libraries. He now has a rather extensive library of his own. I enjoy browsing

through it. Ran across one poem that I particularly liked. It is called
"The Pleasures of the Student." I believe it was written by a Mr. Jamison.
It starts out:

> "And wherefore does the student trim his lamp
> And watch his lonely taper, when the stars
> Are holding high festival in the heavens
> And worshiping around the midnight throne?
>
> And wherefore does he spend so patiently
> In deep and voiceless thought,
> The blooming hours of youth and joyance
> While the blood is warm
> And the heart full of boyance and fire,
> He has his pleasure.

Miriam McGaw's picture was on the front page of the Society Section
of the Nashville Tennessean this morning. There were other pictures
inside. It will be interesting to see if she can continue getting this kind
of publicity and still keep her modesty and charm.

Monday, September 6, 1937 I don't suppose Brother Singleton, whom
I lived with this past year, swapping board for rent of the house, is
much of a preacher or else he would have a church of his own, but at
least, if he uses the title "Reverend" he ought to avoid pettiness in
meeting ordinary obligations. Since he collects laundry and dry cleaning
as a source of income, we had an agreement for him to do the equivalent
of one suit per week for me as a part of our rental contract. Along
towards the end, he let the suits pile up at the cleaners. Over a period
of weeks the count would become uncertain and he could demand extra
money. I hate quibbling over a few dollars, but on the other hand I
hate to be "taken to the cleaners" so to speak, especially by a man of
the cloth. I had to restrain myself to keep from punching him in the
nose. Uncle Walt settled it by paying him off. Saw Miriam for the first
time in a couple of months. She has gained a little weight. I was rather
surprised to hear her talk of matrimony. Said she would get married
before finishing school if the right person comes along. Many of our
mutual friends are married. Guess that influences her thinking. She is
probably also influenced by the fact that her brother Bob and Libby
Early have recently married. In fact they were at the McGaws getting
their things together when I was there. In my class with Dr. Mims, in
January of this year, I remember his saying: "The greatest good that
can come from an English course is to have, at the tip of your tongue,
the wisest and most expressive thoughts that man has ever uttered." I

have already found use for such. In my love life, as it relates to Miriam, for instance, what about George Wither's lines:

> "Shall I, wasting in despair
> Die because a woman's fair
> Or make pale my cheeks with care,
> 'Cause anothers rosy are?
> Be she fairer than the day,
> Or the flowery meads of May;
> If she be not so to me,
> What care I how fair she be."

Tuesday, September 7, 1937 I was intrigued by the movie "Lost Horizon" which I saw at Loews' theatre tonight. It was more philosophical than most movies; a dream of Utopia. Absence of struggle was the keynote. If two men disagreed over a woman, it was courteous for one man to leave her for the other fellow. If he loved her so much he could not give her up, then it was courteous for the other fellow to give her up to him. The place was called "Shangri La." Brother Henry D. and I did a little painting on the Villa Place house this afternoon.

Wednesday, September 8, 1937 Cousin Katherine Anderson, who works with Dr. Ernest Goodpasture in producing serum from eggs, instead of live cows, returned from Louisville tonight with interesting stories about the convention she had attended. Met Tom Short's beautiful sister, Harriet, tonight. She is transferring to Vanderbilt as a junior.

Thursday, September 9, 1937 George Henry "Boots" Tyne was telling me today that his family owns 50,000 acres of land between Nashville and Stevenson. It is the mountainous area near Tullahoma. With that much land, no matter how bad it is, one could create an empire. It is interesting to speculate what the use of the land will be fifty or a hundred years from now. Fred Hume, the Deke alumnus from St. Louis, must have learned that the dream of almost every newspaper man to own and run his own little newspaper, is not the proper stuff of which dreams should be made. He has sold out after a year. "Ma" Clapp is going to be the Deke house mother again this year. Jim Browning, nephew of Tennessee's governor, Gordon Browning, and Charley Majors, were working at the house today getting it ready for "Rush Week."

Friday, September 10, 1937 Went to the Knickerbocker theatre today to see "The Road Back." It was a picture showing how the German soldiers were treated on their return from World War I. The officer's shoulder straps were snatched off by the mobs. Even though Uncle Walton was not going to use his car tonight, he would not let me have it for my date with Miriam. I had to get a U-Drive-It. Miriam and I talked politics for an hour and then we drove out to Hettie Rays night club. Quite a few of the younger set were there: Opie Craig, Betty Lou Vosburg, Paul Clements, Ed Harris and Billy Harper. We danced one or two times and then went home and talked in front of her house for an hour or so. She told me many interesting things. She made a very frank confession. Said that the reason she did not give me certain dates last year was that she just didn't want to have them with me. Said that she dreaded our dates. "Everyone I talked with said you are a nice boy, but somehow I did not like you. No, I had nothing against you. After our last date last Thursday night when we drove a long way down the Memphis highway—I don't know why—but I changed my mind about you." She says that now she likes me and that date did it. I hope she means it. She also told me that I should go on in the invention work. She thinks more of it than she does newspaper work. She is one of the very, very few who thinks that way. Most people are skeptical.

Saturday, September 11, 1937 Went over to the fraternity house and helped the boys paint one of the halls. Mrs. Miles called me tonight and said someone broke into the Villa house and took two faucets off the wall, two paint brushes and a gallon of white paint. George Harmon and I dated Norma Hammond and Elizabeth Carr tonight. We went to Hettie Rays and danced. Don Rust and I slept at the Villa house tonight. We expected the burglars back. They did not come.

Sunday, September 12, 1937 Thought of one other thing McGaw said the other night. In approving my work on inventions she made one reservation, "no war materials." Very typical of a woman. When I told her about my plan to buy Mr. Bender's watchmaking tools she jokingly said: "Now Ben, we'll have to start saving our nickels because we must have those tools." My sister, Mary Wallace, came from Stevenson this afternoon. She is going to sign up for Ward-Belmont tomorrow. I wrote Dad asking for a suit today.

Monday, September 13, 1937 Went over to the fraternity house and helped Jim Browning and Bob Neathery paint. We later went to Loews theatre to see "Dead End."

Tuesday, September 14, 1937 Senator Copeland, who is running for Mayor of New York, has brought up the issue of Senator Hugo Black's appointment to the Supreme Court. At one time in Alabama, Black was a member of the Ku Klux Klan. It has stirred up a furor. I guess the idea is to match one group of people's prejudices against another's, and thereby gain an advantage of the ones you happen to favor. Back in the twenties it was just as necessary for a Democrat in Alabama to belong to the Klan as it was for one in New York to be a part of Tammany Hall.

Wednesday, September 15, 1937 Read some of Uncle Walton's papers that he wrote when he was a freshman at the University of Tennessee some thirty five years ago. The out of town boys are coming in to the fraternity house. After lunch we discussed the prospective pledges that we have dates with tomorrow. Talked to Miriam McGaw on the phone. The Tri Deltas finish their rushing today. She told me my ears ought to be burning because she and Frances Scruggs talked about me all morning. Frances told her there is absolutely no reason why I should not edit the campus newspaper, the Hustler, next year.

Thursday, September 16, 1937 Rushed all day. Met a fine group of fellows. Joe Davis, National Junior tennis Champion, Lucien Lentz, Pat Sturman, from Mt. Carmel, Illinois, Charles Heffron and many others.

Friday, September 17, 1937 I was never so surprised as I was today when I learned that Jimmie Winchester, of Memphis, was Regimental Commander at Culver Military Academy year before last. Granville Sherman told us that he was perhaps the best commander that ever attended the academy. His distinguished bearing and good nature made the boys look up to him as if he were a god. Had a long session with Delbert Mann. We talked about everything but fraternity. Delbert was the third editor of the Fogg Horn at Hume-Fogg. I was the first editor. Had a long talk with Hayes Noel and he advised that I go out for football next year. If I were a little larger I would do it. Charles Majors, rush chairman, made a special comment on the good rushing Jim Tuck and I had done. Bill Shumaker and Bill Steele are the two boys that I think are doing the most outstanding rush work.

Saturday, September 18, 1937 Cousin Osgood Anderson came in from the Yale Forestry School this morning. Uncle Osgood, Aunt Ethel and Kenneth came up here to meet him. He has a little over a week off. Jimmy Winchester came into town from Memphis. Bill Potts, from Abington, Virginia and Elliott Trimble from Mississippi also came. Last night I was feeling pretty good about our rushing prospects, but tonight I am a little down. James Mason, brother of Heywood, has already promised Phi Delta Theta even before we have our first date with him.

Sunday, September 19, 1937 Bill Hume came back to school this morning. Lorraine Matthews, Jimmy Winchester's girl, did lots of good rushing for us today. She is a very sweet girl. I fixed the Zipper on Jimmy's sweater and he was very proud of it. The little Mullens boy, who was a rushee at the house, wanted to buy the sweater and said that if I ever had stock to sell in my Zipper company to come to see him. William Cornelius and Richard Pickens said they were going Phi Delta Theta and that cast a spell because they were really wanted by our boys. The Phis seem to be going us one better at every turn. They got out a larger newspaper last July. They buy a front page in the Commodore, our college annual. Of course, they have a nice goal to work towards.

They, for the past five years, have won the national cup for being the most outstanding chapter in the fraternity. If we expect to stay ahead of them we must work out a plan for doing it and then carry out our plan. Saw the girls come in from freshman orientation camp this afternoon. A girl by the name of Ann, from Shelbyville, sent word to me that she has heard such nice things that she wants to meet me. She has probably talked with the girl from there who went with Tom Happel last year. I hope Miriam heard about her wanting to meet me. The brothers around the house like to talk about my invention and stock company to the freshmen. I had to stand up and be recognized at the dinner table tonight. Harold "Skinny" Huggins came over and did some good rushing today. Talked to Bob McAdam's father. I think he was a Beta Theta Pi.

Monday, September 20, 1937 The freshmen matriculated today. Delbert Mann decided to pledge Kappa Alpha. Charles Heffron brought his father around and we introduced him to all the brothers. He told me about seeing my brother Anderson just before he left Sweetwater, Tennessee. Anderson was sitting on the front porch at Tennessee Military Institute, where he is principal of the junior school, entertaining the kids. I liked Dr. Heffron. He seemed to enjoy his visit with us. Walter King and Andrew Sweat, both good boys, went Deke tonight. All of the four horsemen went Deke except Willie Cornelius and he went Phi. We pledged Richard Pickens, Clark Hutton, and Bobby Stamps. They were the local boys we were concentrating on and we were afraid they were all going Phi. When three out of four went Deke the lid blew off. Robert "Ma" Clapp deserves the credit. He knew all of them well because he taught them in high school. He took them to the fair tonight. The gloom of last night turned to jubilation today. We pledged fourteen. We have the best class on the campus, barring none. We should go places during the next few years.

Tuesday, September 21, 1937 A. T. Levine desperately wanted to pledge Joel Stephens for the A.T.O's but I got him. I enjoyed meeting and talking with his father, who is president of Stephens Manufacturing Company in Nashville. I also pledged Charles Heffron, who is a friend of my brother at T. M. I. Anderson called long distance tonight and asked about my finances. He said he would send $100.00 within the next few days. At the Hustler meeting tonight I was assigned a regular feature about campus personalities. Later, I went to the home of Dr. Chris McClure to celebrate the successful pledging of 16 new boys for D. K. E. The matriculation dance is also tonight and I plan to attend.

Wednesday, September 22, 1937 Dr. Mims introduced the new chancellor, Dr. Oliver Cromwell Carmichael, to the student body in chapel this morning. Dr. Carmichael is an impressive looking man and is a good public speaker. He has a particular squint in his eyes and appears to be looking right through you. He draws out his words in a very effective oratorical manner. I suspect he will make a good chancellor, but he has some big shoes to fill. Dr. Kirkland held the reins 44 years and few men have been so well endowed with the qualities of leadership necessary for running an institution of higher learning. Before the chancellor spoke, Charles Majors and I announced the possibilities open to freshmen in working with student publications. A number of freshmen signed up immediately. I had a talk with Coach Miles about working in the gym, and with Miss Sarah Thomas about an N. Y. A. job. Sarah is a friend of my good friend Louise Dunlop.

Thursday, September 23, 1937 I have never been as sleepy as I was this morning. Went up to see Dr. Mims. He told me he received my letter. I will have English 3 under him this year and Dr. Walter Clyde Curry will take the class during the last two terms. I have Dr. J. S. Morrel in Trigonometry. Went to the Benson Printing Company with James Souby today to proof read the Hustler. I bought a nice dark suit, with gray stripes, at Joe Frank's clothing store. A Mr. Pinkleton waited on me. Ernest Frank, son of Joe Frank, spoke to me as I went out the door and asked me if my Dad were not real tall and practiced dentistry in Nashville over thirty years ago. I told him yes and that I had heard Dad speak of his father many times. The suit cost $40.00, but it is a fine suit and will last me two or three years.

Friday, September 24, 1937 Believe I am going to enjoy Dr. Daniel in Physics, and Dr. Manchester in Spanish. The Spanish is especially interesting under Manchester. Two carloads of us went to town this afternoon to see a movie. Elliott Trimble, Marion Long and I went to see "Good Earth." It was just like the book.

Saturday, September 25, 1937 Landers Seviere came up this afternoon for the game. We opened with Kentucky. It started to rain just before the game and continued to pour all evening. Not many of the ten or twelve thousand people left the game. Bert Marshall, our little quarterback, was sensational. Everything the writers have said is true. I only hope we don't get off to too fast a start and then "run out of gas" when we go against a strong Conference team. Carl Hinkle played his usual good game. Took Miriam to the gym dance tonight. Hated to wear my new suit in the rain but wanted Miriam to see it. She was very popular as usual and I did not get to dance with her very much. I noticed that Bert Marshall, our football hero, danced with her quite a bit. I made a date with her for the 15th, but may want to change it. Both Cousins, Osgood and Kenneth, spent the night with me.

Sunday, September 26, 1937 Got up at 1:00 o'clock today and went to the Hustler office and was signed up for Features. Bill Hall and I dropped by the house and saw Landers Seviere, and his friend, leave for Birmingham. Our freshmen attended the Alpha Omega Pi open house this evening.

Monday, September 27, 1937 Heard this morning that Landers Seviere and Skeets Noel had a wreck going home and were bruised up quite a bit. I don't think Landers was critically hurt. About the biggest thing I have done today is to change my mind somewhat about Mr. Henry Hart. I have previously thought of him as a kind of "stuffed shirt," dedicated to far leftist causes. I had a long talk with him this evening and found out he is not such a bad guy after all. Read an article in the Reader's Digest that a professor had suggested that it would be less strain on the eyes if, in reading, one read to the end of one line and read backwards on the next. I have an idea for a line-o-type machine that will write alternate lines from right to left, just reverse the chute as the letters fall. Had our first "rat court" tonight. I welcomed Joel Stephens into the chapter with a blow of the paddle and someone else welcomed Bobby Stamps.

Tuesday, September 28, 1937 I did not get the N. Y. A. job but got one much better. I am to work at the gym from 4 to 5 P.M. each day and make .40¢ per hour. It may lead to a better job with Coach Miles. Noticed that Ellen Bowers, who lives up near Uncle Walton's Albemarle apartment house, is in my history class.

Wednesday, September 29, 1937 Byron "Red" Anglin was appointed Secretary of the Student Union today. I am almost as happy about it as he. I interviewed Carl Hinkle today and wrote the first installment of his life history for the Hustler. It will appear in the Hustler Friday, I hope. I am liking Spanish under Dr. Manchester more and more. This morning Miriam talked as if our date for Friday the 22nd was off because she had promised to go to the first Deke dance with Elliott Trimble. I worked at the gym for the first time today. Taught a few wrestling holds to the boys who were there. Read in Will Grimsley's column that Hal White had his nose straightened. Grimsley was once editor of the Tatler at Hume-Fogg. His younger brother Elrod was editor at a later time. I started the Fogg Horn a year after the Tatler folded. They never had more than a few hundred subscriptions. We started the Fogg Horn with nearly 3,000 because of a special promotion.

I made a deal with the teachers in the session rooms that if they would guarantee 50 percent participation in their rooms I would see that every student got a paper. I knew that teacher support was essential and that they would give this support if they were financially liable. By having such large volume we could reduce the price of the paper from three cents to one. Selecting the name "Fogg Horn" was a particularly happy experience because it struck people immediately that it was a particularly apt name and it helped to win the widespread support that it enjoyed. Early one rainy, foggy morning I was sitting in the back of Miss Katherine Allen's session room, thinking about the newspaper I was trying to start, rather than my studies, when I heard the low, wailing moan of a fog horn, on the Cumberland river, several blocks east of the school. "That must be a fog horn," I said to myself, "Fog horn . . . fog horn . . . hey, that is the name I have been looking for."

Thursday, September 30, 1937 Frances Scruggs told me today she had talked to Mr. Hill Turner, Alumni Secretary, about doing some writing for the "Alumnus" magazine; no, not for pay, but for the experience. Frances is really my buddy. Had fun in History class. Rush Dozier's dumb remarks were the occasion. Wrestled Jim Ferguson, of South Pittsburg, Tenn. this afternoon and Mickey Carmichael, the Chancellor's son. Dr. Mims gave a very inspiring lecture this morning on the great literary men of New England; centering around Boston. He told the story that when Handel, was watching a rehearsal of his Messiah from the back of the hall in London he shouted "Louder, louder . . ." After about the third shout the choirmaster turned around and said: "Sir, when you wrote that you were hearing the angels sing. We can't compete with them."

Friday, October 1, 1937 Heard an historically important speech on the radio tonight. The Honorable Hugo L. Black, former Senator from Alabama and recently appointed to the Supreme Court by President Roosevelt, answered charges that he was a member of the Ku Klux Klan years ago; he resigned and has never renewed his membership. Went to the Nashville Banner office today and talked to Rousseau Duncan, City Editor, about a job with the Banner. Walter Parks also wants the job but Rousseau is skeptical about his contacts. Had a talk with Hill Turner, Alumni Secretary about doing some writing for the "Alumnus" magazine. My mind does not function well in dealing with the uninteresting details of mathematics, but when I encounter great thoughts and beautifully expressed ideas in Literature, it springs alive and suddenly the world is a wonderful place in which to live. Dr. Frank Owsley is a "fun" teacher who does not hesitate to let his Southern prejudices show. Today he said the Presbyterians came from Scotland and the Episcopalians were sent out from England to establish churches. Lord Baltimore could not get Catholics to come to early America because they were not persecuted enough. The Negro was taken away from his home base and it was more dangerous trying to get away than staying with the settlers. It was different with the Indians: "No attempt was made to convert the Indians into anything but corpses."

Saturday, October 2, 1937 Vanderbilt played in the rain again today but a smaller crowd turned out. Jim Huggins and Bert Marshall made touchdowns and we beat the University of Chicago 18–0. Two or three Chicago students, an Alpha Delt and a Deke ate lunch with us at the house today. I rode home with Dopey Stephens. I ran across a sentence in Emerson's "Scholar" and "Self Reliance" that is the best I have ever encountered about a good writer: "The deeper he dives into his privatest, secretest presentiment, to his wonder he finds this is the most acceptable, most public, and universally true." Owsley reminded us yesterday that it was Stephen Decatur, who in connection with the X.Y.Z Affair and the Barbary pirates off the coast of Africa, who said: "Millions for defense, but not one cent for tribute." I had not realized that Alexander Hamilton and Aaron Burr were rivals for the same girl, as well as rivals in politics. Hamilton was Washington's real chief of field activities during the Revolutionary War. While Washington was conducting the necessary political activities on getting money and supplies for his troops, Hamilton actually ran the war activities. He said Jefferson was a revolutionary and the people were as afraid of him, then, as we are, today, of Kuhn and Browder, Hitler and Stalin's representatives.

Sunday, October 3, 1937 One day, at the end of the last term, while thumbing through the index and telling us what we should read before the end of the term, Dr. Eddie Mims stopped, and said, of a paper I had turned in: "There is a student in this class who does not always prepare every assignment as well as he should, or make as good grades, but every now and then he turns in a paper that warms the cockles of my heart. The other day he submitted a paper, after reading Ulysses, concerning his love of poetry. He tells of his mother quoting poetry in the home, where it ought to be started, of course. I wish I had time to read it." Such a nice thing to say about a student! Rained all day so I didn't go to church. Went to Franklin with Jim Browning for a blind date with Helen Moore, a Ward-Belmont girl from Detroit. We got together with Jack Worley and Sarah Jane Peyton, Charles Majors and Harriet Short, Barney Blair and Whitola Driskill. We harmonized on the way home.

Monday, October 4, 1937 Attended my first Physics lab. and worked three hours on a problem. In a long talk with Byron Anglin this evening he said he could have given me a job for $20.00 per month, managing the Union Play Room. I decided on October 15th as a date for our D.K.E. dance. Had a good wrestling class today.

Tuesday, October 5, 1937 I handed Rousseau Duncan, City Editor of The Nashville Banner, a story and a list of my connections at Vanderbilt. In our political meeting Ed Pardue was elected President of the Confederation. My deal for Anglin worked perfectly. Ellen Bowers looked cute in class today. Saw Douglas Fairbanks Jr. in the "Prisoner of Zenda." It is based on the story of a man who doubled for the king at his coronation. Fairbanks was the likeable villian.

Wednesday, October 6, 1937 Byron Hill and I had a long discussion this morning on patents. Billy Lackey, Louise Sykes, Miriam McGaw and I studied in the library for an hour or so. Miriam talked to me about breaking a certain date that was scheduled for a school night. I invited her to go to Memphis with me but she could not make it. Dr. Mims told us in English class that his first commencement address was delivered at Webb School in Bell Buckle. He was still a student at Vanderbilt. He said that when Ralph Waldo Emerson returned from a visit with Thomas Carlyle and Coleridge in England, he wrote a book called "English Traits" which was one of the best travel books ever written. He added, "Don't die until you have come to know rural England."

Thursday, October 7, 1937 In Dr. Owsley's History class this morning I formulated a plan for another Independent club to split the vote of the Hub Club. Owsley said that Winthrop, father of Mass., came to this country in 1630 for political reasons. The Stuarts of England were attempting to set up a totalitarian state; the Divine Right of Kings. Slater bootlegged, to America, designs of cotton mills and set up the first ones here. He said that Webster changed from a free trader to a protectionist, marking the first point where Industrialism got the upper hand of Commercialism. Tonight I typed a letter on Hugo Black to send to the Reader's Digest.

Friday, October 8, 1937 Carl Hinkle came by the fraternity house today and gave me some more information for my story of his life. Jim Souby took a group of Dekes to Birmingham today. "Blimp" Browning, Eddie Morton, Marion Long, "Led" Adams and I are going to Memphis. We will stay with Granville Sherman. The leaves are beginning to turn and the landscape is beautiful. Here is a feature I wrote for the Hustler.

THE SPLENDOR OF A SETTING SUN
IS SEEN IN CHANCELLOR'S OFFICE

Yesterday I occupied the Chancellor's seat at Vanderbilt University. No, not in an official capacity, but it was a thrill to sit behind the big rolltop desk, in the high backed, heavily cushioned chair of a man who has so capably directed the destinies of a multimillion dollar organization for almost half a century and whose influence has reached the far corners of the earth.

I suppose you are already wondering how I was lucky enough to even get into the Chancellor's office, much less to sit in the Chancellor's chair. Really, its not such a hard matter to get in. You just go to College Hall and walk as far as you can in the south wing. You will come to a door on the right with the name "Chancellor" written in modest brass letters on it.

This being my first visit, I knocked very lightly. I was surprised to hear such a pleasant "come in." I very shyly asked if I could see the chancellor.

"The Chancellor is never too busy to see a student" answered Miss Aileen Bishop, Dr. Kirkland's secretary, "but he happens to be out at this time."

"Do you mind if I sort of look around a bit and see what the Chancellor's office is really like?" I asked. "I understand that in most universities thousands of students spend four years at the university without seeing inside the chief executive's office."

"You may not only look around I will show you around," said Miss Bishop enthusiastically.

The Chancellor's office is different. It has an atmosphere all its own. The serenity of it struck me even when I was in the outer office. One of the fiercest thunderstorms of the season was raging outside, on this late Wednesday afternoon, and the rain was beating against the strong brick walls and window panes with the rapidity and almost the velocity of machine gun bullets. The room was slightly darkened, but not for long. These old walls have passed through so many storms during the past half century, that I would not have had a true picture had I not been there during the heat of a storm.

The heavy rose topaz rug softens the stone floor, but the sturdy concrete beams across the ceiling makes one mindful of rugged strength.

Miss Bishop pointed out that the files on the left contain the university's correspondence, those on the right the Chancellor's many speeches, but the ones in the far corner are the most precious of all. They contain the Iris correspondence.

The large safe in the back corner contains the faculty and Board of Trust's Minutes and the large memorial book contains the volume of warm expressions that the Chancellor received when his fortieth anniversary at Vanderbilt was commemorated.

But this is the outside office. It was almost with reverence that I entered the Chancellor's inner sanctuary. I unconsciously tiptoed. I saw a table in the center of the room with numerous financial and curriculum statements. On top of these papers I noticed a very curious looking whatnot.

"There's a history to that paper weight," explained Miss Bishop, "It was found in an old garage that was torn down to make way for the new hospital. It was the actual knob that was on the door of Bishop

McTyeire's old home, where Chancellor Kirkland lived a number of years." Upon close examination I found the likeness of a railroad engine, with flared smokestack, was carved on the face of the knob. It was the great New York Central's first locomotive.

Had it not been for the ceaseless chugging of that little engine Vanderbilt University may never have seen the light of day.

To the right of the table is the Chancellor's chair and desk. I was not sure that I was not being presumptuous, but I finally summoned the courage and asked, "May I er . . . er . . . sit in the Chancellor's chair?"

"Why yes, go right ahead," replied Miss Bishop, and I did. Having taken my seat uneasily, I looked up over the big desk and saw a picture of the Hermitage and under it a group picture of the Board of Trustees. As I turned to the right, two small, piercing eyes seemed to see into my very soul. It was not necessary for me to know in advance that this great man once said, "It is a disgrace to die rich," this masterful portrait of Andrew Carnegie spoke for itself.

The storm had subsided. I turned my back to the desk and beheld a painting of the most gorgeous sunset that this reporter has ever seen. The brilliance of the colors seemed even to exceed those of the real thing. A placid lake gathered up the fast fading rays as if they were the last. No, there was no doubt that this was a "setting sun" but setting in all the glory that the heavens command.

Saturday, October 9, 1937   I saw the Mississippi river for the first time today. I suppose the river itself is pretty much like it was in 1541 when Fernando de Soto discovered it. It is large at Memphis but somehow did not look as wide as I had expected. The Tennessee river, which I have known as a child in Alabama, is almost as wide. I once swam the Tennessee. It was cloudy this morning and had been raining. We were afraid the game would be ruined but the weather turned fair. Had lunch with Jimmy and Lorraine Matthews at the Winchester home. Joe Agee kicked a field goal, but Bert Marshall was the star. Hinkle did the best blocking I have seen him do. The final score was 17–6 in our favor. Southwestern's best player, a boy by the name of Smith, made a touchdown during the last few seconds and the Memphis people went wild. Twenty of us went to the Deke buffet at Granville Sherman's. Had an interesting talk with Bill Robinson, a Deke from "Ole Miss." He lives in Memphis and his father is president of the largest cotton pickery in the world. He offered to swap me some Robinson stock for stock in my invention. Went to Club "5" in the Nineteenth Century Club and later to the Peabody Hotel. Both were crowded with Nashville people. The Leake girl was with Dan Caldwell and Billy McKee. All were a little "tipsy." Lorraine said she would like to come to Nashville, but if Jimmy were there she could not date any other Dekes. Dick Jergens band was at the Peabody and played slow, sweet music. I dated Louise Douglas. Louis Scutt's father is manager of the Peabody. The dancing was good except that I had on crepe-soled shoes. "Blimp," Bob, and I stayed with Granville's family. Got to bed at 3:00 A.M.

Sunday, October 10, 1937 Jim Huggins, Jim Browning and Charley Majors had dinner with us before leaving the Shermans for Nashville. Mrs. Sherman was kind and gracious and Dr. Sherman, the dentist, is a big talker, just like my Dad. We stopped at Ripley, Tennessee and I had a particularly good visit with Charles Major's father, who is president of the bank there. He has a large family of his own and two adopted children. He showed me old papers published as early as 1865, and took down my address to mail me more.

Monday, October 11, 1937 After the fraternity meeting tonight, Eddie Morton, Jim Tuck and I went to the Confederation political meeting. It was an exciting affair. The Sigma Chi's, the Phi Psi's, and the Pi Kappa Alpha's asked for the presidency of the junior class. The Sigma Chi's finally withdrew their candidate, Ed Hunter, whom they are grooming for Bachelor of Ugliness next year. For withdrawing their candidate, they will probably want, for compensation, the presidency of the Honor Council this spring. That will run head-on into our plans. I suggested an idea for a new political organization. Vorder Brugge and a few others were heartily for it. I rode home with Edgar Uden, who is interested in getting the Kappa Alpha Theta's into our winning combination.

Tuesday, October 12, 1937 Heard President Roosevelt give his 10th Fireside Chat on the radio tonight. It's a marvelous technique, and he has such a magnificent voice, it is no wonder that he has been able to dominate both the Congress and the American people. Saw Miriam with Joe Cummings in the library and she told me she is going on a Student Christian Association weekend party and will miss the Deke dance on the 15th. She also told me that Hartwell Weaver came up to her in lab the other day and said: "I've found something that Comanche (my nickname at the fraternity) can't do . . . work math." Miriam said she could have told him that. In my wrestling class today, one of the boys hit me in the head with his elbow and I have a "goose egg." I don't know when I have felt so bad; almost delirious. It is fantastic the way ideas become disjointed and how the brain conjures up unreal pictures at such times.

Wednesday, October 13, 1937 Received a nice letter from Mr. Dan Majors, from Ripley, today. He sent me some old Confederate money and a copy of a letter from Ripley, England. Spent two hours with Carl

Hinkle getting more details of his early life for my newspaper story.

Thursday, October 14, 1937 Byron Anglin sent me down to the Banner office to see Rousseau Duncan about the job. Someone had talked to Hill Turner and he (Anglin) will be compelled to give up the Banner job. Mr. Duncan talked favorably. In the Intramural wrestling meet this afternoon I met Wilson Lynch, who was champion in the 165 pound division year before last. Wilson is a good wrestler but I managed to pin him. I am probably a little quicker than he is. Clark Hutton was one of my biggest cheer leaders on the sideline. Walked home from the gym with Elise Pritchett and Jane Allen. Ate supper with Mary Wallace, who is making good grades at Ward-Belmont but does not like French. Saw Mr. Gruber assistant principal of Hume-Fogg, on the street car today and he told me the school is better than ever and that the Fogg Horn is coming out next week. I am delighted to hear it is still going strong. Dr. Mims said of Emerson today, "No other American has said so many fine things or made shrewder comments on life." Inspiration is the key word in understanding Emerson. On inspiration, Goethe once said: "The best things I write are given to me." Emerson once wrote that the renaissance is one of the most interesting periods in history: "The man who has seen the sun break out of the clouds at midnight, has been present, like an archangel at creation of life and all the world."

Friday, October 15, 1937 In the Intramural meet today I wrestled Wendell Davis and pinned him. I had so many stories in the Hustler today that I sent copies to Anderson, at T. M. I. and to my good friend Tom Happel in St. Louis. Escorted Louise Douglas to the first Deke dance. She is a favorite of the Beta Theta Pi's, especially John Vorder Brugge. Met Mae Morrison, daughter of the football coach and had a no-break with Harriet Short. Bob Neathery let Homer Howell and me go for our dates in his car.

Saturday, October 16, 1937 Made it to class on time this morning. Later saw Louise and she said she made it on time too. Invited Dr. Mims to have lunch with us at the Deke house some day next week. Said he had been waiting for an invitation. He suggested that some night might be better. Mims talked about Henry David Thoreau this morning. Said he "sucked the marrow out of life. He had no profession, never married, never voted, never went to church, never drank wine and did not know the use of tobacco. He believed in six days rest and one day's work." Mims said that W. L. Fleming was one of the great historians of his day. He was at L. S. U. and later at Vanderbilt. He had to attend to administrative duties because of a lack of financial independence and died with his major works unwritten. Lunny Hollins outshone Bert Marshall and Jimmy Huggins in the game against S. M.

U. today. He made the only touchdown of the game. A whole train load, including a hundred piece band, came from Greenville, Texas to see Marshall and the seven other Greenvillites perform. Ray Morrison's son, Jack, was the big threat from S.M.U. His passes carried them to Vandy's four yard line once. Hinkle played his usual good game. Elliott Trimble asked me what I planned to do after getting out of school. When I answered, "Inventing," he replied, "But how are you going to make a living?"

Sunday, October 17, 1937 The Stamps ate lunch at the Deke house today. Mr. Gatwood, of the Masque Club, gave the Board a report on plans for the year. On Sunday nights Mrs. Miles brings me food on a tray. Reminds me of the story about the scientist who had his food handed to him through the transom on a fishing pole.

Monday, October 18, 1937 It was raining this morning so I had to ride the street car to school. Brother Wade sat in on the fraternity meeting tonight and we discussed organizing a mother's auxiliary to take care of shrubbery around the house and other female activities. Thomas Cummings Jr. invited me to do the honors of initiating him into the fraternity with a blow of the paddle.

Tuesday, October 19, 1937 I was very sleepy in math class today and Dr. Morrell spoke to me about it. His lecture was very dull and sleep inducing. Miriam probably got my letter today telling her how much I think of her but that I am getting pessimistic about hanging around. Saw her uptown when I went to get my picture taken for the college annual, the Commodore. The line was too long so I did not wait. Local writer T. H. Alexander had the featured article in the Saturday Evening Post this week, "They Tried to Capture the Kaiser." He had a story in the Reader's Digest recently on selling bibles in the South. Of James Russell Lowell, Mims says: "He was not necessarily the greatest creative artist, but one of the best all-around Americans." He was a poet, scholar, teacher, critic and letter writer. He was representative of America abroad. On the slavery issue he wrote: "New occasion teaches new duties, time makes ancient good uncouth, We must keep on and upward who would keep abreast of truth." Mims says, Lowell's "Under the Old Elm" is the best poem written about Washington.

Wednesday, October 20, 1937 Had the rare privilege of interviewing Henry McLemore, one of the leading sports writers in the United States, today. He is the top reporter for the United Press. He is a down to earth likeable sort. He would not leave the field until he had seen me for the promised interview. Fred Russell, sports editor of the Nashville Banner, was with him.

Thursday, October 21, 1937 Saw Mary Frances Black coming out of Loews theatre this afternoon and stopped and visited with her and

Virginial Towles from South Pittsburg, Tennessee. Anderson "Big Red" writes me that Henry D. is turning into quite a football player at T. M. I. as well as a track man. He played half a game with the varsity this past week as a pass-catching end, and half with the "B" team. Pop J. wrote a letter that was very flattering to Anderson and me in that he inquired if our brother George L. Jr. would be interested in becoming a counsellor at Dixie Camps. The invitation would be strictly based on his regard for us. Dr. Mims exhibited his most scornful laugh this morning when he discussed Lowell's comment about "Short haired women and long haired men." He also said: "Communities are founded where everything is common except common sense."

Friday, October 22, 1937 Did the craziest thing today. I thought I did not have to go to school until 9:00 o'clock so I leisurely walked over and took an Economics quiz with the wrong class. I never did discover the mistake; although I did notice a few strange faces. I then went to Spanish and found the classroom empty. I concluded we had been given a cut so I dropped by the fraternity house to while away an hour or so. At a quarter of eleven I ran into Roy Huggins and he explained that the Spanish class was the hour before. Went to Dr. Daniels Physics class and got there just in time to prevent getting a cut. Whew! Miriam told me she had received my letter and read it three times. Said it was the best letter she ever received. Buddy Rand and Tom Happel are here for the big game with L.S.U. tomorrow. Page Hill is coming up also. Jim Souby brought me home tonight. I talked to him about the Banner job. He advised me to take it, which means that he is leaning the other way in connection with the Hustler. I don't think I'll accept the Banner job though. Met Ellen Bowers at the Theta dance. Danced with her several times. She is very sweet, but shows that she has been sheltered pretty closely. Ed Uden was her date. Susan Cheek is also a nice looking and good dancing Theta pledge. She came with Tom Scoggins. "Whit" Driskill and Harriet Short were there living it up in a big way.

Saturday, October 23, 1937 I thought we were going to have a quiz in math this morning so I cut it rather than to take it unprepared. Out-of-towners here for the game are: Jimmy Winchester and Lorraine Matthews, Hal Claffey and Claude Estes. Talked to Henry McLemore on the phone. He said that I did a nice job on the write up. I am to see him again in the morning. Morrison planned to score a touchdown on L.S.U. on the fourth play. Sure enough when the fourth play came around, the ball was supposedly snapped and our whole team, and theirs too, ran to the left. When everybody got on the opposite side of the field, Greer Ricketson, who had remained on the right side of the field with Hinkle, picked up the ball and ran for a touchdown. Most deceptive play I have ever seen. We completely outplayed them three quarters but after a deadly penalty in the last period they scored on a pass. They did not connect, however, on the point after and the final score was Vanderbilt 7–L.S.U. 6. Had a surprise no-break with Miriam at the dance. After the dance Bill Lauderdale and I went out to see Elizabeth McEwen. Her mother is from Centerville. Her grandmother is Mrs. Henry Russell.

Sunday, October 24, 1937 The newspaper this morning carried glowing accounts of the Vanderbilt football victory over L. S. U. The now famous "hidden-ball" play worked perfectly. I went to Henry McLemore's hotel room down town and got a story about his reaction to the game. Met his very charming wife. The Huttons and the Neatheries ate lunch with us at the Deke house. Jimmy Winchester and Lorraine departed for Memphis and Tom Happel and Buddy Rand left for St. Louis.

Monday, October 25, 1937 Dr. Mims quoted a hauntingly beautiful passage about college life this morning: "Oxford whispering from her chambers the last enchantments of the Middle Age." Mims, at my invitation, came to the Deke house to have dinner with us this evening. He has a very distinctive mustache and goatee and looks the part of a college professor. I might add that he also plays the part to the hilt. He told us how the local Deke chapter was founded. He was the only member of the Webb school boys "black balled"so the next year he, and a few others, got together and applied for a Deke reorganization. The next fall all of the Webb boys went Deke. At that time "Old Sawney" had already made Webb one of the most famous prep schools in the nation. Woodrow Wilson, when he was President, said that the best prepared students to come to Princeton, when he was there, were from Webb. I talked with Mr. Duncan this morning and told him I was undecided about taking the Banner job. I talked with Anglin and he advised strongly that I take it. He said there is too much politics mixed up with the Hustler editorship. Some robbers broke into the fraternity house tonight and stole several suits. They need an alarm system. I got a letter from Macklin Holder tonight with two cartoons in it that had been published in the Chattanooga News—Free Press. One of them depicted Black kicking the ladder out now that he is on the Supreme Court and another about the Branning Unit plan.

Tuesday, October 26, 1937 Had a tough Trigonometry quiz this morning. I probably did fair on it. In discussing the editorship of the Hustler next year, Jim Souby said the selection would be made impartially, as if it could be. Billy Estes, President of the Honor Council, and I worked several hours this afternoon on a plan for improving the system. Aunt Nell called this evening and said Miss Brooks, one of my old math teach-

ers, had to be removed from the city teaching payroll for mental disturb-
ances. Heard Herbert Hoover speak on the radio tonight. The applause
was tremendous but he is no match for F. D. R. Mims said today that
New England was settled by communities; Virginia by individuals. He
quoted Lowell, who said: "Man has in his brain the geometry of the
city of God."

Wednesday, October 27, 1937   I finally decided to accept the campus
reporter's job with the Nashville Banner, the city's evening newspaper.
Rousseau Duncan, a thin, almost redheaded, likeable sort of fellow is
City Editor and Hilliard Wood, the chief photographer, seems to be
his chief assistant. In chapel this morning the new dean of the graduate
school, John Pomfret, introduced himself to the student body. I went
by the Hustler office this evening and bade my colleagues there farewell.
I will continue writing my column for the Hustler but will no longer
be on the staff. My leaving will probably make it easier for Bill Embry
to get the editorship next year.

Thursday, October 28, 1937   Had two articles in the Banner this afternoon. Dr. Mims gave an interesting account of the first permanent American colony in America in 1620. The group left England surreptitiously
and went to Holland. Bradford gave the following reasons for leaving
Holland a year later: fear of losing their identity, difficulty of making
a living in Holland, and for the purposes of spreading the gospel. Each
man was given one share in the company, if he could pay his way. They
started out on the Speedwell and, when it sprung a leak, turned back
and got the Mayflower. There were 102 people in all. Influenza and
other diseases had wiped out earlier colonists. The great migration
started in 1630. Forty or fifty of the first were Cambridge graduates.
They wished to set up a bible Commonwealth, a Theocracy to regulate
the lives of individuals and bring them into harmony with God. They
considered themselves to be in possession of ultimate political, religious
truth. They considered Democracy to be the meanest and worst form
of government. If the people govern, who shall be governed?

Friday, October 29, 1937   Interviewed Dr. Ernest Eberling and then
went to the Banner office. Sat at the same table with Dr. Powell, pastor
of the First Baptist church, while getting my string ready. We talked
of football and politics. Elizabeth McEwen happened to mention that
Miss Ella Haiman, out at West End High School, told them that the
paper at Hume-Fogg struggled along almost hopelessly until it got a
good name. After they got the name Fogg Horn it was smooth sailing.
That was true to a certain extent but there was a little more to it than
that.

Saturday, October 30, 1937   Riding home to Stevenson on the train
I looked up from my magazine and saw a very beautiful girl looking

at me. Her head was back on the seat in a reclining position. Her eyes were slightly drooped, just enough to accentuate the curve of her eyebrows. She beautifully pretended sleep. All the train seats were taken and I happened to be the only young man in the car. I was identified by a yellow Vanderbilt feather in my coat lapel. She knew my thoughts and I hers, yet we sat there hour after hour looking at each other. Neither of us spoke. I guess if her mother had not been there I would have spoken. Billy Whitson got on the train at Tullahoma. He was going to the game in Atlanta. Got home about one o'clock this morning but got up at eight and walked around town. Could hardly hear the Vandy-Tech game on the radio. They beat us 14–0. Henry D. came home in his T. M. I. uniform. He is taller than I now. We had both chicken and steak tonight.

Sunday, October 31, 1937 On the train back to Nashville I saw Lucy Lee. Our freshmen sang at the Kappa Alpha Theta tea this afternoon. Talked with Ellen Bowers. Picked up Miriam and Louise Sykes at the Tri Delta house. Miriam said she broke up with Billy Lackey this week. I told her tonight for the first time that I think she is the grandest girl in the world. She talked encouragingly. In all of my life my heart never beat so fast. Bill Shumaker is still in love with Elizabeth Carr.

Monday, November 1, 1937 Had a picture of the new literary magazine, "Pursuit," in the Banner this afternoon. I am a member of the publication board. Heard Jim Kilgallen, famous news reporter, speak to a Vandy audience. He told of covering the Dionne Quintuplets birth, Lindberg-Hauptman trial, and other famous news stories. He was introduced by Jack Harris, manager of radio station W. S. M. Miriam told me today that she knew I didn't write the Night Hawk column because it wasn't my type of stuff; very complimentary. Bob Clapp called me aside today and asked that I take a little diplomatic trip for him. He wants me to go to see Mr. Farrell, a neighbor the man who served the injunction on us last year for making noise late at night at the Deke house. He wants me to ask Mr. Farrell to let our cook use his janitor's toilet facilities.

Tuesday, November 2, 1937 Talked to Norman Farrell, the lawyer and apartment house owner and he agreed to grant my request. Bill Jordan and I made plans for publicity for both the Masque Club and for "Pursuit." Dr. Mims said in a class lecture that Hawthorne was at one time perhaps the most discouraged man in the world. Publisher James came to him and asked for something. Reluctantly Hawthorne gave him "The Scarlet Letter."

Wednesday, November 3, 1937 The President of the Calumet Club asked me to write their history but I have too many other pressing duties. Talked to Miriam on the phone. I think more of her all the time. My wrestling class is good for me because it takes my mind off of the numerous activities with which I am burdened. Each night I feel that I can't go on. With a night's sleep I feel better.

Thursday, November 4, 1937 Learned that Sidney Lanier said he never read a novel through in his life. He once started Robinson Crusoe. I, myself, haven't read many. Biographies of great men are my favorite reading. When I was younger my favorite reading material was the Tom Swift books. I guess that, together with my natural mechanical aptitude, and an almost compulsive desire to do things differently and better, led to an interest in becoming an inventor. My Zipper invention will have been in the patent office 12 months tomorrow. So many people have put me down as a dreamer that I have decided to write an essay on that subject. It follows:

ON PIDDLING

Contrary to the great body of literature devoted to urging people to be doers of deeds, there is much to be said for those who delight in doing nothing in particular; nothing important, that is, just a host of little things—the piddlers.

A piddler is not to be confused with a loafer who does nothing at all. The loafer is lazy both physically and mentally. He hangs around the corner drugstore in his youth and around bars and poolrooms in his maturity. He cannot tolerate being alone. His interests are entirely outside himself.

Not so the piddler. He may be physically lazy, but never mentally. His brain is a beehive of activity. He is interested in everything he encounters, and he encounters so many interesting things he finds it difficult to get around to dull necessities. There is always important work to do: his job; the night school to complete the requirements for his degree; putting the finishing touches on the program he had suggested for saving the company money. All these are important and yet the piddler is easily turned aside. The news in the papers is never so interesting as when he should be studying for an examination. He simply cannot put a magazine down. One never knows what interesting information may be lurking on the next page. Always there are clippings to be sorted and pasted, odd jobs to be done around the house, and a hundred other things inviting his attention.

The piddler feels that he can work better, and with greater concentration, when the decks are cleared; when the little things are out of the way. But, in reality, they never are. He spends practically all his time preparing the way for the big things, which he never seems quite able to get around to.

Consciously, or unconsciously, the piddler may have discovered the touchstone of happiness. He is happy by the simple process of avoiding the unhappy. He works with clippings of poems because it is more fun than studying law books. He is late for an appointment because his coffee and cigarette are more enjoyable at a leisurely pace. He may be called an irresponsible dreamer, but he is not a slave to any man. Most of all, he is not subservient to a clock on the wall.

The piddler's constant attention to little things is a subsconscious revulsion to doing more demanding tasks. But, it is more than just this. It is also a genuine delight in a free play of the mind; letting it wander whither it will. If it wants to reminisce, he lets it. If it wants to toy with an idea, or a mechanism, it need not be bound to any prescribed course, because the results of piddling are not important; not important, at least, to the workaday world.

Piddlers are frowned on by their contemporaries, and yet most of the geniuses of the world have been piddlers. Few of the great painters, for instance, were able to make their dabblings in art compatible with the very important job of making a living. Einstein was piddling with theories of Physics and Mathematics when his job in the library called for returning books to their proper shelves. Goodyear was piddling when he discovered how to vulcanize rubber. Spectators must have thought it odd of a grown man, Benjamin Franklin, flying a kite.

Not all piddlers are geniuses, by any stretch of the imagination, but piddling and thinking seem to go hand in hand. Piddling, in many cases, is merely an outside occupation of the body, while the mind is doing its work. The mind chooses it's own conditions. Sometimes it responds to a symphony, or to the frenzied tempo of a night club. Sometimes it prefers long walks in the country, or listening to waves break against the beach at the seashore. One thing the brain must have and that is time. It must have time to turn thoughts over and over and to examine them from every angle. Piddling is perhaps the most appropriate name given to those activities which provide the brain with that precious ingredient called time.

Time never hangs heavy on the hands of the piddler. He never worries about being alone, or not having anything to do. He knows how to entertain himself. There is always more to do than he can get done.

There would probably be less drinking, less gambling and less evil in the world if there were more piddlers. The Devil's Workshop has been associated with idleness. The piddler is never idle.

Friday, November 5, 1937 The last chapter of Mark Twain's "The Mysterious Stranger" says: "There is no heaven, no hell, no anything.

All is a dream." If that be true, then Twain's definition of faith must, of necessity be: "Faith consists in refusing to believe that which you know to be true."

Saturday, November 6, 1937 Met Susan Cheek today. She and Florence Abernathy sat immediately in front of Bob Foote, Elizabeth Carr and me, at the Sewanee football game. Susan is a very pretty brunette, with delicate features and a shy smile. We had a surprise no-break at the gym dance and I made a date with her for the Student Council dance on Thanksgiving night, November 25th. Met Frances Gardner, Ed Kirkpatrick's cousin, who looks a lot like Miriam. Dr. Mims told us of Tennyson's love life this morning. He said that Miss Margaret Gordon was probably the original "Blumine." She took leave of him in a remarkable letter, and shortly married a member of Parliament. Tennyson wrote: "A rat was eating at my stomach." He also wrote: "Every gate is thronged with suitors, all the markets overflow, I have but an angry fancy; what is that which I should do?" It is in Locksley Hall. From "The Princess" are these lines: "Dear as remembered kisses after death, and sweet as those by hopeless fancy feigned on lips that are for others; deep as love, deep as first love, and wild with all regret, O death in Life, the days that are no more."

Sunday, November 7, 1937 I am discouraged about my love affair with Miriam. Tonight at the Tri Delta House when I was talking with her, Joe Little came up and mentioned a compliment he had heard about her. She was all ears and wanted him to sit by her. He would not, so I did. After eating she rushed off into the other room to hear her compliments. Louise Sykes and Winifred Elliot sat with me the rest of the evening. I did not see Miriam again, even to say good-bye. I am afraid she was kidding me along last Sunday evening when she gave me encouragement.

Monday, November 8, 1937 Clark Hutton and Bobby Stamps attended my wrestling class this afternoon. Both of them should develop into good wrestlers. Bud Bray wrestled Wilson Lynch in the Intramural meet this afternoon and threw him. H. B. Tomlin attended his first freshman rat court. Saw Margarete Mahoney on a street car this evening and she told me Paul Slayden and his wife are having matrimonial problems. She is jealous of him. They probably married too young.

Tuesday, November 9, 1937 Mr. H. K. Hunter, Talon Inc.'s representative, showed me a pair of pliers converted into sliders for Zippers. I went straight to Kress' and bought a pair and made one of them. Frances Scruggs told me that Hugh Miser told her I could not hold the Nashville Banner job and that he, himself, would get it. Such egotism! Ed Steele, in the school machine shop, helped me complete the Zipper tool. Had one of the biggest classes ever at wrestling today. The system I have developed for teaching wrestling holds by the numbers, enables me to handle thirty or forty boys on the mat at the same time.

Wednesday, November 10, 1937 Had a nice chat today with Charles Moss, Managing Editor of the Banner. He gave me several assignments for the Educational Issue that is coming out next week. I had Pam Snell's picture on the front page this afternoon. Saw a copy of the University of Alabama's "Crimson White," which is edited by my hometown friend, Walter Bogart. He gave us a good writeup. Peggy Peyton, Anglin's date, wants to have a date with someone else after she gets to Knoxville. The nerve of some girls! My good buddy, Floy Minor, out of a blue sky tonight, said she has a secret passion for me. Says she is hearing so many nice things about me lately.

Thursday, November 11, 1937 William Simpson is home from the hospital. Miriam is thrilled over our leaving for Knoxville tomorrow. Armistice Day seems meaningless this year.

Friday, November 12, 1937 Miriam and I met at the stadium and got our tickets. Byron drove by for me at 2:30 P.M. and we picked up Miriam and Peggy and set out for Knoxville. Miriam and I sat in the back seat and enjoyed every minute of the five hour drive. A cop stopped us because of a faulty tail light. We took Miriam to the Atkin hotel, where she had rooms with Nell Edwards, Louise Sykes, Sarah Goodpasture and four or five other girls. At the gym dance I saw Carolyn Spivey from Scottsboro. She was down from Sweetbriar. She plans to meet her family and go home for the weekend. I also saw Dorothy Winton, who now lives in Oklahoma. We waited in the lobby of the Atkin hotel from about midnight until two o'clock, for Anglin to return. Finally he came in with Mr. and Mrs. Pierce Winningham. They had been to a big cocktail party. We went out to get a bite to eat and then took the girls to their rooms. Anglin and I found lodging in a "one-horse" hotel by the name of Empire. The beds felt good though because we were thoroughly exhausted.

Saturday, November 13, 1937 We met the girls at ten and, after having breakfast we drove around the town looking at the beautifully decorated fraternity and sorority houses. The winning one said: "We have met the enemy and they are ours: one sloop and eleven Commodores." We got to the game early and saw the bands from the two schools parade together. The stadium was packed. When the Tennessee Vols made the first touchdown, everything looked dark. It wasn't too long before we made a touchdown and extra point. The ball shifted back and forth throughout the first half and the score was tied 7–7. The famous "hidden ball" play was tried but it failed. Towards the end of the game, at a very critical point, Carl Hinkle intercepted a pass and made a long run. That turned the game in our favor and we even-

tually won it. Hinkle was the star of the game, but Hollins, Marshall and
Hinton were also brilliant. We went to the Andrew Johnson hotel
after the game and saw and talked to Hinkle. Two boys from Lumkin,
Georgia got Anglin to introduce them to Carl Hinkle, the first all-
American they had ever seen. We went out to hear Duke Ellington, of
"Mood Indigo" and "Sophisticated Lady" fame. Miriam enjoyed it but
I thought he was only fair. I was dead tired. Anglin got to feeling
pretty good.

Sunday, November 14, 1937 We took John Lassiter, a Sigma Chi,
out to Norris Dam with us this morning. The dam and the city of Norris
are impressive. We took the wrong road back to Nashville and did not
get to see Anderson and Henry D. at Sweetwater. Miriam's folks were
glad to see her. They had listened to the game.

Monday, November 15, 1937 I was so tired I went to sleep in classes
several times today. Varsity wrestling coach George Field, came over
to the gym this afternoon to talk to me about the team. He is scouting
out material. Went to bed at ten sharp.

Tuesday, November 16, 1937 In the moving picture that Miriam and
I went to see this afternoon, "Conquest," starring Greta Garbo and
Charles Boyer, Napoleon said that he loved the woman against his will.
That's the way I feel about Miriam. When we came out of the theatre
she saw a few fellows she knew and began talking with them. That's
the way it is all the time. My love is not reciprocated. Went to hear
Palmer Christian, a noted organist tonight. Dr. Mims, in discussing Thoreau's Essay on "Walking," quoted: "A walk will take me to a new world
. . . an old farmhouse as inspiring as an old castle. In his "Rhine Stream"
he wrote: "The foundations of castles is yet to be laid, this is the romantic
age."

Wednesday, November 17, 1937 Handed in my stories today and four
of them came out in the afternoon paper. Jim Christian said he would
take the pictures for my Life magazine presentation so I went to see
John Sloan, President of Cain-Sloans about getting some representative
garments. Sloan liked the Zipper idea and agreed to cooperate. Heard
a lecture by H. B. Abernathy, noted archery expert at the Outdoor Club
this evening. Lieutenant Reeves, of the 105th Ordnance Company,
helped with the rifle work.

Thursday, November 18, 1937 Bought two tickets for the Homecoming
game for Wilson and Dad. They completely sold out shortly after that.
Worked with Jim Reed on the mat this afternoon and showed him a
few holds. Standing on the street corner this morning waiting for a
street car I happened to get into conversation with a shivering old man
trying to sell his last few papers for three cents each. I said to him:
"Standing out in the cold all day is a pretty tough life, isn't it?"

"Not half as bad though" he quickly replied, "as work I used to do on the farm. You can put on clothes to get warm."

Friday, November 19, 1937 At the Tri Delta dance tonight Francis Craig, the orchestra leader, predicted that the score for tomorrow's game would be 6–0 in favor of Vanderbilt. Miriam looked beautiful in a green evening dress. She had on a magnificent corsage. Elliot Trimble was her escort. It hurt my feelings. Elliott is only a freshman at the University, but I have been taking Miriam regularly to our dances for two years. I escorted Miriam to practically every Deke dance and she has never asked me to be her date at any of her dances. I felt so badly about it that I did not dance with her a single time all evening. I think I'll call off our no-breaks for tomorrow night. Here again poetry comes to the rescue to soften the blows of fate:

> "Some girls who no worth respect
> Do so unjustly prove,
> That some shall win by their neglect,
> What others lose by love."

Saturday, November 20, 1937 It was too cold for me to go to the freshman football game this afternoon so I came home and finished typing my homecoming story. Uncle Walt would not let me have his car tonight so I borrowed Mrs. Miles' and took my sister, Mary Wallace, to her first Vanderbilt dance. I introduced her to Carl Hinkle, who told her I am one of his best friends. I also introduced Randy Batson, Don Pierce, Morton Howell, Dick Clark, Tom Shea, Tom Scoggins and Ed Kirkpatrick. I also introduced her to Susan Cheek, Elizabeth Johnson, and Louise Douglas. Miriam, who was escorted by Bob Jordan, chatted with her in the dressing room. Later Mary Wallace told me Billy Lackey was the one she danced with best. I guess Billy's dancing ability is one of the reasons he and Miriam get along so well.

Sunday, November 21, 1937 I worked on the Hinkle story practically all day and this evening, at a party at the Sigma Alpha Epsilon house, I met the publicity man for Vanderbilt, Bob Horsley. He read my story about Hinkle and pronounced it "splendid." He went to the phone immediately and called the sports editor, Fred Russell, and told him all about the story and pictures. I am going to see Fred tomorrow and see if I can sell his boss on it. Hinkle came to my room tonight and gave me the rest of the story. I had given him the wrong directions so I sat on the street, under a street light and read O. Henry's "Municipal Report," a story about Nashville, Tennessee.

Monday, November 22, 1937 Turned in the story of Hinkle to Fred Russell. After the Physics lab. I went to the wrestling practice and then to the fraternity meeting. Homer Howell showed up with multiple pairs of trousers to soften blows from the paddle. Sounded peculiar when he was hit.

Tuesday, November 23, 1937 Fred Russell said my story was worth "dough" and that he would try to get Charles Moss to pay $25.00 for it. We are going to build a wooden horse, a la Trojan war, for our parade float. Dr. Mims cracked today: "Every wag of my eye is significant." In speaking of a well proportioned mind he said: "A well proportioned mind is one which shows no particular bias; one which we may safely say that it will never cause its owner to be confined as a mad man, tortured as a heretic, or crucified as a blasphemer." Mims read from Walt Whitman's works, "Crossing Ferry" and "Song of Myself." Whitman assimilated everything in New York, the theatres, saloons, restaurants, and rode the buses and ferries. He would go to his home on Long Island and run up and down the beaches yelling. Milton and Shakespeare also loved crowds. Whitman was the first to visualize America as a whole. Said of the West: "Where the sundown shadows lengthen on the lone and limitless plain."

Wednesday, November 24, 1937 This is the night before our big Thanksgiving game. I have just returned from one of the largest and most enthusiastic fraternity banquets I have ever attended. Mr. Cason, vice-president of the Chase National Bank of New York, Judge Swiggart, Dr. Mims, Mr. Page Hill Sr., brother of H. G. Hill of Nashville, and Mr. Potts of Abington, Virginia, were there. I made the first talk of the evening, giving a report of fraternity activities. I told of writing the life story of Carl Hinkle and that it would be in the paper soon. Told them that Carl had predicted a win in tomorrow's game. Talked to Charles Hughes' brother, Nat, and he said he would come around to visit us. Finished our Trojan horse just before the parade. A picture of it appeared in the paper this afternoon. The poem read: "The Greeks gave the Trojans a horse they could not ride, With Morrison at the reins, Vandy will fool the Tide." In Dr. Mim's speech he said he had discovered why I was having trouble in English, because of being the political boss of Vanderbilt. Charles Majors and President Eddie Morton made nice speeches.

Thursday, November 25, 1937 The parade was spectacular. Our float, and horse, did not win the grand prize, but the costumes of the freshmen on the float did. The game was splendid. Alabama made a touchdown at the last of the first half. Vandy came right back and pushed one over. Marshall's generalship, running and passing was responsible. Joe Agee kicked the extra point and the score remained 7–6 in our favor until the last few minutes of the game when Sandy Sanford, the boy with the educated toe came in and kicked the prettiest field goal I have ever seen. The final score was 9–7 in their favor. They deserved to win. They pushed the ball deep into our territory several times but always our "iron men," rose to the occasion. Saw several Alabama Dekes at the Dutch supper. Had my first date with Susan Cheek for the script dance tonight. I was thirty minutes late because I could not find her home. It is set several hundred yards back in a grove of big oak trees, hence the name Oak Hill. The solid stone pillars are four or five feet in diameter at the bottom and rise almost as high as those at the Parthenon. The house is brick and stone, instead of wood, and the yard must encompass fifteen or twenty acres. Scarlett O'Hara's "Tara" mansion was never like this. Driving up the winding circular drive and arriving at the front door was more like coming to a state function, rather than a private date. I probably had difficulty maintaining my nonchalance. Entering into the hallway, leading to the circular stairway, was like entering Louis the Fourteenth's palace at Versailles, I imagine. I have never seen a home like this, not even Lee's, at Mount Vernon or Jefferson's at Monticello. It is truly magnificent. Picked up Billy Killebrew, who works at the Third National Bank, and his date Ethel Caldwell, after returning Susan home from the dance. Took Ethel to the home of James E. Caldwell, and Bill to Hillsboro. Bill is a Vanderbilt graduate and he has a brother who is a Deke at Yale. Didn't dance with Miriam at all tonight.

Friday, November 26, 1937 I was tired and sleepy today and glad that the excitement is over. Took a nap at the fraternity house this afternoon and read History all evening.

Saturday, November 27, 1937 Dr. Mims read "Ulalume" from the section of the book on Edgar Allan Poe and then he introduced us to one of his favorite poets, Sidney Lanier. "The Marshes of Glenn" is one of his great poems:

> "As the marsh hen secretly builds on the watery sod,
> Behold I will build me a nest on the greatness of God."

Susan and I got mixed up on our dates and postponed our next one until next Friday. At the private Deke dance tonight Louise Sykes, Miriam's best friend, advised that I should not give up on Miriam but should stick in there and keep fighting. Met and danced with Imogene King, Walter's sister.

Sunday, November 28, 1937 This has been a day of rest. I slept until eleven and when I got up I spent the afternoon reading the letters and poems of Sidney Lanier.

Monday, November 29, 1937 The Masque Club publicity work is beginning to weigh heavily on my mind. There are one thousand things to do between now and Thursday night. Posters, mimeographed sheets, signs and other advertising schemes must be worked up. Bill Hall came by my room to see me tonight. He and I have good conversations together. In reading John Fiske's "The Beginning of New England" I ran across a picture of the "Austin House," the first residence in Cambridge, Mass. Those Austins must have been relatives of mine.

Tuesday, November 30, 1937 Ran around in a whirl all day. Got the circulars and postcards from the printer, Mr. Vandiver, and started getting them out. A letter from Fred Buechel, whom I knew at camp, pledged Phi Delta Theta at his school. Talked with Mr. Draughn, manager of W. S. I. X. radio station, about publicity for the Masque Club.

Wednesday, December 1, 1937 The Banner gave us good publicity on the Mikado; four pictures across the top of a page. I rode to town with Jean Stephenson to put up signs. Had a long and friendly talk with Police Chief Lon Foster before doing it. Chief Foster is a friend of Mrs. Blair, my landlady of a few years ago. I have a feeling that the reason Mrs. Blair had such a wide acquaintance is that she used to make home brew during the time of Prohibition. She is an excellent cook, making the best pie crusts I ever ate, but I doubt that that is the source of her fame. I was told that the West High students almost mobbed Hinkle when he made a speech, at their chapel, promoting ticket sales for the Mikado. I have made exactly $52.00 this month: ten dollars coaching wrestling and $20.00 for the Hinkle story which was sold to the Banner. Dr. Mims told me he was glad I was not one of the students who walked out on his quiz the other day. I am too because they will "pay the piper" for that one.

Thursday, December 2, 1937 Clarence Woodcock dated Sue Craig, Honus' daughter, and I escorted Miriam McGaw to the Mikado, Vandy's first nighter program. It was a howling success. The crowd was large and enthusiastic and the performance excellent. Our publicity efforts were not in vain. My hunch about Miriam seems to be right. I have been rushing her too much. Tonight I didn't even try to make the conversation interesting. I just sat back and took it easy. Didn't even hold her hand. When we got out of the car to go up to her apartment, she reached through my arm and firmly grasped my hand. In saying good night I did not gush all over myself in telling her what a thrill it was being with her; just good night, that's all. It probably works better. This afternoon in the library, she sat by herself at one end and I sat at the other. That's the way it was for a couple of hours. Had a nice chat with Betty Freeland, and Ann Wright asked me about my Zipper invention, which she has been hearing about. Saw Francis Robinson, magazine editor of the Banner, and he said the article on Hinkle was handled well. He will run it this coming Sunday.

Friday, December 3, 1937 This has indeed been a red-letter day for me. First I saw the layout that the Banner is using on my Hinkle story and it exceeds all expectations. There has been some talk of Hinkle getting a screen test, so Francis Robinson took the pictures I had of him and superimposed them on pictures of various movie actresses, as if they were embracing, and ran them on the front page of the magazine section. This afternoon when I got home I found a letter from Anderson with some money in it. Thirdly, the much awaited letter from the patent office arrived. They have definitely granted my first claim and, after adding a few construction limitations, will sanction the rest of them. Being granted a patent, and successfully marketing it are two different things, but a start has been made. I wish I were far enough along to say to my family: "I told you so," but I'm afraid that's a little premature.

Saturday, December 4, 1937 Dr. Mims delivered one of his best lectures of the year this morning. He read from his book "The Advancing South" and gave several stories and anecdotes from his own experience. His story of the fight for freedom of thought at the University of North Carolina was excellent. I already knew a great deal about Vanderbilt's lawsuit to break away from the Methodist Church, but he filled in some blank places. It seems that the Methodist Church wanted to use Vanderbilt as a dumping ground for superannuated preachers and Chancellor Kirkland objected. I had heard much of this from Uncle Walt, whose father-in-law Judge Edward H. East, was associated with both Vanderbilt and the church. In fact he helped select the cornfield in which Vanderbilt was located. The university succeeded in breaking away and established an independent board of trustees. It was a turning point in the life of the university, but there was much bitterness over the court battle. The Methodist Church then established Emory University in Atlanta and wrote their charter in such a way that a split in the future would be unlikely. Escorted Miriam to the gym dance tonight and afterwards we went to the home of George Harmon, where he and Norma Hammond fixed cocoa for us. We had a delightful time sitting before the open fire listening to Guy Lombardo's music. Miriam said she was worried about the way I had been acting during the past two weeks. She was afraid she had done something to make me mad. I explained that I was beginning to love her too much, and since it seemed to be unrequited love, it seemed the better part of wisdom to slow it down. I told her I thought I had been rushing her too much and that I was going to stop. She insisted that I not be rash: "I think too much of you for it to stop like this."

Sunday, December 5, 1937 The article about Hinkle came out in the morning paper. It surpassed my fondest dreams. The pictures of Hinkle and the movie stars were certainly good attention getters. The opening paragraph was as follows:

HIS LIFE STORY

by Ben Austin

"Great football players don't just happen; nor is it purely a matter of training. Great athletes, just like fine race horses, are the result of a long line of sturdy ancestors. War Admiral did not win the Kentucky Derby as a "long shot," or as a "Dark Horse," he was expected to win. The strong line back of him included one of the greatest of all competitors, Man-O-War. So it is with athletes. Jim Thorpe's ancestors were full-bloodied Indians. In writing about the life of an athlete, it is imperative that the background be given."

Dr. Chadwick took some promotion pictures for me of Sarah Cecil, Jean McEwen, Andromedia Bagwell, Lorraine Regen, Harriet Short, Ed Hunter, Donald Pierce and Randy Batson. Last night after George Harmon sang to Norma, Miriam said to me: "Why don't you learn songs and sing them to girls?" I replied that I was not sure I had anyone to sing them to. She gave me an idea, though, I'll learn more songs than George Harmon ever dreamed of, even though my singing voice may leave something to be desired.

Monday, December 6, 1937 Saw Ann Wright in the library this morning and she said she heard two people talking about me. They said I had lots of original ideas and that I had the energy and ability to translate the ideas into reality. They also said how nice I am. I can't imagine who it was that was so complimentary and she would not tell me. It could have been Bill Hall. He is a mutual friend. She said that the remark she made to them was "Zip! Zip! Hurrah!" The political meeting at the Deke House was routine. Heard lots of people talking about the Hinkle article. Lent Rice said it was the talk of the campus.

Tuesday, December 7, 1937 Both the Tennessean and Banner staffs are located in the old editorial office of the Banner. Mr. Duncan handed me a story from the front page of the Tennessean this morning about a boy at Vanderbilt inheriting half a million dollars. The whole thing sounded "fishy" to me. At lunch I found out that it was one of Alan Martin's publicity gags. The boy who was supposed to have been the recipient of the money was Wilson Davis, otherwise known as Zeke. When I showed Mr. Duncan my letter from the patent office he said he himself had worked on a Zipper for a cigarette package. Mr. Tyne and I talked over patent possibilities and decided to take one out in Canada. Aunt Nell called about the newspaper article and stated that Uncle Osgood was elated over seeing it. Katherine told us that he was mightly afraid "Ben's paper" would get lost.

Wednesday, December 8, 1937 I made my first official speech before the entire student body this morning in chapel. I planned to talk about fifteen or twenty minutes trying to get them to subscribe to the new literary magazine, "Pursuit." I told the story of Henry Luce's founding Time, Life, and Fortune. I drew an analogy between Life's auspicious beginning and our own publication and I told them I am appealing to their "gambling instincts" to take a chance on a new publication. That got a laugh. Henry Clay came around to see me after the speech and said he was going to subscribe to the magazine on my account. I hope enough of them have the same idea, so we can go to press. Carl Hinkle spoke immediately after me and got a tremendous ovation. It was an expression of the student body's appreciation of what he is doing on the gridiron.

Thursday, December 9, 1937 Alfred Levingston told me, at the S. A. E. party this afternoon, that Julius Rubel said he learned more wrestling from me in thirty minutes than he had learned from George Field, the varsity coach, all season. That is certainly a compliment because Field is a good coach. To hear such is the pleasure of being a teacher. Saw Miriam on the campus today and she said she was so scared, when I was speaking in chapel yesterday, that I would forget my speech. Andromedia Bagwell complimented the speech highly but asked why I did not smile when I said funny things. I really did not have much time for laughing in such a short speech. This afternoon I finished writing an article I started last night and could not finish. I had to give up at 1:00 A.M. I had gone up to "Blue Heaven," the attic of the Deke House, and went to sleep over the typewriter. It was a theme about my hometown, Stevenson, Alabama, for Dr. Mims. Attended the celebration at the S. A. E. house this evening. It was in honor of Carl Hinkle who had been selected for Grantland Rice's "all-American" football team. Charles Anderson, a big rival of Hinkle, turned out. Bob Horsley told me about being at "Boots" Tyne's last night and hearing about my invention.

Friday, December 10, 1937 I was down at the Banner office and subscribed for a month. Jack Tucker, one of the staff writers said he read my story on Hinkle. Said it was the first magazine section article he had read in six months. I sat across the table from Miriam for three hours this afternoon and never spoke. We would glance at each other occasionally. Once when she glanced at me very sweetly I should have winked, or something, instead of turning away.

Mr. F. L. Castleman Jr, the Engineering professor who advised me to get into the academic school, saw me on the campus this morning and said: "You are turning into a real author, aren't you?" He is a very kind and understanding man. I talked to Susan Cheek this morning and we both agreed that it would be silly for us to have a date this close to exams. She said her mother would be glad to hear of our decision. We made dates for the first gym dance next term and for the Washington Ball.

Saturday, December 11, 1937 Dr. Eddie Mims gave another of his great lectures this morning. He said Matthew Arnold (1822–1888) wrote lyrically of the voices he heard at Oxford University forty years earlier. Arnold was the son of Thomas, headmaster at Rugby, and was steeped in academic tradition, even before going to Oxford. When he got to the great English university and heard the great voices of Cardinal Newman and Thomas Carlyle, and through him, Goethe, and from three thousand miles away, the voice of Emerson, he was transfixed. Arnold said: "The name of Cardinal Newman is a great name to the imagination still; his genius and his style are still things of power . . . Forty years ago he was in the very prime of life; he was close at hand to us at Oxford; he was preaching in St Mary's pulpit every Sunday . . . Who could resist the charm of that spiritual apparition, gliding in the dim afternoon light through the aisles of St Mary's, rising into the pulpit and then, in the most entrancing of voices, breaking the silence with words and thoughts which were religious music, —subtle, sweet, mournful?" It was Newman that Arnold had in mind when he wrote of those "last enchantments of the middle ages." "But there were other voices sounding in our ears . . . There was the puissant voice of Carlyle: so sorely strained, over used, and misused since, but then fresh, comparatively sound, and reaching our hearts with true, pathetic eloquence." It was through Carlyle's translations that Arnold heard the greatest voice of that century: Goethe. "But what moved us most in "Wilhelm Meister" was that which, after all, will always move the young most,—the poetry, the eloquence. Never surely, was Carlyle's prose so beautiful and pure as in his rendering of the Youth's dirge over Mignon!—"Well is our treasure laid up, the fair image of the past. Here sleeps it in the marble, undecaying; in your hearts, also, it lives, it works. Travel, travel, back into life! Take along with you this holy earnestness, for earnestness alone makes life eternity." ' Here we have the voice of the great Goethe. The voice of Emerson is remembered for its most persistent theme: "Trust thyself! Every heart vibrates to that iron string. Accept the place that Divine Providence has found for you . . . Great men have always done so."

Sunday, December 12, 1937 I have been thinking over this past term with Dr. Mims and I have no doubt that he is one of the great teachers of all time. He is dogmatic. He sometime dismisses things like the famous Dr. Johnson did, with a wave of the hand. He is egotistical, but you cannot study with him without realizing how great is his love for literature and his reverence for the good of the past. His predominant theme is that the next best thing to having great thoughts is to have the great thoughts of others at your fingertips. He takes all literature to be his domain, "To look up and down no road, but that it stretches and waits for me." (Walt Whitman). He loved Tennyson and never tired of quoting such lines as: "To follow knowledge like a sinking star, beyond the utmost bound of human thought." and, of course, the last few sentences of Ulysses: "Come, my friends, 'Tis not too late to seek a newer world. Push off, and sitting well in order, smite the sounding furrows; for my purpose holds, To sail beyond the sunset . . . and the last lines . . . Made weak by time and fate, but strong in will, To strive, to seek, to find and not to yield." Dr. Mims had the ability to paint word pictures of the past that burnished themselves into the brain. When he describes Cardinal Newman as "Gliding in the dim afternoon through the aisle of St Mary's Cathedral" I conjure up a mental picture of the glories of the Middle Ages. He could read through the index of a volume of poetry and with one comment whet the student's appetite for reading every poem. John Crowe Ransom, whom I studied with last year, is the great critic. He took poems into the laboratory and examined them clinically. Mims took them to the hearth of your fireside and read them for the pure joy of it. Mims once said he would like it said of him: "On the Muse's hill he is happy."

Monday, December 13, 1937 I took the Spanish exam today. I believe I passed it. The exam that Economics professor, Byron Hill, gave was a scorcher. I never in my life saw such indefinite questions. Maybe I passed it. The tenseness before and between exams was something terrible. Got a letter from the patent office this morning showing that some fellow had a patent issued in 1934 to allow the slider to slip off over the top of a Zipper track, in case it ever got stuck. But he did not provide for a releasable latch at the bottom. The patent office has definitely granted us this releasable catch claim. The other inventor is Robert C. Legat, New Britain, Conn. Assignor to G.E. Prentice Manufacturing Company, New Britain, Conn.

Tuesday, December 14, 1937 I carelessly went to school at nine o'clock to take the examination in Physics. Found that it does not come until two this afternoon. Came on home, after going by the Banner office to collect my salary. It will be mailed out tomorrow. I did only fair on the Physics exam. Think I passed, though. Trig. comes tomorrow. Got off a letter to Burns in Washington suggesting the possible change in the bottom releasable fastener of the Zipper invention. As I have said before, if I could force myself to study every night as I do the night before exams, I would be an honor student. Tonight I learned practically every formula in Trigonometry we have had this term. I learned the proof of the law of signs and cosigns, of half angles and reviewed, understandingly, examples from practically every type of problem we have had this term. Now I hope all this knowledge does not get muddled up tomorrow.

Wednesday, December 15, 1937 That Math quiz was a "burner" this morning. Went to the picture show this evening. Saw a picture called the "Navy Blue and Gold." James Stewart, Toni Brown, and Robert Young played in it. Swell picture. Studied with Barney Blair and William Potts this evening.

Thursday, December 16, 1937 I think I made a good grade on the History exam this morning. Came home after lunch and studied English until four and then went over to meet Dr. Mims and the class in a last minute review. Got my first check from the Banner this morning. It was for $21.15. Did not include the money for the Hinkle story. Mrs. Miles just told me that Don Rust had lost his job. He has been married only a short while and his little baby is only a little over a week old. Such is life. Overhead expense was too great so they laid him off. He was the last one taken on by them. People depend so much on and are governed by the action of others. I go into the fraternity house and see other boys playing around and doing very little studying for exams. I say to myself they are not studying and will make out somehow, why can't I? I see them smoke cigarettes and live, why can't I? I honestly believe that there is not a man in the world who would seriously object to dying tomorrow, if he knew that every other man in the world were going to die too. The thing that disturbs him about dying is that he is going to have to leave all the earthly pleasures to men who survive him. At least that is a young man's view of life and dying.

Friday, December 17, 1937 I took my last exam this afternoon, English, and it was certainly tough. Found out from Dr. Manchester that I made 75 on the Spanish exam. That tickled me. Math, as usual, is the thing that worries me most. Bert Marshall told me this evening that my long lost raincoat is over in his room. He doesn't know how it got there. Tonight I had my first date with Ellen Bowers. We talked awhile, went to the Knickerbocker and then by Candyland and talked for about 30 minutes. I told her all about my invention and finally we branched off on to Medicine and Psychiatry. She said that would be the branch of medicine she would be interested in. As we were driving to town a fellow backed into us and caught our bumper but he did no damage. She is really a nice, sensible girl. Think I'll go out and see her some more. After taking Ellen home I went up to the Delta dance for a few minutes. Saw Virginia Youmans, who is back from Wellesley. Also saw Mr. and Mrs. George Harmon. He was looking a little poorly. Jim and Roy Huggins brought me home. McAdams and Lucien Lentz were pretty well "lit."

Saturday, December 18, 1937 I had a date with Elizabeth McEwen and Edmund Pardue dated Fannie Rose (Dinah) Shore. The four of us went to Hettie Ray's and danced. I have known Elizabeth only since coming to Vanderbilt, but I have known Fannie Rose since we were in Hume-Fogg together. I particularly remember one high school play she was in. She played the part of a Negro "Mammy" and hummed a lullaby that was as hauntingly beautiful as anything I have ever heard on the stage. Later in the evening Miriam came in with a Smith boy. Earlier in the evening I saw Santa Claus taking orders from the little kids at Sears Roebuck.

Sunday, December 19, 1937 Last night, while we were double dating, Elizabeth McEwen was talking about what a wonderful wrestler I am. Edmund Pardue and Fannie Rose were amused at this unintentional humor. Sat by Tom Scoggins at the West End Methodist Church today. He went to sleep. My sister Rebecca, my cousins Katherine Anderson and Frances Ragan visited Uncle Walt tonight and we read poetry. I read "The Man Flamonde" and Katherine read Amy Lowell's "The Patterns."

Monday, December 20, 1937 I left Nashville today for the holidays at home in Stevenson. I did the driving of Uncle Walt's car. I thought about some of the exciting things Dr. Mims said in his last few lectures before the examinations. Charles Dickens wrote of Thomas Carlyle: "I would go farther, at all times, to see Carlyle than any man alive. He first became famous because of his "French Revolution." His "Sartor Resartus" was first published in Boston under the patronage of Emerson. Froude, the historian, wrote of Carlyle: "The present generation will never know what it was to find all lights drifting, compasses dry, and nothing left to steer by but the star (Carlyle). His word was like the morning reveille. His voice was like the sound of 1000 trumpets. Dogma and tradition had melted like the mist . . . I was saved by Carlyle's writing from Romanism and Positivism." Mims says John Morley has written more good books about men than any Englishman—Gladstone, Voltaire and Rousseau among them. Carlyle called Goethe "The clearest, most universal man of his time . . . your work has been a mirror to me. I was once an unbeliever." Mims said that Dr. Johnson was one of the most fortunate men who ever lived. He had Carlyle and Macaulay, two of the best biographers in the world write about him.

Tuesday, December 21, 1937 I had a date with Freda Atwood tonight.

When we were in the fourth grade Freda was a wistfully beautiful little, red haired girl. I was desperately in love with her, but she paid no attention to me. I suppose my method of attracting her attention, such as knocking her books out of her hands, was not a particularly appealing act. In any event, we grew up. I developed interests in other girls, and she came to the conclusion that I may not be such a bad guy after all. What would have happened if we had loved each other, at the same time, at that tender age?

Wednesday, December 22, 1937 When we were young boys growing up, George L. Jr. always stood in awe of my father, but not to the extent of obeying him in matters of smoking. Dad would smell of his fingers and thrash him within an inch of his life if he smelled cigarette smoke. He used to smell my fingers too, on occasion. One day I was out, and couldn't get to the bathroom in time, and had to go in a back-yard, without the usual toilet accouterments. When I got home my father intercepted me before I got to the bathroom to wash my hands. He smelled my fingers, wrinkled his nose, and then looked at me in disbelief. Then he sniffed again, and said: "Son, whatever have you been doing?"

Thursday, December 23, 1937 Percy Armstrong, the local hardware man, was always sort of partial to the five Austin boys, when they were growing up, because they were always into some mischief and it added zest to an otherwise dull little town of less than a thousand population. In fact, the famous Scottsboro Case started right here in Stevenson. I actually saw the five Negroes and two white girls on the flatcar, just before the rape allegedly took place. It was noon and the freight train blocked the tracks as I was going back to school. The incident took place a few miles southwest of Stevenson, near Paint Rock, and blacks and whites were taken off the train at Scottsboro. That night, in 1931, several cars of men made the 20 miles trip to Scottsboro and milled about the jail. It was not because they were bloodthirsty and wanted to witness a lynching, but simply because their lives were dull and they needed some excitement. Percy was a good storyteller and he loved to talk about "Doc. Austin's boys." George L. Jr., who had a slight speech impediment, was the most mischievous one of the lot and was his favorite. He said that George once gathered a basket full of newly born kittens and took them to the home of Mrs. May Rudder to sell. He knocked at the door and said:

> *"Mrs. May, you wanna buy some 'tute little tittens?"*
> *"Wait just a minute George, let me get my mother and see what she thinks about it." By this time George was getting suspicious that he was being put on. When they came back and asked what he had to sell, he replied:*
> *"You wanna buy some 'dod damn tats!"*

Friday, December 24, 1937 The grades from Vanderbilt came out today and the family was upset with me because the grades were not as good as they should be. They want me to give up the Banner job, coaching wrestling, fraternity activities and dating; anything that interferes with scholarship. It is difficult to explain to others, but my grades are no indication of what I am learning at Vanderbilt. If I were preparing for a specific profession, such as the practice of medicine or dentistry, yes, the grades would be important. What I am learning is what the great men of literature have said throughout the ages; how to converse intelligently with, and to plumb the depths of the minds of brilliant contemporaries. I am learning what my place is in society and how effective I can be in changing, for the better, the life around me. In short, I am learning how to live. Only I can grade myself on that score.

Saturday, December 25, 1937 Christmas in Stevenson is not sleigh bells and horses dashing through the snow. It is not the department store's rushing crowds of the big cities. It is not elaborate feasts, or the tolling of church bells. But quiet, simple folk, giving words of cheer to their neighbors. They are a little more thoughtful of each other at this time of year. I know the shortcomings of a small country town; the backbiting and gossip in ordinary times, but in times of sickness and trouble, these people, both black and white, act as one family. It is a rich heritage, from which to send out young people, and I shall always be thankful for it.

Sunday, December 26, 1937 Three hundred dollars worth of fireworks were sold in Stevenson this Christmas and things were really popping. Jimmy Rudder came home for the holidays in the uniform of the Naval Academy. When I dated Freda the other evening I took her a box of candy and told her of my feelings for Miriam. I believe in playing fair, even in the game of love. Dad and Anderson left for a deer hunt in South Alabama and I finished reading "Gone with the Wind," which I started when I was home last Christmas. It is a powerful human drama; an almost pathetic commentary on the fickleness of the human heart. Scarlett did not learn to love until it was too late. Rhett could not win, even thought he played, to perfection, the role of a romantic lover. The circumstances were beyond his control; which is the pathos of all great loves that cannot be.

Monday, December 27, 1937 I have heard public speakers tell of boys going off to college and losing that "old feeling" about their mothers and fathers; their home towns. I have lost none of my feeling of love for the folks back home, as I promised myself I would not do, when I went away to school seven years ago at the age of thirteen. That does not mean that feelings don't change. I realized for the first time, this Christmas, that Stevenson no longer seemed like home to me. It does not have the peace and tranquility that it once had for me. I enjoyed

my visit but I will be glad to get back to my desk in Nashville. It is a
setback to the spirits to return to childhood scenes. As Thomas Wolfe
so aptly put it: "You Can't Go Home Again."

Tuesday, December 28, 1937 I dated Buhl Brown, of Jasper, Tennes-
see and James Mann dated Septima Havron on my last night in Steven-
son. Got up early and caught the train for Nashville. Bill Huddleston,
W. J. Talley, and Bill Simpson saw Mary Wallace and me off. Howard
Canon rode with us as far as Winchester. Saw Myrna Loy and Franchot
Tone in "Man Proof." It was a cleverly written, light show. The hero
was feeling the same way about Myrna that Ashley felt about Scarlett.
Mrs. Miles was surprised to see me walk in five days early.

Wednesday, December 29, 1937 Ate lunch with Uncle Walt and in
the after dinner discussion he was telling me about an article he had
read in the Reader's Digest entitled: "I Live Three Lives." It is the
story of a society girl who spends part of her year in the social whirl,
part on a dude ranch, and the other part in the frozen north where it
gets down 20 to 40 degrees below zero. The keynote is that conventions
vary with latitude and longitude. When in Philadelphia she is a helpless
woman, expecting to be waited on. In the north woods, where she traps,
she takes care of herself. She and her husband enjoy being shut up
together during those long winter months. George Bentley's sister, Flora,
called tonight and invited me to her dinner party tomorrow night at
Hettie Rays. I am to take Mary Paul Parsons. Nashville is enveloped
in a deep fog. The newspapers say it covers the whole of middle Tennessee. I am reminded of the fogs that always seem to be present in London
in the Sherlock Holmes movies. Got out my tux, for the first time in a
long while, to attend the dance at the Belle Meade Country Club. Bill
Shumaker and Sara Jane Peyton came by for me at seven. I don't know
which was more surprised to see me, Miriam or Susan. Susan asked
about my family and suggested that I meet her cousin, and her 14 year
old brother, John Jr., who is attending his first big dance. While Miriam
and I were sitting out a dance I told her that I returned early for my
date with her. Met an artist by the name of Puft, who teaches music at
Peabody. He told me a great deal about Mexico. Lang Wroton rode
home with us.

Thursday, December 30, 1937 I had to break the sad news to Miriam
that I could not date her because I am going to George and Flora Bentley's dinner dance. I called up Joe Cummings Jr., and asked him for a
ride. Said he'd have to let me know later in the afternoon. At 3:30 he
called and said his brother, Alan, had asked for the car first and suggested
that I call Giles Evans. It's hell to be poor; to have no car or money
either. You get into a lot of jams when you make plans, with the same
confidence you would, as if you had both. The party's over and I never

had a better time. Flora is a genius at selecting a guest list. Irene Cason has a unique personality and I told her how impressed I was with her. She liked that. Ileen Swords, whom I know from somewhere, dated J. G. Lackey. Joe Cummings Jr. somehow managed to get there with Louise Douglas. Louise told me how surprised she was when I asked her for the Deke dance. Tom Evans, Ed Walling and Lang Wroton were also there. The surprise of the evening for me was my date, Mary Paul Parsons. What a fabulous dancer she is and she knows a thousand songs. You leave her feeling light and gay. You'd think she doesn't have a care; perhaps she doesn't.

Friday, December 31, 1937 An interesting year has come to a close. One year blends into the next, and I never feel any different, on New Year's Eve, than I do on any other evening, and yet, another unit of time, in a given number, has been used up. We are further along towards what? That is the big question all of us ask ourselves at times. Bill Huddleston, from Stevenson, is in New York this evening making announcements on a national radio network. Paul Dumont is master of ceremonies of Pontiac's "Intercollegiate Variety Show" and Bill is one of the college announcers. Francis Robinson showed me pictures that Carl Hinkle had taken with Jeanette MacDonald and Nelson Eddy recently. Francis asked me what I intend to do after finishing school.

Saturday, January 1, 1938 The New Year's party at the Sigma Chi house last night was mainly an alumni affair. Met Florence Welch, Lu Ray's sister. Jack Worley has a crush on her. The floor was so slick that Louise Sykes fell. Santa Clara beat L.S.U. by a score of 6–0 and California beat Alabama 13–0. It was 'Bama's first defeat in five trips to the coast. The bears won by sheer power. Sanford did not get to use his magic toe. I pasted in my scrapbook while listening to the games. Used up a ten cent jar of paste. A friendly fellow by the name of Woodruff put in my extension telephone today.

Sunday, January 2, 1938 An "EXTRA" newspaper last night carried a story about the death of Hillary House, long time mayor of Nashville. At the West End Methodist Church I walked up the aisle to communion with Governor and Mrs. Gordon Browning. Howard Canon called on me tonight as he passed through on his way to Bowling Green, Kentucky.

e Evening Tennessean

NIGHT EDI

AGES   NASHVILLE, TENN., FRIDAY EVENING, FEBRUARY 15, 1935.   PRICE TE

Exposed Fascist Plot to March On Capital

GEN. SMEDLEY BUTLER
Former Marine commander whose story of an offer to command a "Fascist army" in the United States has been authenticated by the House Nazi committee.

SIMPSON IS OUT; TERA AWAITS JUDGE BROWN

Tennessee's relief administration, responsible for the support of 75,-000 families on relief rolls, was operating under the direction of Field Representative C. C. Stillman today pending the arrival tomorrow of Judge Barton Brown, who is expected to assume charge immediately.

Fascist Plot To Form Army In U. S. Verifi

NEW ARREST IN HAUPTMANN CASE IS HOPE

Authorities Still Think Convicted Slayer Had Help.

NO CONFESSION

NEW YORK.—(UP)— The New York Daily News said today that the alleged "accomplice" of Bruno Richard Hauptmann in the Lindbergh kidnaping was known to authorities who are awaiting a chance to trap him.

The newspaper said the suspect was the man whom Col. Charles A. Lindbergh saw outside St. Raymond's cemetery on the night of the ransom payment.

By SIDNEY S. WHIPPLE
(Copyright, 1935. By United Press)
FLEMINGTON, N. J.—(UP)—Bruno Richard Hauptmann has lost all hope of escaping the electric chair, but will die insisting he is innocent of murdering the Lindbergh baby, the United Press was informed today by a source close

THEY'RE THE STUDENT BOSSES AT HUME-FOGG

Left to right: Ben Ryan Austin, president of the student council at Hume-Fogg High School; Rozelle Wallace, vice-president; and Mac H. Rochelle, secretary and treasurer.
These Hume-Fogg students were elected officers of the council Wednesday. They are all members of the senior class.

Concentration of Wealth Is National Menace, Says
Tax

BUTLER OF LEA OFFER

March On Part of Pl vestigatic

SUPPRESS

WASHINGTO House Nazi in tee reported tod cated charges of D. Butler that I command of march on Was

The committe Congress said, evidence "to sh tween this effo activity of any

The report, r of investigation credited agents were active spread of forei the United Stat Actic

The sharply volved in its im ernments of Italy and the U. tained recomm cisive congressio what it found to Democratic form this country.

Nazi propaga gantic mass me the vilest sort wave radio, the charged one "tr there was "Indi that certain Ga gaged in "viciou propaganda acti

Concerning charge he had a Fascist army ington the com had "received that certain pe attempt to esta ganization in tl

Attemp "There is no these attempts been planned, placed in if the financial expedient," the Butler, the co fied as to Gerald C. Mac latter is allege the "formation under the lea Butler."

MacGuire, th denied these oath, "but you able to verify statements mad ler, with excep statement sugg of the organiza ever, the com corroborated in of MacGuire Robert Sterlin York City."

The report cl R. had failed pledge of stop propaganda. It tee had found b tary evidence a mission of Com the objective o to overthrow by the republican l and substitute government has nation.

The specific munist admini achieved," the r clutionary uphea class hatred, by warfare and by ods."

The "American is definitely un of the third int cow, the report crying the

NORRIS

y of hun-others and

We drag to a point t fall.

had no of individ-r industry en because la plea, he to society, fortune a point ning to in-ess. Such become

no greater money and us to the n enemy to or not, we taxes. Are

"FOGG-HORN" MAKES BOW AT HIGH SCHOOL

Staff members of the Fogg Horn, weekly newspaper published by students of Hume-Fogg High School which appeared for the first time today, are, reading from left to right, Jack Kuhn, circulation manager, Darby Fulton, secretary; Granville Sims, city editor, Harris Abrahams, assistant editor, Irving Schwartz, business manager, and Ben Austin, editor-in-chief.

Top (left to right): Darby Fulton, Harris Abrahams, Ben R. Austin, Granville Sims and Irving Schwartz.

Below: Facsimile of today's issue of The Fogg Horn.

A new weekly newspaper, The Fogg Horn, organ of students of Hume-Fogg High school, made its debut in Nashville journalistic circles today, and was inspected by the staff as the first copies came off the presses this morning.

The Fogg Horn, to be published each Monday, began its career with a circulation of 1,-900, the largest any Hume-Fogg publication has ever enjoyed. It replaces The Tatler, which suspended publication last year.

The new paper will contain Hume-Fogg news and editorials on questions of interest to students, as well as city news pertinent to Hume-Fogg student life. It will confine itself to these types of writing and make no attempt to compete with or displace the Hume-Fogg Echo, which is essentially a literary magazine.

The first editions will be distributed free, and copies of succeeding issues will be sold at a cent each.

Officials of the paper are Ben R. Austin, editor; Irving Schwartz, business manager; Granville Sims, city editor; Harris Abrahams, assistant editor, and Darby Fulton, secretary. Faculty sponsors are W. E. Porter, Miss Emma Brown and Miss Anne Battle.

FOGG HORN

VOLUME I   NASHVILLE, TENN., MARCH 11, 1936   Circulation, 1,900

Hume Fogg Now Has A 1c Weekly

HERE AT LAST

OUR PLAN

LIFE STORY OF NEMO

OUR POLICY

THE PROVERB OF THE WEEK

On Suggestive Selling

The Fogg Horn has prepared an exhibit showing the way it is printed. It includes examples from linotype, press and finished products. Certain articles, columns and editorials were entered separately to be judged on their journalistic qualities. Two first awards and two seconds were won.

Hume-Fogg (0)	Pos.	Central (12)
Walker	L.E.	Whaley
Moore	L.T.	West
Sweetland	L.G.	Suffridge
Berry	C.	Cannon
Woodall	R.G.	Molinski
Austin	R.T.	Sparks
Bomar	R.E.	Seacry
Waller	Q.	Matthews
Mifflin	L.H.	Sullins
Crockett	R.H.	Selby
Trueman	F.B.	Gifford

'FOG HORN' BEGINS PUBLICATION TODAY

Students at Hume-Fogg high school today will receive the first copies of the "Fogg Horn," new weekly publication of the school, which replaces "The Tatler," suspended last year.

Ben R. Austin is editor of the new paper; Irving Schwartz is business manager; Granville Sims, city editor; Harris Abrahams, assistant editor and Darby Fulton, secretary. Faculty sponsors are W. E. Porter, Miss Emma Brown and Miss Ann Battle.

HUME-FOGG CARRIES 30 TO LEWISBURG

Hume-Fogg will carry a squad of 30 players, the school band and the girls' drill team to Lewisburg today for the game with Lewisburg high.

The starting lineup, announced by Coach W. E. Porter, will be: Walker and Bomar, ends; Moore and Austin, tackles; Johnson and Sarvis, guards; Roberts, center; Mifflin, quarter; Jones and Gotto, halves, and Trueman, full.

The complete squad making the trip will be: Austin, Johnson, Waller, Friedman, Boner, Sarvis, Roberts, Berry, Sweetland, Walker, Mifflin, Moore, L. Crockett, Bayer, Trueman, Woodall, Bomar, Gotto, Jones, R. Blackmer, J. Blackmer, Major, Howard, Sanderson, Lowe, Wine, Elliott, Dysart (manager) and Blankenship (assistant manager).

The team, band and drill team will leave at noon, making the trip via bus.

At the extreme left, Richard Flanagan, Knoxville City center, is seen as he reached into the air to knock a pass out of Jimmy Boone's hands in the game with Nashville Central. In the center, Gillard of Knoxville, Central, was snapped as he tore into the Hume-Fogg line in the first quarter Friday for a six-yard gain. Lewis Crockett is seen making the tackle.

WINTER
1938

Monday, January 3, 1938 Classes resumed today. The new literary publication, "Pursuit," made its appearance. Since I am going out for varsity wrestling, I had to give up my coaching job. Mack Peebles, who is ineligible for the varsity, is taking my place as coach of the freshmen and Intramural wrestlers. Ed Kirkpatrick and I worked out together. Tom Happel visited the fraternity tonight and we talked over our stock company. Merrill Stone did me the honor of welcoming him into the fraternity tonight. I hit him lightly with the paddle. I think he was disappointed that I didn't give him one he could be proud of.

Tuesday, January 4, 1938 Dr. Mims stopped me on the campus this evening and said: "I think more of you than I do any boy at Vanderbilt." He went on to say that he understood why I did not make better grades in his course. Nobody can do as many things as you do and make good grades. He said that he had noticed, however, that "The things you get, you get! You remember and use the things you learn." Dr. Walter Clyde Curry delivered his first lecture to us this morning. He said we would study all 37 of Shakespeare's plays; 23 of them this term.

Wednesday, January 5, 1938 Enjoyed all my classes today because I was prepared. I am going to like Spanish much better this term because the emphasis is going to be on conversation and reading, and not so much on grammar. I was tired today from doing too much wrestling with Ed Kirkpatrick yesterday. Coach Field put me with a new man to get him started off on the right foot.

Thursday, January 6, 1938 I took Miriam's advice and went to bed tonight at 10:00 o'clock. I did not go to sleep in a single class and even felt wide awake while studying in the library. I felt so good that I pinned Ed Kirkpatrick in just a few minutes. Bill Daniel, last years captain, paid us a short visit.

Friday, January 7, 1938 Carl Hinkle asked me this morning if Fred Russell had paid me for the magazine section story. I suppose he wants part of it. I don't particularly mind giving him half of it because I do not know the protocol on this kind of thing. Spent the early afternoon reading the "Spanish Tragedy" by Thomas Kyd. Shakespeare's tragedies were modeled after Kyd's. I worked out with Jackson, but will vie in the elimination match with Ed Kirkpatrick. It determines who will wrestle in the next match.

Saturday, January 8, 1938 I was in dread all afternoon of my ten minute wrestling match with Ed Kirkpatrick down at the gym at 3:30. I would have almost given up before starting had there been some easy way of doing it. After seeing the other boys wrestle until they were completely exhausted I decided to take it easy. I took the defense and Ed rushed in and tried to get me off my feet. I landed on top of him and pinned him. He got my shoulders to the mat next time. Instead of riding him to the left and letting him come out of it with his deadly switchback, I rode him to the right side and he was unaccustomed to a person riding him to that side, so he was helpless. I rode him awhile that way and then pinned him with a combination arm lock and half nelson. I pinned him again before the match was over with my favorite hold—namely to get his head and arm in front of him. I felt real proud after the match was over. I took a dreadful cold though while I was up there in my shorts waiting for him to get dressed. Tonight Tom Cummings and Mike Cain came by for me. When we went for Susan, Mr. John Cheek met me at the door and we had a nice little chat before Susan came down. He told me a story that his father, Joel Cheek, founder of Maxwell House Coffee, told him about Stevenson. Mr. Cheek was, at that time, representing some business out of Cincinnati and a group of salesmen were sitting around the hotel after supper one night watching one of their fellow salesmen do sleight of hand tricks. After awhile, one of the biggest customers spoke up: "Please cancel my order. I don't want to do business with anyone who knows all the tricks you do."

Sunday, January 9, 1938 I was surprised to hear Jack Keefe, candidate for mayor, play the piano so well at West End Methodist Church Sunday school this morning. I was there to hear Dr. Mims lecture in his Sunday Bible class. My cold made me feel so badly that I retired early this evening.

Monday, January 10, 1938 Jim Reed jokingly told me today that I should not enter the Intramural wrestling tournament because he may have to meet me and he didn't want that. I had to leave lab. early. Took some castor oil and orange juice and went to bed.

Tuesday, January 11, 1938 Hell week started today for the new fraternity pledges. They have to go through all the hell we upper classmen can think up. I got paid for my Hinkle story today and also for the last two weeks of wrestling. Felt better today so I put on a wrestling demonstration with Partee Fleming. Found out I am going to have to wrestle Bud Bray in the Intramural finals. He is a good wrestler and outweighs me by about ten pounds. Tom Cummings Jr. and I were discussing on the phone tonight what we could do to help his father get elected mayor. I suggested a poll of the students and a write up in the papers. It would be swell if the poll came out right, and it would if you asked the right people. Tom Jr. laughed and said I ought to be his father's campaign manager.

Wednesday, January 12, 1938 Jim Souby, and his Hustler staff, sprung the "Miss Vanderbilt" election this morning. Miriam McGaw, Andromedia Bagwell, Elizabeth Rudolph, Ruth and Sarah King were the leading candidates. I think Miriam will win. I took my story to the Banner after chapel. Sat with Hinkle and gave him half of the story money, ten dollars. Wrestled and got thrown this afternoon by Art Keene. Art wrestles in the weight above me, at 175 pounds, but still I felt the sting of defeat. Think I'll keep working with him until I throw him. Got my lip busted in the furious match. Hartwell Weaver insisted on finding out from me if I intend to take Miriam to our Deke dance. I certainly am not, but I don't want her to know it just yet. Why should I take her? She does not ask me to be her date for her dances.

Thursday, January 13, 1938 I called up Mr. Duncan this morning and told him it was a foregone conclusion that Miriam would be "Miss Vanderbilt." We could "scoop" both the Hustler and the Tennessean if we wished to. After talking it over we decided not to "scoop" the Hustler, but to come out with them simultaneously tomorrow. Mr. Hilliard Wood and I went to the McGaw apartment this evening and took fifteen pictures of her. We had her in jodhpurs, playing the piano, in a tennis outfit and an evening dress. Miriam played for us the "Indian Love Call." That may be the only piece she knows, but she did that one pretty well. Mrs. McGaw thanked me for showing Miriam such a good time in Knoxville.

Friday, January 14, 1938 I was never so surprised in my life when Susan Cheek came by and asked me to take her to her sorority dance January 29th. I was partially in shock because I am not accustomed to being treated so well. Miriam's pictures were beautiful in the Banner this afternoon. We used her studio picture with four different poses around it. The Hustler used the studio picture only. Ellen Bowers and I went to see "Tavarich" at the Knickerbocker. As we came out of Candyland, after the show, a little boy came up and asked for seven cents. I had it in change so I gave it to him. Ellen said: "You're crazy, Ben, for giving that boy money. You're encouraging bad habits." I remember when I was younger there were several occasions when I needed a few extra pennies to go to a show, or to buy something special, and I appreciated the generosity of grown-ups. Ellen says she does a lot of reading and collects stuffed teddy bears and elephants for her room. She takes a trip somewhere every summer and wants to go to Europe next summer. Dropped by the Sigma Chi House, where Francis Craig was playing. He dedicated a dance to "Miss Vanderbilt" and Miriam naturally selected her date for it. She said this was the happiest night of her life.

Saturday, January 15, 1938 I went to the fraternity house and saw raw eggs dropped from an upstairs window into the mouths of gaping freshmen. I was supposed to wrestle Bill Grissom today but he did not show up. In the varsity workout I wrestled Art Keene again. We started out on our feet and I picked him up twice and slammed him against the mat. It was sweet revenge for last week. Bill Lauderdale dated Martha Wade, and I, Louise Douglass, and we went dancing at Hettie Ray's. I enjoy dancing with Louise. Got some bad news this evening. Coach Field told me that the wrestling team is going to be out of town on the 29th, the date of the Kappa Alpha Theta dance to which I am suppose to take Susan. Curses!

Sunday, January 16, 1938 Saw Miriam on the way out of Dr. Mim's Sunday school class. I explained that I had finished his classes at Vanderbilt. I am here because I like to hear him speak. Uncle Walton called today and told me that Aunt Nell told him I was looking badly. Two weeks ago when I came back early from the holiday I asked uncle if I could eat lunch with him for the next three days because my contract with Mrs. Miles did not provide for lunch. He said it was OK, but then called me back that night and told me it was too big an inconvenience, so I did not bother him further. When Aunt Nell told him I was looking sad he probably figured I wasn't getting enough to eat and was sorry that he had refused my request. He said I could come by there anytime I wanted to and could devour everything in the place; just like at home. I am off from 170 to 158, but it is not because of being unable to get food. I am training for the wrestling team and I have cut out the heavy midday meal in order to get into a lower weight category. This incident is of no great consequence, and yet it points up one of the most moving experiences in human relations. When a helpless, or less fortunate, person, asks something of us that we could freely give, and we do not, for superficial reasons, and then later we find out the consequences of our callousness, we are grief stricken. This is the plaint most often heard at the burial grounds. Why didn't I do more? If I had only known!

Monday, January 17, 1938 My date with Miriam last night was a classic. We talked for a long time in her apartment and then we went to the drugstore and talked some more. We walked around the block slowly and talked. We came back and sat on the steps and talked some more. Finally, around midnight I made a move to go in. She reluctantly, almost resignedly rose and walked towards her apartment. I knew what the stalling was all about. She was waiting for me to invite her to the Deke dance, but I never did. Leo Bashinski is taking her best friend, Louise Sykes, and I am sure she is pepped up over the dance and has passed some of her enthusiasm to Miriam. This is the only revenge I have.

Tuesday, January 18, 1938 Hartwell Weaver confessed to me that he and Miriam had been talking over the possibilities of my taking her to the dance. Miriam told him that I had asked her a long time ago for a date for the dance, but that I had probably forgotten. I don't believe I ever asked her for it. I am taking Susan, who reciprocates such courtesies. In the library I had to break the sad news to Susan that I would be out of town when her dance is scheduled. I told her that I had almost as soon forfeit my right to make the trip with the wrestling team. Joe Agee, the football player, started out for the wrestling team today. He is strong and quick and learns fast. I worked with him quite a bit. My going to bed so late last night effected my wrestling today. I met Henry Canon in the Intramural meet today and was as weak as water. I pinned him but I did not make such a good showing. I am going to start eating lunch again to gain back some weight.

Wednesday, January 19, 1938 Dr. Curry said yesterday that life in the Middle Ages was of little importance, just a pilgrimage to the here-after. Chaucer was, more or less, a forerunner of the awakening. Worldly splendor was a characteristic of the Shakespearean era. Shakespeare rarely considers immortality. Sir Walter Raleigh had a hundred pounds of jewelry on his person when he was arrested. Curry said, "Shakespeare had the great ability for putting problems and mysteries of life, but never solving the problems and mysteries."

Thursday, January 20, 1938 Ate a beefsteak for lunch today and it made me feel like a new man. I worked out with Ed Kirkpatrick and he could not hold me down. Made a hundred on the Spanish quiz. Arranged for pictures for the Owl Club, the Scouting fraternity, the new dramatic group and George Morrow, the Engineering scholar, genius. Went up to Hume-Fogg today and talked with Mrs. Henry Claire Blodeau Graham, who is now running 50 libraries in addition to one there. What a friend she was to me, and Theo Mars, Tom Alexander and others. She and W. E. "Slim" Porter were my faculty sponsors when I was editing the Fogg Horn and both backed my efforts to the hilt. Mrs. Graham was one of my favorite people in all the world, when I was at Hume-Fogg and I think even more of her in retrospect. Miss Mary Louise Goodwin invited me to an English teacher's meet. Mrs. Sally Welch, the principal's secretary, is as cute as ever. Miss Dembsky and Mr. Mortimer said hello. Wrestled Dave Patterson, a Sigma Chi freshman in an Intramural meet this afternoon. Dave is a big, strong boy and I did not know whether or not he could wrestle. I decided to take it easy with him for a minute or so to find out. I backed off several times when he lunged at me. On about the third charge I stepped aside, like a Spanish torero, applied a crotch hold in the air as I slammed him to the mat and pinned him. Art Keene was the referee and I thought he would never make the call. He admitted to me afterwards that Dave was pinned long before he called it but that he wanted me to get a good workout. Coach Fields came by after the match and congratulated me. He said: "That is the way it should be done."

Friday, January 21, 1938 It was raining hard this morning so I decided to stay at home and study. Just about the time I got ready to start studying, Lydel Sims called from the Banner and asked me to write some cut lines for the pictures we took yesterday. Also, Mr. Stahlman, the publisher, wanted a story on Vanderbilt initiations. I got the material together and took it to the Banner. This consumed my whole day and I never did get to study. Guess that's one of the answers to the grade situation. It is a matter of priorities.

Saturday, January 22, 1938 Dr. Curry and I had a discussion in class this morning. "Do you believe in love at first sight, Mr. Austin?" he asked. I stuttered and stammered. After a lengthy discussion with the rest of the class he said that love is always at first sight; when you really see that person, as he or she really is, for the first time. Perfect love exists only in the imagination. Artistic love is superior to practical love. Mercutio is a special friend of Dr. Curry's. He is kind of a prince, with wit and a delicacy of mind and fancy. Dr. Curry's description of Mercutio reminds me that the description, more or less, fits Dr. Curry himself. My initiation story made the front page of the Banner. R. A. Gotto also used the little wrestling incident I submitted to him in his unusual sports cartoon. Dot Evans flattered me last night by saying I reminded her of Carl Hinkle; busy all the time, but yet speaking to everyone on campus. Susan told me that the next time she sees me she is going to ask for my autograph. That was probably because some of my fraternity brothers have been referring to me as "Champ" since I have been winning all my matches in the Intramural meet. Edgar Walling told me that my invention was the chief topic of conversation at a 2:00 A.M.

bull session last night when Buddy Rand and Tom Happel came down from St. Louis.

Sunday, January 23, 1938 Did not go to Sunday school because I am behind in my reading. Next weekend I will be in Knoxville with the wrestling team.

Monday, January 24, 1938 William Lauderdale and I had another of our rough and tumble wrestling matches in the Intramural meet this afternoon. Bill is well built, with bulging muscles, but he is a superb boxer, instead of a wrestler, and we both know I can throw him when I want to. Since the outcome is not in doubt and since we are good friends and both like to "roughhouse" it occasionally, we really slap each other around. It appears, I'm sure, to the audience, that we are really mad at each other. I pinned him in four minutes, about the same time as our famous match last year when Bobby Oliver thought we were killing each other. On the phone tonight Miriam complimented my picture in the paper with Susan. We did not discuss the fact that I had not invited her instead of Susan. Miriam is going to attend a summer camp near Winchester. George Morrow's prodigy story appeared in the Banner this afternoon.

Tuesday, January 25, 1938 I was worried about my match with Bud Bray in the Intramural finals this evening. Bud is in the weight category heavier than mine, and is as strong as a bull. My right knee has been acting up so I put a steel brace on it. If Bud had grabbed the knee I would have been in trouble. I was ready for the match. I had eaten a couple of raw eggs and had taken a nap in the afternoon. I took it easy at first. Won the toss and went down first, executed a perfect forward roll and came back on Bud's back before he knew what was happening. Held him practically the whole time. George Fields said it was a good match. John Hood, of the Banner, just missed taking a picture of my roll. Wish he had gotten it. That would have been a classic picture. They gave me my second gold medal. I went down to the fraternity house to receive the congratulations of the brothers, most of whom had seen the match. The Phi Kappa Psi threat of jumping the Confederation is about over. Ed Pardue came by to see me to discuss the political implications of same.

Wednesday, January 26, 1938 When Susan asked me how I came out in the tournament I showed her the medal. She seemed pleased. We are leaving for Knoxville at 7:30 in the morning and will come back Sunday. I am to room with Mr. George Fields, the coach. Just before my match with Bray last night he saw me putting on my knee brace and asked me what my trouble was. I told him it was injured and he said "If in our match I ever hurt it just tell me and I'll let go." I thought it mighty nice of him to say that. He meant it too. Aunt

Nell told me tonight that Wilson Lynch told Uncle Ragan that I won my match last night. He added that I was the best wrestler in Vanderbilt. That was mighty nice coming from Lynch, who himself is no slouch on the mat. "One Man's Family" was particularly good tonight. One of the newly married sons of the Barber family has just had a spat with his wife and they separated. Paul, an older brother-in-law of the family, in a casual chat draws an analogy between handling women and an expensive violin. He says that one person could come along, grab it up, and start sawing away, getting nothing but discords, while on the other hand, someone else might come along, pick it up gently, slipping it under his chin with great care and stroke it gently as it warms up under his light touch. The latter fellow gets beautiful music because he knows how to handle it. He went on to point out that women are the same way. They have to be treated delicately. All the little niceties must be observed. Indelicacies mar the whole scene for them.

Thursday, January 27, 1938 The Vanderbilt wrestling squad: Partee Fleming, Bud Bray, Art Keene, Ed Kirkpatrick, Rush Dozier, Jack Keefe Jr., Scott George, John Pellett, Bob Slayden, Oliver Graves and I left for Knoxville at eight o'clock this morning. We ate in Cookville and arrived at the University of Tennessee gym at three. The match started at four thirty. Just as I sat down on the bench Anderson and Henry D. came up behind me. They received my card and they also saw a notice in the newspapers. I wrestled Silva in the 165 lb. class. Neither of us got the advantage from the standing position. I won the coin toss and elected to take the down position. I executed my specialty, the forward roll, perfectly, and came from the bottom to the top and rode him the rest of the match. I got the decision, but I was completely exhausted. There was talk of getting Carl Hinkle to wrestle Joe Black Hayes, captain of the U. T. football team, but it did not work out. Fleming wrestled and pinned Joe Black. We won the meet 19–13 and I wired a story back to the Nashville Banner. Had a short visit with my brothers before they rushed back to T.M.I. I thought of the last time I was in Knoxville . . . with Miriam.

Friday, January 28, 1938 George Fields and I went to a brokerage office to see the Y.M.C.A. coach. He told us that Art and I did not have to weigh in and that we could eat all we wanted to. We did. I slept all afternoon. The meet started at seven o'clock. I met Householder in the 155 lb. weight. It was the first time I have ever been pinned in a match. Householder cannot be classified as a college wrestler because he graduated two years ago and has been a star wrestler there and at the "Y". The real reason I lost though was a matter of strategy. George Field insisted that I do the forward roll from the down position, even though Householder had seen me do it at Tennessee last night. The surprise element was gone. As I rolled forward he caught my left leg and I was standing on my head with my shoulders on the mat. There is no way to escape.

Saturday, January 29, 1938 I went to the "Y" this morning and put the heat lamp on my injured knee. I could hardly walk. From Knoxville we drove to Maryville College, where we met their coach, and student manager Byrne, who has aspirations of being a cartoonist. Bob Gillespie, student manager of the school paper, was also on the welcoming committee. The University of Kentucky swimming team and football captain, Hinkerbein, as coach, stayed in the same room with us. When they found out we were from Vanderbilt, they shouted with joy. We pulled for them in swimming events and they for us in wrestling. They even sat on our bench. The "Y" coach and Householder also came down from Knoxville. Fleming saved the day for us again and we won. Partee's opponent bit his finger and Partee was ready to fight. We had to restrain him. They finally shook hands and ended the meet on a friendly note. We all had big steaks and retired to the quarters for a joke telling session. We were treated royally and had a delightful time, but Jack Keefe got an elbow dislocation and was in pain most of the night, in spite of sedation.

Sunday, January 30, 1938 We got up early and ate with about five hundred boys and four hundred girls in the dining hall. This is a very religious school and they don't allow smoking, dancing, or the like on campus, but I never saw so much courting in one place in my life. The prohibitions merely enhance the boy, girl relationships. I like the school. Tuition is only about $300.00 per year and most of the students work for at least a part of their expenses.

Monday, January 31, 1938 I had to go to school with a walking stick this morning. While eating lunch with Sykes and McGaw, they were talking excitedly about one date Louise had with Herbert Buchanan. Miriam asked her if she did it. She said: "Yes", and they both broke out in cries of joy. I take it that Louise asked "Buck" to take her to the dance on the 26th. I let Miriam read the theme I wrote on Romeo. She pointed out the sentence: "Rosalin held herself aloof so his ardor was stronger than ever." So that's it, eh? Rode to school today with Ruth Kellar, whom Cousin Osgood has gone with occasionally. Ed Pardue and I went to the Phi Kappa Psi House tonight to soothe some political waters. Algie Choate doesn't seem to have much political clout. It seems that they have a lawyer living at their house who pulls strings behind the scenes.

Tuesday, February 1, 1938 I turned in my "string" to the newspaper this morning. I earned a total of $25.00, but my limit is $22.00. Susan asked me about my trip and my knee injury. Louise Douglas said that she looked all over for me last week to ask me to have a no-break with her at the Theta dance. When Ellen Bowers saw me on a crutch, she said: "I told you so." She loaned me her notes covering the two days I was absent. I went to the political meeting at the Phi Psi House tonight. Pierce Winningham and I struck a bargain. He is to support us for the Honor Committee and one of the Student Union spots, and I am to support him for the Presidency of the Glee Club and one of the four Union or Council jobs. It was a two hour powwow. The Phi Kappa Psi's make an agreement, and still they are not satisfied. My sympathy for their cause is rapidly changing.

Wednesday, February 2, 1938 Dr. Tom Zerfoss put a plaster cast on my knee this afternoon. Dick Matthews and I reviewed the political situation at Vanderbilt and worked up some alternative plans, in case some organization wishes to jump to the other side.

Thursday, February 3, 1938 Dr. Curry got off on the subject of war this morning and talked about it for thirty minutes. He got the whole class stirred up to an argumentative pitch. The main thing he said was that we fight all the time, but we never accomplish anything. He closed by saying that a famous Historian, by the name of Adams, I believe it was, looked back over the blocks of history and said that men are like a pack of wolves, carrying packs across a desert. They stop on the way; a few are killed off; they pick up their packs and move on. Both Susan and Miriam were in the library this afternoon. I came in and asked Ruth Petty if she would meet Mr. Wood and me in a beauty parlor for a picture. She would not agree to it until she asked Miriam if it were the proper thing to do. It was all right after Miriam gave her approval. Tom Cummings Sr. beat Jack Keefe Sr. by 3,000 votes in Nashville's election. The final tally was 9,517 to 6,504.

Friday, February 4, 1938 Partee Fleming told me this evening that Coach Miles told him that I handle the freshman wrestling class better than he does, so he is going to give the job back to me when I finish wrestling with the varsity. Went to the W. S. M. auditorium this afternoon to hear Alfred T. Vanderbilt, President of the American Bar Association, speak. Also heard ex-President Sims, of Alabama. Frank C. Rand, Chairman of Vanderbilt's Board of Trustees, was there, as were several students.

Saturday, February 5, 1938 Saw the third Vanderbilt Chancellor inaugurated this morning. Dr. Isaiah Bowman, President of Johns Hopkins, was the principle speaker. He said all things are academic until we are going down for the last time. Enthusiasm makes a bad councillor, but a good partner. In speaking of a politician's charge that he did not think, the other politician said: "Hell, I didn't come here to think, I came here to holler." Nearly 300 educators from around the world were here to pay their respects to the new Chancellor. Two of Carmichael's brothers were here. Frank Rand presented the University seal of authority. Randy Batson made a grand speech, representing the student body. I went to the gym dance tonight in spite of my injured knee. While dancing the second no-break with Miriam I noticed how small her waist is. Her nice figure and graceful dancing goes a long way towards making her so popular. I can't figure how she manages to feel so light when you are dancing with her. The secret may be that she leans away from you, while dancing, so that only the shoulders touch. Only she knows what her legs are doing. Had the third no-break with Susan Cheek. She has coal black hair, which is always groomed nicely, a broad forehead, and beautiful brown eyes. I enjoy looking at her. She also has a natural effiminate shyness that is tantilizingly attractive. Hilliard Wood, who is covering the Chancellor's Inauguration, for Life magazine, was at the dance tonight and took pictures of "Miss Vanderbilt" Miriam McGaw and of all-American, Carl Hinkle.

Sunday, February 6, 1938 Slept late this morning and did not go to Sunday school and church. Picked up Miriam at her apartment at eight o'clock and as we were driving out to the West end she said she had something both good and bad to tell me. The good—she wants me to take her to the Tri Delta dance. The bad—wants me to change the midwinter dance dates with Ed Kirkpatrick so that she can lead the Junior Prom with him. He is President of the Junior Engineers. I was very pleased over her asking me to take her to her dance, especially after I made it a point to see that she did not get to come to the "Deke" dance. I am still rejoicing over that triumph. We drove around for awhile and then we parked and talked. As time for going home approached, I asked her if she remembered my asking her for a kiss when I left town almost three years ago. She remembered, but said that the answer was still "NO." Then she told me that once this summer she made a dreadful mistake and that things were different from that moment. I did not insist. I believe she got a kick out of my asking her for a kiss though. She seemed gayer from then on.

Monday, February 7, 1938 I had a test in Spanish before going to the Physics class. Jimmy Lanier, President of Sigma Nu, referred me to Wayne Dehoney for a political discussion about their joining us. Went to Physics lab. and to a press conference with Dean Pascall. This evening I went to the Sigma Nu House to talk politics with Wayne Dehoney. If the Sigma Nu's come in with us we will have the strongest political organization ever assembled on the Vanderbilt campus. With their 64 votes we will sweep every election. Went to the Belmont theatre tonight to see "The Life of Emile Zola." He was the French writer who championed truth at any cost. Paul Muni won the Academy Award for his performance. Mrs. Miles hurt my feelings tonight when she suggested that the only reason I wanted early supper was that I was hungry; not that I had to go someplace.

Tuesday, February 8, 1938   Today I am a man. Having reached my 21st birthday I can sign contracts, without my parents cosigning, I can vote and I have all the privileges of an adult. I also have the responsibilities. I am fully accountable for my acts. But that is nothing new, I have been on my own for several years. My 13th birthday was really the turning point for me. I literally sat down and decided what kind of person I would be: honest, or dishonest; responsible, or irresponsible; ambitious, or a loafer. I even decided how I would go about achieving my goals. The keynote was to form the habit of being what I want to be, day by day. It has worked out pretty good so far. Wayne Dehoney and I met at Dr. Taylor's drugstore tonight and thrashed out the details of the merger. The Confederation is favorable to taking in the Sigma Nu's to replace the Phi Psi's, and the Sigma Nu's have agreed to our terms. Morris McLemore, a Phi Psi, saw Wayne and me talking and I am sure he saw the "handwriting on the wall."

Wednesday, February 9, 1938   At General Chapel today the students didn't pay very close attention to the speaker, Dr. Eddie Mims, who was giving some of the high points of the inauguration symposium. They carried on so many private conversations that the speaker could scarcely be heard. At the close, Dr. Mims said: "I thank you for your kind attention, those of you who were courteous enough to listen; to those who did not, I hold no ill will, because I feel that they know not what they do." Anderson sent me $30.00 and news that a Negro wrecked Dad's car. George L. Jr. flew home in one of his training planes and gave the town a thrill. At a Confederation meeting tonight I presented the results of my negotiations with the Sigma Nu's. Morris Burk, as usual, was the chief foe of the plan. They agreed to hold off everything until Sunday when offices are actually distributed.

Thursday, February 10, 1938   Colonel Willard Chevalier, vice-president of McGraw Hill Publishing Company, addressed the engineering students. He told, very interestingly, a story of his first engineering job, that of weighing scrap iron. He had studied hydrostatics but he did not know how to take measurements on the flat boat and figure the displacement of water. The story of the Catskill water tunnel under the Hudson was very interesting. To locate solid rock they made long drill holes but could not tell whether the drill holes were going straight or slanting outward. One fellow thought of putting hydrofluoric acid in a glass container and putting it in the shafts. The glass would be etched and the exact angle of the bottom of the hole could be determined. Took the Miami Triad date list to the Banner. Made a no-break with Susan Cheek. After the dance Mr. Hood, the Banner photographer, showed up just as the first no-break was called. I didn't realize that it was the one I was to have with Susan. I stood her up completely. She forgave me though. Enjoyed dancing with Dot King. Weaver asked me to double with him tomorrow night so I asked Ellen Bowers for a date to go to see Wallace Berry at Loews. Craig played too many fast pieces tonight. Miriam looked real nice. She had on a new dress. Ed Kirkpatrick was giving her a rush. I like Susan more every time I see her.

Friday, February 11, 1938 My knee hurt so badly today that I went to the Student Health Center and had it X-rayed. On the street car today I saw and talked with Miss Ann Battle, formerly of Hume-Fogg and now of West End High. What a delightfully charming person! After studying Physics with Hartwell Weaver this afternoon he suggested that I get a date and go with him and Sarah Jane Peyton to see Wallace Berry in "Bad Man from Primrose." I called Ellen Bowers. She had a cold, but she agreed to go.

Saturday, February 12, 1938 Ellen Bowers did not come to school today. Abigale Robinson told me she must have had a rough night. Started eating at the Deke House today. Charles Sadler spoke to me this morning about participating in an N. B. C. broadcast from the men's lounge of Alumni Hall. He and Jerry Belcher came to the fraternity house to interview me. Saw our freshmen win a match with East High this afternoon. Clark Hutton was very impressive with his win. Tonight, after the basketball game, the varsity wrestled Maryville, in a meet that turned out to be a draw. Miriam was with Charley Roberts. Being injured, I had to sit on the bench. I saw Susan in the audience and she seemed to be enjoying the matches. The score was tied and the outcome depended on Partee's match. He carried the fight, but took entirely too many chances, and was near exhaustion at the end of the match. It was called a draw. Partee cried over the outcome but the Maryville coach was happy. Ed Kirkpatrick wrestled in the slot that I normally would have had. I hated to see him lose before Miriam, but he wrestled beautifully and made a good impression in spite of the loss.

Sunday, February 13, 1938 Went to the Confederation meeting at 2:00. The Dekes got the Presidency of the Honor Council, but no other major offices. We wanted men on the Union and on the Student Council. Even though Algie Choate, of the Phi Psi's, threatened to jump if certain concessions are not made, the Confederation was still in sympathy with them and offered the Presidency of the Owl Club. I think it was a mistake. I had already arranged to cover their departure and hoped they would jump, so we could take in the Sigma Nu's, who have more members. Expressed the Deke dissatisfaction to Pardue and Winningham.

Monday, February 14, 1938 It was a severe blow to learn that Oscar

Odd McIntyre, one of the best columnists in the United States, died today at 53. If he, himself, had picked the day of his departure, it probably would have been on Valentines Day, because his writing was certainly from the heart. I never cease enjoying his whimsical style. Heard that Ellen Bowers was distracted by her little dog and had an automobile accident. A special meeting of the Confederation has been called for tomorrow night. Patton, of the Betas, is the instigator. Dutch Elder, Deke's National Field Director, visited the house today. I resumed coaching the freshman this afternoon.

Tuesday, February 15, 1938 I attended the called meeting of the Confederation at the Zeta Beta Tau House. Patton, seeking to cut the ground from our claim for more offices, made a fervent speech stating how disappointed the Betas' were over their allotment of offices. He finally stormed out of the room. Burk stopped him and engaged him in a long conference, but it broke up the meeting. I suppose participating in campus politics is good training because one learns early not to get mixed up in it in later life.

Wednesday, February 16, 1938 Bill Embry, of the Alpha Tau Omega fraternity, talked to me today about getting the Dekes to jump to the losing political organization and make them into winners. He said he was in a position to offer us almost anything. He admitted that he is not much of a politician, however, because he is not making much progress in his plan for luring away one of the Confederation members. He didn't make much headway with me, either. Bill made the threat to me that if he got to be editor of the Hustler he would give the Calumet Club "hell" if they kept him out. Read McIntyre's article "Winter Is My Dish" in the Cosmopolitan magazine. He quoted the first stanza of James Whitcomb Riley's "When the Frost is on the pumpkin, and the fodder's in the shock . . . His last column started out like this: "We set off in one of those aimless Sunday evening strolls without objective. The city generally was hurrying to the movies and cafes. And that is why a shadowy brick church on the fringe of things, it's bell tolling so sadly, appeared a sudden symbol of neglect. Only an occasional straggler mounted the steps and vanished into the dim-lit quiet. Soft notes from the organ came trembling down the nave in a sort of gentle ballyhoo. And on the impulse of the moment, we too, climbed the steps, the first church going in months. Like many reluctants I am continually assailed, once inside a religious edifice, for my neglect in attendance. It requires only an hour out of the week and there is no place where one may so satisfyingly relax into surprising and almost unbelievable calm." If one is to die unexpectedly, what a wonderful last column to leave as a legacy.

Thursday, February 17, 1938 Saw Ellen Bowers for the first time since her wreck. She had a patch over one eye and the other was swollen almost closed. She certainly must have had a narrow escape. The Banner Society Editor, Miss Kate Talbot, asked me to write a feature story on the Washington Ball for Saturday's paper. She said it would carry a by-line. She told me about the nice pictures she had and about how much space would be allotted for the story. I heard Dr. Oskar Morgenstein, of Vienna, speak tonight. He said Austria was anxious to join Germany until Hitler took control and showed his hand as a brutal aggressor. It is an entirely different story now. I talked with Susan tonight and she told me about enjoying the wrestling matches. She said the people around her said: "I wish Ben Austin were able to wrestle in this meet, he'd sure tear 'em up!" It was a nice compliment, especially appreciated because it was from Susan.

Friday, February 18, 1938 At lunch today I showed Miriam her picture with Don Pierce at the Miami Triad and she wanted to take it away from me. I had to take it out of her notebook or I would not have gotten it back. Miriam's egotism slips out occasionally. She told me recently that the reason she did not make better grades was that being "Miss Vanderbilt" the professors didn't want to be accused of showing favoritism. As I have said before, though, with as much attention as she gets, it would be difficult for one's head not to be turned. I suppose she does very well, under the circumstances.

I met with "Pursuit" editors today. Bernard Breyer is his same old self. I have to exert all my powers of restraint when I am around him. Wrote up a feature on the Washington Ball. Met Mrs. Pride, Dean of Nashville Society Editors, this evening. The Dekes beat the Sigma Chi's in basketball and our wrestling team varsity beat Cumberland. The Chancellor was in the audience. Too bad Mickey Carmichael lost.

Saturday, February 19, 1938 I had a very interesting discussion on humor in Dr. Curry's class. He said humor is when a person treats lightly something he holds dear under ordinary circumstances. Friends may "take off" each other as long as there is no question of friendship or truth in the "take off." In another sense he quoted the famous line: "We are such stuff as dreams are made of." Oh yes, he said: "Clothes make the man and reveal how the woman is made." Our freshmen wrestlers met Castle Heights this evening and we won every match, 36–0. I am proud of my charges. The matches with the University of Chicago were close but they won all except the matches with Art Keene and Partee Fleming. I believe I could have taken their 155 lb. man. Jackson lost to him. Kirkpatrick now has a "hickey" on his knee. A crowd of about 250 seemed to enjoy the matches. Went to the A. E. Phi dance where Fannie Rose Shore was the bright light. She is a tomboy, but always a good sport; always snapping candid pictures and dashing around in her Chevrolet convertible. She has a fantastic figure and is a beautiful dancer.

Sunday, February 20, 1938 Saw in the paper that Mary Wallace made the dean's list at Ward-Belmont. I wrote a paper to be read before the Publications Board concerning the editorship of the Hustler. I will give it to Tom Scoggins tomorrow. Spent the afternoon reading Marquis James' "Andrew Jackson." At Uncle Walt's tonight he read to me O. O. McIntyre's column that deals with going to church. I had already seen it and had clipped it for my scrapbook. On the subject of women Uncle Walt said that they like to be handled. They like affectionate men. I had previously asked Miriam for the O.D.K. dance at the Proms. She had put me off. Called today to demand a "yes" or "no." If she had said "maybe" I had intended withdrawing the request, but she said "yes." Miriam told me that she and Andromedia Bagwell had watched me during the freshman team matches. She said I worked as hard as the wrestlers. In speaking of losing enthusiasm Uncle said he had likened himself to an old fox hound he once had; full of enthusiasm at first, led the race for three or four hours and then just petered out completely.

Monday, February 21, 1938 Paid $10.00 on my tuition this morning. While eating lunch with Miriam, Louise Sykes and Ed Kirkpatrick today we were discussing the Z. B. T. fraternity. Ed said "They are the most friendliest bunch of boys I have ever seen." Louise said: "What?" and he repeated the double superlative. It sounded awkward. Miriam said nothing. I had a good wrestling class this afternoon. We practised our songs at the fraternity meeting tonight. Heard the Publications Board may disqualify Embry, Trimble and Parks because of bad grades. It seems that extracurricular activities and good grades don't often go together.

Tuesday, February 22, 1938 Dr. Curry said today that poetry is the art of indirection. If it can be said it ought to be put in prose. Poetry does not say it but suggests it. The extent to which images are used classifies poetry. Don't push poetry aside to get to meaning. Susan was a little late in getting dressed for the Washington Ball so Mr. John Cheek and I had a discussion. When I mentioned our wrestling team match with Castle Heights, he referred to the alienation of affection suit now being brought against Bernard McFadden, owner of Castle Heights. He said a lady once tried the same thing on him. The gym was beautifully decorated and the temperature was ideal for dancing. Susan looked lovely in a long white evening dress. I had Hilliard Wood take pictures of her with members of the Owl Club. Miriam looked nice too and was presented a loving cup as "Miss Vanderbilt." Saw Matt Pratt, Mrs. Ernest Goodpasture, the McGaw family and Miss Connoll, Society Editor of the Banner, in the balcony. Miss Connoll praised me lavishly before Susan and I felt a warm glow all evening.

Wednesday, February 23, 1938 It was difficult staying awake in class today after staying up so late for the dance last evening. Mr. Wood came out and took pictures of the Ace Club and I rode to the office with him to visit with the ladies in the Society Section.

Thursday, February 24, 1938 Dr. Mayfield attended the Calumet club tonight. Wolf and Van Dusen read the best papers. Tom Scoggins read the worst. Matt Pratt visited. Street Ransom offered some very good criticism. He reminds me of Cecil Abernathy, especially when he smiles. Street, Kirkpatrick and I went to Petrone's where we saw Bill Embry, Jean Stephenson, Pierce Winningham and Jimmy Hofstead eating chili.

Friday, February 25, 1938 My good friend Emily Taggart is getting married so I went to town and got her a silver platter. Mary Paul Parsons recommended that selection. Emily is blonde with a redheaded complexion. She has a deep voice, something like Tallulah Bankhead, with somewhat the same commanding presence that Tallulah has, but in a motherly sort of way. I don't recall exactly what drew me to her, but I have always considered her something special. I took the T.K.A. and Sigma Nu date lists to the Banner.

Saturday, February 26, 1938 "Flip" Timberlake arrived at the fraternity house from his home in Decatur, Alabama. We played a few "Fats" Waller records and then went to town to see Joan Crawford and Spencer Tracy in "Manikin." "Flip" has a special love for movies. His father owned the theatre in Stevenson. To see in person and hear Nelson Eddy sing is to him like taking a trip to Elfland. Nelson made a rapid entrance on the stage of Ryman auditorium at 8:30 P.M. tonight. He sang quite a few classical Italian and French numbers which did not send the audience. Then finally he broke into his famous "Sweetheart, Sweetheart, Sweetheart . . ." and the audience went wild; especially the young girls from Ward-Belmont. It made the show a success. "Flip" and I, who have known each other since early childhood, talked into the wee hours.

Sunday, February 27, 1938 "Flip" and I slept late, read the papers and went to the fraternity house for lunch. He left for home in the early afternoon and I went to a Confederation meeting. It was a love feast, after our turbulent meetings of the past few weeks. Called Susan and she told me that Tom Scoggins has asked her for all of the dances in the Prom series. Said she had rather go with me, however, so that makes me feel good.

Monday, February 28, 1938 After the fraternity meeting tonight Bob Foote and Landis Shaw came over to the Deke House and helped us on our medley of songs for tomorrow night's contest. Wrestled four boys this evening, Chapman, Bernard, Gray and Feinblatt and neither of the four could get me off my feet.

Tuesday, March 1, 1938 Went to a banquet honoring Ben Ames, international reporter for the United Press. I sat behind Charley Moss and Lydel Sims. Francis Robinson was nearby; also Mr. and Mrs. Brainard Cheney. Ames, who was the only reporter at the front in Addis Ababa, discussed the European war situation. Afterwards I went to the fraternity sing and I could not have been more nervous if I had been scheduled for a solo. We sang "Ole Mamie Riley, Sing a Song of College Days and the Alma Mater." The five Kappa Alpha singers won. We did real well though and had lots of fun. The Thetas won for the girls. I thought the A. O. Pi's did better. Louise Sykes and Leo Bashinski went with Miriam McGaw and me to the Tri Delta dance. I was cold and indifferent to Miriam. Any affection that was shown she did the showing. I danced with her only one time, outside of the Special and the first no-break. When we got in the car she sat close to me but I made no effort to hold her hand. When we were discussing O.D.K. she asked me if I were going to have enough points. I answered very caustically: "Why? Do you want to break our O.D.K. dance date if I haven't?" She denied emphatically any such notion. Said she wanted to talk with me about the whole situation. Got to bed at 3:00 A.M.

Wednesday, March 2, 1938 I have never been as sleepy as I was today in classes. The tomato juice and milk I drank last night made me sick and I threw up this morning. Felt better after that. I am very sorry that an embarrasing situation came up between Roslyn Smith and me today. I called the Banner on the bookstore phone and she was waiting to use the phone. I had planned on talking only a couple of minutes, but the city editor got me on the wire after I had talked with Lydel Sims and he kept me longer than I had anticipated. Roslyn got mad and told me never to use the phone again. My freshman team wrestled Dick Givens team at the Y.M.C.A. today and we won.

Thursday, March 3, 1938 I apologized to Roslyn Smith today and she forgave me. Ellen Bowers has a small scar on her nose from the accident. Says she can't decide whether to have her old car fixed or buy a new one. Saw Susan on the steps of College Hall and she said her dad thought we should have won the singing contest. Shows he enjoys the old barbershop harmony. Got paid $9.00 by coach Miles this evening. Read "Much Ado About Nothing" tonight. Dr. Curry said today that comedy is not always happy. In high comedy there are some serious moments. Comedy aims to represent men worse than they are in everyday life. Tragedy represents them better. They are not villains, but are down the social scale. Comedy represents the imperfections of human beings; a lively interpretation of follies and corruptions . . . not crimes. Comedy shows us possible people doing probable things. Exaggeration creates unrestrained laughter; humor to one person only. High comedy should awaken thought; thoughtful appreciation. We don't like the subtle, we want to be hit on the head with a vulgar joke.

Friday, March 4, 1938 The City Editor, Mr. Duncan, told me yesterday morning that Dr. Mayfield is certainly a booster of mine. Part of that compliment may be due to the interest I took in the Ben Ames' lectures which his group sponsored. Some 300 registered for the International Relations Club convention. I went out to see Susan tonight. We went back to the lodge where there was a log fire. Made it nice and cozy, just like what you read about in books. Later we drove down to the lunch stand to get Cokes and when we got back we were met at the door by Mrs. Cheek with a strange looking walking stick. Susan says it is the kind that has a dagger in the end. Susan showed me through the house, pointing out a portrait of her grandfather Joel Cheek, who founded Maxwell House Coffee. He was a distinguished looking old gentleman. His goatee reminded me a little of Dr. Mims'. Lunched today with Fannie Rose (Dinah) Shore, Miriam McGaw and Ed Kirkpatrick. Fannie said she had heard what a good wrestler I am and came to one of my meets and I didn't even wrestle. Miriam explained about my getting my knee hurt and Ed chipped in: "Yeah, if he had not received an injury I would not have gotten to wrestle." It took a lot of character for Ed to admit, before our mutually admired girl friend, Miriam, that I am a better wrestler than he is. Fannie mentioned my dimples and then Miriam went into ecstasy over them. It is the first time Miriam had mentioned them in the three years that I have been dating her.

Saturday, March 5, 1938 I talked to Mary Wallace up at Uncle Walton's tonight. She was preparing for her basketball game at Ward-Belmont and was afraid her club would lose. She was assigned the task of guarding the other team's leading scorer. At the gym dance I saw Grace Benedict and she was as enthusiastic as she could be about her club winning and said that the girl Mary W. guarded didn't shoot but one or two goals the whole night; not any during the first half. The freshman wrestling team defeated the Old Hickory "Y" by a score of 23 to 3. Hutton did well before his family. His mother looked scared. I hate it that Fred Gray did not get to wrestle. I really should have wrestled him instead of Chapman. He was certainly disappointed. Leo Bashinski got a U-Drive-It and went after Louise Sykes, then we went to get Miriam McGaw. Coming back Miriam said that someone had told her how dirty he thought she treated me on the Prom situation. She said that he said "After all you are only a junior once." Miriam said that she had not looked at it that way. Of course she hadn't, she was only thinking of "Miss V" leading the march. She closed by saying she wished other people would tend to their own business. I think it was Bill Embry that talked to her so point blankly. Tickled me.

Sunday, March 6, 1938 Wrote my paper of "Twelfth Night" for Dr. Curry this evening.

Monday, March 7, 1938 Clarence Woodcock and I ate lunch together today. Miriam, Ed Kirkpatrick, Louise Sykes and Leo Bolster came in as we were leaving. I saw the famous Mr. Peterson put on a billiard exhibition tonight. It is the first time I ever noticed that billiard tables don't have pockets.

Tuesday, March 8, 1938 I have never had a spring suit so I went to Joe Frank's and bought a blue gabardine one for $24.50. Picked up my wrestling medal which had been engraved, with my name, at Steifs Jewelry store. Dr. Curry thinks "Much Ado About Nothing" is the best comedy ever written. He considers Touchstone the daintiest, nicest of Shakespeare's fools. He says Shakespeare's psychology of women is excellent. They are always drawn better than his men.

Wednesday, March 9, 1938 It rained practically all day. I saw Susan in the library, but did not sit by her or engage her in conversation. Tom Scoggins escorted her to the S.A.E. banquet and dance tonight and William Nolan escorted Miss McGaw. George Morrow helped me finish three Physics reports. What a marvelous mind he has for Mathematics and the Sciences.

Thursday, March 10, 1938 It seems that I can be tolerant of the big weaknesses of people, but the little things irritate me more than I would like. For the past few weeks Mrs. Miles has been taking the cream off of my milk. I have been noticing it all along but have been trying to think of a way to put a stop to it without causing a furor. Last night I finally decided that it would be an easy way to write a note: "This is the quart of milk that you contracted to furnish your boarder." I thought that might turn the trick. It did just the opposite. At the supper table she really blew up. If I had done the same it would have ended in a fight. I held my poise though and suffered her shrewish comments. Finally she had her say and quieted down. We settled the thing by my bringing the contract to an end April 1st. Talked to Miriam and she bolstered my spirits by telling me of the nice things she has heard about me lately. Martha McGavock had paid me a compliment and Dot Evans had told her I was the nicest and sweetest boy Miriam goes with. Miriam, herself, was a little upset that I told her I may not go to the Proms this year.

Friday, March 11, 1938 Dr. John Daniel reminded me this morning, in my private discussion with him of wireless power, that radio waves are sent out in every direction and thereby weakened so that the impulse that each radio receives is only an infinitesimally small part of the initial energy supply. This faint radio impulse closes a switch and the power plant in each radio goes to work to amplify the impulse. It is more or less a matter of relaying power. I hate the math of Physics, but I love hearing how physical phenomenon works and enjoy speculating how this knowledge can be used to accomplish new and different purposes. One of the most interesting of all phenomena to me is vibrations. It is amazing, but about everything we do depends on vibrations. We hear because sound waves or vibrations, are transmitted through the air. We see via light waves and each color vibrates at a different speed. The sine curve represents waves. The wave length is the distance the disturbance travels between vibrations. The wave length depends on the medium it is travelling through, but pitch depends on the source. Waves require a vibrating body to set them up. They require a continuous medium, not a vacuum. All waves transmit energy unimpaired, weakened only when spread out over a larger area. All waves that go out vary inversely as the square of the distance.

Saturday, March 12, 1938 Met classes for the last time this term. George Wells, whom I knew at Dixie Camps, came up from Darlington to play basketball and came to see me. Thurston Whitaker was with him so we went on over to the A. K. K House and visited with Bob Foote, another Dixieite. Called up Susan and complimented her on her picture in the Banner this evening and made a date with her for April 1st. In the picture she was looking very demure standing on the stairway of Oak Hill Mansion. Seeing a picture of a girl I like so much in the newspapers gives me a sort of cringing feeling. It is like being spurned; as if she belongs to everyone and not just to me.

Sunday, March 13, 1938 The Sunday Nashville Tennessean featured a picture of Miriam as one of the leaders of the Junior Prom. Seeing the picture certainly didn't arouse any gentle emotions in me. I wondered what she was thinking when she saw it. Like Little Jack Horner I guess. I wondered if she imagined what I was thinking, after she broke the date with me, so as to be in the grand march and in the papers. I doubt that she gave it a thought. Spent the afternoon in an Economics class listening to Byron Hill give a summary of what might be expected on the exam. Byron is an exceedingly bright boy, of Rhodes Scholar calibre, but he is not bigger than his subject, as is Gus Dyer, for example. I don't suppose he has the wide experience from which to draw broad and interesting themes and observations. He has to stick to the books and is therefore as dry as the books themselves. Mrs. Miles has been extremely nice to me since our little incident the other day. Glad I was not caustic with her. Getting people told is a highly unprofitable investment in human relations.

Monday, March 14, 1938 Had two of my hardest exams today; Spanish and Physics. The Spanish was extremely difficult but I think I did fairly well on it. I am still having trouble with the verbs. Lunched with Wendell Choate and Charlie Rentrop at Kissam cafeteria. Lydel Sims called me tonight and said that a friend of Mr. Jimmy Stahlmans wrote for press clippings on the International Relations Club conference. The election of their officers came too late for our Saturday paper so we did not have a story on it; consequently no clippings. I called Bob Finney, past president of the club, and he does not know the names of the new officers, nor does Dr. D. P. Fleming, faculty sponsor. After about a dozen calls I found out that my good friend Frances Scruggs wrote a story about it for the Alumnus magazine.

Tuesday, March 15, 1938 Of all the rotten luck! After going to all that trouble to get the I. R. C. story I forgot to call Sims at nine o'clock this morning as promised. At eleven o'clock Hilliard Wood called and said the Managing Editor would like to speak to me. Boy, O, Boy, did he give me the works! He told me to call at nine o'clock, when I told a person I would call at that time. He told me to get the story together and get it down there immediately. I was so nervous that I forgot about an exam that I had scheduled. After the excitement was over I was in the Society department relaxing and Miss Kate told me she was in trouble too. She had put a sentence in the paper stating that Dr. Barr's mother was dead. The whole Presbyterian Church would be on her ear. She, also, had had a talk with the Managing Editor. It was funny after it was all over, but it was some strain before I put that picture into the boss' hand. Think I did well on the Physics exam., except for the math problems. To drown my sorrows I went to town to see Robert Taylor in a "Yank at Oxford." Carl Hinkle had told me it was a punk show but I enjoyed it. I guess Carl didn't like it because it ridiculed college hero worship.

Wednesday, March 16, 1938 Had no exam today so I stayed home and read "As You Like It." I have read it before but never enjoyed it so much. Dr. Curry makes plays come alive. He says: "Life consists of four things; birth, growth to maturity, Love (reproducing one's self) and death. We spend most of our time dressing up the last three. Artistry consists of going the long way around. Beauty dresses up the ordinary functions (eating, for example). Friends during Shakespeare's time were almost deified. "Good music," he says, "Is always sad. Music that sings that evanescent message into the heart of men." Music comes closer to being a reality of life within a reality. One's sadness is in proportion to his appreciation on the one passing away (evanescent) . . . to treasure that which he hates to lose.

Thursday, March 17, 1938 I had an exam this morning at nine o'clock and woke up at ten minutes after nine. I dressed as fast as I could and rushed over. I got there just thirty minutes late and was able to finish the exam. Learned this morning that Francis Robinson had taken a job with W. S. M. and that Lydel Sims is now editor of the magazine section. Got a $25.00 check from Dad. I realized more than ever today that something must be done about the cheating at Vanderbilt.

Friday, March 18, 1938 Had my last examination this evening and was never so glad to get through with anything. I did not know what to do with myself when the pressure was off. Went to the Deke House and loafed until time to get ready for the dance. Amos and Andy were celebrating their tenth anniversary on the air in the Campbell Soup Holiday Hotel program. Bobby Geny and I guarded one of the doors. Don Bestor played for the Prom. I danced a couple of steps with Susan and the third no-break with McGaw.

Saturday, March 19, 1938 This has been one of the most thrill packed days of my life. Got up at 7:30 feeling as if my head would fall off. Phoned in the dope on the Prom favorites and went back to sleep and got up at 1:00 in the afternoon. Went to town and bought a pair of brown shoes to go with my light blue spring suit that I wore to the tea dance. Had many compliments on the suit. Ed Kirkpatrick told me that new suit had him worried. Miriam liked it too. Elizabeth McEwen was my date for the dance. Had the third no-break with Susan, and the fourth with Jeanne Hampton. Dave Seyfried escorted Mary Louise Douglas. Andy Sweat brought Miriam to the Dutch supper at the Deke House. Ed Finch had come up from Birmingham. The food was gone by the time we got there so Alfred Estes gave my money back so we ate at the Toddle House. At the evening dance I danced the first no-break with Miriam and we had plenty of room for dancing. We made long sweeps and there was very little cutting in. Susan said she saw us dancing the "V" Club special. Consequently the next time I danced with Susan we moved around the floor quite a bit more than usual. I don't believe we ever danced together so well. Once while dancing with Lu Ray Welch she told me point blank that she liked me. I told her the same, because I do. I know why Jack Worley thinks so much of her. After the dance Miriam, Alfred Estes, Nell Edwards, Sara Goodpasture, Joe Little and I went to Candyland for refreshments. We drove around for an hour singing old songs. Took Miriam home at 1:30 A.M. We walked slowly to the top of the stairs. When we got there I stood between her and the door. When I finished telling her how much I enjoyed the evening I leaned forward and kissed her. It was the first time I had ever really kissed her. She watched me all the way down the steps, with a puzzled look in her eyes, as if not knowing what to say. I cavalierly bowed and saluted, at the turn of the steps, and walked on out into the night.

Sunday, March 20, 1938 I slept late and then wrote letters to Freda

Atwood, my first love, and to Donald Linton, one of my best friends. Miriam told me last night that she puts vaseline on her eyelashes so they will look bewitching; tickled me. When I was looking up the last O. O. McIntyre column in my scrapbook the other day, I ran across this item from someone who knew him:

> *"One was a columnist. Perhaps the others were. I wouldn't know. Anyway three of them had you on the pan. You were high hat. You were this, that and many other things. I thought of the days I lived across the hall at the Hargrave, of that light under your door and the steady click of your typewriter, so often until daylight. Perhaps you are all they said. I haven't seen you in years and people change. Yet I have a hunch that when I do see you it won't be in a dive, chiseling drinks, telling how good you are and knocking your fellows."*

Nashville Banner

TYRANNIES GOVERN BY DECLAMATION, DEMOCRACIES BY DEBATE — A FREE PRESS AND A FREE PEOPLE ARE INSEPARABLE.

NASHVILLE, TENN., WEDNESDAY AFTERNOON, MARCH 30, 1938   22 PAGES

Competition for Jobs Stirs College Students' Ingenuity

Wins Highest Coed Honor at Vanderbilt

(Pictures on Page 23)

By BEN AUSTIN

With more and more students pouring into institutions of higher education, increasing the competition for part time jobs, ingenious students at Vanderbilt University are finding a wide variety of jobs to meet the heavy financial demands facing them.

Over 500 students, almost one-third of the student body at Vanderbilt applied for the 150 NYA jobs this year which means one out of every three students must raise the whole, or a great part of his college expenses by his own efforts.

A survey of student part time employment was conducted last year by Henry G. Hart, and it was found that while 30 per cent more students were employed under NYA, they earned less average salary per month and their total earnings were less than those of other jobs. Although NYA students reported earnings of $12,275.10 annually, non-NYA students were earning $18,291.60. This total session's earning by Vanderbilt students of $30,566.70 was practically all spent for tuition.

These same students had borrowed an amount of $30,525 to date on their schooling. They said they needed a chance to earn another $11,335.

When asked how much they expected to borrow to finish their education, they said $6,276. Student loans averaged from $124.65 each for freshmen to $565.04 for seniors.

To three outstanding students with literary talents, who have enough money to remain in school during three years of run-of-the-mill reporting and routine staff jobs, goes the editorship of the Vanderbilt publications, Hustler, Commodore, and the Masquerader. The financial returns from these editorships amounts to something near $300 each.

The business managerships of these publications, with approximately the same remuneration, goes to those selling the most advertisements for the publications.

A few students who show aptitude along scholarly lines are given jobs grading papers or private tutoring, but the majority of part-time workers are left to their own resources.

John Gilbert, for instance who is a senior in the school of arts and science, lists about an large a variety of part-time jobs as he has taken subjects. Last year an elderly lady employed him to teach her how to drive her automobile. After six weeks, he advised her to give up the thought of driving, but a telephone call the other day informed him that she was going to make another attempt so he will immediately take up where he left off last spring.

Gilbert has also collected statistical information for a New York concern, fired furnaces, mowed lawns, and worked in a restaurant for his meals and 25 cents a day. He has played in the band, gone out for track, and at present is working in the game room on the first floor of Alumni Memorial Hall. To help keep his mind occupied he is taking a double major in his class work.

Many boys find ready money by operating Honor stores at the different fraternity houses. Others get jobs as special representatives of local department stores, and in many cases work on the afternoons that they don't have lab, at these stores.

Belford Lester and Richard Matthews operate an independent "U-drive-it" system, renting out their cars to other students for dates, dances and the like.

Tom Carney, who is taking a fulltime course at Vanderbilt, passed the civil service examination and is now working part time at the Post Office.

Another ingenious student buys up football buttons and colors for the games and has a syndicate of boys under him, working all the games.

Robert Burgess, who worked seventeen hours every week in the library last year and graduated Phi Beta Kappa, returned this year as a teacher of two Spanish classes, and is working for a library science degree at Peabody College, and still does other work outside the school.

—Staff Photos By James Christian.

Here's the winner of the highest honor Vanderbilt students can pay a coed. She is Landis Shaw after the votes were counted this afternoon. She is shown in three characteristic poses, (left) with her calm, pretty face lighted by a welcoming smile, at her home; at her piano which has won her acclaim on the campus, and finally as the lady of the green car, the way the university knows her best.

hville   Ban

TYRANNIES GOVERN BY DECLAMATION, DEMOCRACIES BY DEBA   PEOPLE ARE INSEPARABLE

NASHVILLE, TENN., SATURDAY   21, 1939

Coeds Elect Landis Shaw 1938 Lady of the Bracelet

By BEN AUSTIN

Miss Virginia Landis Shaw, senior at Vanderbilt University, was named Lady of the Bracelet for 1938 today as the results of the balloting by the coed student body were announced this afternoon. She received 133 votes, while Miss Grace (Pan) Snell received 77.

Selection as Lady of the Bracelet is the highest honor a Vanderbilt coed can receive, and corresponds to the title, Bachelor of Ugliness for men students. Finalists in the voting were announced this morning by the Women's Student Government Board, which announced the names of the coeds selected for final balloting from the candidates of each sorority at the university.

Miss Fannye Rose Shore was the third candidate in the final voting.

Miss Snell, who was the runner-up, was also very active in extra curricula activities and a member of Alpha Phi Omega Sorority. She is the daughter of Mrs. Grace B. Snell, 2210 Acklen Avenue.

Miss Shore, well known on the campus for her activities and musical accomplishments and third in the election, is the daughter of Mr. and Mrs. S. A. Shore, 3745 Whitland Avenue, and a member of Alpha Epsilon Phi sorority.

Other officers elected at the chapel were as follows: president of W. S. G. A. Board, Ruth Petty, Delta Delta Delta; Student Union representative, Betty Penick, Gamma Phi Beta; president of Athletic Board, Betty Friedland, Delta Delta Delta; Senior Class chairman, Floy

(Continued on Page 2, Column 3)

36,000 Grid Fans Jam Knoxville For Tennessee-Alabama Tilt

Odds Favor Vols; Rain Threat Wanes

By FRED RUSSELL
(Banner Sports Editor)

Knoxville, Oct. 21—The largest crowd ever to witness a football game in the State jubileed into Knoxville today to see Tennessee take on Alabama in the season's top battle of the week.

With the Big 13 championship, and a probable Bowl bid at stake more than 36,000 wildly enthusiastic fans were to overflow Shields Watkins Field for the Dixie classic, starting at 2 o'clock.

A fast, dry field and a blazing hot afternoon were in prospect for the game. This morning there wasn't a cloud in the sky and the day threatened to be as hot as the one Vanderbilt played Kentucky. There was very little breeze and the East Tennessee sun was hear-

(Continued on Page 2, Column

Pre-Game Festivities Mark Homecoming

By BEN AUSTIN
(Special Correspondent)

Knoxville, Tenn., Oct. 21—Enthusiasm almost reached a point of hysteria this morning in Knoxville as thousands of frenzied football fans jammed the city streets flashing their colors and yelling with the two student bodies before that titanic clash between the University of Tennessee, unbeaten and untied for two years, and the famous University of Alabama team from Tuscaloosa which this season already has defeated a strong intersectional rival, Fordham University.

Early ticket sales indicated today that some 36,000 people, the largest crowd ever to witness a football game in the State, will be on hand to see the game. It is conceded to be the top contest of the nation.

Clarence Buddington Kelland, Jock Sutherland, former Pittsburgh University coach, and three

(Continued on Page 2, Column

Pretty Josephine Tate (upper left) is shown selling a school pennant to Freshman Pollard Parsons, Jr. And vivacious Polly Anne Billington (upper center) peddles a subscription to the Masquerader to W. A. McIlreath. Racking 'em up (upper right) is John Gilbert, a senior who is gameroom manager. Anne Lee Crowell, (lower left) is working on the Union library catalog, one of the NYA projects. Scholarship is not exactly usual among athletes.

Way for Advance 500 Vanderbilt Students Work Way   R, FRIDAY, OCTOBER 7, 1938

Nashville Banner.

TYRANNIES GOVERN BY DECLAMATION, DEMOCRACIES BY DEBATE — A FREE PRESS AND A FREE PEOPLE .

Full Leased Wire Services of the Associated Press, United Press and International News Service.

NASHVILLE, TENN., FRIDAY AFTERNOON, APRIL 8, 1938

Most Individual Coeds Named | Vanderbilt's Most Typical,

Discovered at last are the most typical and the most individual coeds at Vanderbilt University! Following a complete and mind-searching series of questionnaires sponsored by The Hustler, Vanderbilt newspaper, Miss Sarah Goodpasture, upper left Delta Delta Delta, daughter of Dr. and Mrs. E. W. Goodpasture, 408 Fairfax Avenue, was rated most typical Vanderbilt coed (among other things, she does not go to the beauty parlor more than once a week); and Miss Henrietta Hickman, upper right, daughter of Judge and Mrs. Litton Hickman, 2618 Gallatin Road, and Kappa Alpha Theta, was named typical coed by national standards at Vanderbilt (she refuses to make dates more than ten days in advance). Lower left, the runners-up are Misses Landis Shaw, Lucile Johnson, and Grace (Pan) Snell, Delta Delta Delta, Kappa Alpha Theta, and Alpha Omicron Pi members respectively. Lower right, the two who least fit the mold as made by national and local averages—Misses Frances Evans, Delta Delta Delta, and Jeanne Hudnell Gamma Phi Beta who are seen in one of the most unconventional pictures ever taken of Vanderbilt girls. But even though they are unconventional, even they go domestic only on rare occasions.

Miss Sarah Goodpasture Named Most Typical Vanderbilt Coed

NASHVILLE BANNER, FRIDAY, JANUARY 13, 1939

Photogenic and Glamorous Is Miss Vanderbilt

National Standards Apply Best to Miss Hickman

By BEN AUSTIN

Advanced students in research at Vanderbilt University have at last solved one of the institution's most baffling problems The most typical, as well as the most individual coeds, by Vanderbilt standards and by national standards, have been classified, and the long pages of statistics and questionnaires employed in the survey have been filed for posterity.

She who most nearly approaches the Vanderbilt norm is Miss Sarah Goodpasture, Delta Delta Delta, daughter of Dr. and Mrs. E. W. Goodpasture, of 408 Fairfax Avenue. Miss Henrietta Hickman, Kappa Alpha Theta and Phi Beta Kappa member, gave opinions and preferences which ranked her as most typical Vanderbilt coed by national standards.

The two norms employed were those compiled from all Vanderbilt questionnaires and those from questionnaires made all over America. In that manner, the most typical local and national students—ratings which might be confusing to one not versed in statistics and advanced research—were decided upon.

Fascinating by their individuality were the two girls who deviated most from the two averages. Miss

(Continued on Page 8, Column 3)

Andromedia Bagwell Honored by Men Students In Annual Election Sponsored by Hustler

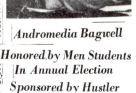

By BEN AUSTIN

Andromedia Bagwell, a sophomore, reached the pinnacle of coed fame today when it was officially announced that she had polled the largest number of votes in the 1939 "Miss Vanderbilt" election which was sponsored by the Hustler, campus newspaper. Ballots were handed out in general chapel Wednesday and the entire male student body participated in the election which named Miss Bagwell the most glamorous coed in the university this year. Bill Embry, editor of the Hustler will present her a handsomely engraved loving cup at the Washington Ball in February.

Miss Bagwell has brown hair and gray eyes, uses very little make-up, and has a ready smile.

She is fond of sports, being captain of the basketball team of her sorority, Alpha Omicron Pi, a member of its tennis team and one of Vanderbilt's most ardent football fans.

For the past two years she has led the cheering section and has been very active in the Junior Athletic Association which has done much towards increasing interest in athletic programs.

She was chairman of her freshman class, is on the board of directors of the Student Christina Association, and is a member of the Woman's Student Government Board, the Lotus Eaters, Sophomore Honorary Society, and is one of the founders of the Vanderbilt Players. She has also served on the Honor Council.

Being called "Miss Vanderbilt" is not her first campus recognition. She rated the beauty section of the yearbook during her first year at Vanderbilt and was selected as a favorite at the Senior Prom. She ranked third in the "Miss Vanderbilt" election last year.

Miss Bagwell's accomplishments at Vanderbilt are practically a repetition of her many honors in high school.

She laid the foundation for her activities at Hume-Fogg where she was head cheer leader, a member of the Student Council, a member of the dramatic club, active on the Fogg Horn staff, and was elected Best All-Round and Most Popular girl in the graduating class of 1937.

Miss Bagwell is the daughter of Mr. and Mrs. N. L. Bagwell, 1801 18th Avenue, South, and is the youngest of a family of three boys and three girls. She was born in Murfreesboro, but moved to Nashville when she was three years old and has lived here ever since.

She loves to dance, can cook a meal, when the occasion demands, likes to read, does not smoke, and hopes some day to travel extensively.

She dates only on week-end nights and has a tremendous acquaintance of men on the campus.

Besides the three leaders, nine others of the twenty-five candidates polled some of the Hustler's ballots received more than 1,200 points each. In order of their totals, these were: Betty Lu Vick, Whit Drake, June Burke, Sarah Goodpasture, Elizabeth Carey, Marguerite Wallace, Ruth King, and Aline Hyden.

Second to Miss Bagwell in the "Miss Vanderbilt" election was Jean Smith, a Kappa Alpha Theta senior from Greensboro, N. C. Madolyn Bidwell, a sophomore and a member of Alpha Omicron Pi sorority, from Pleasant View, Tenn., was third. In a point system of counting the votes, Miss Bagwell received 3,415 points, Miss Smith, 2,680, and Miss Bidwell, 2,006.

SPRING
1938

Monday, March 21, 1938 I got off to a good start in the Physics Laboratory. We are starting in Electricity and I think I am going to like it better than what we have been studying. Passed Miriam on the walkway this morning and she seemed a little shy.

Tuesday, March 22, 1938 Had a long talk with Bill Jordan this evening about using the literary publication, "Pursuit," to do something about the Honor System at Vanderbilt. Professor Irby Hudson came up while we were talking and suggested that we talk it over with Dean Pomfret. Miriam is pretending to be mad at me since that kiss the other night and won't divulge whether or not I can take her to the Deke dance. Dr. Curry talked about Richard III this morning. He was born with teeth, a shrivelled left arm and a hump on his back. He was horribly ugly, abhorred by his mother, but his father admired his energy in battle and his brilliant mind. He had a tremendous will; perhaps the strongest will Shakespeare created. Curry says some hate is not admirable, but complete hate is. Noble feeling is usually giving yourself into somebody else. Love is completely selfish. In Act V, Scene 1 Richard III said: "That high all-seer which I dallied with, Hath turned my feigned prayer on my head."

Wednesday, March 23, 1938 Attended the memorial service of Dr. George B. Winton. Chancellor Kirkland made a beautiful speech, explaining that Dr. Winton, who was a member of the Board of Trustees during the church fight and was also editor of the Christian Advocate, foremost Methodist Journal. He sided with Vanderbilt and ultimately lost his job. He later became a history teacher at Vanderbilt and then Dean of the School of Religion. Talked to Mr. and Mrs. Louis Davis about camp for Louis III and they are responsive.

Thursday, March 24, 1938 Johnny Black was at the house for lunch today. He was the one who first called me "Comanche". One day, while riding to town with a car full of Dekes, I was telling a story and mentioned that the folks were yelling like a bunch of Comanche Indians. It tickled Johnny and he called me Comanche from that point forward. He is in school at the Babson Business University and is home for the spring holidays. He says there are a lot of rich boys in his classes and that there is no cheating. There should be none anywhere. Eddie Morton told me today about a Phi Beta Kappa who is one of the biggest cheaters in school. I was surprised to learn this about G. Johnny explained to me how they make money in the U-Drive-It business. They have their own financing company and each unit pays a large rate of interest on each car they take out. His father owns Dixie-Drive-Yourself. Mary Wallace was the only member of her club to make the Ward-Belmont varsity.

Friday, March 25, 1938 Took my first hitchhiking trip today. William Simpson and I stood on the road an hour and a half before we had any luck. Finally a man picked us up and carried us all the way to the forks of the road at South Pittsburg, Tennessee. We then caught a ride to Stevenson. After a big steak dinner I had a discussion with Mother about manners and home training. I expressed to her my appreciation for the guidance she has given me. She had Miriam's picture above my bed.

Saturday, March 26, 1938 Had a date with Freda Atwood tonight and called her Miriam only once. She pretended to be mad. It rained all afternoon. I rode down to Coffey's ferry with James to pick up Mr. Ernest Mann's fishing chair that had been left there on the creek bank.

Sunday, March 27, 1938 Barney Hale flagged the Dixie Flyer and William Simpson and I boarded it about 2:00 P.M. for Nashville. Saw Louis Liner from Chattanooga. Arrived in Nashville at 5:30 P.M.

Monday, March 28, 1938 As I was walking to school today Susan passed and picked me up. Her new Dodge is really good looking. She thanked me for being so nice about helping her get out of a date mix-up last week. Made a no-break with her for Friday night. I told the City Editor today that Landis Shaw would be a good one to gamble on in the Lady of the Bracelet election next week. We are going to do a layout in advance.

Tuesday, March 29, 1938 Jim Christian and I went out to Landis Shaw's house and took several characteristic poses. It is a long shot picking one girl out of six and shooting the works on her, but if we guess right everything is hunky-dory. Tonight the first wrestling banquet was held in Kissam Hall. Dr. Tom Zerfoss, Master of Ceremonies, pulled the first crack on me. He said I had been applying my knowledge of wrestling in other fields. Bill Schwartz, Hill Turner, Dr. W. P. Fishel, Dean Sarratt and others spoke. Schwartz told us that if interest continues at the present level wrestling will one day be a major sport. I wrote the banquet and the Lady of the Bracelet stories tonight.

Wednesday, March 30, 1938 Sent both stories to town by Mrs. Miles and phoned in the final results after Women's Chapel. My guess was right so the presses went into action with the pictures and the stories on the front page. Got my first by-line on the front page of a city newspaper. We made a big gamble but the reward was proportionate to the risk. This kind of excitement is why newspaper work is attractive to so many people. This is why they say: "Printer's ink gets in the blood."

Thursday, March 31, 1938 Byron Anglin honored me today by asking me to hold down his Student Union job for him while he is away over the weekend. He has done a lot for me and I will certainly reciprocate whenever possible. Aunt Nell sent copies of my front page story to mother and to Rebecca. She seemed proud of me, but she would not tell me so. People, especially loved ones, are reluctant to express feelings, why . . .? Harris Abrahams saw me talking with Miriam today and he said to her that he would have to tell Susan about this. Miriam said I blushed. Miriam also told me I would not enjoy the movie "Tom Sawyer" but I did. Don't know when I've cried so much over a movie. Tom's getting into so much trouble and being treated so unjustly by his Aunt Polly coincides with my own treatment from my Dad. It was perhaps one of the reasons I was a little closer to Mother. I suppose it is a driving force in many young men's lives to grow up and "show their father . . ."

Friday, April 1, 1938 At the "Pursuit" editorial meeting I read my paper "To Hell with College" and several other staff members volunteered to write papers of their own along the same line. Partee Fleming and James Penrod supported the ideas completely. What I said, basically, was that the routine demands of assignments stifled creative activities. Leo Bashinski, Louise Sykes, Miriam and I went to Bitsy Napier's open house and then to the Deke Barn dance. I wore a tuxedo shirt with farmer's overalls. Had the first, the Special and the Surprise no-breaks with Miriam, the lightest dancer at Vanderbilt. Had the second with Dot King and the third with Susan. When I first danced with Susan she said: "How does it feel to rate the front page with a by-line story?" I assured her it was a great feeling. Tom Scoggins broke on Susan quite a bit, as did several other admirers. On the way home Miriam said to me: "You don't think as much of me as you used to, do you?" I merely said: "Don't jump to conclusions."

Saturday, April 2, 1938 Professor A. N. McPherson gave us a cut in math. Louise Douglas and Ellen Bowers were discussing the fact that Ellen's boyfriend was slightly inebriated last night. I suppose it was Jimmy Hofstead. Leo Bashinski and I went to see Jeanette Mac Donald and Nelson Eddy in "Girl of the Golden West." It was only fair. Dr. Curry said today that tragedy is represented on the stage by a protagonist of gigantic proportions who, because of some weakness of character, or some tragic fault, is brought into conflict (external or internal) and so is brought to destruction. The spectacle arouses in the audience pity and terror and there is a catharsis (purge). One has an exhilarated feeling coming away from a great tragedy.

Sunday, April 3, 1938 Mr. and Mrs. Cecil Robertson came by and we had a talk about camp. Their daughter, Martha, knew me when I was President of the Hume-Fogg Student Council. I made more friends at H. F. than at any other time in my whole life. I walked home with Miriam. As we were talking things over she said that my kissing her the other night was the last straw. She gave me the idea that we were all washed up. I accepted her statements with a smile and a joke, as if it did not matter. I told her to "shoot the works" because I could take it. Her attitude seemed to change a little before I left. I told her that I was spreading out and wasn't concentrating on one girl of late and was doing so much better. She said that she was glad for me. Called Susan from the union office and asked her for a date. She asked me to take her to the Theta (her) dance on the 29th. I really feel good about that. The Theta's have had only two dances this year and she has asked me to take her to both of them. I was out of town on the first one though. I am really crazy about Susan. She is so poised and ladylike at all times. I believe that she likes me just a little maybe because I have a little dignity and don't carry on so much horseplay around her. I don't rush her off her feet either. I really don't dance with her as much as I would like to, just for that reason. Came by Uncle Walts and saw Katherine Anderson and Mary Wallace Austin. Mary was telling me that some girl at Ward-Belmont was telling her about my taking a wrong quiz one day and making a good grade on it. Uncle Walton told Katherine and me to come back again, that it was very lonesome around the apartment at times. First time I have ever heard him speak of being lonesome.

Monday, April 4, 1938 After the fraternity meeting Jim Browning, Jim Huggins, Ed Morton, W. T. Adams, Elliott Trimble and I went to the street carnival. Elliott spent a couple of dollars in no time. Finished reading "Unmasking Wall Street."

Tuesday, April 5, 1938 Bill Embry gave me the dope on the Typical Coed story this evening and talked to me again about getting us to jump combines. I told him there is no need to make political changes when you are winning. Got a letter from Henry D. telling me about his track activities at T. M. I. Dr. Curry said that all great crusades of principle are advanced by martyrdom and suffering. He cited the life of Martin Luther and Christianity itself as examples. He said Shakespeare wrote Julius Caesar to prove that the artist can write a play that will strike deeper than hero worship.

Wednesday, April 6, 1938 Rousseau Duncan liked the prospects of the Typical Coed story so he assigned Lydel Sims and a photographer to help get it together. Bill Embry and Joel "Dopey" Stephens helped us tabulate the results of questionaires. Henrietta Hickman, Landis Shaw, Sarah Goodpasture, Jeanne Hudnell, Frances Evans, Pam Snell and Lucille Johnson cooperated with us in getting pictures in typical coed situations. Henrietta and I danced a step or so at the Theta House and Sims took her to dinner.

Thursday, April 7, 1938 Jim Christian and I took some more pictures today; Jeanne Starr, Dorothy Hutchinson, Anne Moore Snell and Annelle Macon. Talked to Susan on the phone tonight and she told me she was going to the Phi Delta Theta dance tomorrow evening instead of having a date with me. It seems that there is no such thing as a woman who won't do a bit of bargaining when a better proposition comes along. Curry said in Macbeth, Shakespeare had a lot to say and very little space to say it. Lines sometime break under the weight of content. It is the most compact of his plays. It is concentrated . . . much under the surface. Deep drama goes inward; melodrama outward. It is the most classic of all Shakespeare's plays.

Friday, April 8, 1938 The Typical Coed story crashed the front page, giving me my second by-line story in a matter of days in a metropolitan newspaper. Lydel Sims and I had stayed in close touch with each other all morning in case there were any late breaking developments. The scoop was complete. We ran the story concurrent with the campus newspaper, the Hustler. We let them use our pictures. Stopped by the Banner office late this afternoon and had Cokes with Sims. He told me about his ambition to have his own small newspaper and invited me to handle the business end.

Saturday, April 9, 1938 Dr. Curry stopped me after class today and said he expected me to write a good thoughtful paper for him this time. I guess he thinks if I can write articles for the front page of the city newspaper I ought to be able to write a fairly decent term paper. Dr. Curry is a marvelously humorous man. He is precise, meticulous, neat in appearance and carries a folded umbrella as if he were a boulevardier with a gold headed cane. His manner reminds me of a person who may have been reared in a large family of girls, or old maid aunts, but his wit crackles like a whip. After listening to his lectures these past few weeks I can understand why he is considered one of the great Shakespearean scholars. Mr. John Cheek met me at the door tonight when I went to pick up Susan for the gym dance. He had just returned from Philadelphia. Susan and I sat by the fire and talked before leaving for the dance. She told me how much she enjoyed the article in Friday evenings paper. We missed the first no-break but made up for it with a couple of specials they threw in. At one point Susan said to me: "You are a nice size for dancing." I was thinking the same thing; how well we fit together. This was one of my most enjoyable gym dances. After taking Susan home I stopped by the Deke House and Wilson Kingsboro and I went to Melfis for chili. Saw Jimmy Hofstead and Ellen Bowers there. Hamilton Douglas, who works full time for the Banner, was about half tight and made some remark about my getting front page by-lines. A little jealousy showed and he caught himself quickly: said my copy was better than most of the regular staff's.

Sunday, April 10, 1938 Mary Wallace told me that when she was spending the night with Jean Burke a Mrs. Harding was there and when she found out that Mary Wallace was Frances Ragan's cousin and my sister she and Mrs. Burke got into an argument over whether or not my article explained that Landis Shaw was a member of the Tri Delta sorority. Mrs. Harding said she read it over three or four times and could not find it. Mrs. Burke said she was positive it was quoted in the article. It was a bad oversight, but attracted more attention by the omission than if it had been in the article. Mary Wallace told me that Ann Carolyn "Bottle" Gillespie was very complimentary in telling Jean Burke, of Ward-Belmont, all about my activities at Vanderbilt. When Ann Carolyn graduated from Ward-Belmont last year her parents gave her a blue convertible Packard. We lost another office at the Confederation meeting tonight.

Monday, April 11, 1938 Gene Strayhorn, the Tennessean reporter, said his boss gave him "hell" for not having any dope on the "Typical Coed" story. They had about a two-inch squib on it. Saw Dr. Mims speak to Susan in front of the bookstore. She did not see him until he spoke and it frightened her. Mims is pretty gruff looking. Susan Scoggins gave a "trade last" in the bookstore. She said her brother Tom had remarked what a keen looking suit I had on at the gym dance Saturday. He may have put her up to that compliment because he is afraid I may keep him out of the Calumet Club, thereby lowering, if not completely destroying his chances for making O.D.K. He has already made a date with Susan for the O.D.K. dance. If he is kept out I will not be the one to do it, even though I did not think his paper was very good. Elliott Trimble was appointed editor of the fraternity newspaper Gamma

Gossip and Val Hain and Joel Stephens will help. Frances Scruggs has been appointed director of publicity for Vanderbilt.

Tuesday, April 12, 1938   Talked to both Susan and Miriam on the "Pell Mell" in front of Calhoun hall today. Susan said she heard that I am the writer of the infamous Night Hawk column. I told her that I didn't have anything to do with it, that I didn't have time for such gossip, even if I wanted to. She replied that I seem to have time for quite a few things (an apparent reference to a comment that was made in the column that I had dated other girls on a trip in spite of a knee in a cast. The statement was completely false). Landis Shaw told me today that she voted for the Dekes in the recent Confederation meeting. That would have given us a total of five votes. The Betas couldn't possibly have won. I secured signatures of the other four who voted for us and called a special meeting of the Confederation at the Tri Delta house tonight. Morgan Patton and I argued for hours to no avail. Having called the meeting, I opened by suggesting that we handle the dispute as if it were a law case. I will speak to the Confederation members as if they are a jury and Morgan can do likewise. Pierce Winningham took up the idea and suggested that it be treated as a contested election and that the results stand unless the Dekes could produce sufficient new evidence to merit a reversal. Ed Pardue presented the statement of the case and I presented the evidence I have, the names of five people supporting the Dekes. Morgan, Bud Beasley and I left the room and they deliberated for nearly an hour. Pierce handled our case magnificently and we were given the office by a 6–2 vote. Algie Choate added his vote to our cause. I appreciated that. I am happy over the outcome. Strayhorn came by and took my picture for tomorrow's paper, as the prospective president of the Honor Council.

Wednesday, April 13, 1938   This day has been memorable. The big spring elections came off at chapel this morning and the Confederation swept all but three offices out of a total of eighteen voted on. I won my office by a score of 64 to 49. Partee Fleming told me that it was unfortunate that the women's votes didn't count because all the women voted for me. Our man George Morrow tied with the very popular Joe McGinniss for the senior position on the Union. Walked over to chapel with Susan and gave her that clipping about her cousin, Helen Cheek, that was in Charles B. Driscoll's column. Miriam told me on the phone tonight that she and Susan are double dating for the Alpha Chi dance. The report of the election was on the front page of the Banner this evening. I got the final vote count in to the City Editor about ten minutes before the deadline at 1:30. The Betas are a little disgruntled over losing their office. Tommy Alexander called tonight and in congratulating me on being elected President of the Honor Council said: "This is one time when machine politics put the right man in office." That was certainly a nice thing to say. He offered his services if ever needed.

Thursday, April 14, 1938   Saw Susan in the hall this morning and told her I understand she was out pretty late last night. She replied: "I know who you have been talking to." Heard President Roosevelt make another of his Fireside Chats. In closing he said that a nation is like a ship. If it is to reach port it must sail and not remain anchored or drift. Went out to see Mr. Rose, who is about 45, and his wife who is about 30, about getting their son to go to camp with me. Mrs. Rose has the prettiest lips I have ever seen; full and pouty.

Friday, April 15, 1938   Saw Tom Happel, who had come to town for the weekend, and did some harmonizing with Barney Blair, and Homer Howell before going to see the new Lynnmeade lunch room the Ragans are building. Got a letter from Anderson with some clippings about George L.'s flying activities. He is doing a lot of barnstorming. Was surprised to see Mrs. Blair, the lady I boarded with a few years ago, on the street car this afternoon.

Saturday, April 16, 1938   Dr. Curry said that "King Lear" is the greatest of Shakespeare's tragedies. Lear is a Gothic structure. It begins with stepping stones (sub-plot). Dividing up his kingdom does not seem important at first, but the whole tragedy turns on that point; again showing that tragedies are based on characters and their reaction to events. Lear, himself, was selfish. He had always been king or heir apparent. The whole universe revolved around him. His character was of colossal proportions. He believed the king could do no wrong. He had complete control of his subjects but never learned to control himself. He never learned the value of love or friendship. He gave only lip service to truth. He could not recognize the sincerity of Cordelia because he had never known sincerity. Dr. Curry also said that Cordelia is Shakespeare's most perfect character. She restores our faith in women. She was denied the informal love of her father; he was always formal with her. She was more or less a female Christ. Act III, Scene VII is the most sublimely beautiful writing in all of Shakespeare's works.

Sunday, April 17, 1938   In talking with Susan on the phone this evening she told me what a wonderful time she and her roommate, Miriam had on their overnight outing. They both woke up at 4:00 o'clock in the morning trembling. There was a tremendous storm raging and the thunder had awakened them. A fuse in her car blew and they had to drive all the way back from Murfreesboro by flashlight. Nello Andrews, Henry Clay and Andromedia Bagwell were with her. Jim Browning told me that his uncle, Governor Gordon Browning, called him the other day and kidded him about "Deke" politics. McKellar, the governor's rival, is a Deke.

Monday, April 18, 1938 From a classroom standpoint, this was one of my most interesting days at Vanderbilt. In the first place Dr. Daniels gave us a very elaborate demonstration in Physics. He rigged up tubes and showed radiation through different kinds of gases. The X-ray demonstration was particularly interesting. He said that a scientist by the name of Leonard is the one who actually pioneered the X-ray field and made all the quantitative measurements. Roentgen, who is generally credited with being the father of X-ray technology, merely applied Leonard's findings to their present use in medicine and other fields. Instead of lab today we went up to the the third floor of the Physics building and saw Dr. Francis Slack give a demonstration of short waves. He demonstrated how airplanes can be guided to an airport by short waves; vertical and horizontal antenna systems. Dr. Underwood explained Cathode rays. Dr. Rudnick gave a demonstration of polarized light, two screens that are polarized at right angles to each other. The colors of mica and celophane were interesting, also the stress on a transparent fork bent by projected rays.

Tuesday, April 19, 1938 Carl Hinkle and I went over to Centennial Park to see the Parade of Progress display by General Motors. The manager of the unit, Mr. J. M. Jerky, saw us and said to Carl: "Aren't you Carl Hinkle, all-American football player?" He called several other men over to introduce them to Carl. His son is a Psi Upsilon at Kenyon. He told us how thrilled Kenyon was to get, from Vanderbilt, Professor John Crowe Ransom and asked how we felt about it here. I told him we considered it a great loss. He said the Dekes rate highly there. Ray Manning has been selected as editor of the Commodore. Anglin reported to me that Tom Scoggins was helping Susan wash dishes at the S. C. A. and that he was driving her around the campus this afternoon.

Wednesday, April 20, 1938 Scooped the Tennessean again on the publications board selections. I was opposed to Bill Embry getting the Hustler editorship at first, but now I have softened up a bit towards him and am glad he got the job. It would have killed him if he hadn't. Dr. Mayfield said to me this afternoon: "I have only one regret in the matter and that is that you, yourself, were not in the race as his competitor." Mr. Duncan had the Publications Board story already set up for me when I called in to confirm that our guesses had been right. At 1:37 he had already ordered the story released because he said he assumed I knew what I was talking about. He said it was nice work. A story of the election in women's chapel will run in the sports edition of the Banner. Alice Beasley, the girl friend of Gene Strayhorn, my rival correspondent won the Presidency of the W.S.G.A. Board. Gene asked me today if I had the story on it and I didn't say yes or no. This evening I jokingly sent him this note:

Dear Gene,

If you want information on the election today see the sports edition of the Banner.

Your most humble competitor,
Ben Austin

Tom Scoggins handed me a paper to read, just before the final meeting of the selection board of the Calumet club, and said: "Just to show you I can write." They turned him down again.

Thursday, April 21, 1938 Dr. Walter Clyde Curry delivered perhaps his best lecture of the year today on Lear. He discussed the two sides of the man and pointed out that the ultimate goal of man is development of the human spirit, and not just happiness, as so many people are prone to believe. I went up after class and told him that more new ideas were given me today than in any other lecture that I have attended at Vanderbilt. Frank Gunter, the Banner photographer, came to school to get some pictures for me. He wanted to take some random pictures for "art's sake" so I took him to the library to get a picture of Susan and other girls that might be there. Joanne Hampton was my date for the gym dance tonight. Francis Craig's orchestra was better than I have ever heard it. I did not get to dance the Special with Susan as I had planned. When I danced with Virginia McClellan she said: "Congratulations."

"Congratulations for what?" I asked.

"You know what!" (She is Susan's best friend.)

She said that Susan thinks a lot of me and that she has been talking up my stock all year. Any port in a storm, I thought to myself. I thanked her for her kindness in speaking in my behalf. This reminded me of the kind of leaders who find out where the crowd is going and then place themselves in front of it. Joanne is in the same club with Mary Wallace at Ward-Belmont, Angkors. Dave Atkinson and I took Joanne to Peggy Wrights where she was spending the night.

Friday, April 22, 1938 I am brooding over an incident that came up between two of my closest friends, Carl Hinkle and Walter Bogart. I felt duty bound to take Walter Bogart's side because I was partially responsible for his getting into the hassle in the first place. Walter had been promised a free pass book to all functions of the Scholastic Press Convention if he would conduct one of the discussion groups. He arrived late because of duties in connection with his own paper, The University of Alabama's Crimson White, at Tuscaloosa. When he arrived his pass book had been given to someone else. Consequently he had not registered at noon today and did not intend to until the matter was straightened out. When I first saw Walter I told him what a fine fellow Carl was and insisted that he go meet him. The minute I introduced them, Carl hit Walter for a $14.50 registration fee. I argued and pleaded with him to no avail. Finally after a lengthy conference Carl agreed to cut the fee to $10.00. After that settlement I asked him where I could get a ticket to the luncheon. Hinkle informed me, in a harsh manner, that cut to the quick, that I could pay for one just like the others do. I assured him that I had no intention of going in as a member of the press, that I only wanted to know where to buy one. When I telephoned in my story, Mr. Duncan told me to tell Hinkle that if he wanted the banquet covered tonight he would have to send tickets down to the Banner office for their reporter. When I told Carl this he said that "Publicity will do us no good now," so there will be no need for a Banner reporter being there. When I reported this to Mr. Duncan he was furious because Mr. E. B. Stahlman is the principle speaker at tonight's banquet. It is all the more aggravating because Hinkle tried to make Lydel Sims, a Banner reporter, pay for the banquet last night. Carl has ruined himself in the eyes of the news department of the Banner, and it will take me a long time to erase the memory of the harsh things he said to me. The thought of this thing has been weighing on my mind so heavily that I could not study or sleep this afternoon. The thing that made it hurt so was the fact that I had given Carl such a build up as a nice guy. If I were a drinking man I'd probably be on a drunk tonight. Carl probably lent his name to the thing in the first place to make money. When he realized that he would probably lose money he turned into a bad sport.

    Saturday, April 23, 1938   Bill Jordan, Partee Fleming and I met at the Phi Kappa Sigma House to talk over our papers we are writing for the symposium of articles for "Pursuit." Tonight I read this in the Night Hawk column of the Hustler:

> *"Susan Cheek, the coffee queen, has been giving Tom Scoggins the run-around and he thinks her actions are 'grounds' for complaint. He says he wants nothing warmed over, not even his coffee. After the luck you have been having, Tom, you had better be content with even dregs."*

    Sunday, April 24, 1938   Today, for some unknown reason, I began to think about Anderson, my older brother, whom we call "Big Red" to distinguish him from Henry D. and Wilson, who are also redheaded. The patterns of large families, I suppose, are pretty much the same. One of the children, usually the eldest, or next to the eldest, takes it upon himself to look after the younger members of the family. In our case it was "Big Red" who assumed this role. Once assumed, the roles seem never to change. Those who start giving, give all their lives, and those who receive seem to go on receiving. There is an air of mysticism about "Big Red" and we all look up to him. He almost never comes home from college except at night, when very few people are up to see him. Unlike the rest of the children, he very seldom goes to town to socialize. The townspeople seemed to hold him in awe too. He eventually grew to about six feet three inches tall, weighing over two hundred pounds, and he is as fine a specimen of manhood as ever walked the streets of Stevenson. Everyone respects him but he is close to very few, and those few are not run of the mill citizens, but are the unusual ones. Jake Peacock, "Monk" Cargile and Jack Bible Jr. are among his confidants. He has a great deal of pride and yet would never push himself out front. He may be even a little bashful, or else unconsciously aware that familarity breeds contempt. One summer after he had made an extraordinarily long swim of 86 miles down the Tennessee River and this feat had become the main topic of conversation in the Tennessee Valley, Fred Russell, one of the leading sports writers in the nation, invited him to write a column about his swim. "Big Red" was oblivious to the request. I accidentally saw the letter and made him sit down and tell me the story. I wrote the column for him.

Monday, April 25, 1938 Mary Louise Davis told me the other night that I could put my shoes under her bed anytime. It wouldn't be a bad bed to put them under, either. Wrestled Partee Fleming and almost got my arm broken. Some guys just can't do things gently. They're competing all the time. Charles Sadler and I got our DKE-SAE dance arranged with Francis Craig's orchestra.

Tuesday, April 26, 1938 Susan invited me to a dinner party she is giving at the Belle Meade Country Club this Saturday evening. Charles "Buddy" Rogers showed up for the Sigma Kappa buffet two hours late, but his program was excellent. I saw him when he was younger and in his prime at the Black Hawk restaurant in Chicago in 1933. He had on a dark suit and his hair was coal black. He is turning a little gray at the temples now. Emmett O'Callaghan wrote an article of political satire for the "Masquerador" called: "That's Unfortunate." We were in a hot political meeting one day and, after hearing a very sad story about the plight of one of our members, I remarked: "That's unfortunate." The particular set of circumstances made it hilariously funny. Emmett tried to recapture it, and did a beautiful job of it. Learned today that Mary Lyle Wilson, the famous cooking expert, is the mother of my friend Donald McClaren. Mrs. Talbot asked me to write a column for the first big midweek section of the Banner.

Wednesday, April 27, 1938 I was officially elevated to the Presidency of the Honor Council last night. It is an office that I have been working towards for the past three years because I think something ought to be done about cheating at Vanderbilt. As President, it will be my responsibility to do something, and I expect to make an all out effort to change student attitudes about this very serious problem. Joe McGinnis won the runoff election from George Morrow in chapel today. Even political organizational strength could not overcome the personal popularity of Joe over George. Carl Hinkle apologized to me today for losing his temper last week. He even gave me two complimentary tickets to "Passing of the Third Floor Back." Apologies can be accepted, but the scar of unduly harsh words cannot easily be erased.

Thursday, April 28, 1938 Dr. Curry says that Othello is the most artistic of Shakespeare's plays. In a play of intrigue the foundations must be laid carefully. It is painful. The passions are ugly; green eyed jealousy, red flaming passion, which changes to white heat. It is hard to portray on the stage. He says Desdemona, like all women, wanted to be swept off her feet. Iago was a dirty minded man who loved evil for evil's sake. Rolled it under his tongue like a sweet morsel. Bad characters are hard to draw; Aaron the Moor, "Ae, that I had a thousand other evils." Othello said: "If I do repent it is of any good deeds that I have done." In speaking of personality Curry said it is the number of roles that one learns to play and is natural in all of them. It is the men that are complex, not the women. Men play a larger number of roles. Of women he said, men hold other men to the line, but expect women to lie to them. Jordan, Simpson, Fleming and I had a lengthy chat with Dr. Campbell today about our articles on education. Saw Clark Gable, Spencer Tracy and Myrna Loy in "Test Pilot."

Friday, April 29, 1938 During the Physics examination today I saw a boy look at his book. I will deal with that later. At the Banner office this afternoon a big explosion story broke. When the reporters were slow about telephoning in Charley Moss swore like a sailor. The pictures Frank Gunter had made of Susan the other day were good so I gave her a copy of them. A funny thing happened about the flowers I gave Susan for the Theta dance tonight. I sent her a dollar and a half gardenia corsage. When I went to get her I saw that she was wearing a bouquet of three orchids, costing at least five dollars each. In order not to make me feel badly, she wore mine too. I appreciated her being considerate. Mrs. Cheek's mother and a Mrs. Glenn, from Clarksville, were sitting in the chaperon section, as was Mrs. Witherspoon, Mrs. Billington and Mrs. Scoggins. Susan was prettier than I have seen her in a long time. I danced the first no-break with her, naturally and the second with Sara King, of Texas, the third with Whitola Driskill and the fourth with Ellen Bowers. Always enjoy dancing with Ann Wright and Henrietta Hickman. Oh, yes, John Cheek told me about seeing Strangler Lewis in Honolulu last summer. On the way home tonight Susan and I talked about pretending. I should have been a little more sensitive to Susan's feelings about one of her first sorority dances, as a freshman, and about her social position in the community, and should have stretched myself a little bit to get her a more elaborate corsarge for the dance tonight. Little things often make the difference between winning and losing.

Saturday, April 30, 1938 The Calumet Club took in fifteen new members today, including Bill Jordan, Partee Fleming, Roy Van Dusen, Jim Tuck, Stanford Wolf, O. C. Carmichael Jr., Jimmy Dobbs, Darby Fulton, William Sanderson, Dean Havron, Harris Abrahams, Winston Tipton, Jack Bernard, Trimmier McCarley and D. Y. Proctor. I saw the last part of the U. T. track meet. Met some interesting people at Susan's party at Belle Meade Country Club. Shirley Caldwell and I had a philosophical discussion at our initial encounter. I suggested that she read Bacon's essays. Cora Grant runs her fingers tantalizingly through your hair while she is dancing with you. I wonder where she learned that trick, or, as Dr. Curry put it, "Girls are born knowing how to trap a man." Marion Long and I rode out with Tom Cummings Jr. Johnny Platt was Shirley's date.

Sunday, May 1, 1938 Although my maximum salary is $22.50 I turned in $42.00 worth of copy this month. When Dr. Curry quoted Shakespeare yesterday, "As flies to wanton boys are we to the gods," I thought of Browning's poem about Caliban. A line of crabs were going back to the sea. Caliban raises his club at intervals and kills one. There is no reason why he should kill one instead of another.

Monday, May 2, 1938 Charley Majors got the presidency of the fraternity. I was put up for three offices and was defeated for all three. It hurt my pride to have worked so hard for the fraternity: kept the scrapbook, edited Gamma Gossip, wrote the best letter to the fraternity Quarterly (according to the editor's note), was chairman of dance committee which originated and promoted the DKE-SAE dance, donated a burglar alarm, won the Intramural wrestling championship and coached our teams, and then be defeated in an election, even for an office which I hold now. On the other hand, I have held offices ever since I have been in the fraternity. I have been before them quite a bit and naturally they tire of one person, especially if he is very active. John McReynolds, as a means of soothing my vanity, nominated me again for the position of "Huey Long for the fraternity." Charles Majors, who had led the fight against me on the other offices, saw an opportunity to get credit for my being given the political job so he praised the work I had done and moved that I be reelected by acclamation. Tonight Byron Anglin was defeated for the house managership of the Chi Phi House so he resigned from the fraternity. He took his brother, Leonard, and Emmett

O'Callaghan with him. I wouldn't think of a thing like this over a little election. Someone has to lose. There is no reason for not being a sport about it. As Kipling wrote, "triumph and disaster" should be treated the same.

Tuesday, May 3, 1938 I wrote until two o'clock this morning on an English paper; a criticism of Macbeth. Bill Embry did a great favor for me by helping me type it before class. Randy Batson presided over his last meeting of the Student Council today and Morris Burk was sworn in as the new President. I was sworn in as a regular member. The Embry-Anglin political deal was mentioned to me again today but I passed on it. The Confederation is the strongest political organization the campus has ever had. All each fraternity has to do to continue winning is to sit tight.

Wednesday, May 4, 1938 My Commencement story made the front page of the Banner this afternoon but I did not get a by-line. My first column "On the Campus This Week" did appear with a by-line though. Lots of people have asked me if it will be regular. Who knows? Talked to Gerald Henderson, Business Manager of the University, about getting out a book on the Honor System. He is sympathetic. Jack Worley and Lu Ray Welch went with Susan and me to the DKE-SAE dance tonight. This was our first dance with the SAE's and it was a good one. Francis Craig read over the PA system a note I handed him requesting slow pieces. It got applause. He played good numbers. I particularly liked the medley which included "Just Picture a Penthouse . . ." Miriam thanked me for asking Seyfried to bring her to the dance. Once I noticed her watching Susan and me talk. Susan said she appreciated the mention, in my column, of the decorations she and Virginia McClellan put up for the Theta dance.

Thursday, May 5, 1938 Pictures of Ed Pardue, McPheters Glasgow and Morris Burk were taken for the paper. Pardue and I had a little political discussion. The Confederation is composed of The Betas, the SAE's, the Sigma Chi's, the ZBT's, the Kappa Sigmas, the KA's, the Phi Kappa Sigmas, the Tri Deltas, the AOPi's and the Dekes. It was rather a formidable group that met at the Beta House tonight to consolidate our gains.

Friday, May 6, 1938 The Honor Committee, the Student Council and Student Union pictures came out in the Banner this evening. Susan and I went to the Theta dance with Clarence Woodcock. Mr. Cheek and I discussed the political situation at Vanderbilt, the split up and then the reunion of frats. Had the second no-break with Gail Armstrong and the fourth with Martha Ezel. Willie Cornelius had the second with Susan. Miriam and Ed Kirkpatrick sat facing us in Candyland. I smiled at Miriam as I went out.

Saturday, May 7, 1938 I accepted it philosophically today, a very severe blow. Because of those bad grades I made in math during my first year in Engineering school, I do not have a "C" average and therefore I am not going to make the honorary leadership fraternity Omicron Delta Kappa. I have more than enough points. Strangely enough the primary reason I would liked to have made it would be to kiss Susan; but I would not have been able to do so anyway because Tom Scoggins has the date with her for the O.D.K. dance. Guess it was just another idle dream. Met with Bill Jordan, Don Ross, Bill Simpson and Partee Fleming to discuss our critique of the university. Dr. Curry was philosophical today. He said that physically we never get away with anything; the nerves and the brain don't forget. Neither do we get away with anything mentally or spiritually. For everything in the material world there is something in the spiritual that corresponds. Hmmm! How does he know that? He also said natural laws can never be broken. A body does not always fall to the ground, it may be borne up by other laws, as is the case in a flying machine. Praying for spiritual forces to come in and subvert natural laws is silly. May it never come to pass. He quoted Prospero in the Tempest: "These our actors, as I foretold you, were all spirits and were melted into thin air . . . We are such stuff as dreams are made of."

Sunday, May 8, 1938 Mrs. Miles, who went to the country today, left me a red rose to wear in my coat lapel in honor of my living Mother. It rained and I did not go to church. I put the rose on my desk and looked at it and smelled it's fragrance all day. It just dawned on me that the English language has an inadequacy. There is no appropriate word for expressing the experience of smelling a pleasant odor. The word smell has unpleasant connotations and so does the word odor. Fragrance is hardly adequate. Why not combine the words flower and aroma into one word "flueroma." I have coined a new and useful word.

Monday, May 9, 1938 After the fraternity meeting, at which officers were installed, James Tuck and I went over to the Z.B.T. House for a meeting of the newly organized political machine. All were in favor of going ahead and consummating the union except the Sigma Chis. They wanted to put it off a couple of days. Pierce Winningham was strong at first but backed off when we told him we were going ahead and getting another fraternity to take their place if they do not give us a definite yes or no tonight. Harris Abrahams brought me home. I had a terrible headache; had to take aspirin to get to sleep.

Tuesday, May 10, 1938 Byron Anglin gave me the O.D.K. list this evening. The tapping ceremony is in chapel tomorrow morning. Those who made it are Joe McGinnis, Ray Manning, Joe Cummings, Ed Hunter, William Benson, Walter Hackett, Jack Worley, Lunsford Hollins, Charles

Majors, James Lanier, "Dutch" Clarence Rheinschmidt, Marvin Franklin and a boy by the name of Perkins. The list of those not making it would make up a pretty impressive fraternity of leaders: Bill Embry, editor of the student newspaper, Morris Burk, President of the Student Council, Edmund Pardue, Ed Kirkpatrick, William Estes, D. Y. Proctor Tom Scoggins and the President of the Honor Council. Studied Spanish with Paul Clements.

Wednesday, May 11, 1938 The O.D.K. tapping ceremony is very austere and impressive, but at the same time a little brutal. Members of the group pass through the audience, one at a time, and at intervals slap very loudly one of the chosen on the shoulder. It is dramatic, as the audience does not know who will be chosen, but it also highlights those leaders who, for one reason or another, were not chosen. When Henry Clay lost something of value to him once, I soothed his feelings by saying: "Henry, there is one thing better than winning, and that is deserving to win." He liked that. I hired Bob Slayden to take pictures of the O.D.K. men so we could get it in the afternoon paper. I very explicitly told him to deliver them to the City Editor. He was in a hurry so he left the pictures with the man at the front reception desk. Consequently the pictures were still at that desk when I went down at 12:30. Luckily we took a group shot and could get it in anyway. After a Calumet club meeting tonight I took Susan to the Kappa Phi, prep. school dance. It was a cool evening and the dance was not too crowded so we got to dance with each other a lot. Francis Craig played a beautiful selection of favorite tunes and we enjoyed the affair very much. We went to Hettie Ray's for intermission. I saw a copy of Edgar Guest's poems on the table in Susan's living room while talking to her father and waiting for her to get ready. Uncle Walt let me drive his new car on the date.

Thursday, May 12, 1938 It was chilly this morning so I wore the sweater with my wrestling letter on it for the first time. Majors was elected President of O.D.K. Dr. Curry said that in "Pericles," Scene III, Act II, is one of the finest pieces of writing in Shakespeare—atmosphere—quaintness—romance—far away. Suggestive of Wordsworth's "Solitary Reeper": "Of old far off places, of battles long ago." His description of a storm at beginning of Act III cannot be paralleled in the language. He quoted: "The sermon's whistle is as a whisper, in the ears of death unheard." Shakespeare's writing is great in that Shakespeare himself is lost in what King Lear thinks and does; what Lear ought to think and do. He does not care to change history. Henry VI is a dramatization of a block of history, the 100 Year War and the War of Roses, 15 enormous acts. Maybe he did not write all of the play. He reworked and put his stamp of genius on it.

Friday, May 13, 1938 It was chilly this morning and threatening rain. Seems more like the beginning of winter than summer or spring. I did not see Susan or her car all day. Thought she might be sick so I called her home and found out she is at school. Burk and Embry are sore about not making O.D.K. and they are planning a drinking party tomorrow night to console each other. Fannie Rose Shore mentioned something about it to me today. I think she was a little surprised at the number that did not make it. I have a date and cannot join them, even for Cokes. Lu Ray Welch and I danced in her basement playroom and went to the drugstore for milk shakes.

Saturday, May 14, 1938 Joel Stephens had a buffet supper for the five boys from Corinth, Mississippi who came up to visit the fraternity and Walter King and Andrew Sweat specifically. Eddie Morton, John McReynolds, Jim Tuck, the two Seyfrieds and a few other Dekes attended. The only two that weren't Dekes were Sol Komisar and Johnny Hyden. Komisar reminds me of Jimmy Armstrong, the Miami dentist who first got interested in dentistry in my Father's office. Going to the gym dance tonight Susan told me about Mary Wallace having lunch with them today at the Theta House and how much they liked her. I had the fourth no-break with Virginia McClellan and she too told me about Mary Wallace's visit. When I was dancing the second no-break with Lu Ray Welch I told her what I had heard Jack Worley say, that he had found his girl. After our dance I noticed Lu Ray standing behind other people looking at me. Enjoyed the third with Susan. It was much like the DKE-SAE special last Wednesday evening. Sitting in the balcony, Susan told me that her worst fault is being sarcastic. I suppose most people are sarcastic. They see through sham and what is untrue and resent, bitterly, both being used as a weapon against them. On hearing about the columnist Walter Lippman not getting along with his wife and being divorced I thought: How can a man, whose business it is to look behind the surface of the news, for example, not do the same thing at home? How could a woman stand being understood? John McReynolds and Sara Cecil rode home with us. We got refreshments at Uncle Ragan's new tea room. After dropping off the other couple Susan and I discussed how much we enjoy Vanderbilt, but we both hate studying. We will both be sorry when we have to go away for the summer. She promised to give me a picture next Wednesday when we return from the swimming party at Franklin. She seemed pleased at the prospect of giving it to me. She says her father kids her, and me, about being so absent minded. Tells her to write a note to herself to come home. She never drinks coffee; doesn't like it.

Sunday, May 15, 1938 What a rare treat it has been this year to have two professors of the calibre of Eddie Mims and Walter Clyde

Curry. The voices that Matthew Arnold wrote of as hearing at Oxford forty years earlier, I'm sure were no greater than these, and I'm sure his appreciation of them was no greater than mine for these two great men. Yesterday Dr. Curry asked the rhetorical question, "Does Shakespeare picture himself in his characters?" Most critics agree that a writer must be objective, yet Hamlet is Shakespeare. Timon of Athens is Shakespeare. When an artist wants to create a new character he takes a genus from his own being and amplifies it. Shakespeare has no sermon to preach. He presents facts as they are. He has no patience with the sentimentalist who says the good do not suffer as the wicked. The Life Force creates bodies with life in them; then tramples them under foot. Curry delights in throwing out little challenges like this: People take it for granted that there is such a thing as justice and try to connect it with the rise and fall of man's fortunes. Why should we expect a consideration of justice or injustice? How do we know we deserve it?

Monday, May 16, 1938 Susan picked me up again this morning on my way to school. She had already picked up Pat Wilson, who lives out her way. Her initials are carved on the gearshift of her car. I told her that was a good thing in case she absentmindedly gets into the wrong car she can check her bearing. Dr. Underwood told Hartwell Weaver and me today that if we didn't get our Physics report in immediately it would be too bad. Had a fraternity meeting and then a political meeting. We are changing our name to the "Senate." Harris Abrahams and Pierce Winningham were nominated for chairmanship of the new group. Since both of those two had participated in partisan issues I felt that a more neutral chairman should be selected. At the last minute I nominated Senator Field and he was elected.

Tuesday, May 17, 1938 Since Ed Hunter could not sit in on the trial before the Honor Committee today because it effected one of his fraternity brothers, I was called in by Billy Estes, this years President, to prosecute the case. I cross examined both R. and L. and finally got an admission of irregularity out of R. We could not determine, however, which of the two did the cheating. H. was also brought up because he sat on the other side of R. After long hours of interrogation the trial was recessed. I am the new president, but haven't officially taken office yet.

Wednesday, May 18, 1938 Today at 12:00 o'clock the trial opened again. After lengthy questioning L. also admitted irregularities and we could have dismissed witnesses and inflicted punishment then and there. Instead of making a decision ourselves, or of forcing witnesses into the embarrassing position of having to admit the cheating before other members of the committee, I suggested that he tell the whole story to the president in private. Estes came back in ten minutes with a promise of a written confession. Instead of having hard feelings toward me, or other members of the committee, as he might have done if we had handled it differently L. came to me on the campus shortly after the trial and thanked me for sparing his pride. Buddy Stone, Dave Atkinson, and I went for Libby Ragland, Peggy Wright and Susan for the picnic this afternoon. Susan and I had good seats up near the cab going down, but we had to sit on the very back edge coming home and we got very cold. We played softball, promenaded about and swam. It was fun having Susan serve my plate. I got the Coca Colas. We helped each other eat our sandwiches.

Thursday, May 19, 1938 I must have gotten a light touch of ptomaine poison at the picnic yesterday because my stomach has been hurting all day. Miriam had to go to bed and Susan missed school. Curry said today that love is the most precious of all values in human relations. He said the two sisters in Lear reach the lowest depth of any women yet presented in Shakespeare. Women can reach lower depths of iniquity than men; they can also reach greater heights of sublimity. Of Macbeth Curry said that he never considered that his conscience would hurt him. At first he thought only of getting by. Later he tried to do so many horrible deeds that his conscience would not bother him. Shakespeare had the power of explaining an offstage murder so vividly that it is probably more effective than if the audience actually saw it. He says the power of suggestion is even more powerful than speech. Innuendo— a lift of the eyebrow.

Friday, May 20, 1938 I saw Susan in front of Calhoun today and she said that she had brought the picture that she had promised. We walked to her car and got it. I did not open it until after lunch as I was riding the street car to town. The picture is simply wonderful. It was made by Aline Du Pont on 5th Avenue N.Y. It is the one that she had made for her high school at Spence School last year. When I arrived home I called her enthusiastically telling her how pretty I thought the portrait was. She said "Turn about's fair play, you know." I told her I didn't think I had a real nice picture but that I would check up and get her one just as soon as possible. I felt really flattered that she asked me for my picture. She was mighty sweet on the phone. Saw Ginger Rogers and James Stewart in "Vivacious Lady." at the Knicker-bocker today. I liked it as well or better than "It Happened One Night." James Stewart was the typical young college professor, and a very logical, bashful one who fell in love with the "vivacious" lady. It was really a scream. Talked to Miriam on the phone tonight. She is not coming back to school until Monday.

Saturday, May 21, 1938 Talked to Susan twice today. I received a letter that pleased me more than probably any other letter in my life.

My friend, perhaps my best one, wrote a biography of me which is very flattering yet it is not intended flattery but a true expression of friendship—

The paper is as follows:

Don M. Linton
Biography Eng. 21
Mr. Hartsell
May 13, 1938

PUSH, PERSEVERANCE, AND PLUCK

I can't remember exactly when I did meet Ben. It might have been the amusingly exasperated state of one of our professors brought about by Ben's persistent inquisitiveness for detail which first caused me to take notice of him. Or I might have asked who that 160 pounds of muscle and grace was who pinned his final opponent to the mat in a speedy 7 second bid for the Vanderbilt Intramural wrestling championship, and the reply from a neighboring spectator might have been, "Name's Ben Austin—D.K.E.—plenty good, isn't he?" I don't know where it was. Anyway its not so important at present. Later on perhaps, in the years to come, the date and place of our meeting might be well worth trying to remember for biographical data; for there is not the least doubt in my mind that someday his life and accomplishments will be set down in such a manner as to create an inspiring and ennobling study.

Ben was born in Stevenson, Alabama, about twenty-one years ago. He has more sisters and brothers than you can count on one hand, and a father and mother who are just as proud of him as he is of them. Ben had been living in Nashville since he entered high school and the balance of the family, excepting the married ones, live in Stevenson where their Father's monopoly of dental work provides them with much more than a comfortable living.

Ben attended a high school whose enrollment was well over 2,500. Before he graduated he was President of the Student Body, President of the Honor Council, a Captain in the R.O.T.C. and he held several offices in four or five clubs and organizations of the school. Let it not be thought that Ben did not have his share of male genes, for he was one of the best right tackles the Institution has ever boasted of, and a member of the wrestling and track teams. The founding of one of the most popular of the three publications, which the school now enjoys, from one of Ben's frequent inspirational conceptions.

One day while sitting in the library he happened to think that maybe the school could use a new type of culture spreader, so he got busy. In the space of ten days he went through the necessary red tape in order to gain faculty sanction, drew up a staff of assistants, gathered and edited material, and thought he was about ready to go to press. However, a day and a half before the "Fogg Horn" form was to go to the printers the advertising manager strolled up to Ben and sheepishly informed him that he had been able to sell only $8.00 worth of advertising space. Instead of turning over the keys of hell to the boy, Ben turned away smiling (and I have this from a reliable authority), dashed out of the building and returned in a day and a quarter with enough advertising from Nashville merchants to cover expenses.

Since Ben matriculated at Vanderbilt his activities have been practically a repetition of his high school days. Such a record of achievement accomplished as a result of the inspiration afforded by institutional environments are great enough in themselves to classify Ben as an up and coming young man, but my reason for attempting to crown him with added laurels springs from the fact that aside from what he has been in and out of on the campus, he has managed to do the following

(1) Read the Bible nightly
(2) Fill two very large scrapbooks full of worthwhile clippings, articles, and editorials
(3) Fill two notebooks with ideas of anything and everything, just as they come to him.
(4) Keep a diary.
(5) Secure protection on two of his inventions through the United States Patent office.
(6) Write 2 Sunday supplement feature articles for a leading southern newspaper.

But wait! I shouldn't forget to mention that this post-adolescent learner finds opportunities to ogle the opposite sex (in a most Quixotic fashion), to sip tea, and to sit in grandstands, elegantly immobile and superbly useless. But his control over his probable desires for excessive wanderings in these tempting fields is beautiful. Never have I know a powerful duty shirking incentive to get the best of his use of time utilization.

Long before Dale Carnegie dared hope that someday he would write a book (How to Win Friends, and Influence People) which would sell well over half a million people, Ben Austin had been applying the principles which this best seller advocated.

Early one fall evening three years ago I walked up on the porch steps of Ben's home (owned by Ben's Father but leased to a Nashville family with whom Ben lives). I rapped on the door and then took a quick look at the number above the door to check it with the one I had written down on a leaf of my Spanish book. Suddenly the door was flung open to permit a smiling face to pop out into the darkness and inquire, "Yes?"

"Hello, Ben," I ventured as soon as he recognized me as being a member of his Spanish class a sharp but pleasant cry of surprise darted forth, followed by such hand shaking, back slapping, and general jubilant jabbering, as might be accredited to a campaigning ward heeler tanked up with the spirits of election. I even thought for a moment or so that perhaps I just happened to be a case of mistaken identity. Since then, however, I've often watched him admiringly as he greeted other near strangers in the same happy and attentive manner.

Many boys have acquired that knack of meeting people in the pleasing fashion that Ben does, but their technique is usually employed for the purpose of creating a temporary impression and letting it go at that. Now Ben's unusual abilities of handling people develop from the same seeds as were sown to produce his other accomplishments, you'll probably find them in a package labeled "consistencies." Ben's interest in people is genuine; hence, it is in no way spasmodic—but constant. When ever I am in his presence, talk to him over the telephone, or even read a letter from him, I seem to receive the same elevating effects of his personality that I experienced the first night I studied Spanish with him.

Ben is not a genius—but he's not so very far from it. He is exceedingly remarkable, however, in that his unusual amount of energy is forced to exert itself continually in constructive and worth while channels, through the pressure brought to bear on it by an unusual amount of common sense and determination. This enviable quality has been an important visual companion of Ben's character from early teen age, which makes it even more admirable, considering that the majority of boys who grope through this "foolkiller" stage apparently never nurse a serious thought of self-discipline or any of its various correlatives.

It is then, this abundant amount of energy controlled by a secret desire to give destiny a well remembered struggle, that is in whole responsible for the sturdiness and beauty seen in the foundation which this Mr. Austin has carefully laid down.

(1,214 words) –30–

(He enclosed this paper that he had handed to his English professor. His grade was A– and the teachers comment was as follows: "vivid, interesting—I hope not over enthusiastic." To this Don added (oh! Hell no, teacher)

Sunday, May 22, 1938 Read History almost solidly from nine this morning until three this afternoon. Chas. Majors called up to remind me of the buffet supper we are giving for freshmen at the house today at 4:00 P.M. Among those attending were: Henry Coile, Billy Northern, Bill Mills (Katherine's brother), the two Swiggart boys, Billy Whitaker and Mac Dickinson. Learned that "Biz" Johnson is going to marry Ed Purdue's older brother. "Blimp" Browning is taking it pretty hard.

Monday, May 23, 1938 This is a very important day in my life. I received word from my patent attorney that my Zipper patent had been definitely granted. If I should be asked what my greatest ambition was I might be tempted to say that it is to take out more patents than Thomas A. Edison. You could not help bettering society with that many inventions.

Tuesday, May 24, 1938 After the Calumet Club banquet tonight Dr. Herbert Sanborn, head of the Philosophy department, Dr. Claude Lee Finney, Dr. Lyle Lanier, Dr. George Mayfield, Dr. Tom Zerfoss, Bill Jordan, Partee Fleming, Morris Burk and I got together for a real old fashioned Calumet Club Round Table discussion. My point about the "Individual Diploma," rather than the mass one, seemed to strike a favorable note with all of them. I was pleasantly surprised to find that many of the professor's ideas coincided with those of the students present. I particularly liked Finney's and Sanborn's comments. We did not break up until after midnight. This was the kind of after hours discussions between teachers and students that made Oxford and Cambridge famous.

Wednesday, May 25, 1938 Emmett O'Callaghan has been selected as next years editor of the Masquerader. I was a little surprised that Roy Van Dusen did not get it. I called up Susan tonight to make our late date for the June 3rd finals and she yelled very enthusiastically "Congratulations." I asked her for what and she said that in the library somebody told her about getting my patent. I'll bet it was Ann Wright because she is the only girl I can think of that I told it to other than Miriam. I have never heard Susan so enthusiastic before. Said she wanted my autograph.

Thursday, May 26, 1938 Yesterday I showed the Zipper invention to Dr. Underwood. He thought it was good. Showed it to Dr. Eugene Ellison, a boy from my hometown, who happened to be with Dr. Underwood at the time, and he reacted to the letter granting the patent, with a cynical grin. Can't figure that guy out.

Friday, May 27, 1938 Carl Hinkle was elected Bachelor of Ugliness today by acclamation. It is the second time in history that the candidate has been unopposed. Randy Batson nominated him and Ray Morrison, Varsity coach, spoke in behalf of former B. U's. The big party of celebration took place this afternoon.

Saturday, May 28, 1938 I am not too worried about Byron Hill's Economics examination but my memory was not too good on the Spanish this morning. Saw Susan walking across the campus with Tom Scoggins and felt my stomach flinch as if I had drunk a glass of ice water. Miriam told me, on the phone, tonight that she would like to go to the Deke house party with senior David Seyfried and quickly added, "Let me go to the breakfast with you." I was previously scheduled for both dates. Jim Reed and I were talking today and he said he was more impressed with me than any other boy at the Deke House during rush week. "I thought you weighed 190 pounds."

Sunday, May 29, 1938 I read Physics all day. It started raining about ten o'clock and made it all the more pleasant for studying. One of Dr. Curry's thoughts flashed through my mind: "The great man is he whose ardor to do great deeds for the world is not dampened by the realization that he can never expect anything in return."

Monday, May 30, 1938 Dr. Newton Underwood helped Weaver and me get through with the Physics reports this morning. Took us two hours. Dr. Underwood is a prince of a fellow. Saw Susan immediately after the English exam and talked with her a few minutes. It was almost as if by chance, after returning from a furious battlefield, the one you love soothes your wounds. I asked Byron Anglin how he came out in his asking the Managing Editor of the Banner for a job. Said he did not do so well. Mr. Moss told Anglin he would have to look after Austin first. I appreciate the fact that he would be willing to give me serious consideration for a permanent job but I am not certain I want to get that deeply involved in the newspaper business. I guess Mr. Moss thinks that the reason I turn in about twice as much copy as my quota allows me to get paid for is that I want a job when I get out of school. I do it because my job is to cover the news at Vanderbilt; not to make some artificial quota. The last issue of "Pursuit" came out today. My article on "Education" was in the lead position. Partee Fleming's and William Simpson's followed. I was amused at Bill's remarks in introducing me in his front page notes: "Ben Austin has been in every conceivable activity in Vanderbilt and has been in both the Engineering school and the College of Arts and Sciences. He knows Vanderbilt pretty well . . ."

Tuesday, May 31, 1938 Had no exams today so I stayed home and studied mathematics. Hope I get the "monkey" off my back this term. It has weighed me down like an albatross all of my college days. Felt terribly bad this evening. Had pains down the center of my arms, like rheumatism. I don't suppose it is a psychological reaction to mathematics. Maybe I am alergic to it.

Wednesday, June 1, 1938 Think I did well on my History examination this morning.

Thursday, June 2, 1938 Mother came from Stevenson last night and to see me this morning. She told me about Anderson's wreck. Swapped his Oldsmobile for a Chevrolet. She and Mrs. Miles seemed to like each other. Took my last exam in English this evening and it was tough. As much as I like English, I have difficulty remembering who said what. I am more concerned with what was said, and how it was said, than by whom. When I went to get Susan for the Prom this evening Mr. John Cheek met me at the door and talked about his recent trip to New York. He told me about seeing John Pierpont Morgan at the graduation of his granddaughter at Spence School last year. Once before he had seen Mr. Morgan. It was the occassion when he participated in the sale of Cheek-Neal Coffee Company to General Foods for some $40,000,000.00 in 1928. He asked me about the progress of my invention. Said he himself had an idea for an invention; a revolving scarecrow in the shape of a man with a gun in his hand. The Prom was delightful. Didn't get Susan home until about 2:30 A.M.

Friday, June 3, 1938 I was hoping to sleep late this morning but Mrs. Kate Talbot, of the Society Section of the Banner called me at about 8:00 o'clock to get some information about the Prom. At noon Dr. John Pomfret, Dr. Mulloy, Bill Jordan, Partee Fleming and I met in the private dining room of the Canary Inn to discuss our reform movement at Vanderbilt. I like Dr. Pomfret. I think his popularity will eventually approximate that of Dean Sarratt. Partee's brother Bill drove me home. Took Susan to the tea dance, at which Jimmy Dorsey's orchestra played, but had to take her straight home so Jim Souby and Charles Anderson could take her to dinner. I escorted Miriam to the dance tonight. I thought I would be bitter about the O.D.K. kissing ceremony but I got a kick out of watching it, just as the rest of the audience did. Mrs. Cheek was one of the spectators in the balcony. I am sorry she could not see her daughter kissed and I should have been the one doing the kissing. Switched arrangements again and rushed Miriam home early so she could go to the Deke breakfast with Seifried. Steve McGaw complimented my article in "Pursuit." Said it coincided with his experiences in school. Steve is an artist and that's what I wrote about; routine school assignments interfering with artistic inspirations. I was supposed to pick up Susan at 2:30 A.M. but she did not arrive on time. I drove out of her driveway just a few minutes before Tom Scoggins brought her home. I turned out my lights and waited for him to leave and then drove back. That added a touch of intrigue to the affair. We were a little late but arrived in time for grapefruit and eggs. We were hungry and the breakfast was good. It was beautiful watching the sun rise above the pavilion. We sang songs and closed with a soft rendition of the Alma Mater. There is no college song quite so moving as the old Scottish folk song from which Cornell University, Vanderbilt and other schools adapted their school songs. "On a cities western border, reared against the sky, proudly stands our Alma Mater, as the years roll by." We drove home very slowly, seeking perhaps unconsciously to prolong the spell of one of the most poignant of all experiences, a sentimental college farewell. The early morning air was fresh and crisp. The world seemed aglow like youth at springtime. One of us, at least, I knew was in love. When I bade good night at her door, the look in her eyes was a little different, a little sweeter than usual. Driving home alone, along half empty commercial streets, I saw the world around me much as Wordsworth once did when he wrote: "There was a time when meadows, groves and streams, the earth and every common sight, to me did seem apparelled in celestial light, the glory and the freshness of a dream." Instead of going to bed I stayed up and Lydel Sims, Jim Christian and I drove around town getting pictures of potential Founder's Medalists, including Lucille Cate and Bob Sturdivant. We guessed right so we used all six pictures on the front page of the Banner Saturday afternoon.

Saturday, June 4, 1938 Yesterday blended into today since I did not go to bed. After finishing with the picture taking, however, I fell into bed and slept all afternoon.

Sunday, June 5, 1938 I listened to the commencement address over the radio this morning and then went to school to discuss Honor Committee plans with Richard Pickens and Bill Travis, of the Engineering school. Later I talked with Hill Turner, the Vanderbilt Alumni Secretary, about the Zipper invention and he immediately said he would buy stock. Showed Uncle Walt the letter from Don Linton tonight and he took it to make some copies.

Monday, June 6, 1938 I got up late, made out a schedule, and started out on it. Saw Fred Russell in the barbershop and Boots Tyne in his office. Dr. Harris, the Cheek family doctor was at her home when I went to pick up Susan and he told us about the automobile accident Joe Wallace had. Susan and I went to Hettie Ray's for dancing. It was a relief to get away from a lot of "breaking" and to have a little room for dancing. She had on high heels tonight, the first time she has worn them all year. It made her taller and easier to hold. Once when our bodies came together she pretended not to notice, but on the next step she pushed away just the least bit. Got her home exactly on time. Her father told us that Billy Eason's father had died. The Easons lived in Jackson, Tennessee. Susan told me her mother planned her summer schedule for her; no more than three dates per week, no typing or anything but tennis lessons and complete rest. She says her family makes all her decisions for her. I told her it was just the opposite for me during the last eight years.

Tuesday, June 7, 1938 Called Donald Linton on the phone and talked with him for the first time in months. Lydel Sims and I went to Loews to see "Three Comrades." When we got out it was raining so we stood for a long time talking about our future plans for a proposed newspaper. At the Senior Farewell dance tonight I passed Ann Elizabeth Fahey without noticing her. She grabbed me by the arm. I have always been physically attracted to her. She is heavily built through the hips and her eyes always seem to be a little puffy and pouty as if she had been crying, or else had kidney disease, but overall she is very sexy looking. Reminds me of a comic strip character "Tilly the Toiler," especially the risqué versions I have seen. She said Dewitt Smith told her I was in love with Susan. I was standing by the door when Susan left the dance and she gave me a glance that made my heart flutter.

Wednesday, June 8, 1938 I arrived home from the dance at 2:00. Got up in the early afternoon and went to the Banner office and demonstrated the Zipper to Managing Editor Charles Moss and Fred Russell, Sports Editor. Fred said: "You can't miss." I asked R. A. Gotto to do some illustrations for me. Saw John Sloan at Cain-Sloans and Mr. Stroud. Hilliard Wood took pictures of Jean Starr and Sarah Cecil. Lallie Ricter loaned us some sports garments.

Thursday, June 9, 1938 Don Linton came by and took me out to Susan's. When I found out Eleanor Richie did not have a date I asked Susan to invite her downstairs for a date with Don. She came, even though she did have belladonna in her eyes. We played the piano, danced and talked. Mr. Cheek told me that several people had tried to interest him in inventions; the colored movie man, and the Puncture Proof Tire Company, in which Chancellor Kirkland and John Daniels had an interest. Guess Mr. Cheek thought I was trying to get him interested in my invention.

Friday, June 10, 1938 Learned from the Bursar that I owe him $26.00 in tuition. Talked to Gerald Henderson about the Honor Committee booklet. He is Business Manager of the University. Met Mr. Henry Tyne, Arnold Peebles and Stratton Foster, a Clarksville newspaper man, in Elliston Place Pharmacy. Rode to town with "Red" Sanders, former Riverside Military Academy coach and now with Josh Cody at the University of Florida. At the Banner dark room I had a talk with Colonel Armstrong, Headmaster at Castle Heights. He is getting prints made of Floyd Gibbons, who was shaking hands with Bernard McFadden at the school last year.

Saturday, June 11, 1938 Packed, kissed the ladies good-bye and closed out another year at Vanderbilt. Departed for home in Stevenson, Alabama and for another summer at Dixie Camps in Wiley, Georgia, high in the mountains of North Georgia.

FALL
1938

Wednesday, September 7, 1938 I returned to Nashville to prepare for the coming year at Vanderbilt. Went to the Bursar's office and paid them $16.00. That leaves a balance of $10.00 owed from last year. Saw Mr. A. B. Miles in Gerald Henderson's office and he said I could have my coaching job again this year. Dropped by the Banner office and had a reunion with City Editor, Rousseau Duncan, photographers Frank Gunter and Hilliard Wood, artist R. A. Gotto and Society's Mrs. Connoll. The new City room is beautiful. Saw Shirley Temple in "Little Miss Broadway." Used Uncle Ragan's car for my date with Miriam. We danced at the Stork Club and then took a long leisurely drive down the Memphis highway. The moon was full and we talked intimately. Spoke with Mr. Sam McGaw when we returned to her new home on Richland Avenue. Her brother Howard had bought it as an investment.

Thursday, September 8, 1938 The Ragans have taken Belle Meade Police Chief, Mr. Boyd, to Primm Springs with them. Douglas Lambeth, a law student at Vanderbilt, was at the Lynnmeade lunchroom today and we had a chat. Mr. John Cheek told me tonight, when I went to get Susan, that he had just returned from Daytona Beach where he had sold his winter home to Mr. Robert Woodruff, President of Coca Cola. Susan was prettier than I have ever seen her. She was sun tanned and had taken off a little weight. She was in a high-spirited mood so we went to the Stork Club in Franklin and danced to the nickelodeon. What a marvelous selection of romantic pieces, "I'm no millionaire,

but I'm not the type to care, 'cause I've got a pocket full of dreams,"
the everlasting favorite "Sleepy Time Gal" and the "Waltz You Saved
for Me." Doc Wallace and Dot King, from Franklin were there dancing,
too. Susan asked me if "Red" Austin, who did all that swimming, were
my brother. There are times when one senses a blending of spirits.
Tonight was one of those occasions. I could feel the warmth when she
looked up at me while we were dancing. When she said good night
she winked at me through the screen. This very evening I should have
asked her to marry me. If I only had the courage!

Friday, September 9, 1938 At the paint store this morning I saw Susan's car parked directly in front. She was not in it at first but a few
minutes later I saw her bid the boy good-bye and she drove off. She
had on a very pretty broad brimmed hat. Seeing her preyed on my
mind so that I forgot to pick up Mr. Ragan's mother, as I was supposed
to do. Worked at the Lynnmeade lunchroom this afternoon and had a
long talk with Mike Cain.

Saturday, September 10, 1938 Saw Mrs. Henry Graham, the Hume-
Fogg librarian, going to town today. What a friend she had been to
me! I never worked in the library for her, but she and Mr. "Slim" Porter
served as faculty advisors for the Fogg Horn. She suffered with me
through the birth pangs of the paper and she fretted with me when it
looked as if I might not pass those double French courses I had to
take in order to graduate. Miss Handly, the French teacher, worried
too, and I am sure the principal, Mr. C. T. Kirkpatrick would not let
my name be put up for the Civitan Medal because he was afraid I would
not graduate. In spite of the difficulties I came through with colors
mildly flapping in the breezes. What a blessing it was to have such
wonderful people pulling for you. Tonight Susan is at Camille Stone's
and Miriam has an open date on her social calendar only on September
19th.

Sunday, September 11, 1938 Helped Uncle Walt cook a lamb roast
today. Cousin Kenneth Anderson and his sister Katherine came to the
apartment this evening and we helped Kenneth straighten out his fraternity rush card.

Monday, September 12, 1938 On my date with Susan tonight we went
back to the lodge room, danced and played Ching Kong, which she
won. At the Stork Club we danced to more sentimental music "I'll get
by, as long as I have you." When she heard the words, "Though poverty
may come to me" she said: "Oh, that's why this piece makes you sad,
eh?"

"No, not really," I replied, "The part that makes me sad is the suggestion of having to get by without you." At least that's what I should
have said. In talking about Margaret Mitchell's "Gone with the

Wind" she said her grandmother likes stories with happy endings so she was trying to comfort Susan by saying, "Oh, Sugar, he'll come back."

Tuesday, September 13, 1938 I was a little surprised last night when Susan told me she would be twenty in March. I thought she would be nineteen. Chatted with Dr. A. M. Harris, head of the Public Speaking department. What a grand old gentleman! I once heard him tell a story about the giant of a man, Robert Toombs, a Senator from Georgia, who called the very brilliant Alexander Stephens, vice-president of the Confederacy, "A shrimp which I could swallow whole." Stephens replied that if he did he would have more brains in his belly than he ever had in his head. As Dr. Harris told that story I thought of Dr. Harris himself as being somewhat like Stephens, small of stature, but proud, quick of mind and dramatic. When Dr. Harris quotes the great orators he throws back his shoulders and assumes the role. His head is held erect and his eyes flash. He is too kind a man to do more than imitate. He lacks the hardness of a Bryan or a Webster.

Wednesday, September 14, 1938 Mary Wallace introduced me to Jean Burke, daughter of the Dean of Ward-Belmont. She seems to be very intelligent and a sweet girl. She is almost a redhead. Mr. Henderson agreed to pay $33.00 for publishing the Honor Committee book so I took it to Mr. Daugherty and will pick it up Tuesday. I have arranged with Mr. Henry Hart and Harry Burks to give it out at freshman camp.

Thursday, September 15, 1938 The war situation is getting desperate. Prime Minister Neville Chamberlain, of England, is flying to Germany to see Hitler today. I suppose it is the first time in history such a thing has been done. Too bad all wars can't be settled by a direct confrontation between two heads of state. The wanton killing of most of the young men of any country is too horrible to contemplate, and yet there seems to be an inexorable movement in that direction. Who knows what the future holds for my classmates and me?

Friday, September 16, 1938 Tommy Alexander was pessimistic, but cards are beginning to come back subscribing to "Pursuit." We got back nine today. Bill Jordan and I went to town to sell advertisements for the magazine. Got twelve dollars from the National Life and Accident Insurance Company for an ad and the same from Nashville Surgical Supply. Zibarts bookstore also bought an ad. Got back from the director of the Georgia Tech Y.M.C.A. two copies of the poem "You in Her Thoughts" by Ella Wheeler Wilcox, that I had written for.

Saturday, September 17, 1938 Bill brought Lyrabeth Fitzpatrick with him for selling ads today and we contacted the Coca Cola Bottling Company, 7-Up and the Greyhound Bus Lines. Saw Harris Abrahams with

Bill Embry at the Kappa Sigma House and wondered what he could be doing there. Political exploration? Senter Field, the boy I nominated and got elected president of the new political organization "The Senate" is not returning to school this year but is going to Cumberland law school.

Sunday, September 18, 1938 Today was like Easter Sunday. The churches were full of people praying for peace. It is sinking in on a lot of people that we may have to fight Hitler. Dictators, gamblers and robbers seldom know when to quit. Mr. John Cheek expressed his gloom over the war situation. He also told me about people, he has helped, beating him out of money. He gave several examples and left the room. In a few minutes he came back and told me about one more example. Susan and I had a parlor date. We sat around the fire and talked. There was ample opportunity to talk to her seriously about us but I did not have the courage. Somehow or other I cannot conceive of her wanting me. It is only with her that I feel that way; have an inferiority complex. I blame it on the slightly crooked nose that I got from a baseball accident. Instead of being bold, as I was saying good night, I meekly said that sometime I am going to ask her for a kiss. I never saw her blush so and seem so embarrassed. Finally she said: "Maybe, sometime."

Monday, September 19, 1938 As I fall more deeply in love with Susan I become more relaxed with Miriam. Tonight I picked her up at the Tri Delta House. We got to Hettie Ray's for dancing and then drove down the Memphis highway to Belleview School and parked. I reminded her that she had once told me I could kiss her and that there would never be a better time than now. She characteristically said: "No." But remembering that a woman's "No" does not always mean "No" I proceeded to kiss her gently on the cheek and to work around to her lips. She did not cooperate, neither did she fight hard. The best I could do was to kiss the moist corner of her mouth, but that was enough to feel a glow of warmth. I could feel her arms stiffen at her side, and her heart was pounding against my chest. She acted mad the rest of the evening. Said that she hated me and didn't want any more dates with me, but I didn't believe a word she said. Jordan, Mae Reinke and I closed out a $50.00 ad with the Union Bus Company this afternoon.

Tuesday, September 20, 1938 This evening Bill Jordan, "Jelly" McClain, Tom Alexander and I drove down to the Vanderbilt freshman orientation camp. A group of editors and student leaders made speeches. Most of them spoke in the open and it was bitterly cold. Fortunately the dinner bell rang so Harry Burks told me I could speak in the dining room immediately after eating. That was a break because the audience would be warm and comfortable. I spoke as follows:

SPEECH BEFORE MEMBERS
OF VANDERBILT FRESHMEN CAMP 1938

Perhaps the reason many of you are entering Vanderbilt University this fall is due to the fact that you have heard so much talk about a college education helping you to get a job.

Your high school teachers back home have perhaps told you that only the college trained men stand a chance today. The principal of your school probably called the seniors together at one time or another and read a list of statistics showing that men who have college diplomas make more money than those who don't have college training.

If Mr. Hart will excuse me I will tell you what the great humorist, Mark Twain, said about statistics. He said: "There are three kinds of lies. Plain lies, damn lies and statistics."

Seriously, though, a college education is a nice thing to have. But getting a diploma is not the most important thing in your life, even at the present, and don't let anybody tell you that it is.

There are a lot of things more important than getting a diploma and I wish to discuss some of those things with you here this evening.

There are some brilliant people, even geniuses in certain fields, whose minds don't run along academic lines. In many cases they have a hard time making good grades.

There are other honest-to-goodness, God-fearing boys and girls whose minds are not brilliant along any lines. This group, which perhaps includes most of us, has to struggle for every grade that is made. It is this group that has a hard time in college. It is they who have to burn the midnight oil and sweat blood over assignments.

The temptations for these students to take a short cut to good grades is sometimes pretty strong. The temptation to look on someone else's paper during an examination has overwhelmed some students. And I say to you, as a three year man on the Honor Council, the saddest and most pathetic experiences that I have had while attending Vanderbilt, were those occasions when my schoolmates, and sometimes close friends were brought to trial. It was always a humiliating experience and one never forgotten.

Gentlemen, I stand before you today as President of the Honor Council and beg of you to cooperate with me in maintaining a high sense of honor on the Vanderbilt campus, and throughout your lives.

If I, myself, were a brilliant student and could make good grades with very little effort, I would consider it no great honor to be able to refrain from cheating, and to be standing here today. But I am not a bright student and it is a struggle for me to make even passing grades. Sometimes I don't even do that.

I flunked freshman math five times and I am proud of it. No, I am not proud of flunking, but I am proud of the fact that I had the will power to sit through four extra sessions of it without stooping to crookedness to get by.

Certainly it was a great sacrifice to make. It would have been easy to look on someone else's paper. But I am happy to be able to stand here today and tell you that I did not cheat and that I finally did pass the stuff, even though it took five terms.

That was the greatest test of my life. It was my greatest thrill when I learned from the professor that at last I had passed the course with a grade of eighty five.

Confidentially, boys, don't stoop to cheating. It isn't worth it. Old Sawney Webb became famous for drilling into his Webb School boys this one thought: "Never do anything on the sly." I am starting my fourth year at Vanderbilt. You are just beginning yours. My greatest hope is that four years from now you can say, as I am now saying: "I have not cheated a single time since I have been at Vanderbilt."

Some of you may have to suffer if you make such a resolution. You may have to spend an extra year in college. But it will be worth it.

If you will make a pact with me, or with your closest friend, not to cheat, come what may, and will come to me four years from now and tell me you have kept your word . . . I will tell you that this day in freshman camp four years ago was the most important day of your college career.

Wednesday, September 21, 1938 As I was talking with the city editor, Rousseau Duncan today, the managing editor, Charles Moss came up and asked about the Zipper invention. I happened to have a good working model and as I was demonstrating it the publisher, Jimmy Stahlman, came up to watch. Mr. Stahlman said: "One day when you drive up in a Rolls Royce I'd like to talk to you about buying the Banner." Who knows when a publisher of a large metropolitan newspaper, and President of the American Newspaper Publishers Association, may be of assistance. He was a close friend and adviser to Dr. Herty, developer of the slash pine paper industry. As I was talking with Virginia Sturdivant, Polly Ann Billington, Ellen Bowers and Louise Douglas at the Theta House this evening I saw Susan doing the serving of tea. At Petway-Reavis this afternoon, after failing to sell an ad, Mr. Jack Minton said: "If you can sell clothing like you sell ads I'd like to hire you." I jokingly told him I might be around to see him. Merrill Stone and H. B. Tomlin were voted into membership at Delta Kappa Epsilon tonight, but F.

was blackballed for no apparent reason, except perhaps that someone didn't like his looks. That kind of thing hurts me.

Thursday, September 22, 1938 Fraternity rush week begins this morning. About this time three years ago I started keeping a record of each day's happenings. At first I did not know how faithful I would be to the task, but to my surprise I have done it pretty thoroughly. A little poem I ran across recently, expresses my predicament perfectly:

NOTE

"Oh, once I kept a diary
Of what I did and thought,
And, looking back, I'd laugh to see
The changes time had wrought.

Well, now I merely have a pad
On which my dates to keep;
It won't record the fun I've had,
But I get a lot more sleep."

—Sis Willner

The fraternity house is in fine shape after spending about $1,200.00. Nobody had to be assessed. Bitsie Napier and Elizabeth Rudolph helped me get the girls together at the Delta Delta Delta House to show them the pictures Frank Gunter took of the rushing activities. Miriam spoke casually to me. She seemed to be a little shy but none the worse off for having lost a little kiss. The Kappa Delta Theta pictures were in the Banner this afternoon. Mrs. Connoll told me that Mrs. John Cheek called her to make favorable comments on them. I rushed Mose Waller, who was a friend of Anderson and Henry D. at T.M.I. I liked Bill Anderton, from Winchester, Tennessee, Billy Clark, from Little Rock, Roger Morrison, Fisher Oakes and Bill Acuff. Our blackball session lasted until one thirty in the morning.

Friday, September 23, 1938 I was supposed to make a speech for the Honor System at the girl's orientation camp but I did not make the proper connection for transportation.

Saturday, September 24, 1938 The Honor Committee books had to be taken to the freshman girls orientation camp this morning so I called Betty Freeland and drove to the camp with her. We arrived just in time. Floy Minor's greeting was that she wanted me to make as good a speech as I did the other day to the boys, since some of the other speeches might not be as good as they should be. The girls were all sitting out in the sun on some hay. They had on their camp clothes.

Miriam and Susan were sitting close together so I walked in and sat close to both of them. Miriam was real pretty. So was Susan and her shorts showed off her well-tanned legs. She has a beautiful coat of tan. Floy was a splendid Mistress of Ceremonies. She asked me publicly if I were not going to speak for the Student Council. I told her "no." So she said, "He is on so many things at Vanderbilt that one forgets just which one he is representing this time." I was the first speaker. "My first remark was that I understood boys, what they think about, their reactions to certain things, but when I face a group of girls, or *even one* girl (they chuckled at this) I am at a loss for words. I told them about the honor store, the funny paper story, and 600 prisoners at Sing Sing who were allowed to attend Mrs. Lawes' funeral. They (the prisoners) were on their honor, and none escaped or even attempted to. Related also Dr. Sutton's story of the District Attorney of Ala. whose life was almost ruined because of drink and made a bargain with Dr. Sutton not to drink. I asked each of the girls to make a pact with her roommate not to cheat and at the end of four years to come to me, or to her roommate, and say that she had lived up to the promise. The speech seemed to go over well with them. Mrs. Hart and I had a talk about Dr. Sutton. She knows him and said that she would cooperate with me in getting him to come to Vanderbilt. She said he is the only speaker she ever saw who was able to get people in the audience so excited that they would stand on tables to applaud at the end of his speech. Miriam invited me to eat at her table and so did Susan. I decided to keep myself "out of a jam" by not eating there at all. I came back to town with Landis Shaw, Elise Pritchett and Alice Beasley. I met Dick Henderson, Bruce's brother, this afternoon. He is a Deke transfer from the University of Virginia. Seems like a nice fellow.

Sunday, September 25, 1938 Rushing started at eleven o'clock this morning. Eight or ten boys that we wanted have agreed to pledge Deke. The question of how many local city boys we want was hotly debated in our blackball meeting.

Monday, September 26, 1938 We put pledge buttons on twenty boys this afternoon. This evening I went to the registration desks in Kirkland Hall and sold thirty subscriptions to "Pursuit."

Tuesday, September 27, 1938 We pledged the following: James and Billy Swiggart, John Hutton, Frank Kirkman, Thomas Sappington, Port Arthur, Texas; James B. Smith, Shreveport, La; Robert Seyfried, Tampa, Fla; Douglas Cochran, Corinth, Miss; James Hardin, Birmingham, Ala; Harvey White, Birmingham; Allen Cheney, Allgood, Ala.; Webb Follin, Bell Buckle, Tenn.; Lindsay Bishop, Chattanooga; Richard Brassfield, Dresden, Tenn.; Tom Blair Pierson, Ripley, Tenn.; Edmund P. Patterson,

Savannah, Tenn.; Mose Waller, Lenoir City, Tenn.; and Jesse Walling, McMinnville, Tenn. The Phi's were "hot" after Mose Waller, but he finally decided to come our way. "Blimp" and I went after him tonight. Betty Lou Vosburg got me a date with a pretty freshman, Mary Elizabeth (Betty) Bell for the Matriculation dance tonight. Betty is attractive and made a big hit at the dance. I expect she made a dozen dates while at the dance: Joe Scull, Joe Davis, Mickey Carmichael, Dickie Hardin, John McReynolds were among her most ardent pursuers. Reggie Childs played.

Wednesday, September 28, 1938 Signed up for classes. Tryouts for cheer leaders were held tonight and the Student Council made the selections. The story is going to be held until Friday when it will appear simultaneously in the student newspaper, the Hustler, and the Nashville Banner. Partee Fleming, the new correspondent for the Nashville Tennessean, was furious. Got my coaching job back and started signing up wrestlers.

Thursday, September 29, 1938 Clark Hutton, Richard Pickens and I went to Loews to see Clark Gable and Myrna Loy in "Too Hot to Handle." As we were coming out of the theatre in the late evening I saw in the early morning edition of the Tennessean, a front page picture of Mimi Reisman, the band sponsor for Saturday's game. Was I burned up! Mimi promised me she would not let Fleming take her picture. I later found out that the Tennessean morgue just happened to have a picture of her.

Friday, September 30, 1938 Attended Dr. Curtis Walker's class in English History this morning and then went to lunch with Bill Embry at the Kappa Sigma House. Susan and I went to the Student Union Open House, where I made a short speech, and then went to Hettie Ray's. Finding a fifty cent cover charge there we decided it was not worth it so we went to Candyland for ice cream and talk.

Saturday, October 1, 1938 Two days ago Prime Minister Neville Chamberlain, of Great Britain, flew to Munich to meet Adolf Hitler, Edouard Daladier and Benito Mussolini. The fate of Czechoslovakia, and perhaps the world, hung in the balance. The Czechs have one of the best small armies in the world, and yet they were sacrificed to appease Hitler. It sounds so easy and so reasonable; a small price to avoid the bloodbath of a world war, and to have "peace in our time." But, is it possible to satisfy the greed of a dictator, once he has tasted blood? Only time will tell. Mary Wallace and I moved into our apartment at 1909 20th Avenue South. Read an article about Westbrook Pegler. He is a caustic individual, but what a fantastic ability he has to mold words into powerful writing. We beat Western Kentucky 12–0. I had no-breaks at the gym dance with Miriam, Opie Craig and Susan.

Sunday, October 2, 1938 Cleaned up our beautiful little apartment today. Jordan and Simpson came by to make plans for the first issue of "Pursuit." Had a chat with Dr. Tom Zerfoss at the drugstore and he agrees with many of the ideas we are going to propound in the columns of "Pursuit."

Monday, October 3, 1938 Mary Wallace and I bought groceries for the first time. The bill came to $3.35. Rode to the fraternity meeting with Bob Neathery. I was appointed Chairman of the Supervisory Committee for the fraternity. At "Rat Court" I welcomed Mose Waller into the fraternity with a lusty blow with the paddle. Arch Trimble called and invited George Morrow and me to dinner tomorrow night.

Tuesday, October 4, 1938 At a Senate meeting at the Tri Delta House Bud Beasley was elected Chairman. Mrs. Majors, Charles' mother, ate lunch with us at the fraternity house. She is a charming lady. Bill Jordan, Tom Alexander and I went to Sam Goldner's Jewelry shop and swapped an ad for a large loving cup.

Wednesday, October 5, 1938 I made an announcement about the Honor System in freshman chapel this morning. Bill Embry, Bud Beasley and I checked the number of political offices and got a list ready for the political meeting tomorrow. I told Susan the date of our dance and she said she already had a date for the Beta dance for the same evening, but she would break it if her mother would let her because she would rather go with me. The fact that she would rather go with me is reward enough.

Thursday, October 6, 1938 An historic political meeting took place at the Deke House this evening. The Bachelor of Ugliness, being the highest honor that a male student can be voted, was first to be discussed. Everyone assumed that the Sigma Chi representative, Pierce Winningham, would ask for it. Ed Hunter, Captain of the basketball team, was the logical choice. Pierce played it cool, as if he wasn't particularly interested in the office. He thought, since he had the leading candidate, that by feigning a lack of interest he could get the B. U. without having to sacrifice other offices. My memory is long; when this subject was brought up last year, as a possible stumbling block to the efficient working of our new constitution, I resolved the difficulty by saying that if this office ever went begging the Dekes would take it. I never dreamed that any politician would ever be so foolhardy as to risk this ploy. I was therefore surprised when Pierce played innocent of interest when the subject came before the Senate. He called my hand and I responded by saying we would take the office. I named Charles Majors as our candidate. The constitution worked perfectly. We did not have to take a single vote between fraternities seeking the same office.

Friday, October 7, 1938 Before the political meeting last night Jim

Tuck said to Charles Majors: "The only thing wrong with Austin as a politician is that he is too honest." Charles replied: "Yes, he doesn't make secret deals as the others do." Frances Spain told me that when Dr. Mims was making up his "20" class today he said that the reason Austin is not taking it is that he has to run the campus another year. Dr. Irby Hudson and I discussed the procedures for bringing speakers to the campus. We got a picture of the political meeting last night and had it in the Banner today.

Saturday, October 8, 1938 Bud Beasley and Abigale Robinson got me out of bed this morning to talk politics. "Aby" is interested in getting the Kappa Alpha Thetas lined up on the winning side politically. I went to the freshman football game with Clark, John and Joe Hutton and saw us lose.

Sunday, October 9, 1938 Cleaned up the house this morning and went to the library this afternoon. Met Lydel Sims there and he talked to me about his affair with Miriam. Said she told him she thought she loved him and then turned around and broke dates with him. I dated Susan tonight and told her that I had rather take her to the dance than anybody. We turned the radio down real low and danced to slow, soft music. She leaned against my cheek and I could feel her breathe deeply and the pump, pump, pump of her heart.

Monday, October 10, 1938 Dr. Curtis Walker, my professor, is an excellent History teacher. The reason I haven't quoted him is because of the nature of the subject. English teachers, if they are good, deal in ideas. History teachers deal, supposedly, with facts. Dr. Walker was always interesting, but he seldom got off the subject and into controversial areas and therefore was not as challenging as the other professors. He did engage in one gory description of King Henry VIII's open, ulcerous, running sores from syphilis and I could never thereafter think of him as romantic, no matter how many wives he had. I'd certainly like to get a "B" from that course. Got a check from dad for $41.00 and a letter congratulating me on getting the patent.

Tuesday, October 11, 1938 Today I thought of a lecture that Dr. Eddie Mims gave almost a year ago on refinement and the social graces. There is always a choice between beauty and ugliness. The street sounds of New York City, for example, are cacophonous, but, on the other hand they have the great Philharmonic Orchestra and the Metropolitan Opera. When one goes to England he can visit Westminster Abbey and the great art galleries, or he can spend his time in the pubs or the king's stables. Such choices are always with us. Philistinism is the opposite of culture and a continual fight must be waged against those who would lower our sense of good taste; against crudities creeping into our cutlure at all levels. Without the great men of literature, such as Arnold, Herbert and Spenser, and, of course, the writers of the Bible, to constantly remind us of our cultural heritage, we would slip further down into the mire of indifference and closer to savagery. Without these beacons of good taste, as check points, we would even begin to doubt the validity of our standards. Mims said that refinement and the social graces reached a peak in the golden era of the French salons. I enjoyed his story about Mrs. John Henry Hammond, great granddaughter of Commodore Vanderbilt, who, on a public occasion, quoted great poetry for an hour and a half, and then, after a long tiring reception, sat down at the piano and for forty minutes played classical music without referring to a sheet of music. It was Matthew Arnold who wrote of the harmonious expansion of all the powers that make the worth and beauty of human life. He listed the powers as: 1. Intellect, 2. Beauty, 3. Social life and manners, and 4. Conduct, which he broke down into two categories, a. Righteousness and morality, and b. Efficient ordering of life. Of the mind he quoted: "My mind to me a kingdom is." He listed as characteristics of the mind, accuracy, concentration, clearness, memory, intellectual curiosity, awareness and open mindedness. The Germans come closest to applying science to life. Beauty is synonymous with symmetry, form, proportion and balance. "Beauty is its own excuse for being."

Wednesday, October 12, 1938   Today I had a great experience. Chancellor Oliver Cromwell Carmichael, in general chapel, handed over to me the official book of the Honor Committee. I made a twenty minute speech on the principles of the Honor System. After my first remark or two, one or two boys in the back of the room whistled. After another remark it was taken up by others and on the third it became a chorus. I stopped completely, and when there was absolute quiet I said: "I assure you that what I am saying is in utmost sincerity. Some of you who are whistling may, yourselves, be brought before the Honor Committee some day and . . ." at this point the audience laughed and vigorously applauded, indicating their disapproval of the discourtesy. From then on it was easy sailing. I told them of my experiences as a freshman and about attending my first university dance and "holding the beautiful girls in my arms . . . with the lights low and the music slow." This brought down the house. When I told of seeing my first case of cheating and that I turned around to "get a better view of the situation" there was another storm of laughter, and the merriment continued throughout the speech. In telling the story of prisoners at Sing Sing making the Honor System work, I once referred to the students as inmates. I brought the speech to a very dramatic close and the intensity of the applause more than offset the heckling at first. Dr. Carmichael came to me after the speech and said I hope you will be able to do something about the cheating here. Dean Madison Sarratt, the very kind gentleman whom all students love, came to me quickly on the stage and said: "I hope you did not take the early heckling personally." Dozens of people came to me afterwards and congratulated the speech. One girl said it took a lot of courage to say what you said, especially about the faculty being responsible for fifty percent of the cheating. Dot King, of Franklin, said: "Your speech was so good that I could hardly study my Spanish lesson for listening." Nearly every student I met on campus commented on the impact of the speech. Overcoming the early heckling added to the drama of the overall effect.

HONOR SYSTEM SPEECH

Dr. Carmichael, members of the faculty, and fellow students—

Two weeks ago I visited the freshman orientation camps and told the new students what the Honor System is all about.

They were interested. I could tell by the way they listened. I could have heard a pin drop at almost any time during the speech. They were literally sitting on the edges of their seats, weighing every word that was said—why? Because they were interested in learning something about the university they were entering.

As I stood there before this eager, enthusiastic, idealistic freshman class, my thoughts suddenly went back three years, when I was a freshman just as they are and I was being talked to rather than doing the talking. How beautiful I thought it all was then.

My father had been a Vanderbilt man thirty years before me. The prominent doctors and lawyers in my hometown were Vanderbilt men. My experiences up to that time had been—to say that a person is a Vanderbilt man is the same as saying that he had the culture and refinement of a gentleman.

> *(Note—About the third time that a roughneck in the back of the auditorium whistled, I stopped the speech completely, and after a lengthy pause, during which a deathly silence fell over the audience, I pointed to the back and said firmly: "You who are whistling had better be listening, because one day I may get you before the Honor Committee, and . . ." My last few words were drowned out by the applause and I continued the speech as if nothing had happened.)*

I had not considered going to any other school than Vanderbilt. I signed as a freshman and put on one of those crazy little freshman caps. Rush week was everything that it should have been. I have never been treated so nicely. Such hospitality, I have never seen the like! Boys came and got me in their cars, showed me around, and entertained me royally for a full week. It was great. Vanderbilt seemed even better than I had pictured it.

Then came the dances. A big name band was brought down from New York for the first dance. I had never seen such beautiful girls. Just to look at them was enough—but, as the lights were turned low and the music played softly—to be able to pick out and break on the most beautiful girl on the floor, and to hold her in my arms—well, I just couldn't find words. (Joke) Nor could I find the girl when I went back the second time. (Laughter).

Yes, Vanderbilt seemed a great place, It was everything I had hoped it would be.

But time flies swiftly when one is happy and having a good time. Before I knew it the first term was over and examinations started. On Friday, the last day of school before the Christmas holidays, I was scheduled to take my last exam—math.

I shall never forget the look on the faces of some of the students in the class as the exam was written on the blackboard. It was the hardest exam I have ever seen. Five problems were put up before I found one I could work. The professor, after answering a few questions, lighted a cigarette and left the room. I was in desperation, but so was the majority of the class. I began to worry about what I was going to tell the folks, if I flunked the exam. Then this thought came to me— surely they won't flunk us all. If three fourths of the class flunk, the exam might be considered unfair and according to the curve system all of the grades would be raised.

But as the end of the hour approached, I learned to my amazement that three fourths of the class was not going to flunk. Directly in front of me I saw one boy write out the solution to a problem and hand it to another boy. My blood ran cold. I turned around in my seat to get a better view (unintended laughter) of the class and several other students were comparing answers.

The temptation, at that time, was to join in with them. It was my only hope—and then something inside me said "No, it isn't worth it."

The next morning a pass list was posted on the door of the classroom. The names of several boys, whom I had seen comparing answers, were on the list. I searched in vain for my name, but it was not there.

I was bitter when my report came home with an "F" in math. Gentlemen, that was three years ago. I remember getting down on my knees at that time and swearing that God being my helper I would do something about cheating at Vanderbilt.

Today I stand before you as President of the Honor Council. On that certain night three years ago, I made a vow to myself and before God—a few minutes ago I took a vow before nearly two thousand of my fellow students—to uphold the Honor System, and to discharge the duties of my office to the best of my ability.

I did not take that oath lightly and I beg of you not to take it lightly. I have never been more serious in my life.

I would be ashamed if one of those freshmen, I spoke to, would see a Vanderbilt upperclassman cheat. And, if it is humanly possible to stop it, there won't be any cheating at Vanderbilt this year.

Up to this point I have discussed cheating from the student's angle. But the students themselves are not entirely to blame for any cheating that may go on at Vanderbilt. I sincerely believe that the faculty is responsible for fifty percent of it.

Why do I make a bold statement like this? Because in some classes, under certain professors, there is absolutely no cheating and in other classes, under other professors, cheating flourishes.

I am not speaking from hearsay. I have been in both kinds of classes and I know.

Under a perfect working Honor System, it might be all right for a professor to light a cigarette and go out of a classroom while an exam is going on, but we do not claim to have a perfect working system here.

You professors are not treating the majority of the student body right, when you put an exam on the blackboard and walk out. It is your duty to stay in the room and see that we get a square deal.

It would be just as unfair for Ray Morrison to walk out of the dressing room next Saturday at the Mississippi game and say: "Well, boys, I've taught you all I can. Now it's up to you. I will not be at the game. I'll be downtown at a picture show."

In closing there is only one other thing I would like to say. There is such a thing as an Honor System and it can work.

I read only the other day in Dale Carnegie's column that an Honor System even works at Sing Sing prison, where some of the world's toughest men are grouped together.

It seems that Mrs. Lewis E. Lawes, wife of the Warden, had won the admiration and love of almost every prisoner by seeking favors for them, by writing their letters, and by visiting their friends.

One day the news reached the prison that Mrs. Lawes had died. There was a mysterious silence at the prison. Finally one of the inmates asked if some of the prisoners might pass by the body and pay their last respects.

The Warden agreed, and six hundred prisoners walked out from behind iron bars. There was only one guard with them, and he did not have a gun.

That night the roll was called and six hundred prisoners answered. Not a man had escaped.

How could a thing like this happen? Simply this, they were put on their honor.

If the Honor System will work at Sing Sing prison, don't tell me that it won't work at Vanderbilt. It will work here.

My last plea is this: Cooperate with me this year and we'll show the world that it will work. We'll make it work!

Thursday, October 13, 1938 Homer Howell told me that on a quiz today the teacher left the room but there was absolutely no cheating. Homer and I talked with Norman Farrell about getting the injunction, against making noise, lifted from the Deke House. Fred Russell called and asked me to be the agent for selling his book "Fifty Years of Vanderbilt Football" on the campus. Bill Embry said he would help me. Took pictures of Jeanne Hudness as band sponsor for Saturday's game.

Friday, October 14, 1938 I sold seven copies of Fred Russell's book today. It is really a natural for anyone interested in Vanderbilt football. At my wrestling class today I took on a couple of heavyweights, Dayton Manier and Dan Sanders. Coach Field, of the Varsity, came over to look at my crop of 135 pounders. I escorted Susan to the Deke dance at Alumni Hall tonight and she asked me to take her to the Theta dance November 19. She has asked me to take her to every dance her sorority has given since she has been at Vanderbilt. I am unaccustomed to such kind treatment. If she is not careful she'll be turning my head.

Saturday, October 15, 1938 "Ole Miss" and Vanderbilt played one of the most exciting games I have ever seen. It was nip and tuck to the very end. It was 7–6 in their favor until the last minute, when Hardy Housman caught a long pass to put Vanderbilt ahead for the win. Max Benson, Fred Russell's coauthor of the book, asked me to get a couple of boys to help sell it at the game. George Morrow and Jack Foley agreed to help. I, myself, sold five copies at the Phi Delta Theta House before going to the game. Susan accompanied me to the gym dance. It is always a good dance when I am with her.

Sunday, October 16, 1938 The folks arrived from Stevenson in the new Oldsmobile "8" they bought from Hal Word Chevrolet Company in Scottsboro. It is a big car with all the latest gadgets, including hydromatic transmission. Bill Jordan and Tom Alexander had been working with me in getting together the series of articles for "Pursuit," so we all went out to Lynnmeade lunch room to eat.

Monday, October 17, 1938 A telegram from Russell Long at L.S.U.

today invited all members of the Student Council to the game at Baton Rouge this week end. Russell is a Deke there. At dinner this evening Uncle Walt was "blowing up" the home folks about "What a great guy Ben is." He compared me favorably with one of his all time heroes Bob Taylor, the famous Tennessee orator and politician. He was trying to sell them on the idea of buying me a car. Too bad he didn't succeed.

Tuesday, October 18, 1938 After carefully explaining the meaning and significance of the Honor Committee oath this evening, especially the part about reporting anyone they see cheating, Dan Sanders and Bill Travis refused to take the oath. It is an encouraging sign. It shows they are taking the oath seriously. Took pictures of the Rhodes Scholarship candidates but ran only the Nashville boys. Scooped Partee on the Bachelor Maids story.

Wednesday, October 19, 1938 Margaret Waller, Mose's sister, told Miriam McGaw that Mose pledged Deke on my account. Miriam was also very complimentary about my speech in chapel the other day. "Pop J." Jamison, director of Dixie Camps, wired me that he is going to be in Nashville this weekend. That knocks out my plans for attending the L.S.U. game in Baton Rouge. Took pictures of Miriam McGaw, Billy Sanderson, Joe Wright and Sam Yarnell, class officers who were voted on in chapel.

Thursday, October 20, 1938 Charles Whitworth, a very intelligent young student, had lunch with me at Dr. Taylor's drugstore today and told me he supports 100 percent the effort that is being made this year to reawaken a sense of honor among Vanderbilt students. Bought pants, shirts and ties at Joe Morse's for $19.00. Learned that Mr. Tyne's secretary, Virginia, lives with my hometown friend, Elizabeth Woodruff just a couple of doors away from the Albemarle Apartments.

Friday, October 21, 1938 Max Benson told me that Fred Russell has been worried about who to get to distribute his book on the campus. When he finally landed on "Ben Austin" he said, "He's just the right man." Speaking of leadership Dr. Mims quoted yesterday a statement he wrote while lecturing at Trinity College, Oxford, England last year: "Don't get too far ahead of the people if you want to lead them." Mims is a hopeless Romantic who has a special yen for the Middle Ages. He said that he regrets having missed Phillip Brooks going through the Communion ceremony at Trinity Church in Boston on Sunday afternoons in the dimly lit cathedral.

Saturday, October 22, 1938 Pop J. called this morning at nine and we went out to see Miss Leila Pound at Scarritt College. Next we went out to see the Louis Davis Sr. family, where John Shumaker met us with photographer Jim Christian and the picture and story appeared in the paper this afternoon. On my date with Susan we went back to

the club room of Oak Hill and listened to the Vanderbilt-L.S.U. game.
Vandy really outplayed the other team but lost because of failing to
score at a crucial moment. At the door saying good night I asked Susan
to let me bid her farwell properly. Again she said "Sometime."

Sunday, October 23, 1938 Caught up on my sleep today and wrote
an article about Matthew Arnold. I had in mind both Dr. Mims' class
and "Pursuit." The general theme was: "What would Arnold say if he
were at Vanderbilt today?"

Monday, October 24, 1938 Met with the freshman Honor Committee
this evening to discuss plans for enlisting their support for the overall
campaign to improve the system this year. Eleven people showed up,
which was very encouraging. Norman Hutchins and Bob Jordan were
new ones in my wrestling class. I wrestled with Jim Reed.

Tuesday, October 25, 1938 The Honor Committee met this evening
and we wrangled over the constitution. Those who have not taken the
oath want to "gut" the document of any strong stand whatsoever. That
I will not accept. You do not strengthen a system by weakening the
document upon which it's strength rests. If we have to elect two new
members to replace those refusing to take the oath, we'll do it.

Wednesday, October 26, 1938 Bill Jordan, at a "Pursuit" meeting at
the Phi Kappa Sigma House today promised me he would report any
other cheating he might see in his Physics class. I had a note put on
the front page of the Hustler that anyone seen cheating on the upcoming
midterm examinations would be reported to the Honor Committee, and
that we would prosecute. Dean Pomfret made a very clever speech in
chapel this morning. He told the story of how Hal White graduated.

Thursday, October 27, 1938 For the big homecoming game with Georgia Tech., today, we scooped the Tennessean on the band sponsor story.
We ran a big picture of Sara Goodpasture on the front page. Had an
Editorial Board meeting of "Pursuit" at the Canary restaurant and Jean
Smith, who was there with her father, invited me over to meet him. I
was flattered. Dr. Mims quoted Matthew Arnold as saying: "The flower
of culture is conversation on a high plane. He said of Darwin that in
his devotion to science he lost his appreciation for poetry and religion.

Friday, October 28, 1938 In logic this morning Tom Scoggins made
the remark that he knows he is brighter than some people. I thought
to myself that he ought to be smart enought not to make a statement
like that if he is so bright. Most of the students at school were dressed
up in costumes of the 1900's. I have never seen such an elaborate display
of clothes. At least fifty cameramen were there taking pictures. Bill Embry
went to the Banner offices with me to write a story about the 50th
anniversary of the student newspaper, the Hustler. The Banner used
several pictures of the homecoming costumes. In the afternoon I went

to the T.M.I. vs M.B.A. game. Saw Colonel Endsley, Jim Holmes, Coach Haynes and my brother Henry. Page Hill, Landers Seviere and Johnny Black were up from Birmingham.

Saturday, October 29, 1938 The big parade came off at ten o'clock this morning. It was really elaborate with over thirty floats. The Pi Kappa Alphas won with the "Flit Gun" idea. The book we are studying in logic was written by a fellow named Patrick; some insights into Philosophy. It starts with wonder, but in modern times usually with doubt. Philosophy may be defined as the art of thinking things through. The habit of clarification is the disposition of the philosopher. To philosophize is to seek cleared notions. In technical language, Philosophy is the critical analysis of concepts and discovery of relations between them. It hopes to integrate our knowledge, to unify and interpret it. Logic is the most essential part of the philosopher's equipment. Philosophy is an attempt to use scientific methods to understand the world in which we live. Herbert Spenser defined it as completely unified knowledge. Philosophy is wisdom, or at least the love of it.

Sunday, October 30, 1938 The Honor Committee meeting had to be called off tonight because some of the members could not be present. Dr. Eddie Mims was once asked if he were a Southerner: "Some kind, not all kind." His talk of John Ruskin wanting England to go back to feudalism, reminds me of the Agrarians here at Vanderbilt. They longed for the peace and quiet of pastoral times. Ruskin points out that in England a large number of people are not related to any class; empty of pocket, empty of mind, empty of soul. Under feudalism at least there was a relationship; also under slavery and reconstruction. Whether we like it or not the greatest statesmen in America were produced in the south during slavery. The same was true of Athens.

Monday, October 31, 1938 I was notified this morning that I have been selected as one of Vanderbilt's representatives in Who's Who among College and University Students. At the fraternity meeting tonight I sold twenty subscriptions to "Pursuit." I must be their top salesman.

Tuesday, November 1, 1938 The first issue of "Pursuit" came out today. I liked the article written by Bitsie Napier. She is a smart girl. Spent some time in the library studying. The day is not complete unless I see Susan and we somehow seem to meet in the library.

Wednesday, November 2, 1938 Received a forty dollar check from Dad and collected thirty-one from Mr. Miles. I still need more so I asked Mr. Rousseau Duncan for a raise. I took an exam in Logic today but purposely cut Spanish. Saw a movie about a doctor in England. It was called "Citadel." In Logic recently, it was pointed out that all animals are concerned mainly with three things: food, protection, and reproduction. The Epicureans believe that individual pleasure is the greatest good. Bentham modified that to "The greatest good to the greatest number." People don't crave happiness, but specific things. Most people do not value happiness, certainly not pleasure, as the greatest good. Our biographies are not written about happy people—Jesus, Socrates, and Lincoln. Other things such as genius, self-sacrifice and originality are higher. In the western world we rank intellectual activities high, but creative work even more—invention, exploration, initiative and adventure. Nietzsche said men want two things—danger—play. It is life that is the highest good . . . Maybe so, all three of the basic animal needs are in that direction.

Thursday, November 3, 1938 Richard Poindexter came by and got me this evening to go to a Kappa Phi, prep. school meeting. James Stewart, Miller, Bob Simmons, Guy McComas, and I met at Guy's house and proceeded to the home of Gilbert Dickey where the meeting was to be held. The fraternity was on the verge of splitting. In fact, this meeting was called for the sole purpose of writing a new constitution and going local instead of national. I have never heard such bitter remarks as went back and forth at that meeting. They were really divided into two camps which were fighting mad at the other. Miller made a speech accusing the president (Dickey) of high treason comparable to that of Benedict Arnold. Finally I got up and talked to them about the spirit of brotherhood and friendship and pointed out that I did not know anything about either side before coming to this meeting and that my advice was to iron out the kinks and to "present an unbroken front to our enemies." I told them I thought myself to be fair minded, cited that I am President of the Honor Committee at Vanderbilt with the power to exclude students from school. I compared the fraternity to the church in that it is not the materialistic things that you get out of a fraternity but the intangible things that are worth while. One boy objected to my bringing the church into a fraternity discussion and I cited Jesus' own words "Love Thy neighbor," "Even though you do it to the least of these, you do it unto me"—Then I asked "Does not fraternalism mean the same thing and isn't it driving towards the same goal?" Finally an expression of almost every boy in the room assured us that they were sticking with Kappa Phi and all was well. They agreed to resolve differences and to build a greater Kappa Phi. I suggested that we form a mystic circle, repeat the Lord's Prayer in unison and adjourn. We did and everyone left happy and with the feeling that all was well. It was a great meeting and I had a very elevated feeling because of the little part that I had in getting the fraternity over these rocks.

Friday, November 4, 1938 Gathered this years crop of Phi Beta Kappas for a picture for the newspaper. They are: Tom Alexander, Bernard Breyer, Dick Christian, Harry Cates, Ovid Collins, Eloise Davidson, Morton Howell, James Lanier, James Lassiter, Charles Majors, Tom Scoggins, Henry Warder, Louise Watkins, and John Webb. Bill Jordan told me that he and a group of fellows were listening to President Roosevelt speak the other day and that they noted that Mr. Roosevelt and I use exactly the same approach in arguing a point. I thanked him for the compliment.

Saturday, November 5, 1938 I took Spanish exam. Doug Abercrombie a Deke from Colgate, dropped in today at the house and went over to the Sewanee game with us. I helped to introduce him around to all the boys and picked out a seat in the Deke section at the game. I saw Susan though and whispered to him that I was going over and sit with her. Jean Gibson sat behind us and also Marcella Driskill, Damaris Witherspoon, Mary Helen Simpson, and other Thetas. We had a nice time. I won a Coca Cola from Damaris. I escorted Josephine Greer to the gym dance tonight. She and her brother have an apartment like Mary Wallace and me. John McReynolds, Mary Bell, "Nookie" King, and Mary Helen Simpson went with us. I took Josephine over to Mary Brown's pretty late. I had the second no-break with Susan and flipped the coin with Nello Andrews for the fourth and won that one. I really enjoyed both of them. We danced by Tom Scoggins and he yelled "Come out of the trance, Austin," but I pretended not to hear him. I did not mind, however. Margaret Jackson was real sweet and pretty tonight. I like her quite a bit, though I have never had a date with her. I did not dance a step with Miriam and I saw her just as I was leaving. She asked me where I had been all night.

Sunday, November 6, 1938 Tom Alexander brought some extra copies of the magazine "Pursuit" by and I addressed one to Adolf Hitler and another to the Reader's Digest. At four I went to the Theta Open House. The other boys got there early and Susan said she was afraid I was not coming. She helped serve me when I did get there though and I asked her to come and sit by me while we were eating and drinking tea. She did and showed me the Theta scrapbook. There was a picture of her and me at the Deke dance last spring. I missed the "Pursuit" meeting today but I talked to Jordan on the phone beforehand. Made a date with Susan for the Washington Ball. Mrs. Connoll called up today and said she would like for me to write the column anytime I saw fit.

Monday, November 7, 1938 How could I be so stupid! I made rotten grades on the midterms. I ate lunch today as a guest of Dean Sarratt, who was explaining to about 60 of the student leaders the ideas behind the Joint University Library project and its importance to Vanderbilt. It was a very interesting and worthwhile meeting. Susan, Bill Jordan, Abigaile Robinson, Jean Nolan, Virginia Sturdivant and I ate at the same table. Afterwards Susan and I went over to see the new Student

Center. I told her the story of the little boy in Atlanta, Georgia, by the name of Atticus Green Haygood, who said he could contribute $10,000.00 to the building of the Methodist Church on the site where the Candler Building now stands. When questioned he said: "I can hand up the bricks." I heard the famous orator Dr. Willis A. Sutton tell the story. Bill Jordan and I have discussed at length what should be done about cheating at Vanderbilt. Bill is a very smart person, with a strong personality. I have felt that he is the one person I could depend on to help me get a test case before the Honor Council in order to warn the student body of our intention to prosecute cheaters vigorously. Sure enough, after a Physics midterm examination, Bill told me there had been cheating in the class. I said: "Ok, give me the names and I'll bring them before the committee."

"Oh, no," said Bill, "I am not going to get myself into the role of an informer." Therein lies the weakness of the Honor System. If a person of Bill Jordan's stature will not report on cheating, who will? After much soul searching, I finally concluded that if we ever expect to do anything for the Honor System we are going to have to go on the offensive and seek out the cheaters. At the very next meeting of the Physics class I entered the room at the beginning of the hour and asked Dr. Daniels for a few minutes of his class' time. I announced to them that I am speaking in my official capacity as President of the Honor Council. "I have been told that at least five persons cheated on the recent mid-term examination and I expect all persons who cheated to report themselves to the Honor Council within 24 hours." This was a bomb shell! From one end of the campus to the other groups huddled in animated conversations. The most frequent question asked was: "Is the SOB bluffing?" I know generally who the cheaters are but I need stronger evidence to go to court. I called a meeting of a few key student leaders and explained to them that we are not out for blood but that we want to get a message to the student body that we mean business and will not tolerate flagrant cheating. It is extremely important that we bring these cases to court. I asked their help and cooperation.

Tuesday, November 8, 1938 It may not work out as well as I expect but tonight Honor Council history was made. After the Student Council meeting, and after a long talk with Anglin, I happen to walk into the Student Union office and heard Mac Glasgow, Morris Burk and Bill Embry discussing the Honor System and the alleged cheating that took place in that Physics class. I joined the discussion and after an hour or so of heated argument, we decided to have a few student leaders contact the five suspects and persuade them to come clean, if they really did cheat, and help us make a beginning towards a better Vanderbilt. We selected five boys to make the contacts and gave them the names of the suspects and scheduled the meetings for noon tomorrow. At a meeting of the Honor Council on Thursday evening these five boys will be escorted before the bar by a member of the honorary Leadership Fraternity, O.D.K. and each shall be given an opportunity to confess or plead "Not Guilty." The strategy behind this maneuver is that it will tie in this prestigious student organization with the work of the Honor Council and it will give the offending students an opportunity to make amends for their transgressions.

Wednesday, November 9, 1938 At general chapel today Chancellor Carmichael, Mr. James G. Stahlman and Dean Madison Sarratt made powerful speeches to the student body explaining the importance of the Joint University Library project and asking the students to support it. Dean Sarratt's appeal at the close of the hour was particularly effective and the students rose in mass to support his appeal. Even the janitors contributed $4,000.00. The Deke fraternity subscribed 100%, averaging over five dollars per year, per person, over a five year period. We were the first to turn in a record so impressive.

Thursday, November 10, 1938 The Honor Committee met tonight and four boys signed statements that they received aid on the midterm examinations. They are: P., N., R., and M., Mac Glasgow, a prelaw student sat in on our meeting and acted, more or less, as a prosecuting attorney. We agreed to summon the whole class before the committee and get testimony from each student. There are about ten others in the class who are suspected of cheating who did not volunteer to come in with the four who have already confessed. We must get to them. They are the ones who deserve the full treatment because they have done nothing to right a bad situation. The meeting lasted from seven thirty until eleven. R. told me today that the reason some of the boys gave for not coming to the original meeting was that they heard I had cheated on the Physics examination last year. I expected something like this to come up; some trumped-up charge that would make me alter my course of action. I will be even more determined in the fight. I sent word to these boys that I am perfectly willing for charges to be brought against me, either publicly or privately. I am not in the least worried about my past record in this regard. It will withstand the assault of any group of students. I was amused at the reaction of some of my friends. Partee Fleming made a humorous statement on this subject. He said: "Nobody who makes as sorry grades as Austin, cheats." That about says it all.

Friday, November 11, 1938 The Deke banquet and dance was scheduled for this evening. The highlight of the evening was an address by Dr. Edwin Mims. He first pointed out that Charles Majors had established a wonderful record. He has been able to combine the outside activities and scholarship. He excells in both. His balance is as it should be. Then he brought up the subject of the fight the Honor Committee is now in the midst of. He said the chapter should feel proud of the fact that one of its members is making the fight. "He is going to make enemies" Dr. Mims said, "But the fraternity must show him that they are backing him. This situation must be corrected." He said he was also proud of the fact that within two hours after the speeches in chapel, the Deke chapter turned in a 100% record of over $25.00 per person. Thanks to Jack Worley's efforts. Dr. Mims opened his Honor System remarks by referring to my statement in my general chapel speech about holding the pretty girls in my arms, but the speech got over. He also mentioned the reaction to Jimmy Stahlman's remarks about the Honor System in his chapel talk. He compared our fight to the one Thomas E. Dewey is making in New York City. He pointed out that Dewey's life had been threatened, and every kind of pressure that could be thought up, but Mr. Dewey kept right on. I went by the Alpha Omega Pi House dance tonight to finish off the day. Met a very pretty University of Tennessee coed by the name of Edwine Powers from Knoxville. I had the third no-break with Margaret Jackson. She told me this morning that she was "down in the dumps." She confessed that the reason for it was that she was afraid that I could not come to the dance tonight. Margaret is such a fine girl and I wish I were not attracted elswhere. I walk with her from the Spanish class every day and even though I have never had a date with her, there is some feeling between us. She asked me quite awhile ago to take her to the A.O. Pi steak fry but I had a previous engagement. She did not go. She was beautifully radiant tonight.

Saturday, November 12, 1938 Ray Manning is going to take charge of the committee which handles publication fees. Eugene Cox talked over the Honor System plight with me. He advises against kicking the first boys out of school. He thinks they ought to be flunked only. I told him we had no intention of taking drastic action on these first cases. We want to use them as a warning to the student body. At the fraternity house today there was quite a few alumni present: Price Carney, Hal Claffey, Page Hill, Landers Seviere, John Black, and Alfred Estes' father. Jim Browning, Homer Howell, Walter King, and I sat together at the football game. Jean Gibson sat directly in front of us. Ray Morrison had a trick play cooked up for the kick off. One boy ran across the field with the ball, passed to the opposite side of the field where the ball was kicked for only a short distance, hoping a Vandy player would recover it. The Tennessee men got offsides, but still U.T. was given the ball by the referee. Vanderbilt outplayed Tennessee during the entire first half, but slumped during the fourth quarter. That seems to be the story of Vanderbilt athletics. We lack depth because of recruiting failures and our atheletes participate in a hectic social life which pre-

cludes getting a normal eight hours of sleep each night. Then too, you
cannot spend long hours on books and long hours of muscle hardening
exercises. There are simply not that many hours in the day. The final
score was 14 to 0 in favor of U.T. I escorted Susan to the scrip dance
tonight. I enjoyed the dance even though I did not have a single no-
break with her. After the dance we went to the home of Damaris Witherspoon for a reception. Billy Eason, David Patterson, David Comey, and
one or two boys from the University of Tennessee were there. Mrs.
Glenn met me at the door when I first went for Susan this evening.
She told me Mrs. Cheek had returned from Baltimore, but that Mr.
Cheek would remain there for three months. I wonder why. Maybe Susan
and I are both guilty of the same prideful fears. Maybe our families
are ordinary individuals and not the paragons of virtue that our youthful
idealism projects. Maybe I should ask her if there are any skeletons in
her family closet. Then I could tell her that there are perhaps some in
mine too, and we could both laugh at our own immaturity. Elizabeth
Zerfoss told me tonight that she knew someone who had a crush on
me—her mother. She knows I go with Susan. I received a couples bid
to Henrietta Hickman's tea dance at the Belle Meade Country Club
next Friday evening. I will take Susan.

Sunday, November 13, 1938 Caught up on my newspaper reading.
Jean Burke and Mary Wallace drove me over to the campus for a "Pur-
suit" meeting in Bill Jordan's room. Paid Tom Alexander $21.50 for
"Pursuit" collections. I went to bed at 9:00 o'clock.

Monday, November 14, 1938 Everywhere I turned today I got encouraging words from the students concerning the Honor System fight. Makes
me think the effort is not in vain. Marcella Driskill said: "I just can't
tell you how much I think of you for making the fight you are for the
Honor System. You are the only person in the school strong enough
to make the fight." Jeanne Stephenson interviewed me today for the
column she writes for the Hustler. Said she would try to do something
for the cause.

Tuesday, November 15, 1938 Thirty-seven members of the Physics
class were brought before the Honor Committee tonight to testify. The
four boys, that had already admitted that they received aid on the examination, sat in on the meeting and listened to the testimony of the other
students. We believed that other cheaters would be reluctant to swear
falsely in front of their fellow students who knew the truth. This would
remove any inclination to protect anyone who would be willing to let
others take the rap for him. M., P., R., N., and S., have already made
statements that they received aid on the midterms. The balance of the
class took oaths that they did not cheat. They tell me that M., S., T.,
and K., cheated on the exam, in spite of their testimony that they did

not. It was a three hour meeting. I believe we are beginning to get somewhere. I was studying in the library this evening with Margaret Jackson when Susan came in. Susan did not look so pleased.

Wednesday, November 16, 1938 Found out that Bob Meyers was the boy who turned in the name of that girl to the Honor Committee several years ago and then the Lady Dean stepped in to quash the deal. Such a thing could not happen today. Talked to Dr. Tom Zerfoss and Mr. Jim Buford in the student center this afternoon about the effect of campus opinion on the outcome of the Honor System fight. The pressures are divided at present; some for and others think we're going too far. Had about 35 students out for my wrestling class.

Thursday, November 17, 1938 I was elected President of the Calumet Club, Vanderbilt's literary society, at the first meeting in Alumni Hall. The club has a long and honorable tradition. Some of the literary giants of America have been memebers of this local club. Talked to Dr. A. F. Kuhlman, director of the Joint University Library system, about library work. He said that the profession needs men with personality; that the field is not crowded. He suggested that I ought to look into the possibilities. Tom Scoggins told me that the boys at the S.A.E. house are talking down the Honor System and me personally as head of it. Partee Fleming brought me more news about the bad reactions of other students. It is a terrible pressure sometimes to stick with something, because you know it is right, in spite of the censure by some of your peers.

Friday, November 18, 1938 The Tennessean carried the story this morning about my being elected President of the Calumet Club. We scooped them on the "I.Q." story though. The Hustler, this afternoon, ran an article listing a series of statements from campus leaders. Some of them expressed skepticism and others were very flattering and very encouraging. I suspect it is a fairly representative cross section of student opinion on the campus. Ed Kirkpatrick said: "It is possible that an over-zealous President makes a farce of the Honor System." Willie Cornelius said "There is plenty of room for improvement, and I believe that this improvement will be found under Ben Austin's leadership." Andromedia Bagwell said "Right now the system isn't so good, but I believe that it will improve with Ben Austin as President." Miriam McGaw, "This is the first year that the council has really tried to stop cheating and I believe that they will accomplish their purpose." Marcella Driskill, "The present system is pretty sorry, but if Ben Austin is allowed to go ahead with his plans, I think we will really have something." Ray Manning, Charles Majors, Billy Sanderson, Alice Beasley, Tom Scoggins, Sam Yarnell, and Mac Glasgow also made statements. Much has already been accomplished in that the students themselves are interested in the problem. They are aroused. Jeanne Stephenson was aroused to the point of interviewing me and writing a very flattering column this week. She is a very clever writer. Took Susan to Henrietta Hickman's debutante party this evening at the Belle Meade Club. Arrived very early and were among the first to greet the Hickman's; *the Mrs.,* Henrietta, Litton, Jr., and the Judge himself. Francis Craig played. Susan told me that her mother, when on her way to Florida, took particular pains to take a look at Stevenson. Susan asked me if I did not live in a colonial-type house. I told her that it was a little on that order. On thinking it over, I'll bet they were thinking of the Walker House at Bass. Told Susan tonight that I would possibly take a law course after finishing this year's work. She was careful to figure up—"That will take two more years, won't it?" Yes, I replied. She told me her dad had always regretted that he had not taken a law course. Fred Russell told me this evening that he studied law after finishing his undergraduate work at Vanderbilt. Decided to pass up the Tri Delta dance tonight.

NOTE: Article written by Jeanne Stephenson and published in "The Vanderbilt Hustler," Friday, November 18, 1938.

VANDY VIGNETTES

by Jeanne Stephenson

Ben Austin, idealist, reformer and philosopher, is the most serious minded of the group so far who have "bared all" in order that their fellow students might acquire an intimate glimpse (tongue in cheek) of their lives on and off campus.

Ben has a list of activities that, as he told me about them, made me sit back in astonishment. Not only has he held various offices in Delta Kappa Epsilon for three years but he has also been on the board of the Masque Club, a member of the Hustler staff, and twice winner of the intramural wrestling meet in the 165 pound division. This year he is coach of the freshman wrestling team, the campus correspondent to the Banner, a member of the Calumet Club and has the fortunate or unfortunate position, according to viewpoint, as President of the Honor Council. To top it all, if the reader will kindly look at the Official Gazette of the United States Patent Office, within the next week or two, he will find a patent on a new type of Zipper (Serial number 109791) issued to a certain Ben Ragan Austin of Nashville, Tennessee. This energetic young man made me feel as worthless as "Step'n Fetchit" looks, and how he finds time to be an English major is beyond my powers of comprehension.

He obviously likes to talk, has fixed ideas concerning all he has ever thought about, which I am firmly convinced is everything, and of all subjects touched on during my chat with him "the points are these"— he's an ardent pacifist, likes football, thinks Roosevelt is all right but disagrees with some of his policies. Ben is definitely for the Student Center. "It shows the liberal trend that the faculty and student body are taking"—and frivilously speaking, likes his music sweet and slow and his girls simple and sincere.

Ben is in a sense the man of the hour as far as campus intrigue is concerned. It has become his duty as President of the Honor Council to see that the Honor System is either enforced or abolished. His job at this particular time is undoubtedly of an unsavory nature and though he termed it a "touchy subject," I feel sure we all agree with Ben when he says, "We must abide by the code and laws that we, the students, have set up." Perhaps the above mentioned Zipper is to zip up the morals of Vanderbilt!

Saturday, November 19, 1938 At one today, four car loads of Dekes started out for Bell Buckle to play a game of football. The field was muddy and sloppy, but we beat them 24 to 6. I got to play about fifty minutes—right tackle. Homer, "Blimp," Charles Major, Estes, and all of us had a good time. After the game we went up to the Follin's home for dinner. It was a buffet lunch and I had a nice long talk with Mrs. Follin. She is a very genteel person. Four of the Webb students live in the Follin's home. We got back to Nashville at about eight thirty. Called up Susan to let her know I was in town. Mrs. Cheek answered the phone and as she was ringing Susan I made an awful break. I was disgusted over getting back late so I used profanity right into the mouthpiece. I don't know whether she heard me or not. I hope not, but I'll never know. I was a little late getting out to Susans. She had on a solid white evening dress and a purple bow around her neck and streaming down her back. The orchid matched perfectly the dress she was wearing and she was extremely pleased with my gift. I never saw her look so beautiful. She got one of the biggest rushes at the dance. I had the third no-break with Shirley Caldwell. She asked me to have it with her and she was extremely flattering in her discussion of the article that she had read in the Hustler about me. She said that I had more " 'umph" than any person she had ever met. Said I was very practical yet also had an appreciation of esthetic beauty. She herself had on a very beautiful evening dress. She dresses more distinctively than anyone I have ever known. She knows how to wear clothes to the best advantage. Susan and I went by Candyland after taking Walter King and Miss Mary Helen Henry home. Had a nice talk as we went home. Told her that if there were not such a thing as inhibition, I would be able to tell her all the nice things I would like to. When I told her good night and that I had had a delightful time, she replied that the reason she had such a good time was that she had such a nice date. Coming from Susan that means a lot. She is not much for flattery and throwing bouquets. She is a wonderful girl.

Sunday, November 20, 1938 Helped Mary Wallace clean the apartment and put up curtains. Called Susan just for the fun of it. Reviewed my notes on Logic. The Normatic Sciences are: Logic, norm of truth; Esthetics, norm of beauty; Ethics, norm of conduct. Etymology, science of the laws of thought. Zeno, 450 B.C. developed the concept of reductio ad absurdum and the Eleatic thesis of the unity of being and the unreality of motion or change. On the other hand Herodotus propounded the idea that nothing is unchanging except the law that everything changes. Plato lived from 427 to 347 B.C. and taught rationalism. Aristotle was one of his pupils. John Locke believed in empiricism, that people are born with ideas. Kant was the father of criticism. The Socratic approach consists in causing an opponent to make certain concessions which are contradictory to the original thesis. He maintained that truth resides in perfect definition. Thought draws people together; feeling separates them.

Monday, November 21, 1938 Ate lunch with Bill Shumaker and Merrill Stone. Frances Spain, Jean Adams, and Edna Murry Davy are going to Birmingham with us. Made arrangements with Mr. W. A. Benson to publish our Honor Council booklet. Almost broke my arm wrestling with Bill Shumaker this afternoon so I didn't go to the fraternity meeting.

Tuesday, November 22, 1938 Mary Wallace told me she heard a freshman from Vanderbilt talking the other day. She said: "It is certainly hard at Vanderbilt. I'd cheat but I'm afraid to." Dr. Tom Zerfoss X-rayed my arm and rib today to see if I had broken any bones. Susan passed by in the library without noticing me. In a few minutes she came back and asked about my arm. We went to the Student Center and talked until it was time for me to go to my wrestling class at four.

Wednesday, November 23, 1938 Frances Spain and I sang practically all the way to Birmingham. I love to try to sing the lead, second tenor, and she knows how to harmonize. We left at about two o'clock in the afternoon and got there at five. We went to Eddie Morton's house to freshen up and then went to the station to meet the train that brought the team to Birmingham. There were about thirty Dekes out at "Pop's Place," a favorite hangout for the younger set. Too much drinking disgusts me. Spent the night with George Morrow's family.

Thursday, November 24, 1938 It was snowing this Thanksgiving morning in the very southern city of Birmingham. I did not know what to think. Bill Shumaker, Merrill Stone and George Morrow went with me for turkey dinner at the Hardins. Mr. and Mrs. Hardin, Dickie, and his two sisters were perfect hosts and hostesses. The meal was excellent. Among the 30,000 spectators at the game I saw Ollie Rudder and Bill Bogart from Stevenson. The field was muddy and it was very cold. Alabama attempted a field goal, the ball stuck the upright and bounced back fifty yards. Preacher Franklin picked it up, but instead of running for a touchdown, which he could have done very easily, he gounded the ball. We possibly could have tied Alabama with this touchdown, but they outplayed us in most of the game and deserved to win. Went to Leo Bashinski's for one of the best meals I have ever eaten. Thirty five Dekes were there. There was turkey, ham and beef, dressing, salads and vegetables and several kinds of deserts. We talked, sang songs and had a good time. Because of the foul weather, Mr. Bashinski called Chancellor Carmichael in Nashville and asked if he would excuse cuts for anyone staying over an extra day. The Chancellor talked favorably. Went from the Bashinski's to the Birmingham Country Club for dancing and other forms of merrymaking. Ed Finch, Alfred Estes, George Morrow, the Bashinskis, John Black, Tommy Tart Brown and Bud Bray were there. Met the much talked about Sara Hogen. She is pretty cute but throws in a little acting on the side. Met Milba Tate, Miss Sample and Miss Tite, a very good looking girl. Eleanor Edmunds, daughter of the well-known minister whom Uncle Walt knew at the University of Tennessee, just before the turn of the century, was very vivacious. Marion Long and I spent the night at the Bashinskis.

Friday, November 25, 1938 We left Birmingham at about eleven o'clock and had a long philosophical discussion about love. It was interesting and at points enlightening. I took a nap as soon as I arrived in Nashville and was feeling fine for the Beta dance at the Hermitage with Johnny Hamp's orchestra. Before the dance I called Susan about nobreaks and she told me she had gotten mixed up on her dates and had promised someone else the date for the Washington Ball. The other person was mad about it. I told her it was perfectly all right and she could go with whomever she pleased and I would not be mad because I myself am bad about getting dates mixed. Susan then said "Ben, you are the most understanding person I have ever known." Later on at the dance a general no-break was announced. I went to have it with Susan. In a few minutes Levi Wade came up and said he had it with her. I offered to flip the coin with him for the dance but he flatly refused and told me that he would dance the first chorus and I could dance the last. The piece was shorter than I had expected and before I knew it Wade had danced the whole no-break. When the music stopped I went up and explained that it was shorter than I had expected but Levy butted in and said, "Aw, you were just trying to gain sympathy by giving up the whole no-break; by being big hearted." He then reached down and took Susan's hand and struck me on the face with it. I did not know what to do or say. Susan was also embarrassed and attempted to stop the slap, but too late. Levi was not man enough to slap me with his own hand, but had to use a woman's.

I did not say anything at all but started dancing when the band started playing. I spoke to Bud Beasley about playing a surprise no-break and he obliged by getting one played. I had it with Susan and it was the best of all. They played four nice slow pieces. Rode home with Merrill Stone. His sister told me that she had been told of the trouble that the Kappa Phi fraternity was having and how I was instrumental in smoothing out the troubled waters. She says the fraternity brothers, both old and new, were grateful to me for that contribution.

Saturday, November 26, 1938 The Army beat Navy by a score of 14–0 before 105 thousand spectators. Carl Hinkle's name was mentioned. Duke upset Pittsburg 7–0. In discussing Carlyle in class today Dr. Mims quoted John Morley as saying Carlyle preached the gospel of silence in 39 volumes. Mims says Carlyle's most striking feature was his eyes; those portrait, painting eyes. His greatest characteristic was his ability to draw portraits; portraits that just fit. He picked his heroes to write about, not by "carrying coals to Newcastle" or following the crowd. He picked Dante because the English knew very little about him; Mohammed because the English thought he had set up a false religion; Rousseau because the English thought he was a worthless dreamer. He turned the whole verdict of history on Oliver Cromwell from a usurper, as Hume thought, to an honest and sincere man.

Sunday, November 27, 1938 Don Linton came to my apartment this afternoon and later Joe Moss came by for him. Both Don and Joe are discouraged because of their lack of progress towards a college degree. Don says it seems that he is never going to get one and Joe has quit trying. He is taking a law course at the Y.M.C.A. night school. I gave Don my copy of "Making the Most of Your Life" and Joe a copy of Dale Carnegie's "Strategy in Handling People." I think these volumes will cheer them up and encourage them to go on and achieve their goals. I, myself, always feel better after a session like this if I feel that I have helped someone through a trying period in his life.

Monday, November 28, 1938 The Masquerader carried Emmett O'Callaghan's article on the Honor System today. It was pretty strong but voiced a fine sentiment. He said: "If you can't abide by the rules, get the hell out. Vanderbilt is no place for cheaters." Bill Jordan and I talked Bill Embry, editor of the Hustler, out of running the very strong Honor System editorial he had planned for this week's edition. We were concerned about the explosion it might set off. Embry agreed to wait awhile.

Tuesday, November 29, 1938 I had a talk with M. today and he said that he had given his word of honor that he did not cheat and that was all he would say. The freshmen at the Deke House get their Christmas paddles signed by an upperclassman giving them a blow with the paddle. I presided over my first meeting of the Calumet Club tonight as President. The meeting was held at the home of Dr. George Mayfield. Scott George was taken into the club after he read a very fine article on "Americanism vs. Communism." Leonard Frank was also taken in. He submitted a story about dictators. Scott George also offered a critical paper on Robert Browning's works. Dr. Finney and R. Mayfield gave talks on their experiences as Calumet Club men in days past. It was a very enthusiastic meeting. Dr. Mayfield, who is professor of German, said it was the best meeting in ten years. Mrs. Mayfield served very delicious refreshments. Earlier this evening I had a heart-to-heart talk with H., who had been reported for cheating on a math examination. It was with tears in his eyes that he told me about never studying in high school and being passed anyway because he was a good football player. Now things are closing in on him. He knows he can't get by forever on his football ability, and he is not prepared to cope with the competition he encounters in the classroom.

Wednesday, November 30, 1938 Dean Madison Sarratt called me in today and asked a briefing up to date on what was happening in the Honor Council crusade. He gave encouragement. He mentioned that he had heard reports of excessive paddling at the Deke House. I told him I would speak to them about it. From there I went by to see Dean Ada Bell Stapleton, whose office had been picketed recently. Susan Cheek was in her outer office and Byron Anglin was inside talking with her. I told Dean Stapleton that my paper would print any dignified statement she would care to make on the picketing. She was very emotional in her expression of appreciation and said she would write a note to my City Editor, Rousseau Duncan. When I was at the Banner office this afternoon, Mrs. Connoll, Society Editor, was telling Fred Russell and me that she had had a talk with Mrs. Cheek, Susan's mother. Fred asked Mrs. Connoll if Susan were my girl and she said: "And how!" I don't know what Mrs. Connoll and Mrs. Cheek were talking about, but I hope they know.

Thursday, December 1, 1938 I had a meeting with Mc. and P. and got statements from them concerning the other boys that cheated on the exam. They said M., who flatly denied cheating to us, had told them after the exam that he had cheated. I went by for Susan at a quarter of ten. She had already read the Night Hawk column which said I took off my sling when I got to Birmingham last week and showed a University of Alabama coed a few holds. It was an infamous lie! I did not even have a date there. That's the kind of irresponsible reporting that can be expected from an anonymously written column. We spoke to Francis Craig about playing slow pieces and he did not play but one or two fast ones all evening. The music was the best I have heard in a long time. It was terribly crowded. It seems that all the good looking girls on the campus turned out for this dance. Homer Howell and John McReynolds, the baritone and tenor of our fraternity quartet, went with Susan and me to Candyland for refreshments at the intermission. In the Deke special the orchestra played the "Bells of Ward-Belmont" and "I wish I had a girl like you for D. K. E., the sweetest girl in all the world to me. I love you, and need you, please promise to be true. There's only one beneath the sun, and that one dear is you just you." The music is based on the well-known tune "When Day Is Done." They played it very slowly and Susan responded beautifully; even when we said good night.

Friday, December 2, 1938 I went to Mrs. Haggard, the Registrar's office this morning and got my patent papers notorized. I also got from her a complete statement for my whole year's tuition. I had my picture taken at Loveman's and then went to see "Brother Rat" at the Knicker-bocker. Beatrice Kemsey asked me to take her to the Sigma Kappa dance so I went by and got her at 9:00. The house mother sent word for me to come upstairs. I did and she said "I have a picture of you?. It was a miniature of the one that I gave to Susan last spring. It was the best picture I have seen of myself so I bought it, $1.25. After the dance Beatrice and I went to Morrisons and then parked for a while in front of her house. Had a pretty good time.

Saturday, December 3, 1938 In a fine lecture this morning Dr. Mims said there are two great monuments to the English language, Shakespeare and the King James version of the Bible. This is one point that even the English department at Vanderbilt can agree on; the Ransom school of criticism and the Mims school of appreciation of the beauty of poetry . . . they both praise these monumental works. *He* said Carlyle's "Past and Present" was written as a warning to England not to follow in France's footsteps in a revolution. We have the ages for our guide, but not the wisdom to be led. In Carlyle's 1838 essay on Sir Walter Scott he said Scott never became a man until adversity took charge of him. He quoted Tennyson's description of what a true university should be: "Thought kindling itself at the fires of living thought."

Sunday, December 4, 1938 Studied all day and this evening went to the fraternity house for the initiation ceremonies. Merrill Stone, H. B. Tomlin, and William Hastings were formally taken into the lodge. Jim

Browning, Polly Ann Billington, Charley Majors, and Harriet Short brought me home.

Monday, December 5, 1938 Borrowed $98.00 from Uncle Walt to cover the fall term tuition. I wrote him a note for the $250.00 he had previously loaned me in times of financial crises. I liked this definition in Logic: Character—The general reliability to act in conformity to duty.

Tuesday, December 6, 1938 The Honor Committee met tonight for the trial of four boys. Only two showed up. M. was brought before the committee but he refused to make any statements until he is faced by his accuser. I called a recess and attempted to reach our witnesses but I was unable to do so. I went back to the meeting and, at the suggestion of Mac Glasgow, asked M. if he were aware of the fact that cheating was going on in the exam at the time he was taking it. He said he was aware of it but that he did not do, or say, anything about it. He shut his eyes to it, thereby violating Section 9 of the code which requires all students to report any case of cheating they may see. He was subject to trial for that, in addition to the other charge that he himself cheated. He still refused to testify. Evidently his father, or his uncle, who is a lawyer, was outside and he sent word that he would like to speak to Mac Glasgow. Mac had been sworn in as a special prosecutor for this case. I cautioned Mac that his leaving the courtroom to talk to anyone for the defense would be equivalent to jury tampering and that he should not go. He insisted on going and came back speaking as a Defense Counsel rather than the Prosecutor. I immediately disqualified him. The trial was postponed until a later hearing could be arranged. The deeper I get into this thing the more convinced I am that the faculty ought to be handling this cheating situation. As I see it they are paid not only to teach but to see that each student has an equal chance to compete with every other student for a diploma.

Wednesday, December 7, 1938 Tonight I saw Henry Clay fight Percy Allen, who fought in Golden Glove Championship fights in Chicago last year. Jim Reed, Jack Keefe and Henry's girl Katie Heitzburg, were at ringside in the Times Building pulling for Henry. Later on I went to the sorority swimming meet and saw the Tri Deltas win, mainly on the diving form of Katherine Brown and Betty Freeland. While we were waiting for the decision at the sorority event a group of girls got together and gave a yell: "Austin for B. U."

Thursday, December 8, 1938 I was called in again by Dean Sarratt in connection with the Honor Committee. He said that Chancellor Carmichael wanted to see me and that I was to see him between two and three o'clock. Dr. Sarratt told me just before seeing Dr. Carmichael that we were not bound by any laws, or rules, other than our own honor code and to act as I thought best. I appreciate that expression of confidence and his reassurance. The Chancellor and I talked for about thirty or forty minutes and he expressed his approval of how the thing had been handled and he also warned against convicting a person on evidence that would not hold up in a regular legal court battle. I explained the whole set up, thus far, to him, and he said that the legal courts would not consider as grounds for conviction a man's own testimony, or statement, unless it is in the form of a confession of guilt. He asked me point blank not to convict on the evidence that we have on M. I explained that I was in sympathy with his views on the case and the saneness of his request, but I refused to answer a point blank "yes." Tonight he called me and asked that the trial be postponed until Monday, also that I come to see him again tomorrow afternoon. I agreed to both. I met with the Pan Hellenic Council tonight and explained the set up of the Honor Committee and asked their advice and support. Dr. Mayfield also made some very pertinent remarks and then we had a general discussion. The presidents of the fraternities were very sympathetic in their views and very enthusiastic in the ideas that they submitted for making the Honor System work. It was a very fruitful meeting.

Friday, December 9, 1938 Met with Chancellor Carmichael again this evening and then again with Dean Sarratt. They suggested that Dr. M. and Dean Sarratt be allowed to sit in on the questioning of M., the son of the doctor. I had no specific objections to the two spectators and Dean Sarratt thought it might be good for the father to see his son's trial. Might teach them both a good lesson. Bill Embry would not hold off any longer and ran the devastating editorial on the front page of the Hustler today. It shook the University. Here it is:

Vanderbilt Hustler
December 9, 1938

THE HONOR SYSTEM . . . WHITHER? AN EDITORIAL

Vanderbilt's traditional Honor System has faced its biggest crisis in recent years during the past few weeks. From fraternity "bull sessions" to informal gatherings, the major topic of the month touching on anything of a sensational nature has been the latest efforts of President Ben Austin and his Honor Council.

For over three years we have watched the Honor System on the Vanderbilt campus. From the outset we have realized that the Honor Code at Vanderbilt did not carry the weight which it should; and it is our earnest conviction that the system has waned since the class of 1939 entered school.

The HUSTLER appreciates Austin's efforts to curb the present wide-spread cheating. We have backed the Honor Council President one hundred percent in his efforts. And, should we believe that there remained a chance for him, with the aid of his Council, to improve the conditions, we would be absolutely consistent in our views. But we believe that the task too large for a single individual, or a small group of individuals; and we have reached the conclusion that campus opinion is definitely against retention of the Honor System and the integrity for which it stands.

It is quite possible that President Austin, whose intentions are unquestionably the best, is far too idealistic in his reasoning. We are of the belief that he overlooks the facts of the case—facts which show the amount of cheating done in the academic school during each exam period. Our most conservative estimate would place close to 75 percent the number of students who have cheated, in the sense of giving or receiving help on an examination, at Vanderbilt during their residency here. Many students will admit their violation of the Honor Code—"I have neither given nor received help on this examination"; and they have reached the state where they look askance at the student who claims to be simon-pure—a fine situation, truly. Vanderbilt students have grown very tolerant of the violations, although they do not, as yet, hail the violators.

Vanderbilt professors, to whom much of the blame for the increasing dishonor must fall, must be catagorized in one or two classes. Either they are laboring under the misapprehension that there is little cheating being done in their classes or they realize what is going on, but hesitate to complain for various reasons, chief of which, probably, is the desire not to offend the student body with reflections upon its collective integrity.

It appears that the whole Vanderbilt community realizes that the Honor System is just about played out here. With campus opinion against a solution, there is little need to attempt to analyze the reasons for its decline with an eye to a renaissance. We who have seen cheating, pure and unadulterated, going on in all save one of our classes fear that it is now too late. Vanderbilt students, or any students, have certain qualms when they realize that by taking an exam honestly they may make grades considerably lower than certain fellows—and that "certain" is generally more than one or two. A clear conscience is a fine thing to have, but a clear conscience is far less material than the grade card that is sent home; and the student at Vanderbilt who cheats cannot be too highly censored, even if caught, when there are several hundred others employing the same tactics.

As even Austin will admit, the backbone of the Honor System is the reporting system. Violators must be reported, if the system shall work. And it is unnecessary to point out the contempt that Vanderbilt students have for the "snitcher"—much of this contempt is had for the Honor Councilor who does his duty. This idea may not be the ideal one, but it's the one present now!

There is no need to beat further around the bush. We must realize and face the facts. Cheating is flourishing, as matters stand now. Is the Honor System, time-honored at Washington and Lee, Virginia, and other institutions, outmoded at Vanderbilt? Has the student body gone too far?

The HUSTLER takes its stand with certain misgivings. The losing of a tradition such as the Honor System would be a blow, both to our self-respect and pride as individuals and as Vanderbilt students. But we see no other way out of the present predicament save the substitution of the monitor system, which entails, more or less, policing examinations.

We sincerely hope that Ben Austin can prove himself the superman we feel that is needed to change the Honor System to its former self. If we are to have the Honor System, let's have an Honor System that means something, not a farce. WE CANNOT GO ON LIVING THIS LIE!

Saturday, December 10, 1938 Dean Madison Sarratt met with the Honor Committee today and presented his case for sitting in as a specta-tor at the upcoming trial. The Committee accepted his recommendations and extended an invitation to Dr. M. and him. Triple dated for the gym dance with Merrill Stone, Corrine Howell, Alfred Estes, Betty Fay Witherspoon, Susan and I. The no-breaks were extremely good. They played three or four fraternity songs on each. I had the first and fourth with Susan and the second with Miriam. Miriam's hair was very becoming tonight and I told her so. She said she had something nice to tell me, sometime. While dancing with Bitsie Napier she said she had heard so many nice things about the work I am doing for the Honor System. She said: "You are the best thing that has come along at Vanderbilt in many a day."

Sunday, December 11, 1938 Studied all day. Wrote a history paper for Dr. Walker.

Monday, December 12, 1938 The big trial came off this evening. Mem-bers of the committee put on their black robes and took their seats in front of the courtroom. Dr. M. and Dean Sarratt sat in the back. We carried on the trial as if they were not there. After thorough questioning of M. and the witnesses, we could not establish direct evidence that he cheated. We had only the statements that he made to the witnesses after the exam; his own evidence and that, hearsay. The witnesses did not actually see him cheat. Under the circumstances we had no choice but to acquit him. After the trial his father asked that we give a statement of exoneration. The committee voted to state only that there was insufficient evidence to convict.

Tuesday, December 12, 1938 Discussed the Honor System with Dr. Mims. A freshman told me he made a speech to their chapel stating he did not want to teach in a school where policing is necessary. Talked to Dean Sarratt on two separate occasions this evening. He was doubtful over the fact that two boys would voluntarily make statements that were untrue about M. He told me Chancellor Carmichael is going to talk on the Honor System in chapel tomorrow. He talked to the faculty tonight.

Wednesday, December 14, 1938 Chancellor Oliver Cromwell Carmichael delivered one of the greatest orations, this morning to general assembly, that I have ever heard. He announced that the two million dollar library drive had been completed. It was oversubscribed. Then he went on to his main discussion, that of the Honor System. He said that the editorial in the student newspaper had caused him much alarm; that the situation was more important than the Joint Universities Library project. He pointed out the irony of building greater libraries and fine facilities when the very heart of the whole system is questioned. He scorned any mention of putting in a monitor or proctor system. He said that this question and its outcome is more important than any other single event at the university. He said his first interest in Vanderbilt was due to its reputation for sound scholarship, but if that editorial is true "I am not sure I did not make a mistake in coming to Vanderbilt." This statement stunned everyone. An unusual quiet settled over the campus. It was just before lunch, a usual boisterous time at the fraternity houses, but today students spoke in hushed tones. Never in my experience have I seen a speech have such an impact on a group of people. The battle was over and won.

Thursday, December 15, 1938 I have heard several students speak of Dr. Carmichael's address. They were moved by it. One boy said he ought to make a speech like that about once a month. Homer Howell said it was the first time since he has been at Vanderbilt that he has really broken loose and showed some emotion. He came down off his pedestal and showed warmth and concern over a student problem. What a fitting climax to a long, drawn out battle!

Friday, December 16, 1938 Took my Logic examination yesterday and my Spanish today. Many people came to me with glowing reports of absolutely no cheating in their classes, especially the freshmen. There is a very small group, however, that no one will ever reach. They are the hard core cheaters and they are the ones who should be dismissed from the university. In one of the Spanish classes R., H., and K. and a few others survived the best way they could and in my section K. left the room several times. I am not concerned now, and never have been, that an occasional student stoops to cheat, what does worry me is the student body condoning cheating. That is not acceptable. The battle that has been won is a changing of student attitudes from that of tacit consent to an adamant censoring of cheating.

Saturday, December 17, 1938 Studied all morning and got my English History term paper ready just in time to go to the exam. I was rather jittery about the exam; Bill Embry was almost hysterical. Think I did pretty well on it though. Called up Miriam and talked with her about an hour. I was reading Thomas Caryle's chapter on Romance in "Sartor Resartus." I read her several passages and several poems. Sometimes when I sit in the solitude of my room I think of such beautiful things to say to Miriam or Susan, and I speak them out with no halting or hesitation. Here I feel worthy, but there, no. Here I am brave and strong; there weak. To paraphrase Hamlet: "Perhaps me care too much."

Sunday, December 18, 1938 Dr. Mims lectured yesterday on the political crisis that took place in England during the time of Ruskin and Carlyle. Across the world from us today is a developing crisis as serious as any that has taken place in days of old. Hitler has given Czechoslovakia an ultimatum. Where will it lead? In speaking of concern for human welfare Carlyle called it: "Sweat of the heart." An eminent Frenchman once said: "Most people hear a tale of woe, sigh, eat a meal and forget." On art, Mims said, Michaelangelo never made a figure. He saw the figure in stone and chipped away until it came out. Leonardo da Vinci called poetry, "The antiqued symmetry."

Monday, December 19, 1938 Mc. called me this morning to tell me the Lady Dean had called him in and talked to him about cheating. I had heard nothing about it and I think he wanted to break the news to me before anybody else did. Robert Burgess told me of two cases of cheating that came up in the Spanish class. Dr. Manchester is going to report them to the committee. Dr. C. E. Crouch reported R. this evening. He said that R. used notes for about 20 minutes and that he walked up to him unawares and took the notes out of his hand. R. later admitted his guilt and said he was sorry. R. was up before the committee last year on a similar charge. Dr. Crouch wrote up the charges and presented them to me. He also gave me the notes that were taken out of R.'s hand. Bill Minton stopped me in front of Calhoun Hall today and asked me if I knew Paul Schultz of Roswell, New Mexico. He said Paul had told him to look me up at Vanderbilt. Paul said he did not know whether I would remember him or not, but that he used to be a friend of mine, as we were growing up in Stevenson, Alabama. I will never forget Paul Schultz. He was one of those people who fit into a special category. All of us, throughout our lives, have people that we look up to as better than ourselves. It has nothing to do with sex and it may be because of their personalities, their aloofness, family position, money, or perhaps even athletic prowess. Whatever it is, we hold ourselves apart from them and indulge in, sometimes unconscious, hero worship. Young Paul Schultz fit into such a category for me. When he suggests that I may not remember him, I realize that he may have thought of me pretty much the same way that I thought of him.

Tuesday, December 20, 1938 I have just read Carlyle's chapter on "Natural Supernaturalism" and declare it to be one of the finest pieces of writing I have ever run across. There is more philosophy, more religion in that one essay than most of us realize in a lifetime. I had a talk with the Lady Dean this morning and she told me about the evidence concerning M.'s cheating in her German class. It looks conclusive. As I left she told me she would stick by me to the end, "If all others go back on you I'll be right there." I thought, "how nice!" Had a short chat with my good friend George Bentley in the library and bought a tuxedo collar from Eugene Pigg. Paid a small insurance premium to the man who runs the National Life Insurance Company debit.

Wednesday, December 21, 1938 Got my schedule mixed up and missed my English examination this morning. Went to take it at two o'clock and found out it had been at nine this morning. Went to town with Devon G. Minchin of Sydney, Australia and George Bentley. We just strolled around town showing the Australian a bit of America. We met Flora Bentley at Wilson-Quick Pharmacy at four and had their famous milk shake. Uncle Walt forgot that he had promised me his car for a date tonight so I was thirty minutes late getting started. We arrived, however, before the Kappa Phi banquet got underway. Our place cards were at the front of the room. We started out with shrimp cocktails and then a real good chicken course and then a combination of fruit salad and ice cream for desert. Susan said the food was the best she had ever eaten at a banquet. After the meal was completed, and the dishes taken, several members and alumni were called on to speak. Finally I was introduced. Gilbert Dickey, President and Toast Master, said, "We are very happy and feel honored to have with us a distinguished person. All of us who know him like him. He is Ben Austin, President of the Honor Council at Vanderbilt." I addressed the Chair and then said "To me this is not just a social function, but a great victory banquet. We in Kappa Phi have gone through much together in the past few months and the presence of this distinguished group here tonight is evidence of our success. In many respects, this marvelous banquet is similar to one of the most famous victory banquests in history; the one at which Cleopatra entertained Mark Antony. We have not the beautiful waterfront, nor the barge laden with gold and the decks strewn with flowers; the girls are not dressed as sea nymphs, but there is one thing that I am confident of and that is that the girls we have selected for this occasion are just as beautiful as those in Cleopatra's Court. (The boys applauded.) Seriously, though, it is a great banquet, a great group of people, and I am looking forward to our meeting again under similar conditions next year." Susan remarked that it was nice offhand speaking. George Burnsides band was really good—nice slow music with plenty of rhythm. I had five no-breaks with Susan and enjoyed everyone of them immensely. There were not too many stags and we got to dance with our partners a great deal. I especially enjoyed dancing with Martha Wood, Elizabeth Zerfoss, Jean Plumlee, and Elizabeth Hall. It was pretty cold so Susan and I did not get to talk very much over our hot chocolate cups at Morissons. Going on home I told her I was going to give her a dance favor, and Christmas present at the Deke dance. She said "I will give you your present tonight." When we arrived at her home we went in and she made a Christmas very happy. My courage did not fail me and just before leaving I leaned over and kissed her gently on the side of her lips. We were both a little cold from the weather and her lips were cool and soft. She did not exactly cooperate nor did she turn away. The look in her eyes afterwards was not that of wrath. It was a little thing but it meant everything. It was a very sweet parting until I return from the holidays. It was and will be very soothing to my mind. I will not fret and worry as I am prone to do. Instead I will live over and over again that moment.

Thursday, December 22, 1938 Got up at nine this morning and packed for going home. I went by the city room of the Banner to tell Mr. Duncan good-bye, and by sports for Fred Russell and by Society for Mrs. Connoll. George Mitchell, from Chattanooga was on the train so we sat in the Pullman all the way. Arrived in Stevenson about five, just in time for a good supper.

Friday, December 23, 1938 Mary Wallace and I drove the Oldsmobile into Long Island this morning to pick up Rebecca. We got there too late for the Christmas program but some of the kids performed for us. I was pleasantly surprised how efficiently Rebecca handled the class. Practically all the kids showed signs of poverty but their faces were bright and cheerful. We ate dinner with Miss Bessie Maxwell, sister of James Maxwell of Flat Rock. It was a lavish meal so I can see why Rebecca is so fat and sassy looking. She looks better than I have ever seen her. Hugh J. Rudder, principal and Amanda Allison rode back to Stevenson with us.

Saturday, December 24, 1938 I have been fighting, with all my will power, to keep from opening Susan's present before Christmas morning. Tonight George L. Jr., and I went to Ruth and Jack Dennison's dinner party honoring their visitor, Virginia Richey, from Corinth, Mississippi. Virginia sat on Ruth's right and I sat on her left. Jack was at the end of the table. Carolyn Spivey, George L. Jr., Mary Anna Rudder and William Simpson were in between. It was a nice treat. Virginia, a cousin of Ruth, is a beautiful and charming young lady. Her hair is coal black and her complexion is strictly peaches and cream. Her eyes are almost oriental and flash when she smiles. The young people rode to Scottsboro together to take Carolyn home.

Sunday, December 25, 1938   It was wonderful being at home with the whole family for Christmas: Rebecca, Anderson, George L. Jr., myself, Mary Wallace, Henry D. and Wilson, listed in descending order. It is a rather sobering thought to Mother and Dad I guess, having five sons of military age and the peace of the world crumbling as fast as the dictators can provoke one nation after the other. These are happy times though. The first thing I did this morning was to open Susan's present. It is a beautiful leather bill fold with my initials in gold. Anderson and our cousin, Edward Austin, went down to Marietta, Georgia to pick up another cousin, Leon. After breakfast Mother, Rebecca, Mary Wallace and I drove over to Flat Rock, on Sand Mountain to visit my father's two maiden sisters, Aunt Belle and Fannie. Dad's younger brother, Uncle Bill, was there with his family: Billy, Virginia, Dan and Bob. Dad's older brother, Uncle Jasper, came by later and there was a big discussion of family experiences and politics. I had another date with Virginia Richey tonight. She is staying with Kelcy Graham's family. We drove to Bridgeport, drank Coca Colas and talked for about an hour about love, romance, and marriage. She said that lots of her ideas crystallized in our talk. We drove to Battery Hill, parked, listened to the radio and watched the lights flicker on the river. She answered my question about kissing by saying that most girls would like to but are afraid of what the boy will think. We did not leave the hill until midnight. She said she thought I was a very nice blind date and I told her I considered it a grand evening. I am sorry she has to leave in the morning.

Monday, December 26, 1938   Got a letter from Bill Potts this morning with money in it for a copy of the book "Fifty Years of Vanderbilt Football." Went to the telephone office to inquire about rates for a call to Nashville to get Fred Russell to mail Bill a copy. Decided to write a letter instead. While at the telephone office I asked Maud Timberlake about Grace. Later in the afternoon Maud called Grace and found out that she did not have a date tomorrow night so one was arranged.

Tuesday, December 27, 1938   Stevenson is a small town of seven or eight hundred people. Its main industry over the years has been railroads.

As early as the Civil War Stevenson and the neighboring town of Bridge-port were important transportation centers. The Nashville, Chattanooga, and St. Louis joins the Southern here and they use the same tracks going East to Chattanooga, a distance of about 60 miles. Many railroad men make their homes here and patients from hundreds of miles up and down the tracks come to Stevenson to get my Father to do their dental work. In a more picturesque era, before the advent of dining cars, the trains used to stop here for the noon and evening meals. It was a colorful sight to see the Negro waiters, in white coats, peaked caps and black silk trousers, balancing the giant trays of food high above their heads and dancing through the crowds as they delivered their wares to the patrons on the trains. Little colored boys found it lucrative to clog and do the buck-and-wing dances for the coins tossed from train windows. I guess the first money I ever made was when I joined in with them and learned to shuffle too.

Wednesday, December 28, 1938 This was one of those days when everything goes wrong. Had a date with G. and had an accident. The side wall of one of my back teeth gave way and there is an irresistible urge to keep rubbing the rough surface with the tongue. She told me that as she was trying to think up something clever to say in the telegram to me, her friend, the Starkey girl, told her to say "come and get it." Said she had to laugh in spite of the fact that the station agent was there. She told me about her early experiences. S. was the boy who started her off. She was staying with a newly married couple in Scottsboro and going to school there. On one occasion S. dated some other girl and she was so jealous that she let him do anything he wanted to. She did not enjoy it at first but gradually began to look forward to it. She says it will make a person love you quicker than anything else in the world. This went on for about three years and the usual thing happened. She went to Dr. Banks in Chattanooga and was operated on. The boy was with her all the time. His folks knew about it and paid the bills. Her folks never did know. She asked me if G. L. knew about S. and her marriage. I was supposed to pick up Henry D. at Mary Elizabeth Talley's but ran out of gas and had to borrow some from her brother W. J. Jr.

Thursday, December 29, 1938 Sidney Ballard and I drove towards Scottsboro tonight for a dance at the Recreation Center.

Friday, December 30, 1938 Got up early this morning and caught the train for Nashville. Mary Wallace tells me that cousin Kenneth Anderson has bought a tuxedo and is making the rounds of parties. Frances Ragan told me that he flunked three subjects at Vanderbilt and may go to Wallace Preparatory School next quarter. Went to Loews theatre and saw Gary Cooper in "The Cowboy and the Girl." It is another one of those pictures where a rich girl marries a cowboy and has a hard time adapting herself. The father of the heroine, Judge Smith, had an obsession to be president. His daughter had to make many sacrifices in his behalf. When she told him she was married, he did not consider her happiness, but how the news would effect his chances for nomination. When he realized his mistake it was a big relief to everyone. It brought home very keenly the folly of being too ambitious; ambition to the point of losing one's sense of values. It has been very appropriate and encouraging that I have been studying Carlyle's "Sartor Resartus" and "Heroes and Hero Worship" this term. The struggles of the men I have been reading about are not entirely foreign to the struggles that we have gone through in the Honor System fight at Vanderbilt. There was a time when it looked as if we were fighting a losing battle, but then like Mohammed we got a few converts and gradually the whole movement took a turn for the better.

Saturday, December 31, 1938 This is the last day of a very eventful year. It brought the culmination of a plan that extended over a three year period; a determination to get into a position to do something about cheating at Vanderbilt. In a sense we have succeeded beyond our wildest dreams, and yet we realize that it is a fight that must be repeated each and every year if we are to maintain the standards we expect at a great university. Has it been worth it? Yes, I think so. Sacrifices have been made, but I have learned that patience and perseverance will usually win battles and that right will eventually prevail. I have learned that young people will attempt to live up to their ideals if they are reminded occasionally of what those ideals are. But above all, I have learned the value of courage; the ability to stand straight and not flinch in the face of great odds, is often the difference between success and failure.

Sunday, January 1, 1939 Seems strange to write that the year is 1939. I called Susan last night and she was surprised to learn I am back in town. Said she was just writing me a letter. I begged her to finish it and mail it to me. Said she would just hand it to me Monday. After getting the information from Tom Cummings Jr., about his reception and dance, I called Susan back and arranged for no-breaks. Said she was helping her mother prepare for a party Eleanor Richie is having. Each Sunday night at nine I listen to a very sentimental program called the "American Album of Familiar Music," sponsored by Bayer Aspirin. It is not only that the music is sad and nostalgic, but it represents the end of the day . . . and week. It reminds me that I am alone and have nothing to do but go to bed. The bitter thoughts of love that may never be; the waiting and the uncertainty of it all is maddening. What a heavy burden providence places on young people. Nature says the time is now; society says wait.

Monday, January 2, 1939 I went to town this afternoon and bought an overcoat and a couple of pairs of sox. The first coat Ernest Frank put on me was a fine fit and nice looking so I bought it for $18.50. Went by the Banner office and found the society staff hovered around the radio listening to the Tennessee game. Mr. Hoffman, a staff writer, looked at my overcoat, with the raglan sleeves, and asked me what I would take for it. He guessed it cost $50.00. Said it was the only one he has seen that he really likes. Came home and listened to the Texas Christian-Carnegie Tech and then the Duke-Southern California game in the Rose Bowl. I am excited about seeing Susan tonight. I am going to take her to Tom Cumming's party and then to the S.P.O. dance. Just think! I will be with her from seven o'clock until two thirty in the morning. She was ready at seven thirty, which made us late, but Mrs. Cummings saw to it that we got waited on. We played numbers and Susan stayed at the head of the table longest. She is very bright; did not miss once. The S.P.O. dance was at the Belle Meade Country Club. John, Susan's younger brother, was there and danced the second no-break with her. It was one of my favorites, the penthouse song, "When We're Alone." I would have enjoyed it more than John, but that's life. Going home from the dance I told her how much I appreciated her picture and she answered a question I was curious about, how many pictures she has in her room. She volunteered to tell me that the only other picture she has in her room is Virginia McClelland and her family. We talked about a certain lady's no-account husband and how often fine women marry sorry men. Susan's parting glance at the door was very expressive.

THE VANDERBILT HUSTLER

Aristocrat of Southern College Newspapers

NUMBER 8   NASHVILLE, TENN., NOVEMBER 18, 1938   ESTABLISH

Students Ask Change In Honor System

By Richard Donaldson

In a poll conducted by the Hustler yesterday, the opinions of Vanderbilt students in regard to the school's Honor System fell in general into two categories. With few exceptions the freshmen and sophomores were optimistic, while the upper classmen were decidedly pessimistic, perhaps because of the varying lengths of experience during exams.

Ed Kirkpatrick, Pi Kappa Alpha: "The present Honor System is not what it should be. I think the teachers are as much to blame as the student body, because they give unfair examinations, stressing small points that haven't been dis-

cussed in class. Honor is a personal thing with each man and I don't think that students should report cheating, if they saw it, to the Council. It is possible that an over-zealous president will make a farce of the Honor System."

Willie Cornelius, Phi Delta Theta: "There is plenty of room for improvement, and I believe that this improvement will be found under Ben Austin's leadership."

Andromedia Bagwell, Alpha Omicron Pi: "Right now the system isn't so good, but I believe that it will improve with Ben Austin as president."

Miriam McGaw, Delta Delta Delta: "This is the first year that the Council has really tried to stop

cheating and I believe that they will accomplish their purpose."

Tom Scoggins, Sigma Alpha Epsilon: "The present system is a flop. The future is doubtful if the students don't give cooperation. The faculty should not encourage cheating by leaving their classes during exams."

Billy Sanderson, Beta Theta Pi: "The past history and conduct of the students toward the Honor System has been bad. I believe that if the Council had more power it would succeed."

Bitsy Napier, Delta Delta Delta: "It doesn't work at all. I think they should put in the monitor system. If the Honor System doesn't

(Continued on Page 3)

Vanderbilt Students Get U. S. Honor

Bur H   Mack Glasgow,   Kirkpatrick,   Ben Austin,

Who's Who, for American Colleges and Universities, announced today the names of Vanderbilt students whose biographies will appear in this year's edition, which gives recognition to the outstanding students in practically every college and university in the country.

In the top picture (left to right) are: William Sanderson, Beta Theta Pi, Memphis, president of the senior class; Miss Alice Beasley, Gamma Phi Beta, 2108 Compton Avenue, president of the Women's Student Government Board; Charles Majors, Delta Kappa Epsilon, Ripley, Tenn., president of Omicron Delta Kappa; and Ray Manning, Phi Delta Theta, Chattanooga, editor of the Commodore.

Second picture: Marvin Franklin, Sigma Alpha Epsilon, Birmingham, captain of the football team; Byron Anglin, Chi Phi, Lumpkin, Ga., Student Union secretary; William Emory, Kappa Sigma, Memphis, editor of the Hustler; and Robert Brubaker, Chi Phi, Greenfield, O., president of the Pan Hellenic Council.

Third picture: Morris Burk, Zeta Beta Tau, 2302 Dixie Place, president of the Student Council; McPheeter Glasgow, Beta Theta Pi, Gulf ... last ...... of the 9...

Wrestling Men Begin Advance Training

The present outlook for the Varsity wrestling team of 1939 is very favorable, if advance word of the coaches is reliable indication. Some of the candidates for places on the team have already been taking regular work-outs at the gym in the afternoons, although official practice does not start until the Monday after Thanksgiving. The official work-outs are scheduled to last about two weeks, during which time Coach George Field will get some further idea of the coming team.

The regular wrestling season does not begin until shortly after the first of January; however, all men who wish to try out for either a place on the team or an assistant manager's job must report to the old gym for the first practice.

A strong team seems evident, considering that ten letter men are returning from last year. This group includes Graves, Keefe, George, Dozier, Pellett, Bray, Keene, Kirkpatrick, Fleming, Austin, and Carmichael. The following men are expected to come up from last year's frosh team: Womack, Beauchamp, Hutton, Gray, Manier, Feinblatt, Sherrell, and Lancaster.

Dr. Gustavus Walker Dyer

ALT HUSTLER

VANDY VIGNETTES
By Jeanne Stephenson

Ben Austin, idealist, reformer and philosopher, is the most serious minded of the group so far who have "bared all" in order that their fellow students might acquire an intimate glimpse (tongue in cheek) of their lives on and off the campus.

Ben has a list of activities that, as he told me about them, made me sit back in astonishment. Not only has he held various offices in Delta Kappa Epsilon for three years but he has also been on the board of the Masque Club, a member of the Hustler staff, and twice winner of the intramural wrestling meet in the 165-pound division. This year he is coach of the freshman wrestling team, the campus correspondent for the Banner, a member of the Calumet Club and has the fortunate or unfortunate position, according to viewpoint, as President of the Honor Council. To top it all, if the reader will kindly look at the Official Gazette of the United States Patent Office, within the next week or two, he will find a patent on a new type of zipper (Serial number 109791) issued to a certain Ben Regan Austin of Nashville, Tennessee. This energetic young man made me feel as worthless as "Stepin Fetchit" looks, and how he finds time to be an English major is beyond my powers of comprehension.

He obviously likes to talk, has fixed ideas concerning all he has ever thought about, which I am firmly convinced is everything, and of all subjects touched on during my chat with him "the points are these"—he's an ardent pacifist, likes football, thinks Roosevelt is all right but disagrees with some of his policies (I'm beginning to feel as if I'm conducting a straw vote when it comes to that question). Ben is definitely for the Student Center. "It shows the liberal trend that the faculty and student body are taking"—and frivolously speaking, likes his music sweet and slow and his girls simple and sincere.

Ben is in a sense the man of the hour as far as campus intrigue is concerned. It has become his duty as President of the Honor Council to see that the Honor System is either enforced or abolished. His job at this particular time is undoubtedly of an unsavory nature and though he termed it a "touchy subject," I feel sure that we all agree with Ben when he says, "We must abide by the code and laws that we, the students, have set up." Perhaps that above-mentioned zipper is to zip up the morals of Vanderbilt!

—Fred Keising, Andromedia Bagwell, Jack Perry, Oscar ight, Virginia Harlan, and Jack Keefe III. (Center right)—

Vanderbilt's cheer leaders—left to ...

Willard Parks, drum major.

1. Lucia Bellinger. 2. Vanderbilt Engineering camp at Sparta, Tennessee, 1936: Front Row—Left to Right: Gus Dyer Jr., Al Hutchinson, Dean Fred J. Lewis, W. A. Coolige and F. L. Castleman. Ben Austin is behind the transit in the second row. 3. Jesse Madden and a camper are with Austin at Dixie Camps in Wiley Georgia. 4. Miriam McGaw. 5. Ben Austin in a Hume Fogg High school football uniform. 6. First year Engineering students studying math. 7. Dr. Willis A. Sutton, Superintendant of City Schools in Atlanta, Georgia. 8. George L. Austin Jr. 9. Walton Anderson Austin. 10. Left to Right—Bill Shumaker, Jim Browning, Ben Austin, Robert Seyfried and W. T. Adams. 11. All Star Basketball Team, Left to Right—Mary Lou Vosburg, Mary Wallace Austin, Marguerite Wallace, Louise Sykes, Catherine Brown and Elizabeth Love. 12. Front Row, Left to Right—Ed Finch, John Black. Second Row—Tom Happel, Paige Hill and Jimmy Huggins, in front of the Deke house. 13. Officers and the dates at a Deke dance. 14. Donald Linton. 15. The Trojan horse used in parade.

WINTER
1939

Tuesday, January 3, 1939 Dr. Gustavius W. Dyer, occupant of the White-
ford R. Cole Chair of Economics at Vanderbilt, has been listed as one
of the ten best public speakers in America. I attended his class for the
first time this morning and it was a scream. I never laughed so hard
in my life. He is perhaps the most original thinker I have ever encountered. He says he has no system of teaching whatsoever. He told how
unsystematic Henry Ford was and that he never kept an engagement
unless he wanted to. He said that Henry Ford's cousin was once head
of the Vanderbilt Pharmacy Department and one of the saddest days
in the life of the university was when they did away with that department.
This, of course, got a big laugh because of the way he said it. He talked
for thirty minutes telling how silly some of the things taught in formal
economics really are. The law of diminishing returns, for example—
everyone knows that if you put too much fertilizer on a crop it will
not only not produce more, but will kill the crop. That's just common
sense; not necessarily economics. He comes nearer being an ideal teacher
than any I have ever had. Not only does he say things that will be
remembered a lifetime, but he is almost unique as a teacher in that
he has absolute scorn for the nonessentials . . . such as grades. Leo
Bashinski told me today that his dad kept on raving about me. He said
that I was one boy who had some sense. Leo said he told him I just
had a gift of gab, but that I did have the toughest job at Vanderbilt
and handled it very well. Hell week is just starting for the freshmen.

Called Susan and made the date definite for the Deke dance on the 20th. "Ma" Clapp jokingly told me that he would like to buy some stock in my "gal." He said she is so poised and dignified. I told him I agreed but that I did not know for sure if I myself owned any stock in her.

Wednesday, January 4, 1939 The Lady Dean called me at the fraternity house today and gave me a news break. Said if I ever needed anything else just to let her know. George Morrow told me also that Mr. Bashinski was sold on me. He said: "That boy has as much poise as a forty year old man." Marcella Driskill and I had a long talk in the Student Center. I told her how much I appreciated her kind remarks in the newspaper interview the other day. Bill Jordan told me he would go with me tomorrow night to take Susan and Eleanor Richie to a show but his mother called and made him promise not to go out.

Thursday, January 5, 1939 Gus Dyer was hot again today. After criticizing Roosevelt's emergency programs for five or ten minutes he said: "It's a wonder the Writer of the Ten Commandments did not say 'Thou shalt not steal . . . unless it is an emergency!' " He said that with the great humor, sarcasm of which he is a master. His great technique is to make a serious point and then to illustrate it with humor. Dyer is, of course, so ugly, and his smile so contagious, that one cannot help being swept along at his hilarious pace. I took Charles Heffron along with me to date Eleanor Richie tonight and I dated Susan. We went to the movies to see "Sweethearts" and I enjoyed it all the more because I was with mine.

Friday, January 6, 1939 Homer Howell and I worked that old trick of asking embarrassing questions of the freshmen at the formal initiations tonight. We told them horror stories just before feeding them a bunch of junk, such as raw oysters. Collected from the Banner and bought Susan some pencils with her name engraved on them. Bought a sweater from Eugene Pigg. In the wrestling class I worked out with Leo Bolster.

Saturday, January 7, 1939 I made my first speech in Dr. Harris' class this morning. I was pretty nervous and put my hands behind me. I weakened the speech by saying that President Roosevelt spoke of this, that and so forth. Dr. Harris quoted from the famous speech by Bob Ingersoll on Napoleon. We were given two cuts so I spent the time in the library studying and talking with Shirley Caldwell, Virginia McClellan, Peggy Norton and Susan. Miriam was my date for the gym dance tonight. Susan was with a fellow a little older than our set and I saw her glance my way when I was dancing the first no-break with Miriam. When I was dancing the second with Susan they played the Deke theme song: "I wish I had a girl like you for DKE" and Susan said: "It's the grandest song on earth, isn't it?"

Sunday, January 8, 1939 I will study Victorian English with Dr. Mims this term. In 1869 there was a Meta-Physical Society in London. Its membership consisted of many of the great men of England: Dean Stanley, Cardinal Manning, James Martino the Unitarian, Frederick Demaurice, scientists Tyndal and Huxley, John Morley, statesmen Arthur Balfour and Gladstone, Freud, Lesley Stephen, Fred Harrison, John Ruskin and Alfred Lord Tennyson. They discussed the great philosophical questions: Who and what is man and where is he going? Mims contrasted Plato and Bacon. Plato's idea was to make men perfect; Bacon's to make imperfect men comfortable. P., exhalt man into a god; B. to supply vulgar wants. P. aimed at the stars, B. hit his target. Bacon's philosophy: "An acre in Middlesex is better than a principality in Utopia." Bill Shumaker called and invited me to a steak fry with him, his brother John, Ben Grace, Billy Woody, and a couple of sisters whose names I have forgotten. The steaks were good and we had a nice time singing.

Monday, January 9, 1939 Saw Susan in the library this morning before nine. Miriam was at a table nearby so I avoided this area of the campus. Went to town and got a copy of Omar Khayyám's *Rubáiyát.* Susan's pencils were ready so I picked them up. Clark Hutton was selected as rush chairman for next year.

Tuesday, January 10, 1939 After the luncheon Pursuit meeting I went to the library and talked with Susan and Billy Eason. Every time I see her she is with him. Obviously she likes him but I don't see how she could take him seriously. He is always so silly around her. At one point he said: "Susan and I are going to spend the spring holidays together in New York." She bristled at such a ridiculous statement and replied: "You certainly have a good imagination." There was a long silence. Wrestled Ted Feinblatt this afternoon and tonight I am completely exhausted.

Wednesday, January 11, 1939 We had a violinist and soloist in general chapel today. Susan sat directly across the aisle from me and my heart was on that side when they rendered "I'm falling in love with someone," "The Indian Love Call," and "Maytime." Dr. Humphrey Lee, the former Vanderbilt Theological School Dean, who is now President of Southern Methodist University, was the principle speaker. He told the joke about the great philosopher Hambone who said he knew it was a ghost because when he reached out to touch it it was not there, and when it reached out to touch him, he was not there. As a topical joke he told of one graduating class that adopted as a motto: "W. P. A. here we come." This evening I was studying in the library and Susan came in and sat by me. I did not notice her until she had taken her seat. I was so pleased. She told me she was planning on changing her Public Speaking class to Biblical Literature. If so she would be in my class, but unfortunately,

in Billy Eason's too. There was a conflict and it could not be done so
I urged her to stay in Public Speaking. I think it would help her to be
a little more outgoing. Uncle Walton brought me an American Magazine
so I read a very interesting article about Felix Frankfurter, who was
recently appointed to the Supreme Court. There was also an interesting
article about Jeff Dickinson, an American who is promoting sports events
in Paris. Shirley Caldwell made me feel ashamed of myself today. She
said she was looking up the grades of the Theta freshmen in the Registrar's office and she ran across mine and she was disappointed. Doesn't
it hurt to disappoint someone you think highly of and who thinks highly
of you! That is one of the great crushing experiences to the human
spirit.

Thursday, January 12, 1939   Scooped the Tennessean on the Miss
Vanderbilt story. We took pictures of Andromedia Bagwell and plan a
beautiful layout for tomorrow's paper. We ran the four most likely candidate's pictures this afternoon. Fleming was hopping mad. He is not a
very good loser. Wrestled Leonard Garrard, Bill Shumaker, and Rush
Dozier this afternoon. That's a pretty good day's work. Jim Browning
dated Marcella Driskill and I dated Virginia Richey, of Ward-Belmont,
whom I met this summer, and we went to the Stork Club in Franklin
for dancing. I am still smarting over disappointing Shirley Caldwell in
my grades. I have to admit it I am no student. My mind refuses to be
channeled into routine assignments, it has a will of its own and becomes
active and enthusiastic only over new and challenging subjects. It balks
like a mule at dull repetitious material, or merely turns itself off. But
when I think something has never been done before, and that maybe
I can think up a new way to do it, I become as excited as a child. I
recognize in myself the rebel spirit; the yen for pioneering and inventing.
One would think that such a mind would care only for the sciences,
and not literature, but the great expressions of literature are new and
challenging too. A thought expressed exactly and precisely is unique
when it can only be said that way.

Friday, January 13, 1939   I was anxious to see the Tennessean this
morning to see if Partee beat me on the final announcement about
"Miss Vanderbilt," but he ran pictures of three girls instead. I guess
he was afraid to take a chance on a wrong guess, or maybe his editor
would not let him do so. I sat up until two o'clock this morning writing
my story and turned it in at ten. I saw the layout before it ran and it
is the prettiest we have done I think. Mr. Wood, the chief of the photo-
graphic department complained about Frank Gunter and me taking so
long with the pictures, because Frank was working overtime, but after
seeing our shots he was well pleased. When I went out for Susan tonight
she said she had something to talk over with me. She said she had

rather I take her to the Theta dance but that Billy Eason had been so nice to her that she felt she ought to ask him. I told her that if she had rather be with me I did not care whom she was actually with. I assured her it was OK with me. Later on she told me she was planning a dinner soon in honor of Judith Browning, who is marrying a Wilson boy, and that she wanted me to be her date at that time. I said I would be delighted. She also asked that I have the second no-break with her at the Theta dance. Earlier in the evening, I told Susan about the first time I ever saw her . . . at the football game about a year ago. She remembered too and said I had a paper over my glasses as a sun guard. She remembered my asking her for no-breaks at the gym dance that night. I got a "by-line" on the front page "Miss Vanderbilt" story and Susan complimented me on it. She asked when I wrote it and I told her between twelve an two this morning. Why did Susan ask Billy to take her to her sorority dance if she had rather be with me? Is it that she feels compassion for him because he acts so like a child at times? Maybe she is more relaxed around him because of it. Are Susan and I too prissy and prim around each other; holding each other perhaps in too high esteem . . . afraid of each other? What a devastating thought! Let the devil take tomorrow, however, tonight is mine. Susan kissed me!

Saturday, January 14, 1939 Andromedia handed me a nice letter this evening thanking me for the fine article I wrote about her. My muscles are tight and tense from the wrestling I do every day and when I get excited and the Adrenalin begins to flow, such as when I start to make a speech, my leg muscles quiver as if I am scared to death or shivering from the cold. It happened in Public Speaking class this morning and I shook the wooden stage in the old West Side building. It is embarrassing, and if I had not had quite a bit of experience in public speaking I would be absolutely mortified. As it is I tough it out and consider it in the same light as the challenge of the speaking itself.

Sunday, January 15, 1939 Cousin Osgood Anderson returned my copy of "Marcus Aurelius" this afternoon. Bill Jordan and Bill Simpson came by and picked me up at five this afternoon and we went to the drugstore to eat supper. I was highly amused at what they were saying about their Phi Kappa Sigma fraternity brothers talking about them. I imagine the average fraternity man does consider them a couple of queer ducks. I guess my saving grace is that I can associate with "Brains" like Jordan and Simpson, but have somewhat of a reputation as a wrestler too.

Monday, January 16, 1939 Gus Dyer, in commenting on seniority in the railroads, said it will kill any business. What if the manager of a Major League baseball team said: "No, that fellow can't play, he hasn't been with us long enough. We'll have to let the fellow play who has seniority." Dyer told the story of four Negroes attempting to move a rock. After grunting and groaning ("You know how Negroes grunt") they could not move it. Finally they came to find out that three of the Negroes did not even have their hands on the rock. When Dr. Gus threw in that parenthetical expression: "You know how Negroes grunt," I thought members of the class would have apoplexy laughing. I have never seen anyone tell a story as effectively as this self-effacing, homely man. The way he looks is a part of his genius. You can hardly look at him without laughing, but when his face breaks into that famous grin, with the deep lines running up his scrawny face from a ridiculously tiny chin, nobody can keep a straight face. Dr. Harris once asked him what advice he would give to his Public Speaking classes: "Tell them to remember that the speaker is seen as well as heard," said the greatest orator that I have ever seen on a platform.

Tuesday, January 17, 1939 I could not attend the Student Council meeting this evening because we had to have a business meeting of the Honor Council. Had a talk with Mc. about new reports of his cheating. Some people never seem to learn. Worked out with the varsity wrestling team and both of my opponents, Bud Bray and Art Keene were in the weight class above me. Wears you out fast but it's good training for wrestling in your own weight.

Wednesday, January 18, 1939 Last night I dreamed pleasantly of making my first trip abroad, to France. I saw beautiful landscapes and tried to make myself feel the thrill of seeing a far away land for the first time. It was beautiful and exceeded all reality or hope of reality. When I went to Chicago for the first time five years ago I got the thrill of seeing my first big city. My room faced the lake and the wind was cold, even in August. As the wind blew the curtains of my room I thought of the lyrics of the song that had just come out: "Can it be the breeze that seems to bring the trees right into my room." How wonderful it is to see the world through the eyes of the very young. It never looks the same again. Coach Field, Dr. W. P. Fishel, Partee and I are making elaborate plans for the wrestling meet Saturday. I wrote a story and turned it in to the Banner today. Susan and I studied in the library this afternoon until I had to go to my wrestling practice at four. Her hair was dark and radiant and she looked beautiful.

Thursday, January 19, 1939 Jim Buford came to me this evening and told me I had to take my English exam immediately or I would not be eligible for the wrestling meet Saturday. I went post haste to Dr. Mims, Dr. Glenn and Dr. Pomfret. I came home, got my book, studied for an hour and took the exam from three until five this afternoon. I think I passed it OK. At a meeting of the Calumet Club at the

Deke House, Partee Fleming read an article satirizing campus activities and John Covey read four short poems. John was elected to the club. Homer Howell, Roy Huggins and Walter King helped serve refreshments.

Friday, January 20, 1939 Worked out lightly at the gym and took a nap before picking up Susan for the Deke banquet dance. I gave her the pencils with her name on them when I arrived at Oak Hill at six and she commented on the originality of the gift. The banquet had started when we arrived. Trying to stay below the 155 pound wrestling division I had eaten only a bowl of soup all day. I was hungry but I ate only the steak. Several of the skits concerned my activities. There was something about the President of the W. C. T. U. at the Deke House because I let the freshmen know that I object to their learning to drink in our chapter. There was also something about the "U-Cheatum-and-Me-Shipppum-Club." One freshman parodied my general chapel speech: "Fellow students, etc." I danced the first and second no-breaks with Susan and the Special, but I was pretty weak from not eating and was not sorry when the dance was over around two A.M. Susan turned her cheek when I attempted to kiss her good night. Everything makes me love her more.

Saturday, January 21, 1939 Slept through Dr. Mahew's Biblical Literature class but got up for Public Speaking and Dr. Dyer's Classical Theory. Dyer told the story about the Negro who said: "Mr. Whiteman, I is black and don't know as much as you white folks, but if you could just be a Nigger for one Saturday night you never would want to be anything else." The house was packed for the matches with Appalachian tonight. Three or four hundred people were there. Mr. Jack Keefe did a masterful job of announcing. The freshmen wrestled Castle Heights and then the Varsity took on the North Carolina boys. We lost by a score of 28 to 8 but it was a good show. Rush Dozier won by a decision and Partee Fleming pinned his man. My opponent was Hobart Perdue, a brother to the Perdue that blocked the punt in the Duke-Pitt. game which enabled Duke to win. I lost by a decision. I had to take the bottom first and the boy kept pushing me off the mat. I had to take the bottom once when I shouldn't have because I broke his advantage. The referee also would not let me use my headlock. Perdue deserved to win, though. He has thrown Householder twice during the last two years. Went to the dance later and Susan was surprised to see me. The social life at Vanderbilt is too pervasive to permit many students to spend the necessary time in training, and to make the necessary sacrifices required for championship athletes. It is a choice that must be made and I personally prefer the Vanderbilt way.

Sunday, January 22, 1939 I think Huxley's famous definition of a liberal education, as given by Mims, is a little wordy and long but worth noting. "The man I think has had a liberal education who has been so trained in youth that his body is the ready servant of his will and does with ease and pleasure all the work that as a mechanism it is capable; whose intellect is a cold logical engine with all its parts of equal strength and smooth working, ready like a steam engine to turn to any kind of work and to spin the gossamers (fine mind) as well as forge the anchors (strong) of the mind; whose mind is stout with the knowledge . . . , one who is not stunted aesthetically, is full of life and fire, but whose passions are trained to come to him by a strong will, the servant of a tender will; who has learned to love all beauty, whether of nature or art, to hate all violence and to respect others as himself." Had tea this afternoon with John Covey and Bill Simpson in Jordan's room.

Monday, January 23, 1939 Coach George Fields pointed out some mistakes in the Appalachian meet. Met with Bill Embry, Editor of the Hustler, and Bill Jordan in order to formulate plans for tomorrow evening's meeting with key faculty members and student leaders. The idea is to plan for a long range improvement of the Honor System at Vanderbilt. Read the story of Solomon, 1st Kings, 1–11 tonight before retiring.

Tuesday, January 24, 1939 Dr. Dyer was hilarious in class today, as usual. He told the story about going to a hotel and running up a bill and not having enough money to pay out. He also said that back in the country they have an expression of getting someone to "stand for you", meaning, to get someone to sign a note that he will pay if you don't. Dyer's comment was: "I've never known a case where someone stood for someone else that the other person did not lie down." Ate lunch with Miriam McGaw and she told me about writing a story for Dr. John Crowe Ransom's class, English IX, about a boy who broke a date with a girl for a Junior Prom. Said she read it to her brother Steve and he just lowered his head and looked at her. I guess Miriam finally realizes that she could have been a little more thoughtful when she did that to me awhile back. I made a short statement to the mass meeting tonight and retired. Deans Sarratt, Pascall and Lewis spoke on the necessity of retaining the Honor System. Chancellor Carmichael was the last speaker and hot debate followed.

Wednesday, January 25, 1939 Heard the heavyweight boxing championship fight on the radio tonight. Joe Louis knocked out John Henry Lewis in less than two minutes. I read the book "Henry VIII and His Wives" in the library and then went to the gym and worked out lightly with Scott George.

Thursday, January 26, 1939 Got up early this morning at seven o'clock and departed for Knoxville with the wrestling team. Oliver Graves, Jim Tuck, Dewitt Smith, Jack Keefe, John Pellett, Marshall Womack, Bud

Bray, Partee Fleming, Mickey Carmichael, Rush Dozier, Ted Feinblatt, Scott George, Coach George Field, and I made the trip. We stayed at the Milner, formerly the Atkin Hotel. I used the forward roll, which was Coach Field's favorite means of escaping from the down position, and which I too have developed to a fine art. It depends on surprise. It is almost sure fire if the opponent is not expecting it, but murder, if he does expect it. It's a dangerous move but usually pays off. I pinned my man in one minute and fourteen seconds. Partee was the only other wrestler to win by a pin. The others won by decisions. We ate at the University of Tennessee training table and saw Bob Suffrage and several other well-known football players.

Friday, January 27, 1939 Ate dinner at Maryville College and wrestled at eight o'clock. For some unknown reason I was dead on my feet and lost by a decision. Oliver Graves actually threw his man but the referee made them wrestle an extra period and Oliver lost. Mickey Carmichael's bout was stopped because of Mickey's stalling. That gave them 5 points and they won by a score of 16–14. Coach Meher and Householder, from the Knoxville Y.M.C.A. came down to Maryville to scout us.

Saturday, January 28, 1939 I asked Coach Field what move I should use when I draw the down position. "Use your forward roll." he said. I objected, because Householder had seen me use it against U. T. and would be expecting it. I tried it anyway and got caught in midair with one leg in the air and the other under his arm, with my shoulders flat on the mat. Before this happened, however, I got him down, got between his legs and almost pinned him. I wore down after four or five minutes though. Bud Bray got rough and threw his man in practically no time. We got bad decisions on Dozier and Keefe. We should have been given the decision in both but they called them draws. The match of matches, however, was the one between Al Crawford, three time National Champion and our heavy weight, Partee Fleming. Crawford is the best wrestler I have ever seen. He is slightly less than six feet tall and weighs about 175 pounds and has a most beautiful body build for wrestling. He handled Partee like a cat playing with a mouse. Partee is no slouch in the ring. He has been boxing and wrestling since junior high school and he knows how to use his 250 pound weight. Partee is only about five feet seven or eight inches, but is strong and very smart. Crawford toyed with him most of the match; coming very close to pins, but never quite doing it . . . by design or otherwise. This is the only match I ever saw in which Partee was not his usual confident self. He knew he was up against a great wrestler and stayed on the defensive most of the time. Along towards the end, Crawford's arrogance made Partee mad, and Al never had another chance to pin him. The match was given Crawford by a decision, three points. If he had really tried hard in the beginning and had pinned Partee and got 5 points, his team would have won. Instead we beat them 16–14. My brothers Anderson and Henry D. came by from Tennessee Military Institute in Sweetwater to see the matches.

Sunday, January 29, 1939 Got up at six and left for Nashville after breakfast. We got home about one in the afternoon.

Monday, January 30, 1939 I woke up at eight this morning and asked Mary Wallace to set the alarm for ten before she left for school. The next time I woke up it was twelve thirty and I had missed both my English and History classes. Worked out in the gym and pinned Scott George twice in a short time, but he was not feeling well. The extra sleep this morning must have been good for me because when I called Susan I was very peppy and feeling fine. She mentioned that she did not see me today. Actually I haven't seen her for six days . . . seems like six years.

Tuesday, January 31, 1939 Dyer said: "Regulation is a judicial power. Direction of a business is an economic function." Under Communism the state owns everything. State Socialism stands for private ownership with the government looking over your shoulder. Freedom has to be suppressed under Socialism. I was in the library this evening and Susan came in and sat by me. Shortly thereafter Billy Eason came in. Shirley Caldwell also sat with us. Finally I told them I had to leave. Shirley said: "If you leave so early it will look as if you don't love us." Willie Cornelius remarked, jokingly, "Aw, what difference does it make if he leaves?" Shirley answered, "A lot, too bad there aren't more like him." Susan, sitting across the table, looked at Shirley coldly and said: "Too bad I can't think up pretty speeches like that." Wow!

Wednesday, February 1, 1939 Dathan Miles brought me a copy of the current Fogg Horn, the newspaper I started at Hume-Fogg. It appears to be growing in size and importance each year. Mims said it was once said of Edmund Burke: "You may not agree with his conclusion, but he states so many truths in coming to it." If we are intended for great ends we must be called to great hazards. Every great statesman ventures forth from a new notion, a new cause. Every great deed is the result of some person's embarking on a course which seems perilous and succeeding at it.

Thursday, February 2, 1939 Tonight it was my very great privilege to be Susan's escort at the dinner party at her magnificent home, Oak Hill, on the Franklin Road. The party was in honor of Judith Davis Browning who is marrying Billy Wilson on the 23rd of this month. Twenty-one guests were invited, Mr. and Mrs. Wilson and Billy's two brothers. There was quite a stir getting enough chairs in one room to seat so many people. I volunteered to aid them and the first place I walked in was the room where the girls were dressing. I did not realize that it was the girl's room until I had already walked in. I was right behind Billy and Judith in the serving line and as I passed the table where they were sitting I had a hunch that I ought to sit with them, being Susan's date, but I wasn't sure (I didn't see the place cards.) So I went to the wrong table. Judith told me that I was supposed to sit at their table. I got up and moved promptly. Susan was helping get the plates served so Judith, Billy and I were half through before she started. I guess I should have fixed her plate for her or else waited. The menu consisted of delicious corn, peas, some kind of fowl (perhaps guineas) tomato aspic, hot buttered biscuits and ice cream made up in clever little flower pots. It was a fine meal. Eleanor Richie served the coffee. The parents ate in the breakfast room. After eating I talked to Joe Dickinson and his wife for a few minutes and then Susan and I went to the club room with the group where we danced, played pool, bridge, Ping Pong, and danced. Billy Eason was with Eleanor Richie and they acted really crazy. Susan told me that Nello Andrews is going to take Eleanor Richie to the Washington Ball, which will be her first Vanderbilt dance. I talked to Mrs. Cheek more than I ever had before and Mrs. Glenn and I had a real lengthy chat about Clarksville, Dorothy Dix, the Merriweathers, etc. It was a very interesting conversation. Billy Eason rode out with me and I brought him home at twelve o'clock. Susan seemed to have a pretty bad cold. I told her about seeing that picture of her in a bathing suit when Jan Garber was here and she seemed embarrassed. She said "I wish you had not seen it."

Friday, February 3, 1939 Talked to Hill Turner today and he wrote out a check for $100.00 on the Zipper invention. He says that he is merely betting on the invention. If it goes over he will expect a larger rate of interest than a safer investment which pays 4%; but that if it does not go over there is no need for worry. I feel real good over the deal with Mr. Turner. He will be valuable as an advisory partner. He told me to go see Dr. Mayhew and to get him to take the other part of the investment. He says that Dr. Mayhew married one of the Leech girls and he spends their money for them. He told me about a monkey-wrench that Mayhew was interested in. Mr. Turner kids him about it all the time. I had tea with Jordan and Simpson this evening. I wrote Mr. Freeman Owens, 2647 Broadway, New York, Jordan's friend from Pine Bluff, Arkansas, who deals in patents. Mr. Jordan Monk, Bill's step father, writes that this fellow is a good friend of Talon's advertising manager. Last night Susan tickled me telling how Eleanor Richie used to get mad and butt her head against the wall. Judith Davis persisted in telling how she used to try to get rid of her little sister by feeding her beads in hope that she would swallow them; also how she used to try to cut off her head with scissors; how she beat the cats heads against rocks and killed them. That was some conversation for a prenuptial party.

Saturday, February 4, 1939 I saw the finals of the Intramural boxing tournament. This is the sport where Jack Keefe, William Lauderdale and Henry Clay excel. About fifteen Dekes came to my class this evening to learn the fundamentals of wrestling. At eight o'clock Bill Shumaker came for me and we went to the Alabama-Vandy basketball game. We stayed for only part of it and learned later that we beat them 34–32. We drove to East Nashville to pick up Margaret Jackson and then to the home of Edna Murray Davy. The Alpha Omega Pi's had Alumni Hall decorated beautifully. They call this dance the Rose Ball. I had the second no-break with Andromedia Bagwell. Margaret and I always have fun together. Kenneth Anderson took Mary Wallace to the Policeman's Ball at the Wagon Wheel. Bob Neathery's car was wrecked about twelve fifteen this morning. Adams was slightly hurt and was taken to St. Thomas hospital.

Sunday, February 5, 1939 Went to Mrs. Duncan's home for a Spanish lesson this evening. Paid her $2.00. I studied late for Dr. Walker's History of England.

Monday, February 6, 1939 One of the most interesting stories Dr. Mims has to tell is the conversion of Cardinal Newman, in his later days, to Catholicism. He could not find complete fulfillment elsewhere. Kingsley misinterpreted his motives; assumed he was gaining influence, during the twelve years that he was at the very heart of English thought and religion, in order to take more people with him to Catholicism. He was entirely wrong. Newman had nothing to gain, but lost much. He had to give up Oxford, of which he he was the living embodiment. Newman tells Catholics that they must take literature as a whole, and not just the pious side. Newman's writing comes nearer to being a model for prose than almost any writer in all of literature.

Tuesday, February 7, 1939 Bill Jordan and I took Susan and Eleanor Richie to dinner at the Hermitage Hotel and then to the Ryman auditorium to see Ethel Barrymore in "White Oaks." Francis Craig, who was playing at the Hermitage, played a Strauss waltz for Susan and me and it made us late for the theatre. The lights went out just as we entered. I sat behind a post and could see but half the stage, but I enjoyed Barrymore's expression. She played the part of a grandmother to perfection. Susan and I swapped seats with Bill and Eleanor for the second half.

Wednesday, February 8, 1939 Today I am 22 years old. Received a nice letter and small check from Aunt Belle, my Dad's sister. She always remembers. Went to the Belmont theatre to see Tyrone Power in "Suez."

Thursday, February 9, 1939 It was raining so I got soaking wet walking to school. Talked to Dr. Mayhew after class and he said he may be interested in my proposition later. Attended the Student Council meeting and made the motion that we contract with Tommy Dorsey's orchestra for the Junior Prom. Told Susan about it and she was thrilled.

Friday, February 10, 1939 The Kappa Alpha Theta dance tonight was Susan's first sorority function that she had not invited me to be her escort. Billy Eason received the honor this time. I didn't particularly mind because she told me she had rather be with me. Susan had on a corsage and also a bouquet on her wrist. Her mother must have given her flowers as she did last year when I was her daughter's date. Once when I broke on Tom Scoggins he said: "So you want to dance with the flower garden?" Some people have a knack for saying the wrong thing. In this case I suppose it is the little boy in Tom that teases the girl he cares most about because he does not know what else to do. After all, the social graces of little boys are rather limited at very young ages. I had one no-break with Susan and another with Shirley Caldwell. Shirley has a very small waist and looked beautiful in a broad, hoopskirt, type evening dress. She is the nearest thing I know to the belles of the old South. She was born to it too. Sam Boone was her date. Susan told me that Judith Browning was inviting me to her wedding and asked if I planned to attend. I was delighted that she was interested. I have such a bad memory that I asked Susan's sister, Eleanor Richie, for the same no-break that I had planned with Susan. Mrs. Glenn, Susan's grandmother, attended as a chaperon with Mrs. McClellan. Mrs. Cheek came with John Jr., who was home from Castle Heights for the weekend. I went to Petrone's with Jordan and Fleming and talked with Tommy Hale and Henrietta Hickman, after the dance.

Saturday, February 11, 1939 Helped officiate at the first rounds of the Intramural wrestling matches today. Two matches were in progress simultaneously so they got over in a hurry. The Dekes won thirteen and lost only three. My classes must have helped because this is the best start we have made in years. Attended the basketball game between Vandy and U. T. and stayed for the wrestling matches. We won 13 to 12. Leonard Anglin was scheduled to wrestle in the unlimited division but Coach George Field was afraid to take a chance since the score was so close, so Partee got the bid. He had just returned from Castle Heights where our freshman team tied them 16 to 16. Art Keene's match was the best of all. He used some holds that I showed him yesterday, especially the pinning hold, a headlock from in front of the opponent. Walked home with Merrill Stone and stopped by the Vanderbilt hospital to inquire about his grandmother who has pneumonia.

Sunday, February 12, 1939 Arch Trimble, Hartwell Weaver and Bill Jordan had dinner with Mary Wallace and me at our little apartment on 20th avenue. We had steak, asparagus tips, peas, potatoes, a salad and icebox pie. Jordan liked Trimble and is going to invite him to dinner with us at the Hermitage Hotel Thursday. Arch called Barr and asked to join him later at his home rather than here. Barr asked if Susan were at the party. I think he likes her too. Out of a clear blue sky Arch asked me if I loved Susan. I dodged the question because I did not like being asked a serious question so flippantly.

Monday, February 13, 1939 Worked out with Ted Feinblatt today and pinned him twice. Both times I came from the bottom position. While studying with Susan in the library she told me that her parents were giving Eleanor Richie a new car and that she was going to swap her Dodge for a Plymouth convertible. Nello Andrews was there also, and Billy Eason came up before the afternoon session was over. Susan and I sat together tonight when the Thetas beat the Sigma Kappas in basketball, 26 to 4. Charles Majors told me he had a talk with Ed Patterson's dad and he told him that P. D. Houston, who is head of the Chemical National Bank in New York, was sent to the first Pan Hellenic Council meeting by the S. A. E's but that the council asked that he be recalled because he created such a disturbance.

Tuesday, February 14, 1939 St. Valentine's Day used to be such a romantic event. We could, on this day, perhaps get up enough courage to send notes to our best girls, telling them they were our Valentines. My courage is not much better today and cards, even humorous ones, are too obvious. A little less sophistication might help. My first patent issued from the patent office today. I wrote my Washington attorney, Mr. James P. Burns, and asked for copies and also invited his son James Jr., to go to camp with me this summer. Ate lunch with Susan and Jane Vance. Jim Reed came by and began to joke about "Pursuit." He finally said though that the only reason most people bought the thing was because they liked me. That was a nice compliment to be paid in front of one's best girl. She and I studied until one o'clock when she went to the Student Christian Association meeting and I to wrestling practice. I pinned Clark Hutton a couple of times. A slight rain was falling this evening and a light breeze blew in my window. What a wonderful night for sleeping.

Wednesday, February 15, 1939 Had only one class today, History. Made "B+" on my review topics and "B" on my History examination. Dr. Walker said I am improving. Wrestled Scott George this afternoon and was able to "wing" him once. A letter from Anderson related that Henry D. has won the welterweight division of the Golden Glove Boxing championship matches in Chattanooga. He knocked out his first opponent in one minute and the next opponent defaulted. He got a technical knockout in the finals.

Thursday, February 16, 1939 Virginia McClellan entertained at the Belle Meade Country Club last night in honor of Judith Browning. I am sure Susan was there but I don't know with whom. It was Eason I guess. Susan was so sleepy today that she did not come to school. Did some outdoor work and then wrestled Rush Dozier. What an athlete! He knows almost nothing about wrestling, and is not particularly quick, but he is phenomenally strong and has a good sense of balance. From the bottom position he just stands up and there are not many wrestlers his weight who can hold him. He volunteered to tell me one day that the reason he is so strong is that he does not abuse himself.

Friday, February 17, 1939 In the United States Patent Office Gazette, for the week ending February 14, 1939, I saw my patent listed. What a thrill to see it in print. There are a few bright spots in one's life when he feels he has accomplished something. Today was one of them. A first patent is like a first date, or a first public speech. The thrill is not quite the same the second time. Worked out lightly at the gym and at seven o'clock I went to get Susan to attend Bill Jordan's dinner at the Hermitage. Susan had on a beautiful dress with shimmering sequins. It showed up her figure to the best advantage. She looked tall and slender. Met Bill's stepfather, Mr. Jordan Monk, Beverly Bridges, Claire Lee Knox and Margarite Robinson. Susan and I were the only two who would not drink one cocktail. We hoped to get our dessert early so I could get her home for her Washington Ball date. We were a little late. I then went out to get Margaret Jackson as my date. The flags were put up backwards and there was a mix-up on the no-breaks and Susan said: "What difference does it make as long as you have it with the right person?" Hope she meant something by that.

Saturday, February 18, 1939 Weighed in at three o'clock and tried to get some sleep before my wrestling match tonight, but could not. Merrill Stone went by Scarritt College dining hall and picked up Susan at eight-thirty. They got to the gym two matches before mine. I was the aggressor for the first four or five minutes and then I was exhausted. When the match started I paused just a few seconds and then dived for his feet. I almost got him. We went off the mat and I came back acting as rough as I could. I put a headlock on him and then worked Partee's trick for catching a leg. I took the top and rode him for a minute or two. He finally switched and came to the top and got the decision. Wood Everett got the slight edge but it was close and I had a lot of fun. I was so rough with him at one point, before I pooped out, that it took all the aggressiveness out of him. After the match I joined Susan, Bill Shumaker and Edna Murry Davy and we went to Candyland. Susan said she had to get in the habit of getting home at eleven o'clock before her father returns from Baltimore in April. Took her home and Bill, and his brother John, and I went to the Tri Delta dance. Miriam was getting a big rush. Saw a few of the Maryville College wrestlers there.

Sunday, February 19, 1939 Bill Jordan called tonight and said he had had tea with the Physics professor who took Dr. Slack's place. They are discussing nonAristotelian logic and hope to bring others into the discussion group. Dr. Mims' recent lecture reported on the plight of Catholics in England before the restoration of the Catholic Church, which Cardinal Newman wrote about in "The Second Spring." An Englishman could meet a Catholic and put whatever price he wanted on his property. I had not realized it was that bad in England.

Monday, February 20, 1939 Dr. Dyer said recently that when a business is unionized, progress stops. Man has got to feel that his property will be protected. In picking a jury for a capital offense, two questions are generally asked, do you own property and are you the head of a family? One of the distinctive characteristics of our society is that we have respect for a man who makes a great success. The English understand this too, and maybe even go further than we do, they make "Knights" out of exceptional people. When you destroy the distinction that goes with business success you destroy business ability. Men work for distinction. They work for money because it gives distinction. By honoring success you bring out the best in people. This is a fundamental principle that a people must understand if a society is to thrive. Received my patent papers today, but the anticipation has been greater than the achievement.

Tuesday, February 21, 1939 Shirley Caldwell is like a spirited racehorse. She is pretty, sleek, vivacious and thoroughly alive to everything around her. After talking with her in the library this afternoon I realized she is one of the most attractive people I have met at Vanderbilt. She likes me too, which doesn't hurt. Yesterday Dr. Mims quoted a statement made by Dr. Robert Millikan, of California Institute of Technology, expressing his, and about fifteen other scientist's, definition of Science and Religion: "The purpose of Science is to develop, without prejudice or preconceptions of any kind, the facts about the processes of nature. The even more important task of Religion is to develop the conscience. Each of these two activities represent a deep and vital function of man and both are necessary for the life progress and happiness of the human race." Mims says that Walter Pater was the best prose writer of the Victorian Age. He cited the wonderful description of a house, with beautiful surroundings . . . associations, in "The Child in the House" as an example of his writing. "To burn always with this hard gem like flame; to maintain this ecstacy is success in life." He quoted: "Give nothing but the highest quality of your moments . . . The joy of elevated thought." How can anyone fail to be moved by this kind of writing?

Wednesday, February 22, 1939 Susan was rehearsing for a wedding, so, when I called tonight I talked with Eleanor Richie. I said I could probably see Susan at school, if she were not too tired to come to school tomorrow. "No! Susan would never miss a day of school." Maybe her mother will make her. Eleanor Richie then said: "What mother says doesn't make any difference with Susan." One would gather from that remark that Susan has a head of her own. Discussed my financial difficulties with Uncle Walt and he promised to help me by about April 10th.

Thursday, February 23, 1939 It is final now that the Tommy Dorsey band will play for the Proms. Morris Burk sent a copy of the current Hustler to Tommy. At three this afternoon I attended Judith Browning's wedding. Susan was one of the bridesmaids and she was very pretty in a pinkish, blue dress. I listened carefully to the words of the ceremony that Dr. Barr used . . . just in case.

Friday, February 24, 1939 Had the surprise no-break with Susan at the Miami Triad dance. As we were dancing I told her that my evening was complete now that I have had a no-break with her. "Mine is too." she said. On a later occasion when Eason and Susan's date, were discussing who was going to dance a certain no-break, she glanced at me in a kind of winking attitude as if she were not particularly interested in dancing it with either of them. I smiled inwardly.

Saturday, February 25, 1939 Virginia Richey called and asked to postpone our date until later in the evening since a boy friend of hers from out of town had called her and would be there only a little while. I told her that it would be okay to break the date if she wanted to. She did. I called up Susan and told her for certain that I would come to the Don's Club dance. Earlier in our conversation I made several dates pretty far in advance. She said she preferred not to make them on Sunday night because it made her so sleepy the next day. I told her that anytime she wanted to break a date that we had it would be all right. She said, "Oh no, I do not mean that!" I explained that I merely meant that when she felt that she really should stay in that it would be fine with me. When I told her I felt sorry for girls who made dates with everybody. She said, "I don't have dates with anybody I don't like." The freshman, rushee party at the Deke House last night was a success. After eleven o'clock I dropped by the Don's club function. I told Virginia McClellan that joke about "Rolling John" (If his wife was unfaithful he would turn over in his grave). She laughed heartily. Her escort was Billy Eason. Morton McMurray was Susan's date. Barr was acting drunk. Dudley Burton was breaking on Susan quite a bit. Never saw so many crazy costumes.

Sunday, February 26, 1939 I called Susan just as Paderewski, the great pianist was coming on the air over the NBC network. I told her that he was appearing and suggested that she might turn it on if she were not otherwise occupied. Said she would. I am noticing a change in my taste in music. I used to thoroughly enjoy barn dance music, then popular music was my favorite type. Now I am becoming fed up with it. I listened intently to Paderewski's program this evening and enjoyed it tremendously. Perhaps I enjoyed it just a little more knowing that Susan was listening. Went with Mary Wallace and Katherine to the Belmont Theatre tonight to see the English picture "The Edge of the World." Saw several friends there, including Miss Kate Talbot, Mrs. Connoll, Bernard Breyer, Harry Coles, Mr. Brainard Cheney, and others.

Monday, February 27, 1939 I took an Owl Club picture, ate lunch at the Deke House, talked to Susan from two until two thirty (in the car) and then met Frank Gunter and Alice Beasley and took pictures of her for a "Lady of the Bracelet" layout, in case she wins it. The voting takes place Wednesday. Uncle Walt came by and gave me a check for $71.00 for my winter term's tuition. Did not go to the frat. meeting tonight but stayed home and worked on my paper for Dr. Mims.

Tuesday, February 28, 1939 Talked to Robert Cooney Jr. about camp. Louis Davis was out there and we had a nice chat. Robert showed me his trains and other junk in the loft of their garage. He is a bright boy. Wrote the "Lady of the Bracelet" story tonight. I just hope Alice comes through okay in the election tomorrow. I called Susan and got the names of the W.S.G.A. members. On one occasion she called me by name "Ben." Girls don't realize how much it means to a man for a girl he really cares for to call him by his first name.

Wednesday, March 1, 1939 I heard John Temple Graves II speak. His dominant theme was "The Excellent and Full Life" closed by saying that some of the energetic young men in the Rotary Club are attempting to change the slogan of the (Alabama) state which is on the seal, "Here We Rest." Studied in the library with Susan until four o'clock this evening and then I went to the gym and wrestled Clark Hutton. He or Fred Gray are going to wrestle this Saturday.

Thursday, March 2, 1939 The Calumet Club met. O'Callaghan read a paper and Dr. Davidson took part in the discussion. The place of the critic was the keynote, Harris Abrahams and Morris Burk were inducted. I took the Zipper models out to Bob Chunn. I was quite depressed by the shabbiness of some of the houses lining the Saint Cecelia Street car line. Ate supper with Uncle Walt this evening. We did our cooking down at Aunt Nell's. The "Lady of the Bracelet" story came out okay yesterday. I was afraid of Betty Freeland's competition, but it turned out fine. I was never so relieved as when I got the final count and knew that Alice Beasley had won.

Wednesday, March 3, 1939 Susan is twenty today. I sent a birthday card merely expressing sentiments of birthday greeting, but that it means much more coming from me to you and that it is from one who cares. When I went out to see her tonight she said she received it. She also received a telegram from Virginia McClellan who drove to Knoxville to see the basketball game. Dave Patterson went with them. I gave Susan a copy of my patent. We sat in the club room and talked until ten o'clock and then went to the A.T.O.-Sigma Nu dance. Just before leaving for the dance I told Susan that I cared a whole lot for her and that I was ashamed of being so backward about telling her so. I was very clumsy in telling her this much and was afraid I was not going to get it out at all. I explained that it was a matter of too much caring. At this point she helped out by referring to Hamlet; "me think too much." There was plenty of room at the dance and Susan and I had a grand time. We got to dance a lot together. She was pretty tired when it was over. Her nose, which bled earlier in the day, started again.

Saturday, March 4, 1939 It rained. I came home early and took a nap and did a little studying. Bill Shumaker invited me to the wrestling meet, but the "Y" team had an accident at Crossville and did not get here in time. Several of the boys put on an "exhibition." Went to get Susan at nine. Bill and Edna Murray Davy went with me. Craig played the Strauss waltz for the second no-break. I was dancing with Miriam and Susan was dancing with Billy Fitzhugh. Later when I danced with Susan, she expressed the opinion that she wished they had saved it for the third (the one I had with her). I took Bill and Edna home first and then Susan. I unlocked the door and stepped just inside with her. This is the last date I will have with her before exams. I took her hand and drew her closer and gently kissed her and then said good night. I was "down in the dumps" yesterday evening but now I feel better. Susan's actions last night and tonight have made me feel that all is not hopeless.

Sunday, March 5, 1939 Dr. Mims spent a great deal of time in a recent class talking about imagination. He said that, except for faith, it is the most misunderstood word in the English language. Shakespeare's material man associates it with being a dreamer or a madman, or childish daydreams and fancies. But Charles Elliott, the President of Harvard, whom Mims calls the Prime Minister of Education, says the greatest need in education is the development of the imagination. Woodrow Wilson said: "No political parties succeed without appealing to the imagination." S. Parkes Cadman, in his Cole Lectures at Vanderbilt spoke of going beyond reason to intuition, as an aspect of imagination. Someone once said to the painter Turner: "I don't see the sunset as you do." To which Turner replied: "Don't you wish you could." Imagery in poetry is imagination in writing; subtle comparisons which bring out hidden shades of meaning; suggesting more than is actually said. Contrast the imagery in such writings as the Sermon on the Mount, with ordinary prose: "A city set on a hill," "A man built a house on the sand." What about this line: "A glowworm hidden in the realm of dew."

Monday, March 6, 1939 Miss "J" told me at noon today that she would write down something she wanted to tell me and would hand it to me tomorrow. I enjoy talking with Mr. Hill Turner, the Alumni Secretary, about my invention, or any other project we may be mutually interested in. He has been crippled all his life with one leg shorter than the other. He has to wear an elevated shoe. He is small in stature, but what a big man! He has the enthusiasm of a child, but the work he has done to create the benevolent gifts program at Vanderbilt, which he calls the Living Endowment, would make him a giant in any circle of achievement. What a wonderfully pleasant man to talk with occasionally.

Tuesday, March 7, 1939 We had our last meeting of the Honor Council before examinations. We have been able to clear the air, I think, and it will be a long time before cheating on examinations will be an acceptable practice to the student body. That was, and is, our objective. Studied in the library with Susan but Tom Scoggins was on one side and Billy Eason was on the other; a rose between two prickly thorns. This morning Miss "J" handed me that note she had promised. Here it is in full:

> *"Ben, I still don't know how to say what I want to, nor how to start. I wanted to talk with you the night of the Washington Ball, but I didn't know what to say to you at any time that night. Somehow or other I felt funny and never could get started.*
>
> *It all amounts up that I like you so much and I sort of thought you did me too, just from several things you said the first term, but maybe I was all wrong.*
>
> *Ben, you like Susan don't you? I can't blame you because she is so sweet.*
>
> *Life is funny. It doesn't work out like you would like to have it, but I guess it works out for the best and the good of all concerned, and no one can know just how that is going to be. It just wasn't meant that way.*
>
> *Ben, I love you, I love you with all my heart.*
>
> *Please don't laugh because I honestly mean everything I said to you before this and this too.*
>
> *I guess I've put things pretty bluntly, but I didn't know how else to say them.*

(My answer was as follows).

Dear Miss "J":
I assure you that I read with much tenderness and compassion your note this evening. It gave me a kind of sinking feeling and yet it flattered me tremendously to know that someone outside of my immediate family cares for me, a little anyway.

Miss "J", you know there was a touch of pathos in your note. I sometimes wonder why things have to be like they are. But, as you suggested it is all for the best.

Yes, I do love Susan, love her so much that I can hardly think of anything else. Not so long ago I attempted to tell her so and I didn't know how to begin. I stammered and stuttered and was actually ashamed of myself for being so awkward.

Why do we do these things? Why can't we fall in love with the person who loves us? When we do we get married though and I am sure neither of us are quite ready for that, yet.

A few years ago I was desperately in love with a girl who did not love me. For three years I worshipped at her shrine. I thought I could not bear to lose her. As long as I thought of her and her alone, I was in misery. But, finally I broke away, just as one would break a habit (just quit it) and I began to think about and to go with someone else. Before I knew it, the other girl no longer made me shed bitter tears.

It is a trying period we are passing through. I am just as miserable as you are—I am just as uncertain about the future—I dream and plan just as much as you do. I will be so glad when it is all over and I am married to someone that loves me and to the one I love. My mind will be much more at ease, I hope.

We are not by ourselves. I suppose all young people, at one time or another, experience the same things that we are going through now. O. O. McIntyre, the New York columnist, once wrote that this period was the most terrible one of his whole life.

I appreciate the frankness of your note and I have attempted to be just as frank and fair with you. I believe we, and everyone else, should be just that way.

You are an extremely nice person. I have been attracted to you and like you a great deal. I enjoy your company and like to be near you. But my heart is only large enough to love one woman at a time.

Believe me Miss "J" things are never as bad as they seem—you'll see things so differently a few years from now. You'll actually be surprised at yourself for giving a guy like me a second thought. Time alone is the great friend and savior of us all. Wait and see.

As ever,
Ben"

Classes as usual this morning. Saw Marcella Driskill in the student center this morning just after I had shaved and she commented to the Swords girl. "Look how clean he looks." I told her that I had something nice to say to her sometime soon and that I would not forget. Lunch at the Deke House after a conversation with Henry Clay. He is preparing to work for the telephone company. Wrote the letters asking for cooperation from the teachers on the exams. Dr. Reinke was in Dean Sarratt's office when I talked over the Honor System situation today. He offered the use of his mimeograph machine. Sat with Susan again in the library this evening. She was so pretty. She is getting to be a habit with me. After four o'clock I rode to town with Partee Fleming and saw "Huckleberry Finn." It was only fair.

Thursday, March 9, 1939 With my new pen my handwriting ought to improve. Susan told me this morning that she got her schedule finally completed and that she is going to be able to take the Bib. Lit. I am mighty glad because I'll enjoy being near her an hour each day. The "fly in the ointment" tho is that Billy Eason is also going to be in there and that is too much. Susan is going to the dance with Nello Andrews. Tom Scoggins took the dance list down from the S.A.E. bulletin board today and would not give it to me for the paper this evening or for a picture tonight. I was listening to the Maxwell House program on which Robert Taylor and other Hollywood stars appear. Frank Morgan referred to that "Luscious blend of coffee discovered by Joel Cheek." The words 'Maxwell House' suggest a wealth of rich tradition.

Friday, March 10, 1939 Thurston Whitaken said he appreciated the things Bob Foote and I said to him about Vanderbilt, that summer we were in camp together. He has just been given a scholarship of a thousand dollars per year for four years. He must practice medicine in a small town for three years upon graduation. Worked in the library this evening on my Public Speaking paper. Talked to Miriam on the phone tonight— made a date with her for a gym dance. She told me that Steve had gone to work for Jarman Shoe Company. He is in the advertising department under Tom Fuqua. Miriam asked me why I did not try to get on out there. She commented that Time Magazine pointed them out as the fifth largest shoe company in the world. Miriam said if I wanted to we would go by and visit Bob and his wife on the night of the Prom. I told her I thought it would be wonderful.

Saturday, March 11, 1939 I finished the Pub. Spk. paper and turned it in. Ate lunch at the house and went to town and saw George Bernard Shaw's "Pygmalion." Leslie Howard was a professor who was a specialist in phonetics. He took this girl and changed her manner of speech and passed her off for royalty within a period of six months. It was a very clever and different picture. Clark Hutton and I took Margaret Jackson with us. We just happened to meet her on the street. In the show the girl was completely dependent on him and he considered her a millstone about his neck. When she found out his one weakness, that he would have her do anything but go over to the opponent to work, she became independent of him. Then she was a real lady. Reminded me of "Gone with the Wind" 's ending.

Sunday, March 12, 1939 I worked on a history paper practically all day. Took a stroll down to Hillsboro this evening and when I saw that Bing Crosby in "Paris Honeymoon" was on at the Belmont, I decided to attend. It is the first time I have attended a Sunday movie in Nashville. Hit on a new Zipper improvement this morning about one o'clock. The idea is to put moving parts on the slider so that it will open and close easier. Talked to Miriam on the phone.

Monday, March 13, 1939 As I passed a record store this evening I noticed an album of Strauss waltzes (6 records), so I bought it. Think I'll give them to Susan as a present. She is very fond of the waltzes.

Tuesday, March 14, 1939 I studied all day, leaving the house only once or twice. I worked on the history paper until nine o'clock and then started working on my Biblical Literature paper. Got through with this at one o'clock. Called Susan earlier in the evening. She was not at home so Eleanor Richie and I had a chat. I made the third no-break with her for the tea dance.

Wednesday, March 15, 1939 I took the history exam and did fair on it. Bill Embry made a short speech about the Honor System. I was glad to see that Dr. Walker carried out the idea that was suggested in the letter. Ate lunch at the house and took the Bible examinations this evening. Went to town with Jim Browning to get a haircut.

Thursday, March 16, 1939 I ate lunch at the house and returned home to spend the rest of the night studying John Ruskin.

Friday, March 17, 1939 I saw cheating on Gus Dyer's exam. It was wholly unnecessary. The English exam this evening was a scorcher. I did not know a thing about it. As I left the room, Dr. Mims told me to come to his office and get the paper I turned in to him last week. He said, "You write so vividly that you ought to be more careful with your punctuation and spelling. Your exams show carelessness." Val Hain, Eddie Morton, and Bill Hume are here for the Prom series. At nine I went by to pick up Miriam. We got there about ten minutes before they started playing and got a kick out of seeing them tune up. Tommy Dorsey started out as usual with his "I'm Getting Sentimental Over You." The second piece he played was one of my favorites, "Tea for Two." Had the second no-break with Susan. They played "Heaven Can Wait." I enjoyed it tremendously. They played real long slow no-breaks. Had the third no-break with Shirley Caldwell. Kenneth and Mary Wallace rode home with Miriam and me. We went up to the restaurant across from the Hermitage and saw Tommy and his band again. They were eating a midnight snack (2:30 A.M.). We ate sandwiches and then went home.

Saturday, March 18, 1939 Today's dances were best of all. I escorted Susan. I went out to get her at four o'clock. She was not quite ready. Eleanor Richie was waiting for Nello Andrews. The tea dance was crowded but it was not too hot and the music was fine. Susan asked me to dance with Eleanor Richie. I did and then introduced several boys to her. The next time she said, "I saw what you did and thank you." Once when I was dancing with Eleanor Richie she asked me if a large number of Jews did not go to Vanderbilt. I told her yes and that lots of people had thought I was a Jew. E. R. said that people were forever calling her a little Jew girl. Danced the second with Miriam, "Heaven Can Wait" and the third with Eleanor. After the tea dance Susan and I went to the Deke House for the Dutch supper. Wilma Fite, one of the cutest girls in Birmingham was there with Harvey White. Dolly was there with George Morrow; Sarah Goodpasture with Joe Little; Dick Henderson with Alice Lewis and all the other regulars. Susan and I left early and went home for her to dress. Eleanor's second date and another girl were talking to Mrs. Cheek when we got there. Mrs. Cheek was telling about Mr. John writing for pictures of the family. He especially mentioned one of Mrs. Cheek about two years before they were married. Mrs. Cheek said it was so bad that Susan would not let her send it. Her mother and Susan both had told me to lie on the couch in the guest room and rest. I took them at their word and got so comfortable that I almost went to sleep. We got to the dance just after it had gotten well underway. I had the first and Student Council special with Susan. A number was dedicated to Francis Craig. As we were getting in the car to leave, Susan told me that Al Osborn had asked her to the Phi Psi dance next Friday and that she had accepted. Later she looked on her calendar and found she had a date with me. She asked me if I had just as soon come for dinner that evening so that she could go to the dance also. I told her that it sounded good to me. We went to Candyland and sat with Bill Shumaker and Edna Murray Davy. At the first dance Susan handed me a note with the words to the song "I Promise You" on it. I had asked her to make a copy of it. The first verse is as follows.

> "I promise you
> with heart sincere
> That I will always love you, dear
> and when you need me, I'll be near
> I promise you."

I told her, "Too bad that is just a song." She smiled sympathetically. It was about one o'clock when I took her home. I opened the door for and let her in. I stepped in . . . there was a slight pause. . . . The happiest moment of my life—an energetic K.

Sunday, March 19, 1939 I read the papers and walked up to the Albemarle tonight and talked with Uncle Walt and Aunt Nell. Had a splitting headache all evening. Answered the University of Illinois' questionaire about honor systems.

VANDERBILT CAMPUS ABUZZ WITH PLANS

FOR JUNIOR PROM

Vanderbilt students are getting themselves and the campus in general refurbished for the Junior Prom dance series to be given Friday and Saturday.

The series includes the Prom, the Pan-Hellenic tea dance and the Student Council dance.

At the upper left, John Hutton and Charles Beasley put in their bids for no-breaks with Elizabeth Surles and Carolyn Campbell. In the next picture Ed Wilson struggles with that too tight collar. Maurice Holdgraf and Marguerite Wallace, who will lead the Prom Friday evening, stroll across the campus. At the upper right, Madolyn Bidwell, Miss Vanderbilt of 1940, and Walter Parkes, Hustler editor, examine the cup Madolyn will receive—officially—at the Student Council dance Saturday evening.

In the second row, Henry Clay and Elaine Haile practice new dance steps as Catherine Simpson accompanies them, at the left; and Susan Cheek takes advice from Ann Stahlman on a Prom frock shopping tour, at the right.

Just below in the third row, Shelly Welch's Titian locks get a good scrubbing in preparation for the Prom, left; and Blair Batson, president of the Student Council, tacks up Hal Kemp's Orchestra poster as Helen McMurray, and Virginia Youmans look on, right. The orchestra will play for the entire series.

1. Left to Right—John Hutton, Elizabeth Surles, C. P. "Bud" Beasley and Carolyn Campbell. 2. Ben Austin teaching wrestling by the numbers. 3. Austin giving pointers to John Hutton and Kenneth Anderson. 4. Roy Huggins and Clark Hutton. 5. George Field and the varsity wrestling team. 6. The Turtle Trudge. 7. Henry Clay coming out of a "Giant Swing." 8. Ben Austin "rough-housing" with Shirley Caldwell on "Informal Day." 9. Charles Renfro, Jack Dempsey, Partee Fleming and Ben Austin.

SPRING

1939

Monday, March 20, 1939 I got a "B" on History and Public Speaking. I just did pass English though. Down at the Banner office today Mrs. Connoll mentioned something about my having a certain look in my eye while dancing with a certain girl at the dances Saturday night. She said Mrs. Bryon noticed it also. I don't know Mrs. Bryon but she told Mrs. Connoll she had heard of me. Mrs. Connoll tells me that Mrs. Bryon is one of Susan's mother's best friends. The Deke dance was decided on at a meeting tonight—for the 4th of April. I have a date with Susan anyway. I also have a date with her for the 14th.

Tuesday, March 21, 1939 At the first meeting of Bib. Lit. Susan got to the class just a little late. There was a vacant seat by me, and one by Billy Eason. Susan did some quick thinking and did not sit by either one of us, but took a front seat. When the class was over, Billy jumped up and walked over to where Susan was and started walking out with her and talking. They walked on over towards the bookstore and I went to the library. I think more of Susan than I do any other person in the world, yet I am not going to be so undignified as to tag along after her, nor am I going to quibble over the privilege of sitting by her. Wrestled with Clark Hutton today in the new gym.

Wednesday, March 22, 1939 Walter Stokes, tax commissioner in the previous state administration, spoke in chapel this morning. After it was over I went up front and listened to his answers to questions. Read Tennyson's "Princess" all evening. Just before going to gym I browsed

179

through some files of Harper's Weekly. The particular volume I looked at was for about 1832 or some date close to that. Thomas Nast the famous cartoonist was in full swing. Tilden was in politics. Many of Nast's cartoons concerned him. Bill Jordan came by the gym for me this evening. We went out for lunch and then down to the Vanderbilt hospital amphitheatre to hear Dr. Albert Szent-Györgyi, a Nobel prize-winner from Hungary for 1937. He is a famous biochemist. He discovered two vitamins. One of them is the famous vitamin "C" which is in cabbage. He started his experiments in this field when he began to wonder why people turned brown when they died and why some plants do the same and others do not. He found by mixing juices of those that do and those that do not, that neither turned brown for awhile. The difference was due to what came to be known as vitamins. Vitamins, he said, are a cog or wheel that can be taken from one machine (vegetables) and will fit into another (minerals). Called up Susan and made a no-break with her for the dance Friday evening. That is after I have dinner with her family. Billy Jordan said that Susan was the most civilized girl in Vanderbilt University. That, I think, sums it up pretty well.

Thursday, March 23, 1939 Susan came early and was in the second row with a vacant seat on each side of her when I got there. I sat down by her and in a few minutes Hartwell Weaver came in and sat on the other side. Eason had to sit in the front seat. As we were walking out Eason stepped in front of me at the first door. By the time we reached the second door he realized that he was a little rude at the first door so he stepped back gallantly at the second door and let me go out first. Gus Dyer gave us a cut so I went to the library and studied with Susan. She told me about her new car arriving. Located that Zipper cartoon that appeared in the New Yorker, February 26, 1938. Wrestled with Swiggart and then came home and ate a beefsteak. Mary Wallace showed me her gold miniature basketball for making varsity two years in succession. It was presented to her in chapel this morning.

Friday, March 24, 1939 I ate with the Cheeks this evening. It was the first time that I had eaten with them, other than at a party. I went out at six o'clock and Susan showed me the tennis court, garden, lawn, etc. They have quite a place there. At about six-thirty dinner was announced. Mrs. Glenn took a seat at the head of the table and I sat at her left. Susan, after calling Eleanor Richie, took a seat opposite Mrs. Glenn and Eleanor sat opposite me. The dinner was served in courses, chicken, cauliflower, butterbeans, celery, pickles, olives, coffee, Coca Cola, and ice cream with strawberries for our dessert. Mrs. Glenn told us about her activities in the D.A.R., her trip to Washington for the convention and how she thought people were foolish to spend all their time on studies; others things are equally important she contends. Eleanor Richie had a headache and was not very talkative. Neither Susan nor Eleanor ate as much as Mrs. Glenn and me. I don't know but what she kept eating just to keep up with me; to be sociable, so to speak. After eating, Susan and I connected up Eleanor's phonograph and played dance records. We danced and talked until about eight-thirty. I came home and wrote part of the fraternity chapter letter and then went over to the Phi Kappa Psi dance. I was enthusiastic over the start that I had made on the letter and was feeling fine. Susan said she had a slight fever, but she danced well. Eason showed up right before intermission. During intermission, I went with Harris Abrahams to the Tally-ho and then to the Noel Hotel to see Miss Battle. One of her classes was having a soirée. Saw Gilbert Dickey.

Saturday, March 25, 1939 I got to class early. Susan and Eason came in later. Susan came on back and sat where she did yesterday, by me, and Eason sat on the front row again. When the class was over, Eason walked on out and to his class without waiting to talk to Susan. I have never seen him do that before. Dr. Dyer discussed the wage situations in the South in his lecture and also advised that manufacturing plants should be built in small towns rather than large ones. I made my first speech in Mr. Miller's Public Speaking class this morning. When I first got up, my knees were shaking so much I could not stand still. It seemed that the whole room was being shaken by my vibrant motions. I paid as little attention to it as I could though, and proceeded to drive home point after point about the little group that I am planning on organizing for visiting different industrial plants around Nashville. I was vitally interested in the subject and before I was through with my speech I had overcome the nervousness and had gotten over more fully my points. After the speech was over, Mr. Miller said that it was the best speech that had ever been given by any student at the opening of his course. He said it was a good example of the fact that "It can be done."

"When he started out," said Mr. Miller, "I saw how ferociously his knees were shaking, but it did not upset him. Most people would have stopped, but it seems that Mr. Austin is not made of that "kind of stuff." He showed us he could think on his feet, despite handicaps. He completely mastered the nervousness." I appreciated that, especially since it came from Mr. Miller. It is better to attempt to overcome such an embarrassment rather than to live with the memory of failure. Enjoyed a talk with Mr. Hill Turner. Mr. Williams, the unversity bursar, joined us later.

Sunday, March 26, 1939 Had tea with Jordan at four. I fixed his radio, phonograph for him and we played my six records of Strauss waltzes. "Vienna Blood" and "Artist's Life" are my favorite. I am going to give them to Susan as a present. I know her favorite is waltzes. As Bill and I were playing them this evening, telephoned Susan and let her listen to parts of them. I told her to be good and I would present them to her next Firday evening. I helped Bill clean up his room and then he drove with me to Uncle Walt's. Uncle and I discussed a few philosophical points. I suggested this: A radio, by itself is no miracle, nor is a transmitter in a distant city so much of a miracle. But, when the two are coordinated; when voices are picked up a thousand miles from where they are spoken, you have a miracle. So it is with man in his relation with God. Man unto himself is nothing but when in harmony and coordination with God he has infinite capabilities.

Monday, March 27, 1939 I wrestled Billy Swiggart this afternoon and got kicked in the head. The blow raised a big bump. Mailed the Quarterly letter to D.K.E. headquarters tonight.

Tuesday, March 28, 1939 After lunch at the fraternity house I took George Morrow with me to see Bob Chunn. Forty people attended the wrestling banquet tonight. From the faculty were Dr. Tom Zerfoss, Dean Lewis, Dr. Fishel, Dean Pomphret and Sarratt; Professor Robins, Jim Buford and the man from Peabody who refereed for us, Mr. Andrews. They gave only ten letters this year (I was not one) and Bud Bray was elected captain. Telephoned Susan and had a nice comforting chat with her. I did not laugh boisterously as I am in the habit of doing. I've got to break myself of that. Partee Fleming called me "cackle" Austin tonight. That's an awful adjective to use in connection with a person; not dignified to say the least. Funny how I took the lead in seeing that everything went well for everyone else at the wrestling banquet this evening and my own head was put on the chopping block. Discussed with Lorraine Regen this evening the very serious subject of marriage. She said she did not know of any person who could live with her. "I am too mean," she said. She also said that she could not be happy if she had to worry about security. We both agreed that the present economic condition is hard on youth. It is preventing early marriages.

Wednesday, March 29, 1939 Mickey Carmichael told me he felt that Tuck and I got a raw deal on the wrestling letters last night. Bill Shumaker came to me in the library and said it was the dirtiest deal he had heard of. He said that I had done more for Vanderbilt wrestling than any man on the team. Partee Fleming told me that he did not understand why Buford did not give the letter. He pointed out that I had wrestled in five meets. To all of these I counselled that it did not make any difference and to forget it. Funny thing, the Banner copied the Tennessean story this morning and spliced my name in. They evidently thought it was a mistake.

If outsiders caught the mistake immediately, why didn't Jim Buford who was on the scene? Jim is a peculiar fellow.

Thursday, March 30, 1939 Partee Fleming told me today he had had a talk with Jim Buford and that I was going to get my letter. They say it was a misunderstanding. The committee thought I only wrestled in two meets. At the Sigma Chi dance tonight I saw Joe Little and he told me about having a talk with Jim Buford. He said Mr. Buford wanted me to come to see him. I was reading "In Memoriam" tonight; finally decided to call Susan and ask her if she would be at the Sigma Chi dance. She said she would and she insisted that I come. I decided in favor of going so I started dressing at nine o'clock. Talked to John Caldwell on the streetcar. He is with the United Press. Got to dance with Susan quite a bit. She had a couple-bid with Billy Eason. I had Gunter take a picture of Ross Hanna and Ed Hunter. Ross was unanimously elected captain of the basketball team tonight. Rode home with Trimmier McCarley, Tom Shea, Buddy Stone, and Jack Foley.

Friday, March 31, 1939 Took the waltz album to Susan. We went back to the room at the end of the hall and played them. The room was pretty chilly and at ten-thirty Susan made me go. We played the pieces, listened to Guy Lombardo and then I showed her the analysis of my handwriting. The statement written by Dorothy Carner was as follows: "Clever and discerning mind, adaptable and versatile, but with good concentration, too. Somewhat nervous energy. (It is possible that you start things with more enthusiasm than you finish them) Very good at organizing and composing material. Somewhat impulsive in affections." In the chart she had "law" "literary" checked as traits. "Parting," as Shakespeare put it, "is such sweet sorrow."

Saturday, April 1, 1939 At the Banner office Tommy Morris showed me through the plant. Saw them make up the front page; make a mat of it, mold the metal into cylinders for the giant presses which turn out 10,000 papers per hour. They come out folded and ready to be distributed. The engraving room pleased me most of all. I studied very carefully how the pictures were taken in and put through the various stages to be made into a cut. Went to the dance at the gym tonight. Danced with Susan quite a bit, as usual. Eleanor Richie and I were talking about how one person in a family gets all the brains. She said "Like Susan and me for example." Dudley Burton was her date. Talked about Henry Clay when I danced with Katie Heitzburg.

Sunday, April 2, 1939 Homer Howell and Walter King went with me to the political meeting at the S. A. E. house. It was a very interesting meeting. Harris Abrahams was elected President of the Senate for next year. I took Homer Howell and Bud Beasley in on my Industrial Tour idea. They both like it. Bill Jordan and I discussed the possibility of forming a new political party in the South. To regain the past glories of our section. He said that Professor Owsley and Davidson are in favor of it. Read Bertrand Russell's essay "The Free Man's Worship" tonight.

Monday, April 3, 1939 We had an Honor Council trial today and voted to exclude R. from school for another term. He will be eligible to return next fall. I talked to Dean Sarratt and Pascall and both agreed on the sentence as just. Talked over my Industrial Tour idea with Mr. Hill Turner this evening and he agreed that it was a good idea. Went by to see Chancellor Carmichael in afternoon about the Honor Committee funds. He instructed Mr. Williams to pay the account. Dr. Mims was in the outer office when I came out this evening. I suppose Susan got my little note this evening saying, "I love you."

Tuesday, April 4, 1939 Dr. Mayhew gave us a cut in Bib. Lit. Susan and I went over to the Student Center and talked to Billy Eason while he ate breakfast. Then we went to the library. Susan sat right across from me and I noticed her staring into space instead of studying for her quiz. This was the first time she had seen me since I wrote her that letter and she was probably thinking about it. This evening I passed Susan's car and went on up to the library to study. In a little while Susan came up and we studied together until four o'clock. Tonight, Uncle Walt let me have his new Pontiac which he bought today and I drove Susan to the Deke Barn dance. We had a nice time and got home about 1:30 A.M. The only bad part about the dance was the dust brought in by the hay.

Wednesday, April 5, 1939 Susan told me Willie Cornelius asked us to come to the Delta Sig dance but that she was afraid he would forget to bring the ticket. We first went to hear Bertrand Russell at Vanderbilt speak on "Power and Propaganda." We then went to the Student Center for the bid that Willie was to leave for us and then went on to the dance. I got to dance with Susan quite a bit, but not a single no-break. Had a nice short chat with Elizabeth Craig. She seems to be a really fine girl. Bun Dudley was her date. I had the second no-break with E. R. Saw Billy Whitson who was here from Mc Minnville. It was raining when Susan and I left for home. I did not hold her hand or anything on the way home. When we got there though I made the motion to kiss her good-bye. She very bashfully refused. I asked her why she refused and she merely blushed and turned her head to one side. I kissed her hand and said good-bye. I don't understand her actions. Guess I'll have to ask her how much she cares for me, if any. Got to sleep about four o'clock.

Thursday, April 6, 1939 Uncle Walt and I left at nine this morning for Stevenson. Stopped in Manchester for lunch, where we saw Dr. Zerfoss and Tom Bagley who were there on a fishing trip. We also saw

Dick Smith Jr. Drove about 40 m.p.h. all the way. Got there about two o'clock. I went to Hollywood for a date with Grace Jacobs.

Friday, April 7, 1939 I drove Mother and Dad to Chattanooga to see the Baylor T. M. I. track meet. Henry D. ran both the half and the mile. Last week in the intersectional meet Henry ran anchorman on the relay team and took the baton 30 yards behind the last man and with 70 yards left in the mile race and won by about 30 yards. The Free Press played him up as a hero. It was quite a remarkable feat and the people up there are still talking about it. The Free Press also mentioned about his being a Golden Glove Champion. Ross Endsley says he can pick the record that he wants to break at the state meet and break it. Cassavant was with Henry all evening and coached him on his run. We had a nice drive home. Had a talk with Gene Henninger, Sidney Ballard, and Walter Bogart, Jr., tonight.

Saturday, April 8, 1939 Talked to Mrs. Gracie Huddleston about some of her girlhood friends which included Paul M. Davis, President of the American National Bank. Wilson is now five feet eight inches tall and weighs 130 lbs. Anderson and Henry D. drove in this evening. Henry went by to see Mary Elizabeth Talley. I went to the Eastern Star function with George L., Betsy and Louise Bogart. We danced until twelve thirty. Ran into Fred Cargill and his wife, Cam Mac Talley, W. J. Talley, Freda Atwood, Walter Bogart and five boys from Tulane. I danced once with Freda. Betsy Bogart and I had a few dances.

Sunday, April 9, 1939 The sun came out bright and we had a pleasant Easter. Had a lengthy chat with Anderson, Geo. L. Jr., Henry D., Wilson, Dad and Mother. Walter Bogart Jr., came in later and joined the conversation. Enjoyed a nice Sunday dinner and caught the Dixie Flyer for my home in Nashville. Sat with Herbert Dunkerley. Saw Dr. Sanborn, the philosophy professor, on the train. Eleanor Richie Cheek was meeting somebody at the station in Nashville.

Monday, April 10, 1939 Showed Mr. Hill Turner my letter about the turtle races and we made plans immediately for Vanderbilt eliminations. Discussed the idea with Rousseau Duncan, City Editor of the Banner and he agreed so Hilliard Wood and I went to the campus and took pictures of Jane Vick and Elaine Haile weighing in the turtles. We also took one of Dr. Tom Zerfoss looking at one through his glass for dope possibilities. At the fraternity meeting tonight I made a political report and announced that Charles Majors would be our candidate for Bachelor of Ugliness. On second thought I realized that I should not have made it so easy for Charley. I should have let the fraternity select their candidate. They might have selected someone else. I am not so sure Charley deserved it handed to him on a silver platter. On the phone I asked Susan what she had been doing and her sense of humor showed through. "One night I went to the Delta Sigma dance and on another night I went to hear a man speak." I told her the D.K.E.–S.A.E. dance was scheduled for May 5th.

Tuesday, April 11, 1939 It was raining when I awoke this morning so I did not get the Turtle Trudge story to the Banner until ten o'clock. Susan was at school early and her hair was fixed differently. She had some little curls up on top. The teacher mentioned something about marriage and Hartwell Weaver, who was sitting on the other side of us, leaned over and whispered: "You and Ben ought to listen to this carefully." Susan blushed. I knew that the Theta Phis, her prep school sorority, were having their dance on the 12th of May, so I asked Susan if we could still have our date on that night. "That will be fine," she said. In a few minutes she said: "I have something to ask you. The Theta Phis are having their dance on the 10th and I want you to take me." In a few more minutes she seem startled and said: "No, it is on the 12th." I said, "That'll be no problem, we'll combine the two." We were both successful. I got my date with her and she got credit for asking me to her prep school sorority dance. I wrote an article for "Pursuit" condemning our attitude towards the war situation.

Wednesday, April 12, 1939 Had the first Turtle Trudge today and it was a huge success. Everything went off perfectly and the story made the front page of the afternoon Banner. John Shumaker came out and wrote a fine story and Hilliard Wood took some good pictures. Just after chapel the students gathered outside the ropes, around a ten foot ring, and the overflow crowd hung out of windows in Alumni Hall. We waited just long enough to ignite the firecracker, which set the turtles "off" and the race was over in about a minute. "Cap" Taylor kept the crowd well in hand. After the race I went to town and talked with Mr. Shyer, who agreed to donate a cup to the winner. Loews theatre gave six tickets to first place winner, four to second and two to third. My suspense was broken tonight in a telephone conversation with Susan. She asked me for the second no-break for her dance Saturday night. Woe is me! That means I am not taking her. I guess Nello Andrews is since he has had her to several dances and I don't think she has asked him a single time. Guess she's returning his favors.

Thursday, April 13, 1939 Dr. Mims was saying recently that Robert E. Lee was one of the great men of all times, but he did not have the power of expressing a thing finally, as Lincoln did. Lincoln's great use of figurative language was superb: "A house divided . . ." His simple stories had a quality that wasn't even present in Christ's parables, humor. And when he died it could be said of him: "And when some lordly cedar goes down with a shout into the hills and leaves a lonesome place against the sky."

Friday, April 14, 1939 Took the English exam and did better than
before. Headlines in the Hustler announced Charles Majors as the B.U.
candidate but Rousseau Duncan of the Banner did not print my story
on Majors. After talking to Jitney players and picking up my laundry
Jordan and I went to Loews to see "Wuthering Heights." It was a very
dramatic picture of a man who remained a servant so he could be near
the woman he loved. Circumstances led her to marry a wealthier man
and Laurence Olivier who was playing the leading man went away to
America, made his fortune and came back to marry the wealthy lord's
sister. He did it because Merle Oberon, the leading lady would not
come back to him. On her death bed, their spirits were again united.

I was late getting to Susan's tonight. She met me at the door in a
very pretty red dress with, black dancer, cutouts on it. Susan was gayer
than usual this evening. I have never seen her so alluring and tantalizingly
attractive. We sat down in the front room and began to talk. In a few
minutes she said, "There is something about me that you haven't noticed." I said, "Oh no, there isn't. I have noticed all along but I just
haven't said anything." She remembered that I had once said that I
did not like complicated hairdos. I told her that as a rule I do not like
fancy hairdressing, but, that there were exceptions to the rule and I
like it as a change, but not as a permanent thing. In a few minutes we
discussed how hard it is to be frank and to discuss things freely with
people you really care for. She said that when she was by herself she
could think of so many things she would like to say, but that she had
trouble when it came to saying it. There was a very long period in
which neither of us spoke. We just sat and stared into space, my own
heart was pounding and she swallowed with difficulty. We then went
to the room where Eleanor Richey's phonograph is connected and played
a few records. Her new favorite is "Our Love." She played that first.
When she played "Hold Tight" she referred to the girl who sang in
Ted Weem's orchestra and said that every time she started singing,
the boy she was dancing with made a break for the orchestra stand. "I
couldn't compete with her" she said. After playing the best of the Strauss
waltzes we sat down again. I told her the letter I wrote her awhile back
was an expression of my real feelings. She said she did not know for
certain until then and that she had already asked someone else to the
Kappa Alpha Theta dance. "Who?" I asked. When she told me Bill
Eason I thought I would fall through the floor. I have never in my life
been so shocked. This makes the second time in succession. I would
have thought nothing about it had it been somebody that she was obli-
gated to, but Eason, of all people. I could not say a word for several
minutes. Finally I asked her who she really cared for. She said she didn't
know, but that there was no one she likes better than me. She said

that one reason she asked Billy was that he fits in with only a small group of people that know him and that I fit in with any group I happen to find myself in. That is why she asked him to the Vanderbilt dance and asked me to the Theta Phi dance at the club on May 12th. Coming on back from drinking a couple of Coca Colas at the Stork Club I told her that I ought not to go to the dance tomorrow night. She said it would ruin the dance for her if I took that stand. Said that she had made arrangements for the orchestra to play "Our Love" on the second no-break. Her dad has returned from the hospital and she is very careful about getting home on time. When I said good night I asked her for a parting kiss. She refused. I said "Don't you want to?" "It's not that ———I just want to be absolutely sure before I do." I went to the Phi dance after leaving her.

Saturday, April 15, 1939 I sat by Susan in class. I walked with her to her car, between classes, to get a Public Speaking book. She thought she had forgotten it but she promised to bring it Monday. Dr. Mayhew promised me a check for $100.00 on the first of the month for one share in the invention. Saw Bitsie Grant and Joe Davis play tennis this evening. Grant is one of the top flight players in the nation yet Joe won seven and Bitsie won seven before the rain started. Went to the dance at ten o'clock. Saw Mr. and Mrs. John Cheek there but I did not get to speak to them. They stayed only a few minutes. Sure enough they played "Our Love" for the second no-break but they played "Theta Lips" for the special and a Strauss waltz for the fourth. Nello had this one with Susan and I had it with Peggy Norvell. I did not dance with Susan as much as usual. After the dance I went down and had a talk with Anglin. Francis Craig came in and looked over the Hustler. He asked who Major's opponent was. They told him "Boss" so being a true Phi he made the statement that the Phi candidate would win. Anglin informed him that I was Major's campaign manager. Craig and I made a little bet of four dollars on the election. Craig read on down the column and came to the turtle racing article. When he started to make an announcement about that they (Anglin and Walter Parks) pointed to me again and said "Austin managed that too." At this point Craig said, "What about managing my orchestra. We need a good agent and big money could be made out of it."

Sunday, April 16, 1939 I read the papers and wrote letters all day. Jordan came by to see me at six-thirty.

Monday, April 17, 1939 I woke up from a terrible dream tonight. It was thundering and lightening, and storms and cyclones were reported in the morning paper. I dreamed "Flip" Timberlake came to see me. In the dream he was a dope fiend and somehow or other I got doped up too. We were in the little bedroom at Stevenson but instead of sleep-

ing we got up and began to stagger around. We, of course, woke the
family up and when they came back to the room I tried to tell them
what was happening but the dope paralyzed my vocal cords and I could
not say a word. I woke up as I was struggling to get the words out. I
was half frightened. It is on such occasions that one longs for human
companionship; for someone to put one's arms about. I saw Miriam
McGraw in the library today. She was writing a poem for English IX
and let me read it. The theme of the poem was that she did not sit
and stare and dream of her love. She thinks of him only when she
reads a good book or visits a beautiful flower garden that she knows
he would appreciate. In the first fraternity meeting tonight we took
another vote on whether or not the meeting was to be moved back to
7:30. Bob Neathery made the motion and got mad when it failed to
carry. I got up and asked for a revote on the grounds that there was
no discussion on the measure. I explained why it was a hardship on
the boys who live in town to get to the meeting 30 minutes earlier.
Browning and Tuck expressed similar sentiments and the group reversed
their stand. Rode home with Stone and Shay.

Tuesday, April 18, 1939 I missed Dyer's class this morning. I slept
right through it. They tell me he gave a quiz and everyone got up and
walked out without taking it. I studied in the library today until four.
Susan came in and sat by me until about three. We were not very talkative.
She then had to go to the Theta House. I gave her 75¢ for her Public
Speaking Book. Partee Fleming came home with me this evening and
ate dinner. He stayed around until nearly midnight.

Wednesday, April 19, 1939 The Freshmen and Sophomores selected
Student Union, Council and Honor Council representatives today. I
was in charge of the Sophomore academic class elections. I had to explain
to a very large gathering the procedure to be followed. The Senate
won every office and Ray Manning gave me pictures of all of the candidates of whom we did not already have cuts or pictures.

We ran the nine winners this evening. The first Vanderbilt industrial
tour composed of eleven boys whom I picked and invited to go with
us. Went to the General Shoe Company this evening at two o'clock
and Harold Finnon showed us through the plant. The group was composed of Richard Donaldson, Homer Howell, Walter King, Jack Foley,
Buddy Stone, Jim Reed III, Francis Dority, Henry Clay and Mose Waller.
Mr. Alford is the man we contacted. He is personnel manager. They
employ about 1,500 people in this plant and turn out 550 dozen pairs
of shoes per day. I had no idea there were so many processes in the
making of shoes. All of the boys seemed to enjoy the trip very much
and are looking forward to our DuPont trip next week. Dean Sarratt
says he may go with us next Wednesday. Uncle Walt came by this evening

and showed me Rebecca's letter asking aid for getting her degree. He suggested that she do the work at Peabody, which is sensible. Jordan also dropped in.

Thursday, April 20, 1939 I went to the library at nine and sat with Virginia McClellan. Susan passed by the table while I was talking to Virginia and went to the very back of the room and sat down. I remained seated. In a little while Susan went out of the library and came back in a few minutes and sat down in the same place. At the very end of the hour I walked back and visited with her for a few minutes. Changed my date with her for a no-break tomorrow night from the 2nd to the 4th. We talked of the picture "Wuthering Heights." Said she cried at the end. She was sweet and talkative and looked nice. I made a sorry speech before the class this morning. I almost forgot my speech. I stammered around for awhile and picked up the threads. Read the section devoted to Louisville in the book "Five Cities" by George R. Leighton. The story of how Rogers Caldwell traded stocks with Jim Brown, head of Banco Kentucky and left him "holding the bag" was an interesting story. Read the chapter on Birmingham last night. Had a conference with Fred Russell this evening. He told me that they have about a thousand of the football books left. I was surprised. He discussed with me a little plan that he has "up his sleeve" for conducting a campus poll regarding the popularity of the various features and items in the newspapers of Nashville. I am going to conduct the poll for him. He showed me a check for $500.00 from the Saturday Evening Post for the articles on Major Bob Neyland which they are going to run next fall. Bill Embry came by and borrowed $2.00 from me today. He got back in school but the Deans are down on him. The trouble with Bill is that he stays up all night and then can't get to class the next day. Van Irving brought his photography equipment by and took a picture of a Zipper on a busted suitcase tonight.

Friday, April 21, 1939 In the library Shirley Caldwell was writing a poem for a three o'clock class under Dr. Donald Davidson. I had a very interesting discussion with her as to what poetry writing is. I maintained that the trouble with most beginning writers is that they don't know what they are trying to do. They don't analyze the situation. As I see it a person should set about writing a poem as follows: First he should be impressed by some phenomenon and then set about to transfer a similar impression to others. He should have in mind his audience always to whom he is writing the poem. If it is too vague or subtle, if they do not follow through on the poem, it has not accomplished its main purpose and is a failure. Had a date with Virginia Richey this evening. Bill Jordan dated "Droopy" Elaine Ewald. They wanted to go see John Barrymore. It was eight when we got there. I finally won out.

We did not go. Drove out to Lynnwillow Lunch Room, danced for a few minutes, by the Phi Kappa Sigma Fraternity House and then to Candyland. After taking the dates home Bill and I went to the Beta Bowery Ball. I had the fourth no-break with Susan. She told me of having a new combination Victrola and radio and that it really sounds good. Said that she had been playing her waltz pieces. Said her dad and mother are going to Florida next week. Partee Fleming brought me home and we talked politics. His fraternity wants to get on the winning side.

Saturday, April 22, 1939 Dr. George Mayhew's father died last week and instead of giving us a quiz he gave us a cut. Susan and I went to the library to study and Billy Eason came along a little later. After talking with Susan a few minutes he said: "I notice you have on the same blouse today that you had on last night." Susan blushed and I could tell she was furious. Her reply was: "You don't look so different yourself." Ate a steak dinner with Bill Jordan at the Brass Rail, Andrew Jackson's stables.

Sunday, April 23, 1939 At the political meeting at the Sigma Chi House today I said I didn't think we ought to offer the Medical School students a keg of beer as a bribe for their votes in the B.U. election. Everybody else did, so I dropped the matter. Rode home with Belford Lester. Saw George Nelson and Jimmy Stewart in Hillsboro and Jimmy was telling me that his mother's bakery bankrupted a month ago. They expanded to 25 trucks and could not meet the overhead. When I told him something about my idea for going into business for myself he said: "Do it if you want to grow old quickly."

Monday, April 24, 1939 We got a cut in English today because Dr. Mims' mother died. Dr. Mims, himself, is getting up in years so his mother must have been 90 years old. I am always undecided about what to do right after lunch each day. I always have more to do than I can get done so I usually go to the library and hope that Susan will be there. I do get some studying done. Dyer said that Martin Luther was a 19th child and Enrico Caruso was a 17th child. He told the story of two Negroes who were robbing a hen house. The conscience of one of them began to hurt so he said: "Sam, I don't like what we are doing. It ain't right." "That's the moral question. This is a provisional one."

Tuesday, April 25, 1939 The Biblical Literature examination was harder than they have been up to this time. Susan and I went to the Student Center for refreshments and then studied in the library. Eason, of course, came along eventually. Susan was answering the questions asked on the typical coed questionnaire. She prefers marriage over a career; would get married before she gets her degree; would help husband by getting a job, if necessary; does not lose her temper on provocation; does not believe in extensive wardrobes; would not marry for money; thinks three children make the ideal family and thinks personal appearance more important than intellectual achievement. I was interested in her answer to the one about marriage. Harold Nichols and Jack Benton came by to see me about contributing three dollars to the Kappa Phi prep school fraternity dance scheduled for the 19th of May. I agreed. I talked to them about getting Hal Hemp on an adjoining date with the D.K.E.-S.A.E. dance.

Wednesday, April 26, 1939 The History midterm. was pretty stiff this morning. Our political organization made a clean sweep of the elections. Mr. Fitzgerald Hall, President of the L. & N. railroad, pointed out in chapel how the government discriminates against the railroads. He said that six million dollars were paid in taxes last year but that not one cent could be paid to the stockholders. He admitted that the railroads were pretty high-handed when they had a monopoly. He said: "We may have waited too long for reform." Last week Gus Dyer was telling of his experiences with some bankers and industrialists. He said that P. D. Houston was a pet of Mr. Watts, who was his mentor in Houston's rise to prominence; and took him to New York but Watts was not connected with the Chemical National Bank, which Houston headed. In telling the story about Harry K. Thaw killing Stanford White he said that a professor who once lived there said that the only thing he had against Harry Thaw was that he did not kill him before he designed Kissam Hall. He told the story of Fourier, who bought 30 thousand acres of land in New Harmony, Indiana and set up a Socialist party. He did away with competition. It lasted only a few months. Brooks Farms, sponsored by Horace Greeley, was a similar Fourier Society which lasted a short time. Ruskin Cove, Tennessee lasted two years. This is the story of Socialist operations throughout history.

Thursday, April 27, 1939 I went to the Banner and was thirty minutes late getting to class. Susan had her books lying on my desk so that no one would sit there. She is so sweet. Today in the Public Speaking class, which was held in Alumni Hall, I gave a nominating speech for Charles Majors. Mr. Miller spent quite a while discussing the organization and the use that I had made of psychological points suggested in our chapter. He complimented the platform manner and movements. "It was as if he were reasoning with us rather than lecturing." He did not overlook however the awkward spots; in voice and movements. Immediately following my speech, Thurston Whitaker nominated a boy, whom he had been associated with at camp, for the President of the School. He said that the boy had been selected President of the Honor Council at Vanderbilt and even though he knew he was making enemies of a certain element, he pushed through a rigorous campaign for raising the moral standards at this institution and accomplished his purpose. Funny how a speech like that, when it is entirely voluntary and spontaneous intensifies your admiration for that person. It is like Dr. Gus Dyer says, we all crave recognition. Sat with Susan a few minutes in the library this evening. I took pictures to Mr. Rousseau Duncan and had a chat with Fred Russell. Showed him a copy of my speech about Charles. He said it was a perfect angle on him. The Calumet Club meets tonight.

Friday, April 28, 1939 The Typical Coed story appeared in the Banner this evening, but it had been rearranged so I hardly recognized it. It was a mess. I usually call Susan the night before I have a date with her, but the Calumet Club meeting prohibited this last night. Tonight when I was in the tub bathing the thought struck me all of a sudden there would be something wrong when I called Susan. When I finished, and just before leaving, I called Susan and asked her what time I should come. She said, "What!" in astonishment. She said that she did not have me on her calendar for a date tonight. Said that "Johnny Platt is downstairs now." I told her that it was okay because it was probably my mistake, anyway. Bill Jordan dropped in just as I was leaving. Said his telephone had been ringing all night and that he came over to my apartment to study, to get away from it. Said that he was in the lowest mood that he had been in in years. We talked for an hour about politics, fraternities, and his outlook brightened. He said that he and I ought to go into politics. I left him in my apartment at nine o'clock and I went to the Tri Delta open house. Had a nice time dancing with Miriam. Kirkpatrick was her date. Ross Hanna tickled me to death, throwing a fit, while he was dancing with one of the Ole Miss girls. He liked to have scared her to death. She was trembling all over when they got through dancing. I then went out to the Kappa Delta Theta dance at the club. Had the second no-break with Elizabeth Hall. I told her how much I enjoyed her dad's speech in chapel last Wednesday. Ed Pardue was her date. Craig's music was really slick tonight. Saw Nello Andrews at the dance. Said he had wasted an evening since Susan was not there. Henry Clay rode home with me and we talked until nearly one o'clock. He told me that Jack was going to interview some boys for the bank and that he had asked about me. I told him that I was going to go to law school for a year though. Henry told me he and Katie were going to play tennis with Billy Eason and Susan tomorrow afternoon. That news does not make me mad, but it does depress me.

Saturday, April 29, 1939 Susan and I did not mention our last night's mix-up on our date schedule. We had our usual discussion as if nothing had happened. We held our Public Speaking class in Neely Auditoriun this morning. I spoke on James Stahlman's dedication speech of a half nude statue at the World's Fair to "Freedom of the Press." I took the angle that a "freedom" of the press has become license when it attempts to stir up a nation to a white heat over a war situation which is unreal. I spoke better than usual but my ideas were not as well connected as they might have been. Later on I made my presentation speech. I started out by saying, "I want to present this audience an idea. An idea which, perhaps should have come to me years ago but for some reason or other has only come to my mind recently. That idea is the value of the Bible as great literature." I spoke for a few minutes and then asked them to follow the picture drawn in the twenty-third Psalm as I quoted. It made a hit with Mr. Miller. He said that he is always glad when some student gives a speech on something that particularly interests him. We get some of our best speeches on these occasions. This evening I went to the Knickerbocker to see Charles Boyer and Irene Dunne in "Love Affair". He was to marry a rich industrialist's daughter, but meets Irene on the ship and falls in love with her. Just before parting they promise to meet each other six months hence in the top of the Empire State building and marry. On her way there Irene is hit by an automobile and paralyzed from her hips down. She refused to let him know anything about it. After a very romantic scene in which she sat on the sofa, (he did not know she could not get up) he finally found out that she was paralyzed and then they made up and were married. The keynote song in the picture was "Keep on Wishing," and if you wish long and hard enough your wishes will come true. I knew that it would be no use for me to try to study knowing that a certain tennis match was in progress at the very time I was supposed to be studying. That is why I went to the show. After returning home I had to go to the library to return a book. I saw Katie Heitzburg just after she had brought Henry and Billy home. She waved at me. Read in the paper this evening that Mr. William Dan Majors, 57 had been arrested along with three others on charges of embezzling $80,000 from the Ripley bank. I don't believe Mr. Majors would have voluntarily taken money. He seemed too fine a man. When I was at the house last night Charles was dressing. I asked him if he was going to the dance. "No," he said, "I am going home on the late bus." I told him to tell his dad hello for me and that if he ran across any old money to let me know. Strange that I should mention money at this particular time. Of all the times for a thing like this to get out, just before the election which is to bestow on Charles the highest office in the school. My sympathy goes out to Charles and his family. Mary Wallace tells me that she and Bill Jordan rode down to the drugstore for a Coca Cola last night. He stayed until eleven o'clock. I walked down to the drugstore tonight. On the way back I happened to glance

up into a second story window and saw a couple in a long embrace. I
suppose they were newly married. Surely they don't carry on like that
year in and year out. I envied him though.

Sunday, April 30, 1939 This had been a beautiful day. I spent the
bulk of it in my room reading Browning. Called Susan and had her
get out her date book and check with me on our future dates. They
checked okay. I mentioned to her about the house party but I did not
ask her to give a definite answer. She said that she had also stayed in,
studying, this evening. At seven o'clock this evening, after I had spent
the whole afternoon studying, I decided to call up Virginia Richey for
a picture show date tonight. She had just returned from a weekend
outing with one of the clubs but she consented to the date. We went
to see Claudette Colbert and Don Ameche at the Paramount in "Midnight". It was one of the funniest shows I have seen in years. After
the show we drove out to the Toddle House and after talking for an
hour or so, called it a night. For the past few days I have been a bit
despondent about my affairs along romantic lines so I welcomed the
opportunity to cry on an understanding shoulder. Realizing all the while
that it was dangerous business, this sob story stuff, I indulged just
the same. We had a very delightful evening. Next Saturday night when
I take her to the gym dance she promises that she will tell me her
troubles.

Monday, May 1, 1939 Nello Andrews and I rode to town on the
streetcar today. He says that Eason is going too fast with Susan, that
he can't last. Had a long talk with Uncle Walt this evening. He told
me that the animal passion side of marriage lasts only about seven years
at the most and that if companionship and other comforting features
were not present the marriage will likely go on the rocks. James Tuck
was elected President of D.K.E. tonight. Marion Long was elected vice-
president. Tuck was elected by acclamation. Got our political plans underway. Pierson and Smith were initiated. The S.A.E.-DKE function was
called off since no agreement could be reached for a date.

Tuesday, May 2, 1939 I gave a pep speech in Public Speaking class
today. Charles Majors asked me today if I had heard of the trouble
about his dad's bank. I told him I had read something about it in the
paper and that I was glad that he brought the subject up because it
opened the way for me to offer my service if there is anything I can
do. He said that his Dad liked me particularly and that he knew I was
managing Charles' B.U. campaign. He said Father was worried because
of the effect that this thing will have on his children. I told Charles
that I would write his dad a letter explaining that this unfortunate happening will have absolutely no effect on this election.

Wednesday, May 3, 1939 Harris Abrahams was elected President of the Honor Committee tonight. I made a little farewell speech. I urged that they be strong at all times and have the courage of their convictions. Richard Pickens is clerk and Tommy Harrison secretary.

Thursday, May 4, 1939 The Calumet Club accepted tonight Willie Cornielius, Eric Bell, Ed McGee, Marty Lichterman, and Richard Lightman. Tom Cummings was refused admission. I was peeved at the way Jordan voted. His questions were asked in such a way that it appeared that he was attempting to display his brilliance. Partee Fleming was also a little rowdy. Jimmy Bangs made a Cracker Jack of a pep speech this morning. He gave a typical speech that a coach might give on the last minute before a big game starts.

Friday, May 5, 1939 I had a date with Susan tonight. We listened and danced to several records on her new phonograph and radio combination. Drove to Tally-ho. The newspaper stories of recent kidnappings and murders have the Cheeks alarmed. They make the chauffeur Leslie trail Susan to school each day. Went to the Tri-Delta dance after leaving Susan. Especially enjoyed dancing with Floy Minor, Laura Whitson, and Elizabeth Surles. Miriam was not there. She was on a retreat.

Saturday, May 6, 1939 I sat in the back of the room on the Ec. quiz this morning and later on I heard reports that members of the baseball team were really griped at me for doing it. They dared not cheat under the circumstances. Made a 50th anniversary wedding speech in Frierson today. Saw Jack Clay and Eleanor Reed at the ball game and track meet today. Jack asked me if I would be interested in a job at the bank next year. Thanked him but told him that I had planned on entering law school. I escorted Virginia Richey to the gym dance tonight. I introduced her to dozens of boys. They all seemed to like her. We danced close to Susan. She was with Eason. On the few occasions that I danced with her she was extra nice. I noticed her looking at me a bit strangely several times when I was dancing with Virginia. Last night she told me that she dreamed of me not so long ago. Dreamed that she had stuck a long needle through my head. Bill Shumaker, Josephine Green, Virginia Richey and I took a long ride and parked in the moonlight after the dance. Had a nice time. Saw Tom Happell and Fred Hume at the dance tonight. Hap and I had a long talk.

Sunday, May 7, 1939 Mrs. Glenn, Susan's grandmother called me this morning and broke my date with Susan for tonight. Said Susan had a sore throat and a slight temperature and her mother wanted her to stay in and go to bed. Dad came in about two o'clock. Rebecca came with him. We took a long ride and ate dinner with the Ragans who had just returned from a fishing trip to Muscle Shoals. Had a date with Virginia Richey again tonight. Drove to Hettie Rays, danced, back to the Tally-ho, listened to the car radio, went home about 1 o'clock.

She cried on my shoulder tonight and told me of her love for Jack Clay. I said I didn't blame her.

Monday, May 8, 1939 When I saw Susan in the Student Center we discussed her throat trouble. My copy of "Who's Who" arrived this evening and I was listed as one of the honorees. Officers were installed at the fraternity meeting tonight and afterwards I went to the art exhibit in Alumni Hall. George and Flora Bentley rode home with me in Dad's car. Dad is in Nashville for a dental convention and was there all day. When I went to pick him up I met Dr. Beverly Douglas. Uncle Walt wrote me a check for $67.00 tuition and one for $30.00 to help get some miscellaneous bills paid.

Tuesday, May 9, 1939 After Bib. Lit. class today I asked Susan if she would like to go to see a show with me this evening. She said that if it did not rain she was going to play tennis. I went to a show and afterwards dropped by the hotel and met several of Dad's dental friends. Cousin Luther was talking to Dad when I went in. Garnet was out playing golf at the club. Paid Joys, Genys, Joe Morse and Joe Franks all that I owed them this evening. Dad left for home at six. He did not even take time to eat. The Calumet Club banquet was really a scream tonight. I had to ask Mickey Carmichael to leave the meeting he was so hot. Jordan, Fleming, and others were at each others throats. Even the new members, Bill Booth and Willie Cornelius took an active part in the discussions. At the close of the meeting I congratulated the group on the fine points brought out at the orderly part of the meeting and I accepted the blame for letting the meeting get out of line every now and then. I explained that my head was splitting and that every minute of the meeting was painful for me, but that I was sure that everyone would forgive and that everyone would remember only the pleasant. After the meeting, Willie Cornelius came around and shook my hand and said it was a fine meeting. Jordan came up and put his arms around me. Dr. Mayfield said he enjoyed every minute of it. All left the meeting happy.

Wednesday, May 10, 1939 Mr. Moss called me this morning about getting a story about Anne Stahlman's winning the Eta Sigma Phi Latin medal at W.B. I carried it down to him at noon. Mr. Wood got pictures of the O.D.K. group and also the Bachelor Maids. Saw the tennis match with Tulane this evening and the DKE-Kappa Sigma baseball game. We are tied in games. Answered Val Hain's letters concerning my references to the University of Alabama in my chapter letter. They took my references as a "dirty dig" at them which was entirely unintentional. Virginia Richey picked me up in the station wagon as I was on the way home from the singing session tonight. We rode around before going home.

Thursday, May 11, 1939 We met in Neely this evening and practiced our song. We needed a leader so Homer insisted that I do that since he was going to do a short solo. There was a large crowd there tonight and the AOPis won the cup for the girls and the Beta's for the fraternities. I believe we got the biggest applause though. My remark about Homer Howell writing the words to our song got a big laugh and applause from the audience which "broke the ice" for us. Many said we were second. We got a lot of fun out of it anyway. We lost the final game in baseball to Kappa Sigma this evening. Talked to Susan after the contest tonight.

Friday, May 12, 1939 Dr. Mims promised us a quiz today but he did not give it. "Frosty" Francis Dority went all over town with me this evening looking over summer tuxedo coats. They were priced at $12.50 and $18.50 for the complete outfit; that is, the Palm Beach ones. At Petway-Reavis they showed me a tropical worsted one that sold for $22.50. The minute I put it on I knew I would never be satisfied with another. It felt twice as light and twice as comfortable as the others. It was a perfect fit. Uncle Walt made me go by the apartment and show it to Aunt Nell tonight. When Henry Clay saw it, even though it was half dark, he commented on how nice it looked. We went by Katie's and talked for 15 minutes. Mrs. Glenn met me at the door tonight. I played several records while waiting for Susan. She wore a beautiful white dress with ruffles. Spoke to Mr. John Cheek as I went out. I have never felt so completely dressed as I did tonight. Boy, that coat is really a knockout. Shirley Caldwell said it was the whitest, prettiest, coat she had ever seen. Jim Reed III also said it was the slickest coat he had seen. Those Palm Beach coats really don't compare with it. Susan was pretty tired and sleepy tonight. We stayed the whole time though.

Saturday, May 13, 1939 Dr. Mayhew said he would give me a check Monday. Susan cut Bib. Lit. class. I saw her at noon, just as she was leaving for the retreat. She will not come back until Monday. Last night Henry Clay said that he and Susan would take a walk while they are on the retreat. To this Katie answered, "Ben and I are not saying what we are going to do while you two are away." This afternoon I went to see the picture "Union Pacific." The story centered around Joel McCrea's activities in curbing the evils such as gambling and shooting which hindered the progress of the workmen. He did it in such a brave manly fashion that no one could help admiring such a character. It is a noble thing to fight for what one believes and knows to be right in spite of unpopularity and difficulties. It is amazing how much one strong individual can accomplish. I like the sentiment of that song "Give me men who are stout hearted men who will fight for the right they adore. Give

me ten, who are stout hearted men and I'll soon give you ten thousand
more". Started reading Dr. Richmond Croom Beatty's "Lord Macaulay"
this evening. I remember my first encounter with Macaulay was one
evening when I was in the sixth grade. Mrs. Pixie Alspaugh read "Hora-
tio at the Bridge" to me. I shall never forget it.

Sunday, May 14, 1939 I went to the Belmont Methodist Church this
morning. Heard a nice Mother's Day sermon and saw Jim Browning,
and John Shumaker. Took another nap. Bill Jordan came by at six.
On our way to dinner and discussed John Covey's marriage. Bill thinks
Covey's crest has fallen since his surprise marriage. Jordan says his eyes
used to sparkle when he rose to answer an argument, now he just has
a "what's the difference look". He says that Covey is the most disillu-
sioned looking man he ever saw. He explains the marriage as happening
in Covey's first flush of love. We came by my apartment and we discussed the psychology of getting other people to work for you—executive
ability. Shumaker picked me up at nine and we dated Josephine
Greer and Virginia Richey. Virginia says she has been doing some
thinking since our last date and our "No illusions about each other"
attitude. Says she has changed her mind slightly. Said she was going
to get up at seven o'clock and take a thirty minute walk with me in the
morning.

Monday, May 15, 1939 I did get up and Virginia Richey and I had
a nice early morning walk. I came home and ate twice as much breakfast
as usual. I felt twice as good as usual for awhile, but I got sleepy in
the middle of the day. I should have gone to bed earlier last night.
After our regular fraternity meeting tonight we had a meeting of the
Gamma Gossip staff and also a political meeting. Made arrangements
for canvassing Kissam and Wesley Halls for independent votes.

Tuesday, May 16, 1939 Dr. Mayhew gave me a check for $100 this
evening as payment for a share of stock. Made a seven-minute speech
this morning in Public Speaking on the history of Vanderbilt. Mary
Engle McDaniels from South Pittsburg telephoned tonight. "Biffle"
Moore came over and asked me to write a nomination speech for him
to deliver at West End High tomorrow. Had midnight lunch with Bill
Jordan.

Wednesday, May 17, 1939 I got a letter from the President of the
Alabama chapter of DKE. It was very nice and expressed appreciation
for my letter of apology. Met Mr. Dan May and went through the May
hosiery mill this morning. Mary Engle told me on the phone tonight
that Dr. Ferguson paid for a love affair for three years and for one
year of education in connection with Jim. Talked to Mr. Turner for an
hour this morning about my plan of a patent holding company. Ate
lunch with Miss Young today.

Thursday, May 18, 1939 Dr. Dyer was funny this morning. He said that when you are on the witness stand you can't give opinions, you must give facts. A lady was on the stand and when she said: "I think . . ." The lawyer stopped her and said: "We don't want you to think on the witness stand. We want facts." The lady turned to the judge and said: "Your honor, I am not like a lawyer, I can't talk without thinking." He also told the story about the colored preacher who said much of his success was due to the fact that he kept his sermons "short but brief."

Friday, May 19, 1939 I came home early today and attempted to take a nap but could not sleep. Rebecca was here. Went by for Henry Clay and Billy Eason showed me his room's location. Henry was over at Mr. Hart's office getting in the Houston contest for speaking. Dropped H. at Katie's and went on to get Susan so we could get to town in time for the last show. We saw Robert Taylor and Myrna Loy in "Lucky Night." It pointed out the early difficulties of marriage. It showed two entirely different viewpoints of marriage, one the secure side and the other the revelling side where a large amount of money is needed. In discussing the picture, Susan made the remark that some people have the mistaken belief that happiness lies in having money. We got to the dance about ten. Missed the grand march and the first no-break but had the others with Susan. She knew very few people there. Neither did I know very many. When they played "Heaven Can Wait" Susan said "I always think of you when they play that piece. I must have been with you when I first heard it." I whispered to her in a joking way "It's hell waiting though, isn't it?" She laughed. The orchestra played one of the Strauss waltzes for the surprise no-break. Towards the close of the dance they played "I Love you Truly." I was dancing with Susan and I told her that she should think of me when they played that piece. She smiled shyly. Got home at 3:00 A.M.

Saturday, May 20, 1939 Susan was not in class this morning. I saw her at eleven o'clock and she said she slept until nine. She was very attentive when I talked to her. Billy Eason and I studied in the library together this evening for about two hours. Coming on home late tonight I saw Florence Cheek parked in front of the drugstore with Ned Wallace. I had never noticed how beautiful she is. Just as I passed she was running her fingers through her long black hair. Read 44 pages tonight in a very interesting book "The Du Pont Dynasty" by John K. Winkler. Biographies of men and families who do things are my favorite type of reading matter. Jim Reed loaned the book to me. It belongs to his sister Eleanor. I am very fond of both of them.

Sunday, May 21, 1939 Bill Jordan came by for me at five and I went by Simpson's with him and then to his house for his birthday dinner. I have never eaten so much in all my life. Just after talking to Fleming, Simpson, Jordan and two Noland girls, at Bill's party, I remembered Bob's invitation out to his house where the seniors were to be honored. Mr. Neathery gave us all an engraved knife. I went to Miriam's for a date. We talked and reminisced until about eleven o'clock when Jordan came by and picked us up and took us to the drugstore for drinks.

Monday, May 22, 1939 I made final arrangements for the B.U. election tonight. Joe Little and Homer are working Wesley Hall and Tom Cummings Jr., is working Kissam.

Tuesday, May 23, 1939 I served as Toastmaster at the Calumet Club banquet tonight. It was Jordan's job to see that the drinks were taken down and when he came by for me he had the back seat piled up with Scotch and fizz bottles. Dr. Eddie Mims and Dr. Frank Owsley rode down with Jordan and me. Owsley was the main speaker. I introduced the new men and then called on Mims, Davidson, Costellano, Manchester, and Dr. Tom Zerfoss. After Dr. Mims' speech I said, "I believe it the part of a toastmaster to be on the lookout for events, or incidents that may suggest humor. Dr. Mims' remark that he sometimes wishes he could be three persons suggested to me that if it were anyone but Dr. Mims I'd say one's enough." Jordan was elected President for next year, Willie Cornelius vice-president, and Darby Fulton was re-elected Secretary. Rode home with Jordan and Fleming.

Wednesday, May 24, 1939 I scooped Partee on Bitsie Napier and Scott George being made heads of the "Pursuit" and Masquerader. The picture of the Calumet Club speakers was in the paper this morning. I took Susan on the DKE hayride and swimming party. Susan looked real nice in her bathing suit. She is a good swimmer. Went for a walk with Long and Damaris. Going on down, Long asked me if I wanted a cigar—Susan said "No you don't want one of those things." Then I said "no I don't." It tickled Damaris. Rode home after the party with Stone. We sang songs all the way. It was a fine affair.

Thursday, May 25, 1939 I talked with Mr. Hart. He said: "If every student in Vanderbilt felt as keenly his responsibility to the university as you do, Ben, we would have a much better school." He was, of course, referring to the Honor Committee activities. Political meeting this evening to make B. U. plans. I had a run-in with Mr. Miller this morning. Went to the Public Speaking banquet tonight and I made a pretty good speech. Ended by quoting Tam o'shanter, "Pleasures are like poppies spread—". Andy Bagwell in her speech made a remark about my smoking a cigar. When I got up I said that the thing that amazes me is that Andy has been going with cigar-smoking Red Anglin for three years and still isn't used to cigar smoke. Interviewed Dr. Youmans about his grant from the Rockefeller Foundation for work on nutrition. Saw Eleanor Richey's car this evening for the first time. The chauffeur had brought it to her and was riding the rumble seat. The picture that E. R. asked me to have taken of the Peabody Musical came out this evening. Saw Billy Eason and Susan sitting out in the grass studying this evening.

Friday, May 26, 1939 I got the cards that had been printed for Charles Majors. Went out and studied Bib. Lit. with Susan until ten. I had not realized that we would encounter the word circumcision, but evidently Susan did and she got the word behind us immediately. Her mother and father went down to the Castle Heights dance with E. R. Just before leaving we ate a piece of cake and drank some grape juice. We tended strictly to business all evening. Frank Chenault called about the beer that someone offered the AKK house. Joe Little and Homer Howell worked that out though. Bob Neathery trailed me to the Albemarle and brought me back to 20th.

Saturday, May 27, 1939 Bill Jordan came by and we went over to the house and started things rolling. He loaned me his car. We hung a sign over the speaker's stand but Morris Burk made us take it down. Preacher Franklin spoke for Charles Majors and Jimmy Lanier spoke for Boss. Majors won by a landslide vote; 390 to 228 was the final vote. I sent a telegram to Mr. Majors. The party at the house started at noon. The Phi Delta Thetas and the S.A.E.'s were tipsy before they got there. They had played a ball game for a keg of beer. It was the roughest party I have ever seen. Tom Happel and Buddy Rand dropped in from St. Louis. Rand was driving a Buick coupé this time. Merrill Stone told me this evening that Mr. Rand contributed $50,000 to the Joint Library project. Merrill said he knew because he worked in the Chancellor's office. Went to the Student Union dinner which was given in honor of student leaders this evening. Mac Glasgow served as toastmaster. Dr. Carmichael made a fine Founder's Day address. For one thing he said that he agreed with Mr. Burk who said that the biggest thing that has been done at Vanderbilt this year was the rejuvenation of the Honor System. (Burk gave a resume of the year's activities) Escorted Virginia Richey to the gym dance tonight. Jordan argued me into wearing my formal jacket and then he showed up in a blue suit. I brought Virginia to see Mary Wallace while I changed to a suit. After I had changed I showed her some of my pictures. I was with Susan during the ten minute intermission. I asked Susan whom she had a date with and she said Billy Eason and then she asked me whom I had a date with and I told her, and also that Virginia visited in my hometown last summer. I took Susan over and introduced her to Virginia. About that time Eason came up. After the dance we went to Candyland and then drove up on the campus and parked by old Wesley Hall. We had a very interesting chat

about each other, a very affectionate farewell. We got home about
two thirty.

Sunday, May 28, 1939 I saw in the paper that Dr. Willis A. Sutton
is going to deliver the Peabody Demonstration School commencement
sermon. I wrote him a letter immediately. Called Susan and asked her
if she would like to go to the program with me that night. I was surprised
when she accepted so readily. Jordan said it was because I had made
her jealous. She told me last night that she could not go on the house
party the first day. Her mother had accepted another invitation for her.
I went down to Domnicks with Jordan tonight and ate chili. Ran into
Noah and William Smith. I would not have known William. Last night
I happened to be dancing with Shirley Caldwell when she mentioned
Nello Andrews. She said, "I feel so sorry for him because he does not
do any good at all with Susan."

"Don't you feel sorry for me too?" I said.

"No!" she said very emphatically. I hope she's right.

Monday, May 29, 1939 I did not go to school today. Slept late,
cleaned up the house and studied. Went to the farewell fraternity meeting
tonight. The seniors made a few parting remarks. I stressed the fact
that one's enjoyment is directly proportional to what is put into the
fraternity. Mother and George L. came to Uncle Walt's tonight. I went
up to see them at ten. Jordan came by for a snack at eleven and stayed
until twelve thirty.

Tuesday, May 30, 1939 Dr. Mayhew did not come to class so Susan
and I went to the library and studied. I was so tired and sleepy in Dr.
Dyer's class that I slept half the time. Bought my Commodore and gave
it the once over. Went by Mr. Miller's office and asked him to let me
take my makeup quizzes, but he would not let me take them. He told
me that my work was splendid at the beginning of the term but that I
had dropped considerably towards the last. What he meant was that
our relationships are not as pleasant and smooth as they were earlier
in the term. Got the Gamma Gossip to press this afternoon. I am in a
low mood tonight. I am moody over the bungle that I have made along
scholastic lines. I am not dissatisfied with what I have done and accomplished during the past four years; merely dissatisfied with the marks I
have made in scholarship. My reward has been along practical lines.
Dr. Carmichael says that the biggest thing that was done at Vanderbilt
was in connection with the Honor System. That is my reward. In one
sense I have sacrificed selfish marks for other things that I considered
important. I still think I'm right but the resulting pills are hard to swallow.
Funny thing at this moment, I don't care what the rest of the world
thinks, only one girl.

Wednesday, May 31, 1939 The folks left for home this morning. I came home early, cleaned up after them and rejoiced in the silence and solitude. Talked to Dean Sarratt this morning and he told me that he would like to have me around next year and if there was anything he could do that would help out to let him know. I am going up and talk to Dean Arnold about getting in the law school. Mr. Windrow, Principal of the Demonstration School gave me entrance cards to Dr. Sutton's speech which is scheduled for Thursday evening. Called up Susan and she says that she will be ready at five tomorrow evening. Called Shirley Caldwell and asked her to go to the Senior Prom with me. She is going to try to arrange it. We had a real nice conversation. It is so much easier for me to joke and carry on with people I am not too serious about.

Thursday, June 1, 1939 My alarm clock was wrong so I cut the last Bib. Lit. class unintentionally. Came home early and studied. Went by for Susan at a quarter after seven and took her over to the Peabody Demonstration School to hear Dr. Willis A. Sutton deliver the commencement address. The auditorium was hot and packed, but we enjoyed it very much. He stressed, in his speech, the importance of making men and women rather than just turning out graduates. I went by and spoke to him after the address and introduced him to Susan.

Friday, June 2, 1939 The Peabody baccalaureate speaker wired the President of Peabody College that he could not show up so Dr. Sutton was prevailed on to substitute for him. Tonight after Miriam got back from the speech, I called her and asked her how she liked him. She said that she perhaps had had too great a build-up and that she was just a little disappointed. Steve graduated tonight. It was nine when I talked to her so we continued talking for thirty minutes. She had turned out her light and was lying in bed. Jordan and Jean and Hardy Noland came by and took me down to the Tally-ho tonight for a Coca Cola. I did not get to bed until after 12 o'clock.

Saturday, June 3, 1939 Susan sat two chairs away from me as we took the Biblical Literature examination this morning. I probably did fair on it. After eating dinner with Bill Jordan at the Brass Rail, we discussed love and marriage. We concluded that marriage has a tendency to stifle a man's creative abilities; that he becomes self-complacent after the marriage is consummated. When I called Susan later and told her of the conversation she violently objected. She said: "Not if you get the right one." Talked with Shirley Caldwell and she said her mother likes me, even though we have never met. She has read several of my articles in "Pursuit" and agrees with them.

Sunday, June 4, 1939 Dr. Gus Dyer is a great proponent of the free enterprise system. He also believes that large businesses do not have all of the advantages over small ones. He says it is brains that produce wealth. Wealth production is not making things, it is combining parts and things. Karl Marx was obsessed with the idea that wealth is produced by hands. In talking about Adam Smith, author of the "Wealth of Nations," he said Smith was not concerned with public good, that is in the field of morals. "All his thinking led him to the firm belief in spontaneous economic order, founded and guided by self-interest." Of people he said, "Nine tenths of the people who do anything in this world are driven to it by necessity. William James, of Harvard, once said, in a derisive comment about psychology: "The study of psychology ought to be turned over to the Germans. They are incapable of being bored."

Monday, June 5, 1939 Took two extremely hard examinations today and when I had finished I did not know what to do with myself. I was at loose ends, sort of depressed and let down. Jordan invited me to dinner at the Brass Rail with him and his mother. We had delicious T-bone steaks. He had a date with Mary Brock. The other day Dr. Dyer said a member of the Women's Christian Temperance Union was lecturing a man on drinking beer. The fellow replied that his father drank beer and lived to be eighty. The woman then said: "How much longer would he have lived if he had not drunk beer?" To which the drunkard replied: "He got in the way as it was." If I were to pick a single type joke and say it was typical of Dyer's humor, this is it.

Tuesday, June 6, 1939 Jordan came by for me at eleven o'clock and we drove to the campus, aimlessly, and loafed until we encountered Dr. Molloy and then the three of us went to the Log Cabin in Centennial Park to discuss university problems, politics, sex, homosexuality and marriage. I guess the professors are a little disoriented too when the pressure is suddenly off. I particularly enjoyed the last few lectures by Mims, in which he was discussing various aspects of the imagination. In Wordsworth's "Tintern Abbey," for example: "I have felt a presence that disturbs me with the joy of elevated thought." And of memory and reveries, how's this? "What fairy palaces, treasure houses of pleasant thoughts, houses without hands for our souls to live in."

Wednesday, June 7, 1939 The charm of Oxford is the blending of a medieval city with the pastoral background. Nashville, Tennessee, has somewhat of an Oxfordian atmosphere. There is a great university that treasures intellectual conversation and academic achievement above some other aspects of college life. I have been fortunate in associating with the Jordans, the Flemings and Simpsons, and among faculty members the Mims, Ransoms, Dyers, Mayfields and Currys. I have thought often of the statement of Matthew Arnold about the "voices heard at Oxford forty years ago." I am hearing voices at Vanderbilt now and they are probably the same kind of voices that Arnold heard. I am sure

I will cherish them forty years from now, but then, with an added touch of nostalgia.

Thursday, June 8, 1939 Packed my books and clothing today in preparation for going to camp for the summer. Shirley Caldwell's phone was out of order so I could not call her before the dance tonight. Met her little sister Allison, who looks a great deal like Shirley. Stopped by the Deke House on my way to my date and gave two tickets for the dance to Bill Shumaker and Granville Sherman. Sang a couple of barbershop numbers with tenor, Homer Howell, and baritone, John McReynolds. Shirley and I got to the dance early and enjoyed the warm up numbers such as "Wishing" and "The Angels Sing." I don't know why it is but most orchestras play their best pieces first, when there are the fewest people dancing, and later on, when the dance hall is crowded, they play their fast exhibition music, which I don't particularly like to dance to. Tommy Dorsey is no different. Found myself in a dilemma, I had made the second no-break with both Susan and Miriam and when the time came for it they were both standing and waiting. It was tough to make a choice; one was the best dancer on the campus, whom I am quite fond of, and the other, the girl I love . . . now. I hated to do this to Miriam, but she has done a thousand things to me that are worse. It wasn't the kind of revenge that I like to take, but I danced it with Susan. Somebody had warned Shirley about dating Frank Chenault, and she was a little resentful about the advice because she did not consider it any of her business. She asked me if there was anything wrong with him. "Not that I know of. I like him." We stopped at the Toddle House for refreshments and then went to her home. Darned if we didn't talk until daylight. She is a good listener as well as a good talker. We agree on a lot of things; about Virginia McClellan and that Susan is nice but a little hard to know.

Friday, June 9, 1939 Picked up Susan at five for the tea dance. She broke the sad news to me that her dad would not let her go to the house party with me at Rock Island. I was bitterly disappointed but, on the other hand, I never could fully believe that she would go. It would have been too good to be true. Some things just can't happen. Staying out all night began to show on me before the tea dance was over. Besides being fatigued I was despondent over Susan not going with me to the retreat. Had I made O.D.K. I would have kissed Susan before all those people. It would have been acceptable too. She would have an excuse for giving in. She would have had peer censorship had she not. I did not worry too much over this though. It was simply not to be. Johnny Noel and Becky McRee really put on a show. I thought they'd never turn loose. After the dance we went to Rawlings, on the Clarksville pike, for breakfast. Since this was our final meeting of the year, the breakfast was conducted along the lines of a farewell banquet. All the seniors made speeches in a humorous vein. When my turn came I said that I was expecting everyone to be in tears and that I would be different by expressing the joy of completing four years successfully. "Now that the occasion is here, I find everyone else is happy . . . and I am the one in the dumps." I explained that I needed sleep, but that other things contributed to my unhappiness. Susan got the point and was sympathetic. We drove home slowly and I told her that in spite of the things that had happened in the past few weeks I consider her the sweetest girl in the world and nobody means as much to me. We got home about five-thirty and she handed me the key to the door. She walked in and just before handing her the key I stepped inside and leaned forward and kissed her good night and good-bye for a few days. Her lips were full and warm. The bliss of this last minute parting blotted out all physical fatigue and worry and the disappointment of not being able to go to the weekend party with her. I lived this experience over and over again. As Tennyson once wrote:

> "She looked so lovely as she sway'd
> The rein with dainty fingertips,
> A man had given all other bliss
> And all his worldly worth for this
> To waste his whole heart in one kiss
> Upon her perfect lips."

Saturday, June 10, 1939 I caught up on my sleep this morning and this afternoon moved out of the apartment at 1909 20th Avenue South.

Sunday, June 11, 1939 Slept until eleven o'clock and Bob Neathery, Charles Majors, Harriet Short and Alfred Estes came by to take me to the house party. Joan Young was my date. We arrived at the Rock Island cottages about four thirty, just in time for a swim before supper. Dr. Manchester and Dr. Rochdeau and their wives were the chaperons. Whitaker and Westbrook (from the Phi Kappa Sigma house) are cooks. Leo Bashinski, Louise Sykes, George Morrow, Mary Louise Davis, Bill Hume, Kit Weed, Jim Browning, Jean McEwan, John McReynolds, Sarah Cecil, Hartwell Weaver, Willie Matt Beasley, Jack Worley and Lu Ray Welch were there. Hume says that he and Kit are married.

Monday, June 12, 1939 Got up early and after driving to town for a few minutes we put on our swim suits and swam and took sun baths all morning. I almost got sunburned. Sykes and I had a lot of fun singing and joking with each other. Alfred Estes' girl, Lula Rose Furlington, is a good conversationalist and Weaver's date, Miss Beasley, knows my old flame, Freda Atwood. Before going to bed tonight we all gathered around a large table and sang sentimental songs.

Tuesday, June 13, 1939 I got up early and rode to Nashville with Louise Sykes and Leo Bashinski; arrived home about noon and had a long talk with Uncle Walt. I was slightly disappointed in the attitude he took towards my schooling. He has always told me to take it easy and to live now. He has advocated "leisurely scholarship." His tone today indicated to me that what he has previously said has been largely talk and not conviction. He is not above the mundane considerations of grades, jobs and money, as I had previously thought. Met Alfred Estes' mother and sister at the fraternity house. Saw the Bashinskis again. The orchestra played slow pieces all evening and Susan and I talked of our activities of the past few weeks. I reminded her of our parting the other evening and what an elevated feeling I had. She seemed a little embarrassed at first but as we continued to dance the subject changed. As we sang the Alma Mater at the close of the dance I noticed that Susan's eyes were red and a small tear trickled down her cheek. My fondest hopes are that I am among her thoughts at this moment of reluctantly finishing another school year.

Wednesday, June 14, 1939 Tonight I felt keenly the bitter pangs of loneliness. I came by the fraternity house and only the "house mother," "Ma" Clapp was there. The campus was lonely and there were no students at the Tally-ho. I saw only older people at the student hangouts. I was reminded of the old German city of Hamelin after the Pied Piper had lured away all the children and the gaiety and laughter. After signing up the Davis boy for camp I went to town to see a movie, "The Young Mr. Lincoln." One of the best jokes was that a farmer stuck a pitchfork into his neighbor's dog when it bit him. "Why didn't you use the other end?" complained the neighbor. To which the farmer replied: "Why didn't the dog use the other end?"

Thursday, June 15, 1939 Elizabeth Barrett Browning, after publication of Locksley Hall, said she couldn't imagine Tennyson loving any woman without her loving him. It was Tennyson who wrote, in Canto 27, in "In Memoriam," "It was better to have loved and lost, than never to have loved at all." Mims quoted from somewhere, lately, that "The rarest triumph of civilization is a woman of fine character at the head of a family." Of passionate love he quoted: "Sad, and bad, and mad it was, but O how it was sweet." He lightly suggested that perhaps the summum bonum is summed up in the kiss of a girl.

Friday, June 16, 1939 I did something tonight that I have never done before, and would never do again if I had the choice, I let Susan read some of my diary. How could I have been so stupid? I guess one can be so in love, and so desperately afraid of losing, that he will do the very thing that brings about his defeat. I once heard a statement: "A wise man tells a woman he loves her, a fool tries to prove it." If I had searched the world over for the greatest of blunders, I would have been hard put to find a greater one. I know that women, like Susan, who have a wide choice of suitors, and who are not given to romanticism, will probably make the final decision on the basis of the one who arouses her emotions through physical contact, kissing. I also know that Susan is supersensitive about her good name and reputation and attempts to live up to what others expect from one who shares her family's position. Knowing how sensitive she is about publicity and revelations about her personal life, how could I have been so unthinking as to show her a love letter that had been written to me? I did not let her see the name, but that was of no consequence. The damage had already been done. I sensed it too late. From this day forward she'll be forever on her guard. I'm afraid I'll never have the chance to teach her to love me. At every touch she'll think: "How will this look in his diary?"

1. Pursuit staff, Left to Right—Bernard Breyer, Bill Jordan, Ben Austin, Robert Meyers, Bill Hall, Darby Fulton and Delbert Mann. 2. Ace Club. 3. Miriam McGaw. 4. Washington Ball Tea, Susan Cheek is on the extreme right. 5. Bachelor of Ugliness victory party at the Deke house. 6. A "Senate" political meeting at the Deke house. 7. Nell Edwards, Ann Wright and Henrietta Hickman. 8. The O.D.K. kiss, Charles Majors and Harriet Short. 9. Coeds lined up in poses similar to ones struck 40 years earlier by other coeds: Right to Left—June Burks, Edna Murry Davy, Elaine Haile, Mary Davidson, Sarah Logue, Madelaine Bidwell, Helen McMurray, Sarah Kirkpatric, Sarah Kelley, Martha Thatch and Marguerite Willis. The basketball team, Front Row, Left to Right, Billy Woody, Gray Moore and Frances Carter. Back Row—Caroline Stehlin and Jane Chadwell. 10. Susan Cheek, Andromedia Bagwell and Mary Alice Beasley. 11. Maurice Holgraf and Marguerite Wallace leading the Grand March. 12. Alice Lewis and Emmett O'Callaghan. 13. Virginia Blair.

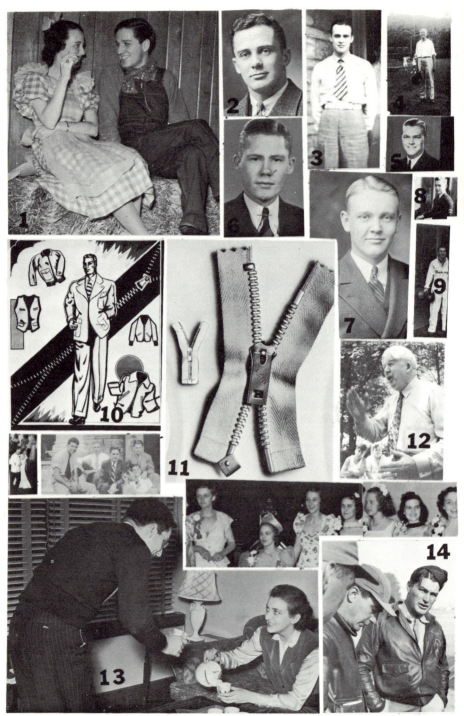

1. Susan Cheek and Ben Austin at a Deke barn dance. 2. John Black, of Birmingham. 3. Tom Happel, of St. Louis. 4. "Pop J." A. A. Jameson. 5. Mickey Carmichael. 6. Byron Anglin. 7. Nelson Paige Hill, of Birmingham. 8. Jim Tuck. 9. Charles Majors. 10. Advertising layout on the "Swivel Zipper" by R. A. Gotto. 11. The "Swivel Zipper." 12. Dr. Willis A. Sutton, speaking at Chapel Island, Dixie Camps. 13. Ben Austin being served tea by Mary Alice Beasley. 14. George L. Austin Jr. with two of his flying buddies in the 36th Pursuit Squadron.

TRIP TO
NEW YORK'S WORLD FAIR

Monday, August 21, 1939 Camp broke today. Jesse Madden, Madge, Barbara, Frank Jones and I got up at four-thirty and drank coffee with Mr. Steele and then started on our trip to New York. I was terribly sick all last night and did not sleep more than an hour or so. We had not had dinner more than an hour until I got sick at my stomach again and threw up all I had eaten. After that I was okay. Barbara did the same thing and then she came back and sat with Frank and me the rest of the morning. We had lots of fun all the way. Came through Asheville, Roanoke, Bristol, Staunton and Lexington. At Lexington we ate at the Southern Cafe and then went to see the campus of Washington and Lee and V.M.I. We saw the Lee Chapel and the beautiful grounds. It was a treat. The atmosphere seems to be restrained. We came over the Natural Bridge of Virginia but did not go down beneath it. Spent our first night at the Valley Lee Camp a hundred or so miles out of Washington. Called and talked to Bill Potts and his dad as I came through Abingdon, Virginia. Bill invited me to stop over with him on my way back. He is working in a bank.

Tuesday, August 22, 1939 Jesse knocked on our door at six o'clock this morning and we got off immediately for Washington. We took the skyline drive up the Shenandoah Valley and we considered it well worth the extra quarter we spent in tolls. It was a grand view early in the day. We ate a short breakfast at Washington, Virginia. Saw headlines in the paper which said that Germany and Russia had signed a non-agression agreement. A later paper stated that the British Parliament had been called into an extra session. Ate at a place called the "Hatchet and Cherry Tree." We got to Washington about 11:30. We passed the White House on the way in to the heart of the city but we were not thinking about it as being in the heart of the city so we did not agree on it unanimously as being the place. It looked a little crowded, too, for the president's home. We drove up Pennsylvania to the Capitol, parked our car and took a tour of the nation's Capitol. We enjoyed seeing statues of Washington, Lincoln, Jefferson, Stephen F. Austin and Ericsson (inventor of screw propellers). Especially were we surprised to see the fine statue of Will Rogers. We climbed to the very top of the dome and saw some workmen busily painting the top of the Capitol, which is steel instead of concrete. It is made like a battleship. The painters located the different buildings for us. On leaving the Capitol, we went to the Congressional Library and saw the original Constitution; Declaration of Independence, Victor Herbert's original manuscripts; the original of Lincoln's Gettysburg address and the Gutenberg Bible. Two copies of every book copyrighted in the United States are supposed to be there. Anybody can read in it, but only government officials may check out books. From the library I called up Mr. Burns and taxied over to see him. He is a prince of a fellow and seemed to be satisfied with the camp experience of his sons Jimmy and Wendell. He said with the early enrollment and two from the same family commissions, it was $150 cheaper than the eastern camp where the boys went last summer. He advised that I sell the invention at a reasonable sum if it is offered as it is purely a structural invention and the claims had to be trimmed down pretty narrowly. He says by selling, an entree into the company might be made. I told him about my proposed trip to Meadville and he thought it a good idea. I drank a milk shake and caught a taxi to the Smithsonian Institute. My stay there was limited to a hurried 20 minutes. I saw the "Spirit of St. Louis," the Wright brothers' plane, "Winnie Mae," the first autogyro, and numerous models of inventions that have been revolutionary in their scope. The sewing machine, incandescent lamp, the steam engine and so on. I merely got a taste of the place and will have to go back when I can stay longer. We met the sight-seeing bus at the Institute at two. We drove through the city seeing the different government buildings, The Unknown Soldier, "Our Country Right or Wrong," Decatur, and were amazed at the small lawns of some of the fine homes. There is practically no yard space, even in the millionaire districts. Saw where Mrs. Longworth, Frances Perkins, Mary Ruth Rhinehart, the McCormicks and others live. Saw the hotel (The Carlton) where Mr. Cordell Hull lives. It is one of the most fashionable of all the hotels. We then crossed the Potomac River on the Francis

Scott Key Memorial Bridge and drove on to Arlington Cemetery and to the tomb of the "Unknown Soldier," one of the most sacred shrines in America. We saw the Arlington Mansion where Robert E. Lee was living when the first shot was fired on Fort Sumter. Lincoln sent for Lee and offered him command of the Northern forces. Lee said, "I hate slavery and secession and I believe in the Union, but I cannot pick up arms against my native state, my home." It is said that Lee paced the floor of the beautiful Arlington porch all night before he made that momentous decision. He and his family packed their things and never again set foot in beautiful Arlington. The Lees, Washingtons and Curtises were very closely related by marriage. The trees in Arlington are the same as they were. One East Indian cedar is the only one of its kind in America. The magnolias are beautiful. We came back by the Commerce Building and got a peek at one of the Patent Office Search rooms. We then went to get a close-up view of Washington's Monument which is 555 feet high (50 stories) and 55 feet square at the base, tapering to 34 feet at the top. Ate dinner at the S and W and then drove out to the Lincoln Memorial. That great statue of him sitting in a chair is the most impressive thing I have seen. The Gettysburg address is engraved at one end of the building and his inaugural address at the other. We left Washington at nine and drove to Baltimore, Maryland. It is larger than I thought. It seems that Washington does not stop until Baltimore begins, although they are more than four hours drive apart. I have never seen so many houses and apartment houses just alike as in Baltimore. I wonder why? I am going to find out if I have to write to the Chamber of Commerce. We stopped at a real nice home for the night—very homey—I am writing from this home.

Wednesday, August 23, 1939 Drove through Wilmington, Delaware the home of the Du Ponts. It was interesting to me having just read John K. Winkler's "The Du Pont Dynasty." We drove to Philadelphia for lunch and saw Independence Hall, the Liberty Bell and the other historic landmarks of the city. I was impressed by the large size and fine looks of the Philadelphia people. Stopped by Lakehurst, N.J., this evening on our way to Asbury Park and saw two or three dirigibles in the giant hanger, including the Los Angeles which is only slightly smaller than the "Macon" and "Akron," both of which fell and were destroyed. I have never seen such a large and impressive piece of machinery in my life. The "Los Angeles" has not been flown since 1936 because of popular opinion since the fate of the other two ships. We were allowed to go up into the ship and inspect the quarters and instrument panels. It took a crew of 40 men to man the Los Angeles. It carried 20 to 30 passengers. I got my first glance of an ocean this evening about four-thirty. I saw the Atlantic from Asbury Park. It was just about what I expected. The breeze was refreshing and I could sit for days meditating over the vastness and mystery of it. The people on the beach seemed to be regular waifs for the most part. We got into a big traffic jam coming into Jersey City and we were detained in getting into the city. We came through the Holland Tunnel though and put up at the Cartaret Hotel after failing to get located at the "Y." Our hotel is directly across from the 23rd Street YMCA that Pop J. used to be head of. Our rooms are with Jesse, Madge and Barbara. Glimpsed the Empire State Building coming in tonight. Frank Jones and I went on a walking tour after supper. Saw Broadway, Times Square. The signs are certainly fascinating. The Chevrolet, Planters and Coca Cola signs I am familiar with from the movies of Broadway. The Camel and Old Gold signs are captivating. The Maxwell House Coffee sign is, of course, of interest to me. Passed by Jack Dempsey's restaurant. Tommy Dorsey, Jan Savitt, Little Jack Little, and dozens of orchestras are in town. Mickey Rooney, Tallulah Bankhead, Frederick March, and Katherine Hepburn are here in person. I believe you could get more live entertainment in New York than any other place in the world. Went by the Park Central to see "Scotty" and Warren Sewell's dad. He seemed like a real nice fellow. We talked of Mr. Worley, Jack Worley and Charlotte. I told him something of my Zipper invention. Says he does not use Zippers at present on the pants but may have to come to them. He was alarmed over the war situation; Russia signing that pact with Germany. Bill Strother walked around the city with Frank and me.

Thursday, August 24, 1939 After breakfast at the Cartaret we went with the Maddens on a grand sightseeing tour of the city. We crossed Times Square, called "the Cross Roads of the World," drove down Fifth Avenue and saw the fine homes and apartment houses of the millionaires and social leaders (the Whitney's and Vanderbilt's) and then after seeing O. O. McIntyre's penthouse we drove over to Riverside Drive and saw Grant's Tomb, Dr. Fosdick's Riverside Church and Charles M. Schwab's fine home. It is the only one that we saw that had any yard space. The guide told us that he has a fine yacht down on the Hudson. The Cathedral of St. John is the most impressive church I have seen anywhere. It is only two-thirds built and it has been under construction for 47 years. They work on it only when they have the money and they don't go into debt for it. When completed, it will be the largest cathedral in the world. It is large enough to serve as a hangar for the giant dirigible we saw yesterday. It is an Episcopalian cathedral. I was impressed by the soberness and vastness of Wall Street. The property near 21 Wall Street is valued at about $1,000 per inch or $12,000 per square foot. The whole of Manhattan Island was bought for $24 from the Indians. It is said to be valued at 16 billion dollars now. I saw the largest apartment building in the world with some 2,500 families with an average of three people per family. The garment center was interesting. The different businesses are more or less grouped together in New York. As our bus drove through the east side slums and other districts the kids would yell "Rubbernecks." Tickled me. Got a view of the Statue of Liberty from the aquarium grounds. Rode on my first subway today. We used one in getting to the fairgrounds. Got my first glimpse of the fair at two this evening. Perhaps the first thing I saw was the Life Saver parachute jump. The Triolan and Perisphere were next. The Coty powder exhibit was first on our list. Heard Ben Bernie (in person). Ben is some kid. Jesse and I almost split our sides laughing at him. Saw the YMCA putting on some wrestling matches at the fair. Saw some A.A.U. champions wrestle. "Tiny" Peterson AAU champion in the 112 pound division was referee. I talked to him after the match and he told me about Al Crawford winning the National Championship for three years in succession. The wrestlers here use lots of leg rides. This fall I think I'll practice some of them. Saw toothbrushes (Dr. West's) being made at the Du Pont exhibit, also combs. They have quite an exhibit. On my way home from the fair I met Billy and Martha Wade from Nashville. They were on the Penna. train headed for the hotel Gov. Clinton. They have been here a week. Martha had just won a free telephone call and had called George Pellett in North Carolina.

Friday, August 25, 1939 Frank stayed with his girl in New Jersey last night. I got up late and went to the Capitol Theatre to see "The Wizard of Oz" starring Judy Garland. Judy and Mickey Rooney were on in person. Judy has a wonderful voice. There were three characters of importance the "Strawman" who had no brains, the "Tinman" who had no heart, and the "Lionman" who had no courage. In places the satire was biting, for instance, the Wizard of "Oz" at last told the straw-man that he had as much brains as lots of people and that there was only one thing lacking, "you don't have a diploma." He was given one. The lion was told that he was not lacking in courage, all that he needed was recognition for it. He was given a medal for valor and his troubles were over. The man who had no heart was advised of his good fortune as far as heartbreaks are concerned. "Oz" said, "The test of a heart is not the number of people it loves, but the number of people that love it." I am forever on the lookout for bits of philosophy with the hope that some application can be made in my own life. As Browning suggested "catch hints of the tools true play." On second thought this is not a bad definition of education. I am forever groping in the dark for a flash of "superphilosophy," superunderstanding, so that I might get a glimpse of that beyond the human intellect. I am forever on the lookout for an original idea. It is a most fascinating study to probe into the unknown,

almost the immortal. I was glad to see the Maddens tonight in front
of the Plymouth Theatre. We went to see "Abe Lincoln of Illinois."
Robert Sherwood's play was put on with Richard Gaines as Abe, Frank
Andrews as Mentor Graham and Muriel Kirkland as Mary Todd. Ann
Rutledge, Lincoln's friend and only real love was played by Adele Lang-
mire who was making her first appearance on Broadway. I enjoyed the
play and so did Madge and Jesse. The speeches were exceptionally good.
Lincoln's answer to Stephen Douglas was excellent and his prayer was
a masterpiece. One joke he pulled on his wife. He says they were pretty
ritzy to spell their name with two "d's" when one was enough. This
was my first Broadway play and I enjoyed it tremendously. You haven't
really lived until you have seen the lights of Broadway and a Broadway
play. Went on a tour through the NBC studio and saw the largest studio
room in the world where Fred Allen's and other big programs originate.
The television display was good but I don't believe it was as good as
some others. I myself was televised. I learned that Kasper Kuhn had
changed to the job of Master of Ceremonies at Ripley's Times Square
Odditorium. Saw a Johnson boy from Chattanooga in front of the "Y"
this morning. He goes to Vandy. I got my theme of the New York
visit today from the "Oz" show. Judy sang it. "Somewhere over the
rainbow . . ." Every time I hear that song from now on I'll think of
the fair. From the Chicago fair in 1933 I brought away "Moonglow,"
"Cocktails for Two" and "Love in Bloom." Saw a cop "bawl out" a
taxi driver today and it tickled me. First time I ever enjoyed seeing a
cop getting tough. Afterwards I went and told the cop how much I
enjoyed it. He laughed. It was on Times Square. The television guide
today said that television is only good for a radius of about 50 miles
(or the vision of the eye). It could reflect the waves from the moon or
a plane. At present the height of the sending tower determines the
distance that the reception is good. A man in Kansas reported television
reception from England.

Saturday, August 26, 1939 Frank Jones and I went to the Maplewood,
N.J., ferry today to see his girl, Virginia Vase. She is a very cute little
blonde. We went to the South Battery and caught a boat for the Statue
of Liberty. The view of the New York skyline is marvelous. We went
to the top of the statue and looked over the harbor. I imagined that
we were immigrants coming to this country for the first time. On the
way over Frank Jones told me of his conversation with Lucia Bellinger.
He said that she told him that I was funny. She related the incident
when I told her to pretend that she was asleep and I kissed her. She
laughed and joked, so he said. She said that she liked Boyd, and did
not want to hurt him, but that there was a boy in New Jersey that she
cared for. I thought of the things Boyd had told me. That he was certain

she loved him. I told him that he had better be absolutely sure before he fell too deeply. We came on back from the Statue of Liberty and went up Wall Street and got a close up view of the street which includes J. P. Morgan's building. I left Frank and Virginia and went to the RCA Music Hall to see Ginger Rogers in "Fifth Avenue Girl" and the symphony orchestra under the direction of Erno Rapée. Met the Maddens at nine in front of the Center Theatre and saw Frederick March in "The American Way." I have never seen such elaborate stage equipment; 280 people were in the cast. The story was the rise to riches of a foreigner in this country and the reaction of the different political elections and wars on his family. It came right up to the present when Nazi propaganda is about. My head was splitting when I came out but I went with the Maddens anyway to the top of the RCA building 65 or 70 stories above the ground to get a panoramic view of the city at night. It is the most impressive sight imaginable. Really worthwhile. I could stay hours up there. It is a favorite courting spot for transients. The Maddens plan to leave in the morning, after church, for Washington.

Sunday, August 27, 1939 I went to morning services at the famous Riverside Church, which was donated by John D. Rockefeller, Jr. Dr. Harry Emerson Fosdick was on leave of absence but his assistant Dr. Frederick W. Norwood was taking his place. It was a fine service. Saw Mrs. Haggard, Vanderbilt's Registrar's secretary, as I came out of the church. She was on her way to Bermuda but the war scare had made them call in all the boats. She had planned to take the trip on a German boat. Went to the fair after church. The next show I attended was the Aquacade. Johnny Weismuller, the fastest swimmer in the world, and Eleanor Holmes were there. The diving by the different champions, the crazy diving, the dancing, music, singing, rhythmic swimming and all were excellent. Whom should I meet as I started out of the place but Dean Sarratt. He was there with some boys from Camp Mandamin. The G. M. exhibit (Futurama) was too crowded today so I did not attempt to see it. Saw the French exhibit, Ford, Western Electric, Chase and Sanborn Coffee, Crossley Radio and others.

Their little car was interesting. At the League of Nations at nine I witnessed perhaps the most spectacular display at the fair; the music, different colored lights, fountains and fireworks all mixed together. It was really the most spectacular thing that I have seen in New York.

Monday, August 28, 1939 Hitler is still in the headlines and his war scare is by no means over. Britain is firm. Peddled my invention on Broadway this evening. Visited several slide fastener places and showed my invention to the first man I visited. Mr. J. Klein, 40 West 23rd Street, New York, N.Y. His company is known as the Universal Slide Fastener Co. He has been in the business eight years. I gave him a demonstration

and he said, "I can see possibilities." He said that he only makes slide
fasteners for short pieces like on the side of a lady's skirt and pocket-
books. He advised me to get a job with some Zipper company in order
to learn about the business. He told me to go out to the Zipper plant
out at Long Island and to call for Mr. Jensen. I had lots of fun visiting
the different places today. Don't know when I have had such a thrill.
On 25th street, where I was today, I never saw so many sewing machine
companies. A nice letter from Susan awaited me at the hotel Park Central.
I saw Scotty and the Dixie group for the last time. Sat down after lunch
and wrote Susan a real long letter. Told her that business was interesting
but nothing compared to my thoughts of her. Also balanced it by saying
that I bet she was as stubborn as a mule and that when she gets mad
the cats and dogs tuck their tails and go into hiding. Her letter said
that Jack Clay and Eleanor Reed were going to get married; also Betty
Butler Field.

Tuesday, August 29, 1939 I got up and got on the subway for Waldes
Koh-i-nor, Long Island City 22, New York. Talked to Mr. J. Brozek.
He seemed interested in the device and said he would take it up with
the vice president. He asked me what I would sell it for and if this
company was the first that I talked to. He told me to write the company
in a week or so and we can go further into the matter. He took down
the number of the patent. I was very elated over my reception there.
When he asked me what I would take for the patent I told him that I
had no idea as to what the invention is worth. I told him that I would
like to see it put into use and that I would like a small royalty. He
said that the large companies had quit buying patents on that basis. I
came back to Times Square ate lunch and went to Loews State to see
Buddy Berigan's orchestra and Maxine Sullivan, the colored singer who
is famous for the record "Loch Lomond." The show was "The Man
in the Iron Mask." It was supposed to have taken place during Louis
XIV's reign. Called up Martha Wade at the Waldorf Astoria and invited
her to go out with Frank Jones and me tonight. She said she is going
to "Hellzapoppin" and that she will go to it with us. After that Frank
and I decided to go to that show but when we found out that there
was standing room only we began to cast about for another show. We
passed by the theatre where "Tobacco Road" was showing and decided
to give it a try. We got very good seats for 55¢. This show, which has
been running for six years, was funny at first but the vulgarity at times
got pretty rough. James Barlan, the main character, was hysterically
funny. Some of his typical profane remarks set the audience to howling.
They did not spare the horses. The hare-lipped daughter of the Jeeter's
family acted out a very pathetic, passionate scene right on stage. I have
seen lots of people and families that were somewhat like the Jeeters

in the South, but they are the exception among the lower class of southern people. These simple families are, as a rule, pretty straightlaced and God-fearing. The conversation in this play seems to me to be more nearly typical of the New York City taxi drivers and drunks. Got a letter from Mr. R. S. Kelley of the Talon Co. telling me that he will be in his office all this week. I will plan to see him about Friday. Captain Eddie Rickenbacker passed Frank and me in the lobby of the Park Central as I was getting my mail. While we were in front of "Hellzapoppin" Alice Faye and her husband, Tony Martin, passed us and got in a taxi. I didn't notice who they were though. Someone told me after they had already gone. I got a good look at Tony though and he was nice looking. Got a good look at Sonja Heine in the lobby of the Waldorf Astoria when I took Martha home. Billy Wade, Frank, and I went by the Stork Club, Club No. 18, and some of the other night spots where celebrities hang out. I left Frank and Billy about 2:30 and went to our room in the Sloan House "Y." I was pretty tired and the play "Tobacco Road" just about soured me on New York.

Wednesday, August 30, 1939 I got up early and checked out of my room in New York. Got on a bus for Waterbury, Conn. Sat by a very pretty Connecticut girl and talked to her most of the way. Arrived at about two o'clock and went to the Kingsboro Hotel. My first visit was to the American Fastener Co., M. J. Kiessling, Waterbury, Conn. I was shown into Mr. Kiessling's office and I demonstrated the invention to him and his brother. Before I got through their father came in and I demonstrated to him. They say they have been in the business 20 years. They have a very modern factory of three or four floors and I would guess that they employ two or three hundred people. They make fasteners with the trade name "Lockfast." Incidentally one of my models was on their make of fastener. I obtained it from Sears, Roebuck. He asked me how I learned their name. Mr. Kiessling told me that Talon is ten times larger than his company but that he has just installed new machines that make his Zipper one of the very best on the market. He says it is even smoother and superior in many respects to the Talon fastener. Mr. Keissling is not a college man, nor is his brother and he says that he considers his company "small fry." The American Fastener Company used to be a corporation but the Kiessling brothers recently bought up all the stock. I mentioned to him that I may be interested in going into the Zipper business and that I would perhaps like to work for his company, that is if I do not sell to another company. From a promotion standpoint I had rather work for a small company rather than a large one. Waterbury is a nice little manufacturing town of about 150 thousand population. It is about a three hour drive from New York and about 2.3 miles from Yale University, at New Haven. I ate a nice dinner not far from the hotel and retired very early. It was barely dark. Lux soap is made here; Scovill also has a plant, the Patent Button Works and numerous other novelty enterprises of copper, brass and nickel are located here. Mr. Kiessling advised me to go to Shoe Hardware and to see Mr. C. T. Manville.

Thursday, August 31, 1939 This morning I went to the Shoe Hardware Division, U.S. Rubber Co. 72 Brown Street, Waterbury, Conn. to see C. T. Manville. I had to wait a few minutes before being shown into Mr. Manville's office. He immediately called a secretary and had her look up a copy of my patent in their files. She brought it in just a few minutes. We had not talked five minutes until we got off on the subject of camps. He is about 45 years old and has no boys of his own but is very fond of boys and he has two nephews staying with him who have just returned from a northern camp in which they caught 52 trout between them on a 15 day canoe trip. Mr. Manville himself is very good at woodwork and he spends some of his weekends at these camps instructing in craft work. His wife has done councilors work and has taught at the University of Texas. We also talked of football and numerous other things. He asked me about Vandy's prospects next fall. I told him "fair" but that the University of Tennessee would be national champs. He seemed to like my invention and said that he would like for me to send him a model so that he could take it up with his engineering and sales staffs when I mentioned the raincoat idea his eyes flashed. He said "you know we are one of the largest raincoat makers in the world." I am going to send him a model and suggest that he have one of them put on an actual raincoat. He outlined to me the different plans that they have used in dealing with inventions in connection with patents. He said that the down payment and graduated royalty basis is perhaps best of all. He is one of the nicest fellows I have talked to and I sincerely believe that he will do what he can to help get the thing on the market. I also mentioned the prospect of working with the outfit that buys the patent. His company makes the "kwick" fasteners. Caught a local bus for Meadville, Pa., for my interview with the Talon people. Mr. Kelley wrote that he would be in his office all this week. Caught a bus out of Waterbury this evening at two and had to go by way of New York City. Arrived in New York about dark and did not leave there until about 9:30 P.M.

Friday, September 1, 1939 I rode all night on the bus. It was a large comfortable one; we would have suffered otherwise. There was a real good-looking blonde sitting a couple of seats in front of me. I was hoping she'd move back, but she never did, not even after I wrote her a note. I got little catnaps all night but it was a poor excuse for a night's rest. Arrived in Pittsburgh at noon. Everyone was listening to the radio and discussing the war situation. Hitler bombed four towns in Poland this morning and Great Britain and France are expected to come to Poland's defense. It will probably mean another world war. The city of Pittsburgh did not impress me very favorably this evening. I spent an hour there walking around. It is kind of dismal and smokey, like Nashville. It was a longer trip from Pittsburgh to Meadville than I had expected. I did not arrive at Meadville until five-thirty P.M. I went to the Savage Hotel, cleaned up and strolled about the town. Learned that the population is 24 or 25 thousand and that they claim to have the best drinking water in the world. They have artesian wells. I walked out to the Talon plant and gave it the once over. Met an old Negro in front of the plant and talked to him about thirty minutes. He told me about Mrs. Walker (the Col's. widow) living in a large house on one of the Meadville streets. Her husband died a few years ago. Her son took over and then he died and Mr. William C. Arthur became President. The old darkie told me that his parents were born in Alabama and that he himself worked for the railroad until he was pensioned at $79.00 per month. Says that he remembers when the Hookless Fastener was just a little hole-in-the-wall building. They now have four divisions in Meadville, and one in Erie. The plant that I visited this evening used to be a boiler factory but it went bankrupt and Talon Co. took over the property. I went to bed at ten this evening.

Saturday, September 2, 1939 I did not wake up until eleven o'clock. The all night bus ride was almost too much for me. The Talon offices closed at eleven A.M. Tomorrow is Sunday and Monday is Labor Day. Seems that I arrived at a very inopportune time. I called Mr. Kelley but his wife said he was at the Meadville Club and would probably not be at home until late this evening. I went to the picture show, "The Star Maker" starring Bing Crosby. After the show I walked around the town. I saw the very lovely Walker home where the widow of the late Col. Walker resides. I have an urge to ask her for an interview tomorrow. I could get a feature story for the Banner—whether they want it or not. I bet I could really get some interesting points from her. Haven't made up my mind as yet but I may do that very thing. She lives on Grove Street. A few blocks from the Walker home is the Talon plant. The plant is set on a hill, very well arranged and the grounds are neat and trim. It is a model factory, if I ever saw one. I called Mr. Kelley at six-thirty and made an engagement with him for nine in the morning. I am to go out to his home. Ate lightly tonight and inquired at the station about train service before retiring. The trip to Stevenson will cost $14.03. I can leave at 8:28 A.M. or at 9:25 P.M. I will either go Sunday or Monday night. Saw a sign in a Meadville restaurant tonight which said "Our beer makes you see double and feel single." Talked for quite a while with the man at the desk tonight. He has lived here all his life and says that this city has not seriously felt the depressions. He remembered the one in 1893. There used to be a big glass factory which closed in Meadville when he was a boy of eight. Col. Walker used to be superintendent of the Sunday school here and taught a class. His son, who died last year, is said to have lived "too fast."

Sunday, September 3, 1939 I took a taxi to the Plateau to see Mr. R. S. Kelley at his home. I arrived at nine-thirty and we went to his beautiful lawn garden to talk. I gave him my regular demonstration and then he studied the claims and complained that they were rather narrow. He says that there is a possibility that if he himself had the patent in charge that he could possibly get a reissue on it. I doubt that though. We discussed the Legat patent which G. E. Prentice owns and also a Sundback patent which suggested a fastener something like mine for keeping the bottom from fastening when it is not in the correct position. Mr. Kelley says that he worked in Washington in connection with the patent office for ten years. He does know his stuff or seems to on Zipper patents. He advises that one good clear-cut patent is superior to a number of patents on the same feature. He said that they figure that they can pay a thousand dollars for a patent that may in the future be of service to the company. The Talon Company owns more patents than any other Zipper company. They own outright over 500 and they have about one hundred pending at this time. He told me that if I would stay until Tuesday he could probably get his company to write out a check that would well take care of my expenses on this trip. When I asked about going through the plant he said, "There is only one objection and that is a personal one. If I showed you through the plant you would probably be pestering me for the next ten years telling me how I could improve it." I told him if he would show me through the plant I'd stay. Then he invited me to go with him and the two fellows from Washington to the Air Races at Cleveland, Ohio. I accepted. He drove me in his Cadillac to the "Lafayette." He said that he would pick me up in the morning at eight o'clock. While Mr. Kelley was in the house I talked to his little girl, who is ten years old, about camp. She went to a camp in Vermont last year (that is this summer) and it cost about $350.00. I think I'll write to Mr. Kelley next summer about getting his daughter to come to Dixie. Mr. Kelley himself says that he plans to vacation some place down towards Asheville, N.C. I am going to the races with them tomorrow and Tuesday I'll be taken through the plant. I'll also probably get to talk to their chief engineer. I went to the show "Stanley and Livingston" this evening starring Spencer Tracy. Livingston was the missionary to Africa and Stanley was the news reporter for the New York paper that sent a party in search of Livingston. I enjoyed the picture very much. Wrote a letter to Susan telling her about my good luck and good fortune here and about my fear of what may develop in the war situation now that England has declared war and that France is prepared for it. Heard President Roosevelt speak to the nation tonight about war. He advised the people to discriminate between rumors and actual facts and to forget prejudice and let the nation be of one thought. He said, "I have seen war and I say as I have said before, I hate war." He assured the people that the government would do all in its power to see that this nation remains neutral.

Monday, September 4, 1939 Mr. Kelley, Francis Stephens, M. D. Pickens and Mr. Hogue came by the hotel this morning for breakfast. Then all of us except Mr. Kelley left for the National Air Races in Cleveland, Ohio. Mr. Pickens, who is Mr. Kelley's assistant in the legal department at Talon, did the driving. He is a large fellow about thirty years old who has been to a half dozen prep schools in the South, including Webb, T.M.I. and Gulf Coast Military Academy. He went to Annapolis and then to the law school in Washington. He worked in the patent office at the same time. He was originally from New Orleans. He is really lots of fun. Mr. Stephens is a member of the firm of Larsen and Baily of Washington. Conway P. Coe used to practice law with the firm before he became Commissioner of Patents. Mr. Stephen's firm is composed of young men, mainly, and they have several large accounts such as Talon. Hogue is a real estate man. Builder of cheese boxes as Pickens calls him. It rained all the way to Cleveland but it slacked up just as we arrived at the airport. The others had box seats $7.95 so I had to agree to the price. It was the largest show I have ever seen. The Army and Navy put on gigantic demonstrations. Each of them had about 12 planes here for the maneuvers. The largest plane I have ever seen was the U.S. Army Boeing XB15 Super Flying Fortress. It had four motors and a cruising speed of nearly 400 miles per hour. It is really faster than the speed planes on a straight course. We saw the plane take off and fly past the stands. The field is so large that these air events do not disturb the regular commerce. Saw Donny Fowlie do a piggyback landing in the air. Saw all kinds of upside down acrobatics, loops and spins. The Thompson Trophy Race was postponed because of the rainy weather and low ceiling. We were disappointed about not getting to see the main feature but it was a good show anyway. We did not get back to the city of Meadville until about ten o'clock. We ate a fine T-bone steak. On arriving we went to Picken's apartment and relaxed for awhile before retiring. Pickens walked part of the way with me and told me about the relationship between the town and the Talon Company. Jealousy exists in spite of the prosperity that the Zipper factory has brought. Half of the golf and country club resigned. They said "Why don't you call it the Talon Club." The company is held up in prices on every hand and taken advantage of often. They have trouble with labor. They can't cut prices to the level that they could if they were not bothered by labor agitations. Back in my head I was thinking all the time about the advantages of a plant in the South. The wages here are sky high. I can see Dr. Dyer's point that small businesses sometimes have advantages over the larger ones. A small business is at least more wieldy.

Tuesday, September 5, 1939 When I got to the Talon plant this morning Mr. Kelley was waiting for me and I was ushered right in. He and the chief engineer, Mr. Noel J. Poux, Research Engineer, Talon, Inc., were discussing the device when I walked in. Mr. Kelley took the drawings up to the office of the sales manager and vice-president, Mr. Sam Kinney to get his advice on the matter. Mr. Kinney's advice was a little disappointing, so Mr. Kelley said, and his throwing cold water complicated matters. While Kelley was up talking to Kinney, Mr. Poux and I had a confidential talk. He said that he had been in the business about 26 years—from the very beginning and he has bought and sold lots of patents over the counter. He looks a great deal like Knudsen who is president of G.M. "Don't be afraid to state your beliefs," he said, "of course you'll get your ears pinned back once in awhile, but don't mind that." In answer to my questions he said, "Cross one bridge at a time. Your invention is on a releasable catch at the bottom. Let someone else worry about the top release. As to the value of the invention, he said, "It is worth as much as you can get out of it." "If I were you I would not be disappointed if I went away without selling, you have plenty of time." I took down his name and address and told him that I wanted to write him later on. He gave his initials and address willingly and said that he would welcome a letter. I can readily understand the position that Mr. Kinney took. It is easier to say "no" than it is to say "yes." After all the man in charge of sales and advertising would bear the brunt of marketing of an innovation. I think we can win him over though. Stephens, Pickens and Hogue then came into the office and we talked over the claims of my invention and the possibilities of getting a reissue on the patent. Mr. Kelley got out of his files a number of patents pertaining to inventions in this field and we checked over them to find out how close they came to my invention. We found one or two devices for opening the tracks at the bottom and also the Legat patent which shows a method for switching loose at the top. I pointed out, however that my invention is the first to combine the releasable catch at bottom and the slide release at the top. I also pointed out that they cannot take part of one invention and use it against an issued patent which is in no way "obvious" in the old patents. Mr. Kelley told the group that I "cleverly" pointed out that my invention is a "combination" patent of old parts to accomplish a new result. Kelley had his secretary write for the history of my case before the patent office. After this conference we went to lunch at the Talon cafeteria and then for a drive around Meadville looking over the real estate prospects. At two o'clock we started our journey through the factory. I was thrilled to see the machines which were putting the teeth on the cloth strips. The "y" shaped wire is fed into the machines, which bite off the teeth, feeds them into a revolving notched disc, where they are punched and pressed into the desired shape, and when each tooth is in the proper space on the chain of cloth, levers come in from the sides and brad the opened mouth of the "y" shaped tooth into the cloth. I had a great curiosity to see how those machines work. They call them the chain machine. We also took a peep into a room where a teacher was conducting a Zipper school. We left the main plant and went to the shop by the railroad where the clips, slides, stops and other miscellaneous parts are made. The people work forty hours per week and are paid good wages, but still their jobs are pretty confining and routine. I had no idea the business was as complicated as it is. About $25.00 a week is the lowest wage to regular work which requires an average factory skill. We left the plant at about four o'clock and Hogue and I bought our railroad tickets. At six o'clock we went to Picken's apartment where he, Kelley, Hogue, and Stephens were sipping cocktails. About an hour later we went to Gray's restaurant for steak dinners. Here the boys drank more and before train time they were feeling pretty good. I went by the hotel and got my baggage and met the boys at the station. Just before the train pulled out, Stephens threw a pebble against the train. It did not make much noise, so he picked up another, quite a bit larger and threw it through the window of the train leaving a hole about the size of my head. They disappeared for a few minutes and as the train pulled out whom should we see at the end of the station all of them waving good-bye.

Wednesday, September 6, 1939 The train arrived at Galion, Ohio at two o'clock and departed at four. From Galion I rode on the New York Central's "Big Four." At eight-thirty or nine we pulled into Cincinnati. From there I got on the L. and N. and at four this afternoon I returned to Nashville. Met Rabbi Marx in the smoker on the way to Nashville. We talked for a few minutes and then he continued reading Time magazine about the war situation. I was tired when I got to the Albemarle. Aunt Bess fell and hurt her arm just a few minutes after I arrived. Osgood and Katherine came by after supper. Osgood had a date with Frances Evans and invited me to go with him. Telephoned my friend Mary Engles and got a date with her. We drove around and stopped awhile and danced.

Thursday, September 7, 1939   I stayed at the house today while uncle and the family were out looking over a farm. After lunch I went to school and told Mr. Turner about my trip through the Northeast and he said that he was going to use the same salesmanship in putting over his Living Endowment Fund. At four o'clock I saw Mr. Tyne and made my report. He said, "Congratulations for the fine work."

Friday, September 8, 1939   I went to the new Theta house to see Susan this morning. She and Susan Scoggins, Katheryn Simpson, and Lucille Johnson were there. I went by and got Uncle Walt's Negroes to help them bring a flower box from the sun porch. Susan's hair was wavy in front, rather in a complicated pleat. I liked it better. Saw she was wearing the silver bracelet. I was certainly glad to see her after so long. Caught the train and arrived in Stevenson at noon. Saw Percy and Claude Spivey the minute I got off. Claude said, "Oh I see why the train stopped now." Told Percy of my experiences. Mother and I went to a show tonight, "San Francisco," starring Clark Gable and Jeanette MacDonald, Spencer Tracy and Jack Holt.

Saturday, September 9, 1939   I spent the day with the folks whom I have not seen in quite awhile. About ten or fifteen letters have arrived while I was gone and I opened and read them. Pop J. sent me a check for $58.00 as commission on my four camp boys. Jean Burke wrote me from camp thanking me for my letter and the pictures I sent her. The letter I appreciated most, of course, was from Susan. She had told me there would be a letter waiting for me when I arrived home. I answered Tom Happel's letter immediately. He has severed relations with International Shoe. Went over to a medicine show tonight. The old doctor was a pretty smooth customer. The music was good and they put on a blackfaced act at the end of the show that was excellent. They sold quite a bit of medicine.

Sunday, September 10, 1939   Geo L.'s picture was in the Birmingham News. He had on his flying outfit and seemed as happy as a lark. He is in something he likes. At dinner today I made the statement that George would have to stay in the service quite awhile to pay off his obligations. Dad made the statement that it would take someone else quite awhile also. (He was referring to the fact that he had paid off the note for me from Uncle Walt.) I said that it would take quite awhile for some of my other relatives to pay off also. This started the fireworks and Dad gave me a lecture on not appreciating what he has done. I do appreciate everything, but I don't appreciate his cutting remarks, at times. Went out to see Freda this evening. Henry went to see "Perk" (Mary Elizabeth Talley). Ran into Mrs. Mabel and Sammy out there.

Mrs. Mabel, of course, asked me about my trip and when I told her about the luck I had in meeting the officials of the different companies she said: "You know what made you get such a good response from them? You discussed points of mutual interest. I can remember when you used to bring my paper and you used to talk to every woman on this street. That was good training for you." Freda and I drove to the dam, and enjoyed visiting a place where we used to have so much fun, years ago, just talking. The dam property is not kept as tidy as it used to be. Anderson said that Dad had brooded all afternoon about our little fuss. Tonight I played five games of Chinese checkers with Dad and Anderson.

Monday, September 11, 1939   I saw Dad and Jim Bennett Austin at People's Restaurant eating. Went over to the high school this evening and watched the boys practicing football. Wilson was running with the first team. Henry D. and I worked out with them for a few minutes. They haven't enough men to have a first-class team. Talked to Jack Dennison and his wife on the street tonight about their airplane. Jack has bought a Stinson and is going to keep it in Chattanooga. Sammy Simpson has just passed his pilot's license examination.

Tuesday, September 12, 1939   Got a note from Freda saying she would like to go swimming this evening. I could not get out there until three o'clock and Freda had come in to the funeral of Mr. Jordan's mother. Carolyn Spivey was here with her Dad delivering flowers from her shop in Scottsboro. Mary Wallace took her riding. Bill Simpson, Mary Wallace, Freda Atwood and I went out to the dam about four o'clock. The clutch in the car burned and we had to get someone to push us all the way from the dam. Bill Simpson got his car and drove Freda and me home. I told Freda good-bye until the next Christmas holidays.

Wednesday, September 13, 1939   Confirmed by mail my date with Susan Friday. Went over to Dick Shofner's this evening and talked to him about his invention of a rubber fastener on a shoe polish can, or the like. Talked to Mr. Percy Armstrong tonight in the drugstore. He was telling about Geo L.'s experiences in trying to get in the Air Corps. Almost everybody in Stevenson is talking aviation now. Mrs. Alice Armstrong said that she wanted to learn before she gets too old. Percy said that George flew over Stevenson and cut a few loops and everyone there went wild over it. Bill Henniger, Sammy Simpson, Mac Johnson and Rice Coffee are among the pilots. Percy said that Dad fussed around while Geo L. was here but when he got off to the air corps, Dad came around and said "well by gad, he made it didn't he." Robby Graham is dating Rebecca tonight and Mary W. has a date with J. Selly McGriff. Wilson is getting mother to help him on his Latin. Katherine Armstrong told me tonight that she is going to study medicine. She'll make a good doctor.

Thursday, September 14, 1939 Had my teeth checked. Gus McMahan was there. So was Mr. Hodges, who used to be coach here. He is principal of the grammar school at Scottsboro now.

Friday, September 15, 1939 Packed my suitcase tonight. Got up early and caught the train at 9:20 and got to Nashville shortly after noon. Saw Walter Parks and Mac Campbell down at the train looking for freshmen. A few were beginning to come in. Called Susan about our date and she said that she had been working at the sorority house all day and that she was too tired to have a date. We put it off until tomorrow night. I went to the Knickerbocker to see Jimmy Cagney and George Raft in "Each Dawn I Die." It was the story of a newspaper man who accidently got in the pen and served four years on trumped-up charges. Raft, the criminal, finally came through for him.

Saturday, September 16, 1939 Unpacked. Mary W. came in at noon. Went out to see Susan at eight o'clock. Mr. John Cheek met me at the door and we talked until Susan came down. Talked of North Carolina and Georgia as vacation spots. Susan and I talked of the sorority house work, and then started for a Coca Cola. We stopped behind the old post office and saw an airplane do some rolls. Drove by the sorority house but no one was there. Then we drove by Hettie Ray's and danced. We were out in the open pavilion and saw Billy Eason come in. Susan and I were about to leave the pavilion but after seeing Billy Eason she said "we might as well stay here." We stayed for awhile and then went up to the closed section. Saw Eleanor Richey Cheek, Tommy Tart Brown, Hensley Williams, Dayton Manier and others from Vandy. Partee Fleming came over and sat with us for awhile. Eason came by and spoke to me. He said: "I'm glad to see you." Louise Sykes told me she sent a card from California to Stevenson. I told her I did not get it. Bud Beasley, Mickey Carmichael and Merrill Stone were there. I took Susan home nearly an hour late but she said her dad would not fuss because Eleanor Richey is sometimes late. It could be that Susan does what she wants to do and uses the parental excuse only when it fits in with her own wishes.

Sunday, September 17, 1939 Susan told me last night that Dr. King Vivian, of McKendree Methodist Church is very much like Dr. Sutton. I decided to go hear him this morning. Dr. Vivian is a Scotsman and his accent reminds one of what was once said of Thomas Carlyle: "His voice is as refreshing as a gush of fresh mountain air." Jean Burke came by and took Mary Wallace to see "Beau Geste." I met her sister Margaret for the first time. Once when I gave Jean a picture I identified Margaret as "some other girl." Jean told me that Susan's mother, Mrs. Cheek, is paying for the refurnishing of one room at the Theta House and Shirley's mother, Mrs. Meredith Caldwell, is paying for another.

Monday, September 18, 1939 I went to the Banner office this morning and wrote a story about freshman camp. John Hood took some pictures of the freshmen departing for camp. I went to practically every clothing store in town this afternoon trying to locate a raincoat with a Zipper in it. I finally found one at Joe Morse's and then Mr. Morse himself had to locate it for me. I paid five dollars for the coat and then took it to Mr. Tyne's office for his approval, since he is going to pay for it. Called Susan at five and she said she and Florence Abernathy would go to a show with me. I went by at eight-thirty and Susan had been trying everywhere to get me because her mother would not let her go. Florence got up at six o'clock this morning and she was already in bed. I stayed only a few minutes. I then telephoned Mary Engles and we drove out to Lynnmeade and danced. We later stopped by 1909 20th Avenue South and then on home. I too was tired.

Tuesday, September 19, 1939 Heard Adolf Hitler speaking from Danzig, Poland this morning. He spoke for an hour and fourteen minutes in one of his most colorful speeches. It is amazing that even though I don't understand a word of German I get a feeling of what he was saying. My emotions respond in accordance with the amount of emotion the speaker is putting into the speech, and the audience reacts also, with no relation whatsoever to the meaning of what is being said. I suppose this is the spell that magnetic speakers cast over their audiences, even those who understand the words. On the campus I saw Bill Embry, Jim Reed III, Roy Kelley and Delbert Mann. They were working at the Panhellenic clearing house where freshmen pledges and dates are recorded. I had a short conversation with Mr. Turner and then saw Byron Anglin in Mr. Gerald Henderson's office asking for an extension on his telephone in his upstairs office in the Student Union building. It seems that Dean Arnold is going to give Anglin another chance as a freshman in the law school. Mary Wallace completed her first day of "rush" with the sororities. She said she saw many friends at different houses. Louise Douglas was warm and gracious to her at the Theta House. Susan told her of our dating difficulties last night. Miriam McGaw and Landis Shaw were especially nice at the Tri Delta House. Tonight I wrote a letter to Mr. and Mrs. Jesse Madden thanking them for the delightful time I had with them on the trip to New York this summer. I wrote a thank you note to Mr. R. S. Kelley at Talon in Meadville and to United States Rubber's Mr. C. T. Manville and to Mr. Kiessling at American Fastener Company.

1. Susan Cheek with Owl Club members Harris Abrahams, Rush Dozier, Leonard Anglin and Bob Seyfried. 2. The Delta Kappa Epsilon fraternity. 3. Chancellors Carmichael and Kirkland. 4. Honor Committee officers, Left to Right—Harris Abrahams, Ben Austin and Richard Pickens. 6. Marvin "Preacher" Franklin gives an O.D.K. kiss. 7. At a Deke barn dance are, Left to Right—Ben Austin, Miriam McGaw, Charles Majors, Helen Ford, Jack Worley and Mary Jane Peyton. 8. Jimmy Weems receives Public Speaking medal from Dr. A. M. Harris. 9. Ray Morrison, head football coach. 11. Andromedia Bagwell. Ben Austin at the Deke house. In the background, Left to Right—Bill Shumaker, George Harmon, and John McReynolds. 13. Grey Moore and Damaris Witherspoon.

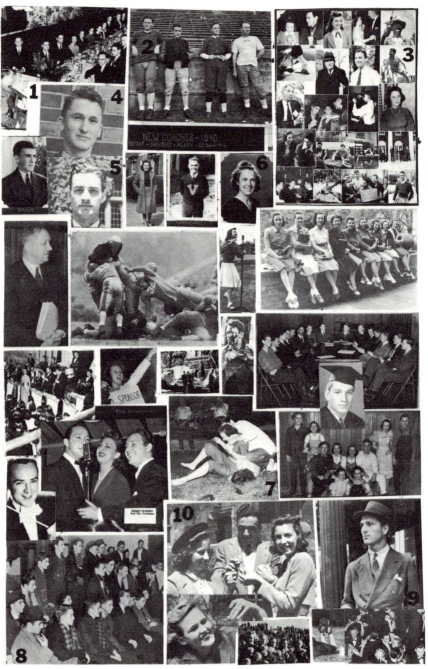

1. Dr. George R. Mayfield at Student Union banquet. 2. "Bear" Bryant and "Red" Sanders, when they were directing Vanderbilt's football fortunes. 3. In this composite Marguerite Wallace, Martha Wood, Hartwell Weaver and Dr. Tom Zerfoss are in the last three pictures of the upper frame. Dr. Edwin Mims and Henry Clay are the two center pictures of the second frame. Dr. Gus Dyer is in the first picture of the third frame. Jim Reed is in the lower right hand corner. 4. Edmund Pardue. 5. McPheeters Glasgow, 6. Elise Pritchett. 7. Ben Austin "rough-housing" with Mary Helen Henry and Shirley Caldwell on "Informal Day." 8. Nashville Banner photographer, John Hood, snapped this photograph of the audience at the instant Ben Austin did a forward roll in the finals of the Intra-mural wrestling tournament against "Bud" Bray. 9. Jack Clay. 10. Holding the winners in the Turtle Trudge are, Left to Right—Mary Frances Dodd, Lester (Dusty) Rhodes and Frances McConnell.

FALL
1939

Wednesday, September 20, 1939 The fraternity brothers are busy getting ready for the beginning of "Rush Week" in the morning. Jimmy Winchester, who is visiting us, reported that he has been accepted by the Air Force. Went to the football game with Joe Little. It was the first time I ever saw a college football team lose a game because of taking out the varsity too soon. Vanderbilt committed the unpardonable sin of doing just this and Tennessee Polytechnic Institute was the winner. Jim Huggins played a beautiful game though. Mary Wallace told us about rushing experiences. She says that there is a lot of sham and acting to it but that a great many of the girls seem to have depth. She complimented Susan on being so refined and ladylike in all of her actions. She seems to think a great deal of the Thetas and, of course, she has a great many friends in the Tri Delta sorority. She very wisely says that she doesn't think she'll have time to pledge any of them. I attempted to contact Jordan this morning. Learned this evening that he also had attempted to contact me so I called tonight and got him. Dr. Mayfield was near the phone and chimed in. Jordan said that on the way back from freshman camp he and Dr. Mayfield had mentioned me. Dr. Mayfield yelled to Jordan that the freshman this year missed a treat in not hearing Ben speak to them. I answered that I appreciated the compliment. Bud Beasley told me today that Harris Abrahams made a nice speech out there yesterday. Saw Abraham at the game this evening. Had a pleasant chat with M. on the street today. He is one of my best friends in spite of the Honor Committee's prosecutions last year. Jordan has a mustache which has been growing three weeks. He is full of his visit with Trotsky last summer in Mexico. I sat up until two o'clock talking to Jordan and from two until three thirty I wrote an answer to Jimmy Stahlman's column.

Thursday, September 21, 1939 I went to the house this morning for the first day of rushing. I enjoyed seeing the boys and joining in on the excitement. Hartwell Weaver arrived this evening and told me that the people in Dixon are crazy about Osgood Anderson and that he has talked to Osgood about taking over a scout troop. Weaver told Osgood that he is going to bring me home with him some weekend soon. Paid "Ma" Clapp $10.00 today and told him I would pay on the balance from time to time. Called Susan this evening and asked about coming over and seeing the new house. She said we would not be allowed to go today but that we can tomorrow. She seemed very glad to have had me call.

Telephoned Virginia Richey this evening for a date for the Matriculation Dance. Said she had to work that night but that she is anxious to see me and to talk over our respective trips. Went to see "Beau Geste" with Weaver and Hume. It is a story of three brothers, by adoption, who stuck together through "thick and thin."

Friday, September 22, 1939 I went to the fraternity house about eleven o'clock. Rode home with George Appelby, who is working for the telephone company. This evening at three I went to the Theta House with Buddy Stone and Tom Cummings to take a look at the new house since it has been fixed. Susan met us at three o'clock and showed us through. It is really nice now. Susan was dressed in a very becoming green skirt and sweater with puffed sleeves. She had on the silver bracelet I gave her and it was very shiny and pretty. I am really proud of it, and she is too. She drove Tom and me back down West End to the corner of 23rd. She did not dare offer to take us down 23rd and to let us out in front of the Deke House. She has the modesty of our grandparents' time. At five-thirty Jordan came by and picked me up at the Deke House. We drove with Dr. Mayfield and Dean Zeigler to the girls' camp. At the camp we saw Dean Ada Bell Stapleton and listened to her pro-British speech, saw Libby Zerfoss, Frances Carter, Mary Wallace, Jean Burke and others who are coming to Vanderbilt. It looks like a pretty good crop of freshmen. Jordan found Dean Zeigler quite interesting and we plan to invite her for dinner some evening. We stopped at the Toddle-house for lunch on the way back and stopped at the Mayfield's for a few minutes. Saw Mrs. Jordan Monk, Mrs. Mayfield, and George Jr. Heard gossip about the new sorority on the campus Psi Phi.

Saturday, September 23, 1939 Saw and talked to Roy Huggins on the way to the Deke House. I found Gray Stahlman a very interesting person. He is Jimmy Stahlman's half uncle. He has attended St. John's Military Academy for quite a few years and was a Captain there last year. Bill Jordan told me to look him up. Saw Bill Borches tonight. "Blimp" and I talked about his and Charley's work at General Shoe. Jim Browning is in the inquiry dept. and Chas. is in the correspondence dept. He used a dictaphone in answering fifty or sixty letters per day. He has been doing this work for two months. Jim is driving a small, new Studebaker. Homer Howell drove me home this evening. I was amused at his saying he is tired of going to school. "I am so anxious to get married and start raising kids that I don't know what to do." I wrote a long letter to Pop J. answering his questionaire about changes next year. I am flattered that he writes for my opinion on such matters.

Sunday, September 24, 1939 I rode to the Deke House with Jim Browning this morning. Had a long and enjoyable talk with Billy Whitson from McMinnville. Mac Dickinson went S.A.E. as I expected. I saw Howard Ball and his new wife drive by the fraternity house. Charles Hughes and Bob Sturdivant stopped by the house to renew acquaintances. I hated to see Gray Stahlman pledge Phi Delta Theta; also Matt Dobson. We have had a lot of competition with the Betas this year. We had about ten pledges when I left tonight. They seem like a good group.

Monday, September 25, 1939 I went by to see Mr. Miles and got my coaching job again this year. I am going to be doing two full hours of work each day. I wrote a feature story on matriculation at Vanderbilt and telephoned it to Jimmy Metcalf. When I went by the fraternity house this evening I learned that we now have fifteen pledges. I visited Hill Turner, Dr. Walker and Dean Sarratt. I received a letter from Jimmy Stahlman, publisher of the Nashville Banner, in response to the letter I wrote him several days ago. It was a nice letter. I was surprised at the reasonableness of it. After all, I am his employee and he could have been nasty, had he chose to do so. Bill Jordan came by the apartment and dictated a story about his trip to Mexico and his visit with the exiled Trotsky. Trotsky was a brilliant and popular leader of post-revolutionary Russia, but he did not do his staff work and Stalin did. Stalin built up an organization that outvoted Trotsky in the politburo. I was sitting on a downtown street, curb this afternoon, waiting for a street car when a couple of boys and girls came by in a car. One of the girls yelled: "Buddy, are you blue?" One of the other girls put a "honey" on her greeting.

Tuesday, September 26, 1939 Went to the Banner office this morning and worked until two o'clock with "Putt" Reynolds getting the pledge lists from the various fraternities. Ate lunch with Jordan at the Tally-ho and then went to school to register. Prof. Blair said "Are you going to have any activities this year"? I said "They are all cut out." He said "Your leadership training was valuable last year but it hurt your scholarship, didn't it"? Prof. Binkley advised that taking the History 450 without the advanced build-up courses would be pretty difficult. "It's the only option open" I told him "so there is no way out." Dr. Mims invited me to come around to see him soon. Called up Susan and found her resting for the frolic tonight. Bill Simpson, Bill Jordan and I went to the Matriculation Dance. I saw several people that knew Mary Wallace and they all complimented her. Someone told me that she captained one of the camp baseball teams. Shirley Caldwell said "I wish I were as sweet as she is." Susan was with Eason and did not stay out long for intermission. I danced the second no-break with Miriam "You Taught Me to Love Again." The floors are extra slick. Miriam is still a good dancer. Drank a Coca Cola with Eleanor Richey. Had the third with Susan and let some dumb "cluck" break on me right in the middle of it. Susan is a greatly improved dancer. She has "limbered up" as Jordan put it.

Wednesday, September 27, 1939 I saw Susan at the bookstore and made a date with her for the first football game and for dinner afterwards. She seemed to like the idea. We drank a Coca Cola and discussed our courses. Levy Wade came up and talked to Susan. When he left Shirley Caldwell sat down with us and talked. I went for my first time to Dr. Herbert Sanborn's class. Alice Lewis, Sara Goodpasture, Mary Davidson and Bitsie Napier, are in it. He is a very interesting person. He pointed out that history is divided into two divisions, personal and impersonal and that it is written from the particular slant or idea of the historian. Went to Mr. Turner's office for a few minutes and we talked for one hour. We talked of fraternities, school politics, alumni work and the imbibing of cocktails. John Cross, the newspaper cartoonist, came in while I was there and I was introduced to him. The first general chapel took place today. Chancellor Carmichael made three specific points and discussed them: The death of Dr. Kirkland on August 5; the breaking of ground for the new library and lastly the effect that the outbreak of war, on September 1, might have on the army of college men and women in this country. In this connection he said that the students of this country must devote themselves to holding up a high standard of scholarship. "Integrity of work," he said, "is necessary." "The greatest thing that has happened since I have been connected with the University," he continued, "was the fight that was made last year to uphold the Honor System at Vanderbilt. Some had considered the Honor System a dead issue, but last year's activities proved that the Honor System at this University is a very live tradition."

That statement from the Chancellor is reward enough for sacrifices that any of us made in the fight. There was a time in that fight everything looked black. There was a time when it seemed as if the whole world was against us. There was a time when we would have given up; I would have resigned from the Chairmanship of the Honor Committee, if there had been any doubt whatsoever as to the righteousness of our cause. I remember saying at the time that no one can question our cause, any more than they can question the morality in Christianity itself. Some people may abuse us now, but later on, when they fully realize what we are fighting for, they will admit that we were right. I am happy now, thank God, to realize that time has already come. Every boy who was prosecuted last year is friendly (even more so than usual) with me now. There was only one exception to this and that boy never did confess and the court was never satisfied that he did not cheat. The thing is still on his conscience. Mary Wallace came home from school and said that William Simpson told her that I was the person that Chancellor Carmichael referred to in his opening address this morning, "Ben is the one who did it," he told her. She also told me about visiting Mrs. Haggard and that she said "Ben had a mighty hard time of it last year but we are all proud of him for it." That was extra nice, coming from Mrs. Haggard.

Thursday, September 28, 1939 I attended Dean Pomfret's History class for the first time today. Miriam McGaw, the Austin girl, Tom Alexander and others that I know are in it. Many of them are graduate students. Henry Clay, Andy Bagwell and several other familiar faces are in my Public Speaking class. Sat with Susan, Katherine Simpson, and Peggy Norvell in the Student Center today at lunch. After Susan left Henry Clay said "she is really pretty isn't she? I like her a whole lot." I said, "I like your gal Katie too." To this Henry replied, "she likes you too. She thinks you are one of the finest boys in Vanderbilt." Henry and Mac Dickson asked me to go to a show with them but I could not. Read "The Rise of American Civilization" all evening. Bill Jordan went to my wrestling class this evening and participated in the drills. I could do him a lot of good if he would stick with the class. Kenneth Anderson also took part in the class. I wrote home with Clark Giles, my assistant coach. Talked with Miriam on the telephone and Martha Wood called about helping her develop some publicity for the freshman Student Christian Association.

Friday, September 29, 1939 Dr. Sanborn gave a lecture this morning, which as usual, gave quite a bit of food for thought. The more I study philosophy, however, the more I realize that the different schools of philosophers vie with each other to see which can express most expertly the incomprehensibility of God. In the bookstore I encountered Dr. Gus Dyer and told him about my business trip to the Zipper plants this summer and that I often thought of, and agreed with, his theory that "large companies do not have all of the competitive advantages." He seemed pleased that I had utilized some of his teachings in my own thinking. He told me about one of his own ideas for an invention. He said why not put a band on the handle of the axe to prevent the blade from coming off. Now they make the blade end of the handle larger than the other end and depend on centripetal force to keep the blade in place. Dr. Owsley's class in Sectional Controversy has great promise of being an interesting one. His irreverent style is appealing. Andromedia Bagwell helped me get this year's cheer leaders together so we could take their picture for this afternoon's paper. Had a short talk with Dr. Kuhlman, head of the Joint University Library program, before joining Jordan and Simpson for lunch at Kissam Hall. Mac Dickinson wrestled Rainey Frierson in my class and I toyed with Henry Clay by rubbing his nose in the mat. It makes him so mad that he can't throw me that he goes over and beats his fist into the mat, as if the mat were me. Got a letter from Anderson which said: Dear Ben: You were right when you said that the speech you wrote for me should go over with a bang. It seemed just ordinary to me until I gave it, but I studied it and had it right on the tip of my tongue all the way through. The boys really did respond. Colonel Endsley just now came out of the dining hall with me and said: "Red, that was the best speech you have ever made here, with the exception of your cigarette speech last year." He must have liked it also. The speech was as follows:

A SPEECH AT T.M.I.

"Many young people today feel exempt from the responsibilities of the world. They say: "What can I do? I am just a kid. Nobody will pay attention to what I do or say."

Let me remind you, though, that some of the bravest and noblest deeds that have ever been done in the world have been done by people no older than many of you are. Our history books are full of the heroic deeds of the young people from all countries. Legends have grown up about them.

The most famous story from Holland is the one about the peasant boy who stuck his finger in the dyke until aid came. This deed saved his town.

In France, a young girl dressed up like a man and placed herself at the head of her troops. The valiant spirit of Joan of Arc set the example which inspired French soldiers on to victory. A young girl saved her country.

And what American does not know the story of Nathan Hale, who said: "I regret that I have but one life to give for my country."

And, to bring it even closer to home, right here in Tennessee, Sam Davis, a beardless boy, stood on the gallows because he refused to give out military information.

The Union Commander, seeing his extreme youth and courage, begged him to give the information so he would not have to be hanged. As they tightened the rope around his neck he turned to the Commanding Officer and said: "I cannot betray my friends."

Where the Atlanta Journal now stands in Atlanta, Georgia, there used to be a famous church. The story is told that when plans were first being made for that church, quite a bit of trouble was encountered in raising the necessary funds. At the close of one discouraging meeting a little boy rose up from the audience and said: "I'll give a thousand dollars towards the building of the church."

The preacher was amazed. He said: "Son, you can't give a thousand dollars," and so he passed on and the meeting was adjourned.

At the next meeting the same boy rose and repeated what he said the first day. This time he was ignored.

At the third meeting, when the boy rose and made his pledge, the preacher stopped and called the boy up front. He said: "Son, I wish you would not bother us this way. How can you give a thousand dollars?"

The little boy looked up at the preacher, and his eyes beamed behind his dirty face, as he said: "I can hand up the bricks."

There was a hush over the audience and the editor of the Atlanta Journal rose and said: "If the boy can give a thousand dollars by handing up bricks, I can give ten thousand," and other large donations followed.

In later years it was this same spirit in Atticus Green Haygood that led to the founding of Emory University, and its rise to eminence among Southern universities.

In meeting the problems of the world today, very few of us can be the ones who can make the ten thousand dollar donations, but we can set the example by "handing up the bricks."

Saturday, September 30, 1939 Dean John Pomfret asked me in class this morning why I am studying history. I said on the spur of the moment: "I've heard historical names all my life. It is interesting for me to learn more about these names and the part they played in affairs." I spoke for the first time in Dr. Harris' Public Speaking class this morning. I was interested in the subject and therefore made a pretty good speech. My friend Henry Clay applauded. After we examined the mimeograph, which I worked on this afternoon, Bill Jordan stayed for dinner with Mary Wallace and me. He and I picked up Susan at a quarter of nine and "Katsy" Aycock at nine. Holley played for the dance. The gym floor was slick and in good condition and dancing was smooth and easy. Susan was beautiful. I danced quite a bit with her at first because I knew she had to go to Nancy Hoagland's debut party at ten-thirty. I had the second no-break with Virginia Youmans and the third with Eleanor Richey Cheek. Eleanor told me about the wreck she had on the way to a dance at Castle Heights. I danced several times with Jean Burke, Mary Wallace's friend. She is a good dancer. Heard part of the football game. Rice was expected to beat Vanderbilt by two touchdowns and had us down 12 to 0 at the close of the third quarter. In the last six minutes of play Vandy scored and in the last ten seconds scored again to win from Rice 13–12. The crowd in the gym heard the final score and went wild. It was an exciting event. After taking Susan home, so she could dress for her debut party, Jordan, "Katsy" and I went to the Tally-ho and talked until two o'clock. "Katsy" has some very definite and interesting ideas about the Honor System.

Sunday, October 1, 1939 I went to the Hillsboro Presbyterian Church with Harry T. Moore, the boy who lives in the apartment next to ours, to hear Dr. Kerr's sermon: "How Big Is Your Life?" Maizie, Jim Frank Rudder and one of their friends dropped in to see Mary Wallace this evening. M. W. studied at the library so I served them tea and Roquefort cheese. Telephoned Mrs. Davis this evening and had a long discussion about their grandson Louis, and his friend Tommy Carruthers. They invited me to dinner next Saturday after the football game. I had a date with Virginia Richey this evening. We drove out to the Belle Meade lunch room and danced and stopped by the campus on the way back. Virginia told me about her Western trip and I told her of my experiences in the East. She said she appreciated my letter about her former boy friend, but that she did not want me to be sorry for her. I hated to see the big tears in her eyes. She told me that Miss Sisson, Dean of Ward-Belmont women, said that it is also a pleasure to live through the lives of others.

Monday, October 2, 1939 I attended the magnificent wedding of Jack Clay and Eleanor Reed this evening at the West End Methodist Church. I had seen Jack, Henry and their brother Gordon, from Georgia Military Academy, at the gym this afternoon. I have known Jack for several years and consider him, and my brother George, as two of the best looking boys I have ever seen. Henry, who was the best man, is one of my closest friends. I have enjoyed many pleasant conversations with Eleanor. She, and her brother Jim, are much alike. They both have an ingratiating manner. I sat by Ann Carolyn Gillespie and the Burke family. Louise

Sykes, and her cousin Valery Axtell, sat behind me. Hayes Noel and Joe Dickinson were ushers. It was the first wedding I have ever attended where I could hear everything the participants said. Jack spoke in a clear, resonant voice. Eleanor was beautiful in her white lace gown. The strains of "Here Comes the Bride" are always thrilling. My heart went out to Bobby Oliver, the loser in this triangle, as I saw him on the way out. He was in a state of camouflaging cheerfulness. Why must there always be a loser . . . even on such a happy occasion as this?

Tuesday, October 3, 1939 In Public Speaking today I gave part of the speech I wrote for Anderson. I started off all right but before finishing my knees began to shake and I had a difficult time mastering the nervousness. Don't know that I ever did. As I entered the Banner office this afternoon, I encountered Mr. James G. Stahlman, Publisher and said: "Hello, Mr. Jimmy." He said: "How ya, Ben?" I was a little surprised at his warm greeting, especially after the letter I wrote him last week. But, after all, what I said was that instead of expecting the reader to sort out truth from false propaganda the professional editors ought to do it. I wrote the letter, though, in imitation of Jimmy's own arrogant style in his column "From the Shoulder." I got some "Anti-war Petitions" from the Banner and got permission from Dean Pomfret to make an announcement in freshman chapel soliciting signatures. Dean Pomfret said to me in the hallway of the administration building, "Well Austin, would you say you are getting a liberal education from my course?" I answered that I was not getting it out of his course alone, but that I am enjoying all of my courses. We walked together into the Registrar's office. The Lady Dean was talking with Mrs. Haggard. Dean Pomfret said to Dean Stapleton, pointing to me "This is one of your favorites, isn't he?"

"Yes," replied the Dean of Women, "And you had better treat him nicely."

"I am going to treat him rough," replied Dean Pomfret, "I have seen him wrestle and he can take it."

Wednesday, October 4, 1939 After listening to a dry talk by Dean Pascall in Freshman Chapel this morning, I got up and made my announcement about the "Anti-war Petition" I spoke as follows:

> *"Dean Pascall, Members of the freshman class. I am not going to talk long. (There was applause.) You will recall that Chancellor Carmichael, in his address to the student body last Wednesday, spoke of the war that broke out in Europe on September 1st of this year. He reminded the student body it must concern itself with things that are going on in the outside world.*
>
> *Some 22 years ago a class entered the university, just as you are doing.*

They were just as unconcerned with world affairs as you no doubt are today. Before they graduated, however, they did become interested in the European war. They fought in it. Inscribed on the walls of Alumni Hall are the names of those students who laid down their lives . . . and for what?

We must not let that happen again. If we must fight, let it be right here and now; on the campus rather than on the battlefields of France and Germany. Let us tell our Congressmen that we don't want war.

The Nashville Banner has provided convenient petitions. Every boy and girl in this auditorium should remain a few minutes and sign this petition against war."

During dinner with Bill Simpson and Bill Jordan, I was told that Bill Payne is marrying a girl from Stevenson next week. Jordan facetiously said: "He didn't get away to the Navy soon enough." When I took the petitions, containing 215 signatures, to the Banner office I learned that Mr. Moss had already been turned down by Dean Sarratt on the petitions and he was delighted that I was able to get them. He put the story on the front page this afternoon. The headline said: "VANDERBILT FRESHMEN OK BANNER PEACE PROGRAM." The story went on to say that I spoke to the student body and the students stood for nearly two hours to get their names on the petitions. In talking with Susan tonight she noticed my hoarseness and said: "Maybe you made too good a speech today." While studying with Susan in the library this evening she seemed a little sweeter than usual. Maybe she cares a little.

Thursday, October 5, 1939 I used the example of Uncle Ragan's gas tank leak, near a pile of smoldering leaves, in my speech today. I was not scared and the speech was much better than my first one. Henry Clay spoke on our trip to the Du Pont Company last year. I studied in the library a long time before noticing Susan was there. I waited a little longer before going up to sit with her. She said she would like to take me up on the invitation to attend all of the Community Playhouse productions but that she would purchase her own tickets. Had a long talk with Dr. Irby Hudson about the international situation. He thinks our involvement in the war is inevitable. Perhaps he is right. When this one is over, how long will it be until the next one? That is the ominous question.

Friday, October 6, 1939 Albert Hutchinson, one of my former engineering profs. sat in on Dr. Sanborn's lecture this morning. Sanborn is a distinguished thinker and lecturer, but I imagine he is going through torment these days as Germany the country he loved "40 years ago," as a student, is acting more and more beastly. His lectures reflect his concern and his defensiveness. In a talk with Blair Batson and Pierce Winningham, the Sigma Chi political representatives, I learned Bert

Marshall may resign from the Presidency of the Student Council. He is too conscientious to remain in the office if he does not have time to do a good job. I also learned that Byron Anglin is trying to get the Chi Phis back in the winning political organization. The senior history seminar, with Dr. Binkley, is fruitful. We examine how history is written. One famous case history of conflicting testimony is "Who burned Columbia, South Carolina, during the later stages of the Civil War?" Another is: "Who fired the first shot in the battle of Lexington?" Virginia Youmans, who was Prom queen at Massachusetts Institute of Technology last year, was present for one of my picture-taking sessions this afternoon. She had her shoe off and asked me to look to see if she had a broken toe. I wiggled it and found nothing wrong. I believe she is the best-looking girl I have ever seen and she has a way of flaunting her femininity, or sex appeal, even in such mundane matters as examining a little toe. I called Youmans tonight, to ask for a date, and she was about to get into her bathtub. She said she didn't have on any clothes. I told her it was too bad that the Telephoto phone system is not in operation yet. Elliott Trimble had a fine letter published in the Hustler today, attacking my speech to Freshman Chapel the other day. I will answer it soon. At nine-thirty tonight I went up to Ward-Belmont and walked around the campus with Virginia Richey. Met the night watchman, Mr. Stamper. I was reminded of the story of the night watchman at girls' school who, when offered his paycheck at the end of the week asked: "Do I get paid too?"

Saturday, October 7, 1939 My "Sectional Controversy" professor, Dr. Frank Owsley, is a very interesting lecturer. He makes no bones about his southern prejudice, in fact he delights in it. He loves to tell such stories as the one about Stephen Foster (not the songwriter), who in about 1835 is reported to have said: "I had rather a harlot fill a New England pulpit than one of the Southern Methodist ministers." He says that even though William Lloyd Garrison is usually thought of as being the leader of the Abolition Movement, the real power behind the scenes was a man by the name of Theodore Weld. Arthur and Lewis Tapping, young, second, generation millionaires from New York, put up the money. The Abolitionist's propaganda philosophy was patterned after the British, who are masters of the technique of tying up a political objective with a moral issue. Ate lunch today with George Marion O'Donnell, Jordan, Simpson and Mrs. Brainard Cheney. O'Donnell is one of the literary luminaries on the campus at present. He came along at the tail end of the Agrarian movement of the famous Fugitive group and contributed some articles of his own. Randall Jarrell, whom I studied with last year, during Ransom's absences, is another. Mrs. Cheney, of the Vanderbilt library, is the wife of Brainard Cheney, a late contributor to the movement. Jordan and I escorted Susan to the Kentucky-Vander-bilt football game. Mickey Flannigan passed for a beautiful touchdown in the very first few minutes of the game. Kentucky then got underway and pushed over two touchdowns. From a running position Jim Huggins kicked a spectacular punt that ended up on Kentucky's five or six yard line. Kentucky won by a score of 21 to 13, but it was an exciting game. It was fun being with Susan. She is always a perfect lady and fits into every situation. Went out to the Louis Davis' for dinner and enjoyed roast beef with all the trimmings. At ten I came by the gym dance and discussed the Anglin proposition with my protegé, Harris Abrahams. Rush Dozier came to me and said: "Ben, you are setting a mighty fast pace for us in that Public Speaking Class, but I suppose it will be good training for us." Gave up the third no-break with Virginia Youmans because she was in a jam. Rode home with my assistant wrestling coach, Clark Giles.

Sunday, October 8, 1939 Heard the last of the World Series. The Yankees won four straight from Cincinnati. Lloyd George spoke again for serious consideration of Hitler's terms for peace. How sensible it seems, to give a little to preserve the peace, and yet, human nature being what it is, it never seems to work out that way. Giving even an inch is most times taken as a sign of weakness and it merely emboldens the other side. How pathetic are human beings in their relations with each other! Tonight I rented Fleming's car and had a date with Virginia Richey. I was in no social mood and neither was she. Both of us would have been better off staying home . . . and yet the restlessness and loneliness of youth drove us out in search of, what for youth seems unattainable . . . peace of mind.

Monday, October 9, 1939 I had almost finished drinking a cup of coffee this morning before noticing that Susan was also in the Student Center. I joined her and we went to the library together. Her sister, Eleanor Richey, had sent me a bid to her Theta Phi prep. school sorority dance. Dr. Owsley was really "hot" today. He caused a general uproar of laughter with his description of the "uncertain parentage" of Alexander Hamilton. He said that Hamilton was accepted in the best circles and married into one of the leading families in New York. He took a crack at Lincoln as follows: "We have had men come from log cabins under similar circumstances and to reach the presidency, but they were not taken into the best families." Spent a quiet afternoon in the library reading Sir Walter Scott. Wrestled Rush Dozier and got the better of him. Ate a full pound of rare beefsteak afterwards.

Tuesday, October 10, 1939 In Dr. Binkley's History Seminar 450 we discussed the value of history. It was extremely hot and humid, however, and I am sure no brilliant ideas were advanced. Elizabeth Zerfoss, Frances

Carter, Martha Wood and I spent some time in the library and in Mr. Turner's office searching for some pictures in the old annuals and alumni magazines. Our idea is to publicize "Coed Day" by getting some pictures of our modern coed sitting in the same poses as the coeds in some of the old pictures. For instance, a very good one was a group of girls in old fashioned bloomers, sitting at different levels of steps going into College Hall. We plan to duplicate that one beautifully. Went to the Tally-ho with Jordan to have refreshments and to read his book review. Saw Marty Lichterman, who was complaining of being sick. In Memphis this summer a golf ball crashed the side of his face. Think I kindled a fire in the minds of Andromedia Bagwell and Louise Johnson about what can be done to strengthen the Women's Honor Committee.

Wednesday, October 11, 1939 Ate dinner at the fraternity house to-night and opened the political meeting at six. I made my usual speech about compromises; about not being so greedy for offices that we lose a whole election. Bert Marshall got the Bachelor of Ugliness nod over Bud Beasley. We got the presidency of the Student Council and the presidency of the Honor Council for H. B. Tomlin and Richard Pickens respectively. I made a motion that the girls give up their chances on the Sophomore Union positions. It failed. The motion for taking the Honor Committee out of politics also failed. I rode home with Pierce Winningham. Walter King proved himself to be a shrewd politician. He made deals while I talked. Anglin was anxious for Andromedia Bagwell to be elected President of the Union. He was opposed to a woman being head of the Union two years ago when Alice Beasley beat him.

Thursday, October 12, 1939 Spent the morning reading Miss Stella Vaughn's article on coeducation and the afternoon at the Banner's office writing my article. Dr. Owsley made some interesting remarks about early America. He said that the yeoman class was a group of people who owned their land outside the feudal system. They made up the largest class in Virginia. The squirarchy was made up of the younger sons of nobility. Winthrop, in 1630, came to Massachusetts to get away from the totalitarian system being set up by the Stuarts; the divine right of kings. The Puritans were Constitutionalists. First there was fishing and fur trading; then there was carrying (like trucking) and selling. The Industrial Revolution started when Slater bootlegged a design of the cotton mill. Webster's change from free trader to protectionist marked the point where industrialism got the upper hand of commercialism. It is interesting to note that Indians were not made slaves because they had a home base to go back to and could bring their tribes down on the heads of the settlers. "There was no attempt to convert an Indian into anything but a corpse."

Friday, October 13, 1939 I saw Margarete Heitzburg, President of Theta Phi, at the dance tonight, Katie and Henry Clay, Frances Carter, Clark Hutton, Martha Wood and Richard Pickens. Merrill Stone went with me. Levi Wade was Susan's date for the Beta Theta Pi dance so we went there for the last half of the dance. Had chats with Byron Anglin, H. B. Tomlin and Jack Peebles. Dr. Owsley noted a point of interest that Alexander Hamilton and Aaron Burr were law partners. They went with the same girl. They were competitors in almost every category and Burr won most of the time. He lost a big one though when Hamilton threw his support to Jefferson in the election of 1800 and kept him from being president. He won the biggest of all when he killed Hamilton, but this was a Pyrrhic victory, as Burr was publicly discredited and thereafter was a fugitive from justice.

Saturday, October 14, 1939 Mrs. Henry Hart conducted our Public Speaking class today. I spoke on "The Cost of War." After quoting some figures about the material costs, I cited the awful losses of human worth . . . the geniuses and the poets. It gave me an opportunity to quote a part of Joyce Kilmer's trees and John McRea's "In Flanders Fields." Both poets were killed in the war.

IN FLANDERS FIELDS

In Flanders fields the poppies grow,
Between the crosses, row on row,
That mark our place. And in the sky
The larks still bravely fly,
Scarce heard amid the guns below.

We are the dead; short days ago we lived
Felt dawn, saw sunset glow,
Loved and were loved, and now we lie,
In Flanders fields.

Take up our quarrel with the foe!
To you from failing hands, we throw,
The torch; be yours to hold it high.
If ye break faith with us who die,
We shall not sleep, though poppies blow
In Flanders fields.

John McRea

I escorted Susan to the football game, which we lost to V.M.I. by a score of 13–20. I took Susan home and then I went to the picnic in

Percy Warner Park that was given by Dr. Carruthers and his family. At the dance tonight I had the "Coed Special" with Susan. Met her cousin Jim Cheek from V.M.I. Without being told I knew he was a member of the family because he has the high cheek bones and copper colored skin tone that is characteristic in most of the Cheeks I know. He has a girl friend here and he is staying with the Robert Cheeks. In talking with Susan I told her "I alternate between supreme joy and utter despair." She said: "I am surprised at your being that way. You always seem so happy." I could have told her that "My disposition depends on you."

Sunday, October 15, 1939 Dot Evans, Partee, and many others complimented the pictures and story of "Coed Day" we had in the Banner yesterday afternoon. They did turn out well.

Monday, October 16, 1939 Studied with Susan until my eleven o'clock class. She asked me what "hedging" on the stock market means. We discussed it quite awhile. I told her I was skeptical about playing the stock market. I told her about my Dad losing $25,000.00 in the Forida land boom in 1925. Professor Owsley was "hot" again today in his story of the New England Junta, which discussed secession long before it was ever mentioned in the South. He was hilarious in discussing the British in the war of 1812. Got one side of my chest injured in the wrestling class today. Coach Miles did it. One of the reasons I am a better coach than Miles, Fleming, and even Henry Clay, is that I do not hurt my pupils. I handle them gently when I am showing a hold or a new technique. Got my first look at our pledges at "Rat Court" tonight. They look pretty good. Discussed with King and Howell the possibility of Huggins as a B.U. candidate.

Tuesday, October 17, 1939 Bill Jordan told me that Dr. Sanborn stopped him on the campus today and asked: "Are you Ben Austin?" I did not dress for wrestling this afternoon because of the knee injury. Ate dinner with Jordan at the Brass Rail and then went to the library. Shirley Caldwell came in and sat by me. She has nearly a perfect figure and wears clothes well. She had on four Zippers tonight. I told her that Jordan and I would take her to dinner some evening so she could join one of our conversations. Jordan and Marty Lichterman discussed with me the possibility of arranging a debate between the Lady Dean Stapleton and Dr. Gus Dyer on the subject: "Resolved: That Education Is a Failure." Dyer would, of course, take the affirmative side. It would be sponsored by the Calumet Club. Suggested to Roy Huggins that he go talk with his professors to map out a program of studies to get him some quality credits for graduation. Jean Burke is spending the night with us. My ribs are aching so that I may have to go to Dr. Zerfoss tomorrow and get them X-rayed.

Wednesday, October 18, 1939 Got up early and saw Jean and Mary Wallace off to school. Talked politics with Pierce Winningham, Nell Edwards and Walter King. Walter is one of the smoothest politicians I have seen in years. The Deke's interests should be in good hands for several years to come. King is one of the few men I know at Vanderbilt that I would like to have as a business ally in future years. He is, I understand, a shrewd poker player. That goes hand in hand with his native abilities. Dined with Simpson, Jordan and Dr. Shoup. Shoup is in the biology department and has a very keen mind. We discussed Communism and Tennessee politics. Dr. Tom said he thought my rib cage injury was strictly muscular. Dr. Mims talked to me about the article I wrote for the Hustler last year concerning a visit to Chancellor Kirkland's office. Says if he has room he wants to use it in his biography of the Chancellor. "Katsy" Aycock went to dinner with Jordan and me at the Brass Rail, and then to Loews theatre to see Leslie Howard in "Intermezzo." It is the story of a great musician, a family man, who falls in love with his beautiful accompanist, and an intermezzo takes place in which he is alienated from his family. Got a telegram from Knoxville which said: "Got one ticket for Saturday." signed, Henry D. Austin. I was amused at the brevity of the telegram. You can depend on that Henry to get the job done. Got a letter from Mother that the house in Stevenson, where I was born, burned Monday. "Monk" Cargile and Aileen Lloyd are getting married. Henry D. is waiting tables at the University of Tennessee for his meals and guards a gate at the football games for his admission. George L. Jr. is coming home before going, from his basic training school in flying, to Randolph Field. I received a nice letter from Jane Ellithorp, of Smith College. I haven't written her in a long time. I called Susan and asked her if Bill Jordan could pinch hit for me on our date Saturday night. She said she would be delighted. They will go to see Mickey Rooney and Judy Garland in "Babes in Arms." I told Susan how much I have been thinking of her during the past few days. I will be going to Knoxville this weekend and, as always, before such trips, I consider the possibility of an accident. I am not quite ready for such an eventuality, yet. Susan has not definitely said: "I love you." Tennyson expressed it this way:

> "O let the solid ground
>   Not fail beneath my feet
> Before my life has found
>   What others have found so sweet!
> Then let come what may,
>   What matter if I go mad?
> I shall have had my day.

Let the sweet heavens endure,
  Not close and darken above me
Before I am quite sure
  That there is one to love me!"

Thursday, October 19, 1939 Mr. Rousseau Duncan, City Editor of the Banner, asked me to write a pregame, color story and wire it to him from Knoxville. I am somewhat fed up with criminal pictures, but I enjoyed John Garfield's "Dust Be My Destiny" at the Knickerbocker.

Friday, October 20, 1939 Told Susan good-bye in the library and dined with Jordan and Simpson before catching the bus at one. Sat with a girl I know from Hume-Fogg. The scenery between Nashville and Knoxville is beautiful at this season of the year. Such drama! The panorama of color, as displayed in dying leaves, is unsurpassed in nature. It was a pageant all the way.

Arrived in Knoxville at five and saw Mose Waller the first thing. Went to town to see friends and to the Barnwarmin' and then met Henry D. in his room. Vic from T.M.I. is Henry's roommate. Jones, another boy from T.M.I. drove me to the Western Union office at midnight and I wrote and wired back my story on the pregame activities. Henry made me sleep on his bunk and he slept on a palate on the floor. Also met Billy King and others in the Athletic Association.

Saturday, October 21, 1939 This morning I met Dad and Mr. Mark Rudder in the athletic office. Visited the campus all morning. Saw Nancy and John Cargile and many Nashville people. Henry went to work early but I saw him at noon. 40,000 people attended the game. Grantland Rice, Ted Husing of CBS, Bill Stern of NBC, Henry McElmore and dozens of other famous sportswriters were there. Clarence Buddington Kelland came with Rice and Jock Sutherland, former Penn coach. The final score was 21 to 0. Johnny Butler's forty-yard run was the feature of the game. It was one of the best exhibitions of open field running that I have ever seen. He was tackled on three or four occassions and still kept on running. Ed Molinsky was outstanding in the line, Anderson, Wilson, John Lloyd and several others met in Henry D.'s room after the game. Mr. Mark gave me his bus ticket and he and Dad came back with Anderson. Saw Bert Weaver, who used to be in my cabin at camp. He looked nice in his uniform.

John Lloyd, Wilson and I came back on the Special. Talked with Coach Hodges and the leading criminal lawyer from Scottsboro. I was particularly interested in this remark that he made, "A man can't be a criminal lawyer without gradually being pulled down by the criminals." He seems to be a pretty clever person and is crazy about his boy, Tom, who was with him. Saw Ed Kennemer for the first time in quite awhile.

He was sobering up. Got home about twelve-thirty. Henry, Mother and Anderson got out of bed to visit with me.

Sunday, October 22, 1939 I called Mr. Barney Hale to get him to stop the Dixie Flyer. He did. Had a nice long chat with the family and caught the train at one. Arriving in Nashville I came by the Banner office and got a couple of copies of the paper (Saturday) which carried my front page by-line story about the Knoxville game. Called Jordan and he reported that, while out with Susan last Saturday evening, he had a wreck. Went to Uncle Walt's after getting cleaned up and then went out for my date with Susan. We went to the game room and played the electric organ. The first piece was "Intermezzo," then she asked me to pick out one. My choice was Shubert's "Ave Maria." Susan sat at the organ and I at the other side of the room watching and listening as if she were actually doing the playing. I told her that "Ave Maria" was perhaps my favorite piece. Drove to the Stork Club for dancing and saw Clark Giles, Virginia McClellan, Sara Goodpasture, Mary Davidson and others. Susan had to go home early to write a paper so I acted accordingly. Showed her a picture of Geo. L. in his flying suit. She looked at the best one very closely. At ten I merely said "Good-bye."

Monday, October 23, 1939 Perhaps the most famous lead sentence to a World War I news story was written by Richard Harding Davis in his description of German troops as the "long gray columns" entering Belgium. An interesting aspect of that story is that reporter Davis wasn't even there when the Germans entered Belgium. Neither was Grantland Rice in the press box when he wrote his famous description of "Four Horsemen" of Notre Dame riding forth on a cold, gray October day. Such bursts of inspiration spring from fertile imaginations and are more powerful than they would have been if the event was actually seen. I thought of this when I got the inspiration for the lead sentence in my color story about the Alabama-Tennessee game on Saturday, October 21, 1939, in Knoxville. While I was in the bathroom shaving on Friday morning, before leaving for the game, I was excited about the prospects of a big weekend and this line came to me: "Enthusiasm almost reached a point of hysteria this morning in Knoxville." Rousseau Duncan, the City Editor, took the story off the wire and gave it a front page splash with a by-line. It is probably the best newspaper story I ever wrote and yet instead of being seated comfortably at my typewriter, in a quiet room, I wrote it on scraps of paper in the telegraph office, at midnight, in Knoxville, while standing at the counter. I handed it to the telegrapher sentence by sentence as I wrote. Besides that, two people were standing around impatiently awaiting my finish of the story so we could resume revelling. Here is the story:

Saturday Oct. 21, 1939

36,000 FANS JAM KNOXVILLE
FOR TENNESSEE-ALABAMA TILT

Pregame Festivities
Mark Homecoming

By Ben Austin

(Special Correspondent)

Knoxville, Tenn., Oct 21—Enthusiasm almost reached a point of hysteria this morning in Knoxville as thousands of frenzied football fans jammed the city streets flashing their colors and yelling with the two student bodies before the titanic clash between the University of Tennessee, unbeaten and untied for two years, and the famous University of Alabama team from Tuscaloosa which this season already has defeated a strong intersectional rival. Fordham University.

Early ticket sales indicate today that some 36,000 people, the largest crowd ever to witness a football game in the state, will be on hand to see the game, which is conceded to be the top contest of the nation.

Clarence Buddington Kelland, Jock Sutherland, former Pittsburgh University coach, and other notables and leading sports writers from all sections were on hand to add their bit to the gigantic show.

Knoxvillians have almost declared a moratorium on business for the past few days and have been thinking only of "What are the odds? Which is the better player, 'Bad News' Cafego, or Jimmy Nelson of the Alabama crew?"

Fraternity Decorations

Fraternity houses have been decorated for this year's homecoming event as they have never been decorated before. The Pi Kappa Alphas turned their front yard into veritable Maginot and Siegfried Lines, with sand bags, pill boxes, and all the trimmings. The dugouts and shell holes are filled with the "Crimson Tide."

The Kappas have turned Shield-Watkins Field into a slaughter house with little pigs in a pen labled "rooters."

The Phi Gamma Delta front yard is staked off into red and white sections representing the State of Alabama. The hometown of the Red Elephants is labeled "Tuscer-Loser" and stars with pictures of Suffridge, Molinski and Cafego on them are suspended over the state. You guessed it—"Stars Fell on Alabama."

A large goose in the front yard of the Alpha Tau Omega house is laying "goose eggs." Those already laid are for Sewanee, Chattanooga, and North Carolina State. The goose is shown struggling with the Alabama egg.

Parade and Rally

The festivities started off at noon Friday when all sororities and fraternities on the campus entered floats and staged a downtown parade. At 6:30 P.M. students and alumni gathered at the Rose Bowl for a bonfire and pep rally. At 8:30 o'clock some 3,000 rooters turned out for the Barnwarmin' in the gymnasium. This spectacle which is sponsored annually by the Agricultural school, consisted of a script dance, at which an elaborate floor show was presented. Gingerbread and cider were served, the award for house decoration and floats were presented, and the Queen of the Barnyard, this year Mickey McGuire, was chosen.

"Bama" Band Absent

The Alabama band did not make the trip to Knoxville. They are given their choice of only two games and they chose the Tulane and the Vanderbilt games, due to the fact that midterm examinations at the university start next week.

Knoxville business men were particularly interested that the "Bama" band accompany the team and telegrams poured into the office of the Alabama band leader. The Milner Hotel of Knoxville even offered its dining room as sleeping quarters for the band members.

The nearest thing to the Alabama band was the mock musicians who got together a couple of tin cans and a washboard and marched in the front of the parade today.

The streets in front of Knoxville's leading hotels were jammed for blocks last night with scalpers, "buy-your-color" boys and fans waving $10 bills in their hands seeking bets.

Highway patrolmen were active every few miles on all the leading highways into the city and it is said that there is not an available hotel or motel room within fifity miles of Knoxville.

Nashvillians seen at the Barnwarmin' were Roy Kelley, Billy Hudson, George Moore, Tom Hudson, Mose Waller, George Wilson, Charles Heffron, Miss Shirley Steele, Dewitt Thompson, all of Vanderbilt, Miss Virginia Lyons of Peabody and Mary Lee Watson of Nashville.

Tuesday, October 24, 1939 At the office today, Mr. Duncan, in his own backhanded way, complimented my story from Knoxville. He yelled across the room to me "Say Austin, who wrote that story that you signed from Knoxville?" He said it was a good story. I told him it was just a case of there being good material for a story at this game. I thanked him, though, for giving me such a good break. Ate lunch with Charley Moss, Managing Editor, at the restaurant next door to the office. We discussed Joe, his brother. Joe is at Cumberland now. Called Susan about our tentative homecoming date for the game and she had forgotten that I had asked her for a date for all of the games. She had a date with someone else. I said "That's okay." Went by Ward-Belmont tonight at nine and talked to Virginia Richey. She took me riding in her new station wagon. She came by the apartment and talked to Mary Wallace and me for a few minutes. I showed her pictures of Jack and Eleanor's wedding.

Wednesday, October 25, 1939 In chapel a man from the American Manufacturer's Association spoke. When the kids whistled he changed his pace from the serious to the humorous immediately. Did it very cleverly. To the Little Theatre with Susan tonight to see "Ah! Wilderness." Jack Keefe took the leading role as the father and Gray Stahlman was the son, Jane Allen the young girl. Henry Clay Evans was good as Sid, the drunken newspaper man. Putt Reynolds as the Yale graduate. Rebecca Rice Lunn was good as the Old Maid. When Gray (as Richard) said that his sweetheart was afraid to let him kiss her, afraid of her old man, afraid of life and everything I was particularly interested in Susan's reaction. Kissed her on the cheek as I said good night. She is so sweet. We lost the engineering classes in the election today and the Junior class Presidency to Maurice Holdgraf. I knew this would happen one day if we didn't throw a sop to the Independents. I have warned about it several times.

Thursday, October 26, 1939 Turned in book review on Herbert Hoover. Saw "Mr. Smith Goes to Washington" at Loews. I was hoping to see Mickey Rooney and Judy Garland in their picture. Mary Wallace says she is planning a tea for some Sunday soon. She is going to have Susan, Andromedia Bagwell, Marie Smith, Jesse Scott (her teacher) and others.

Friday, October 27, 1939 Attended Chancellor Kirkland's Memorial Service. Frank Rand, Edwin Mims, Keppel, head of the Carnegie Corporation, and McCain, President of Randolph Macon, spoke. I was interested in Rand's remark that he was not personally acquainted with Dr. Kirkland when he was a student, "I was not such a scholar as to attract attention nor were my grades poor enough to bring down condemnation. I was one of a large number of students." Keppel said that schools and services rendered to them should not be referred to as southern or northern. McCain came back as follows: "If I were to write a letter to the president of Yale, Harvard, or Chicago, for advice, a nice letter from their secretaries would come in answer. When a Southern educator wrote Kirkland, he knew that "The Chancellor" himself would give some thought to the matter and would answer." Mims spoke last. He spoke for the student body when Kirkland was inaugurated. There was considerable body to his speech. Went to the Tri Delta dance this evening after studying for my history midterm. Met, for the first time, Jimmy Stahlman's daughter, Ann. Frank Gunter took a picture of the officers and freshmen. Enjoyed dancing with Elizabeth Surles. She is sweet and a fine dancer. John Shumaker brought me home. Arch Trimble had to leave early. Johnny and I talked until two o'clock. He confessed that he and practically the whole staff are scared of Jimmy Stahlman. He told me about going to the War Memorial building one night for a story and after finding out that Stahlman was on the program, was afraid to ask for the information. Such relationships are bad from every standpoint. Jimmy is a bad executive. He cannot possibly get the most out of his men under such conditions.

Saturday, October 28, 1939 Think I did fair on the midterms. I went to the Banner office with Partee to view the parade. Governor Prentice Cooper rode with Fred Gray in the official car. The Deke float consisted of a group of little Negro boys who went through the streets yelling "S.A.E." It got more laughs than any of them. Bill and I took Virginia Youmans to the football game. She is beautiful and clever but I am afraid she is a bit spoiled. I don't see how she could avoid it. She says that she has been in love three times and that when she finds that she has a boy she loses interest; quite natural. Used Uncle Ragan's car tonight to take Susan to the dance. Picked her up at eight. She looked sweet in her red and white evening dress. I'll bet she does not wear it much though because I saw another one just like it at the dance. On the way to the dance she said: "We are having our Theta dance on November 23rd and I want you to take me." "Swell," I exclaimed, "I have been wondering when you were going to ask."

"I am doing it because I really want to" she said. Up to this moment I was tired but from here on I felt fine, and I told her so later on. Glen Gray was really good. He alternated between slow and fast pieces and had the ring of a "big-time" band. I danced several no-breaks with Susan and many times in between. Eason carried her away from her spot several times to keep me and others from finding her, but I didn't mind. After what happened tonight I don't mind anything. Coming out of the Tally-ho, Susan asked me if I looked at the check to see if it had a star on it; if so, the bill is paid in full. I told her that I had not and that there was no use to do it. "There is only so much luck that a person can have in one day or else fate would not be just. I've had mine today." She said, "Oh, you too believe in that." On the way home

I told her how much I appreciated her asking me to take her to the dance and I told her I would do everything in my power to make the evening perfect for her. She said she knew I would. Susan doesn't usually use affectionate language (love talk) but tonight her accents were stretched in that direction. On the way home from Susan's I heard Wayne King play "The Blue Danube," a very beautiful Strauss waltz. At the dance Surles asked me who had the upper hand, Eason or me. I told her about Susan's asking me to the dance. She said "Fine." Saw Ken Kavenaugh, the all-American end who caught both of LSU's touchdown passes this evening. He had made about 50 of LSU's 60 points this season. He is about 6 ft 6 and weighs over 200 lbs. He is a natural at end. Over 50 passes were thrown in today's game; razzle-dazzle in its best form. They beat us by a score of 12–0. It was a close game.

Sunday, October 29, 1939 I read papers, cleaned up room, ate dinner with Jordan and Simpson. Called Susan and confirmed that date for Saturday night. She talked sweet even on the phone. Talked with Katherine Anderson. Wrote Wilson and George L. Jr. Caught up in my diary. Translated my notes.

Monday, October 30, 1939 I went to the library and looked up some dope on John Bell. While I was talking to Mrs. Cheney, Susan came in and sat at the very same table where my books were. I was very pleasantly surprised when I looked around and saw her. I feel very complete when I am sitting by her. O. O. McIntyre once said that he could do much better work when his wife was in the room. Nello came in and sat by us late in the evening. At four o'clock I went to the gym class. Ate supper with the Ragans. Read conflicting stories about the battle of Lexington, first conflict of the Revolutionary War. This is a classic example of how difficult it is to get a true story.

Tuesday, October 31, 1939 Halloween! Mrs. Hart was our Public Speaking teacher again today. Told us about one of Joe Parrish's cartoons. Had an interesting discussion with Dr. Binkley in the Seminar this evening. He mentioned human geography and I asked him if it was not a study of the contours of the human body (in fun). All the girls in the class "hee-hawed." He let us out early. I was especially amused at Mary Davidson's and Jean Ewing's reaction to my joke. Susan came in the library this evening and sat with me again. My day is not complete unless I see her. Ate an ice cream cone with her in the Student Center. She was on her way to Bond Davis' fashion show. After a fine gym class I ate dinner with Katherine and Kenneth Anderson. Oysters were the main dish.

Wednesday, November 1, 1939 Independents held the power balance again today and won all but one of the offices in the Freshman class. Maynard Thompson, however, the only boy I was really interested in won the freshman Honor Council election. He and I have already made plans for a revitalized freshman Honor Council. Susan came in and sat by me this evening in the library. Bobby Chalfant put her in an embarassing spot by yelling "come and sit here Miss Cheek." Tonight I went to the community concert with Katherine and Mary Walker, a teacher here in Nashville. Charles Kullman, leading tenor of the Metropolitan Opera Association, was the singer. Stuart Ross was the accompianist at the piano. He sang selections of Handel, Cavalli, Schubert and Martini. The one that thrilled me most was a Strauss waltz. It was a very enjoyable evening and I saw many friends and acquaintances.

Thursday, November 2, 1939 Dr. Harris was back today and we had our speeches as usual. I spoke on "Great Speakers." I gave some interesting points about Daniel Webster and Bob Taylor. I told of my intimate association with Dr. Willis A. Sutton. I told his story about the boy flying the kite. He could neither see it nor hear it but he could feel it forever pulling upward. I concluded by saying "So it is with God. We can't see Him and we can't hear Him, but, we can feel Him forever pulling upward." Took my string to the Banner this evening and Duncan told me about the Tennessean scooping us again on the band sponser. Susan did not come to the library today. Chalfant's remark yesterday was perhaps too much for her. I studied for awhile and then went to the Student Center with Damaris Witherspoon. I like her better than I used to. I used to think she wasn't interesting, but I've changed my mind. Heard today that Bill Embry skipped town owing about $90.00 in football game bets. Hate to hear that. Bill seemed to have possibilities. Its not the first shady deal that I have heard about him pulling, though. I was paid $16.00 by Coach Miles tonight. I signed a much larger check than that though. Mr. Miles folded it so that I would not see the amount unless I made a special point to open it. Henry Clay told me the other day that Mr. Miles does him the same way. Called Susan and told her I missed her today. Said she is through with the library. Asked her for certain about the date of the Theta dance. "Guess" she said. "I think it's the 29th." "Right." "That is exactly 27 days from now, isn't it? Multiply that by 24 and you get the number of hours." She laughed. We discussed going to hear Alexander Woollcot next Monday night. For our date Saturday night we decided to just talk. I am going to show her, at that time, the analysis of her handwriting, which I picked up this evening at the Banner office. Darned if I don't believe I've hit on a perfect fastener at the bottom of my Zipper. It is simply a spring clip that becomes longer when pressed together with the fingers. When it becomes longer the pin is allowed to slip out. I was reading history and while taking a short intermission the idea came to me—I don't know how. I get so enthusiastic when an idea like this comes to me that I can't restrain my enthusiasm. Called Miss Mary Louise Goodwin this evening and asked her the details of a story which she told us in class five years ago; the story of Benjamin Brewster, an eminent attorney, for an eastern railroad, whose disfigured face inspired a nasty remark from an opposing counsel once. Mr. Brewster's reply was classic. "The opposing lawyer's remarks are as follows: "And now gentlemen of the jury, the methods employed by this railroad are as dark, devious, and scarified as the face of their counsel." The audience was horrified at such an inhuman attack and a hush fell over the courtroom as Brewster rose to speak. "Your honor" he said, addressing the judge, "I have never told anyone why my face is so disfigured, but now I am going to. Many years ago when I was a child of ten years old, my baby sister and I were playing together in the parlor when she tripped and fell headlong into the open fire. I saved her but when I regained consciousness, my face was as black and as dark as the heart of my honorable opponent." Henry Clay told me this evening that, after his class with Susan this morning, he looked very carefully at her sorority pin and said, "You know what I thought that was at first."

"Yes, a Deke pin," she said.

"For a moment I thought Austin was really doing some good." Wrote a letter to Miss Goodwin.

Friday, November 3, 1939 I was using the phone in the Student Center when Susan came in for a Coca Cola. I sat with her and drank a cup of coffee. I walked right out without paying and they had to send a boy running after me. Quite embarrassing. We went on to the library and studied together for thirty minutes. She looked extremely nice. Finished Dr. Owsley's first midterm okay. Ate lunch at the Deke House and went with the boys to Webb School to play a game of tackle football. Had a great time at right tackle during the first half. Played quarterback during the third quarter. Ran a series of plays through the same side of the line and then passed for a touchdown. Tom Hudson received the pass. I ran it over for the extra points.

Saturday, November 4, 1939 Few members of our Public Speaking class were present today. I spoke on the theme, "Many of the greatest things that have been done in this world have been done by people attempting to overcome a physical handicap." I did not get to finish the speech. Paid several bills in town after getting my check at the Banner office. Paid Joys $5.00, Genys $2.50 and Morses $2.30. Came home and listened to the Vandy-Ole Miss game. Vandy lost by a score of 14 to 0 but Captain Andrus, playing on an injured knee, turned in a brilliant performance. He caught a pass and scored; running ten yards with a man hanging on to him. Went out to Susan's at 5:00. Mrs. Cheek met me at the door and Mrs. Glenn was back in the game room checking on the open fire. Mrs. Cheek told me about her sprained ankle. Mrs. Glenn and I talked of her sister, Mrs. Hayes.

Susan and I sat in front of the fire and talked for awhile. I showed her her handwriting analysis and we discussed it. Played the organ and then rode down to the Stork Club for a few dances. Then rode down to Radnor Lake and parked for a few minutes. When the first car came around the bend Susan pointed to it and I knew what she meant. We drove on back and threw a couple of logs on the fire. She expressed lack of interest in debut parties. I agreed with her. She said that people asked her if the dance that she and Eleanor Richey are giving is a coming-out party. She said that she told them "No, Eleanor Richey and I both wanted to give a dance so we just planned for it." My guess is that since she is asking me to take her to the Theta dance that it would soothe Eason's wound by letting him take her to that function. A nice way to keep everything running smoothly, if you can afford it. This was the first she had mentioned this dance to me. Her dad and Mr. Newman Cheek are in Florida fishing.

Sunday, November 5, 1939 I went to West End Methodist Church with Osgood Anderson and to a Kappa Phi meeting with Howard Nichols. The same old question was up; national or local. A compromise plan was hit upon. The question will not be decided until after January 1st. I ate supper at Aunt Nells. Uncle Walt and I talked of my getting a law degree and then taking a year of journalism or business at Harvard. He recognizes, and I admit, a vanity which best expresses itself in public life, politics, or newspaper work.

Monday, November 6, 1939 After going to bed this idea came to me. Why not ask Susan to marry me and spend next year in California. She could take her senior year at the University of Southern California and I could take graduate work. It would be like a whole year's honeymoon. That difficult adjustment which is always trying the first year would be minimized. Both of us would be in school, as we are accustomed to being. Both of our minds would be free from outside worries for at least a year; until we could become adjusted to each other. The announcement could be made in June, the betrothal in September, a few weeks before school starts and then a year of academic work and nuptial bliss. Today at ten o'clock I saw her in the library. At twenty of eleven we went to the bookstore. I was determined to tell her of the idea. I simply could not. I had lunch with her in the Kissam Hall cafeteria. The thirty minutes were delightful, but my courage could not be mustered. We studied in the library from two until a quarter of four. The same story. Saw Eason doing his reading in the library this evening. Mazie Rudder, Jean Burke and one of their Peabody friends ate dinner with Mary Wallace and me. Merrill Stone and I went to the War Memorial to hear Alexander Woollcot. When asked, by a group of us after the lecture, how to become a journalist, he said, "Learn to write by expressing yourself in your diary." He is an ardent supporter of Roosevelt but not for a third term. Mr. Woollcot, who is supposed to be one of the best humorists and raconteurs in the country, chose as his subject, "The Confessions of a Dying Newspaperman." On the radio he is known as the "Town Crier." He opened his address by walking on the stage and saying "This is Woollcot speaking." He asked if the public address system was needed; if those in the far back "who want to be alone with their thoughts" could hear. "Those who can't hear, and wish to, wave your hands and I'll not misconstrue this gesture. If a person is going to talk to me I would always rather it be about himself, it is something he knows something about. Can you hear each exquisite syllable" he said, as the address system was turned on. "See if you can't match this from your own experience" he said as he told of knowing Rose Field, the brother of Eugene. "In the case of almost every well-known individual the hometown folks will always say, "you should have known his brother, he was the real character."

"Going to plays will run into money" his parents told him at an early age, "but that's something the Woollcots never did," responded the speaker, parenthetically. He referred to a kiss and hug as a "biological grapple." As a newspaper man I was always fearful of typographical errors" he said—"bottle scarred" then to "battle scared."

A little girl whom Woollcot is quite fond of asked what a war is. "It is an affair at which people dress in different kinds of uniforms and fight" she was told.

"You know what?" the little girl remarked. "Someday I'll bet they have a war and nobody'll come." (applause).

"Thats my story and I'm stuck with it" he quoted somebody as saying. He closed with his heart gripping story of the former Nashvillian Morris Frank, who helped to found the school of the Seeing Eye, where dogs are trained to lead blind people. He related how a dog refused to enter a vacant elevator shaft from the height of ten stories. I went backstage and saw him after the lecture. He reminds me quite a bit of Uncle Osgood. Frank Gunter asked him if he knew Francis Robinson and he said "of course, he helped plan my tour."

Tuesday, November 7, 1939 I rode to town with the Johnson boy and Virginia Youmans. They drove me down to take a Zipper to Mr. Snodgrass, my model maker. Read in the library until nine o'clock.

Wednesday, November 8, 1939 I went to the library, after eating at the house. Susan was in one of the graduate rooms so I studied with her until four o'clock. She has been up late several nights in a row and she shows signs of fatigue. Tomorrow she is through with her exams for the middle of the term. The announcement that I made to the freshmen at the house today was effective and about ten or twelve new men were out for the wrestling class today. It was a very interesting class. Ate dinner with Aunt Nell, and Uncle Walt gave me a check for $70.00 tuition. He pointed out that the opening sentence in my review of Mr. Hoover's book, which was in the Banner this evening, should have been broken down into two or three sentences. He is perhaps right. Dr. Claude Lee Finney spoke at the Calumet Club tonight. This statement which he quoted somebody as saying, interested me, "Literature is an imitation of an imitation, three degrees from the truth." He arrives at this statement thusly: a carpenter visualizes a perfect table and makes an imitation. The poet attempts to describe this table. To the Tally-ho with Simpson and Jordan Fleming.

Thursday, November 9, 1939 I resumed where I left off in my "Physical Handicaps," speech. I spoke last and my story of Benjamin Brewster got over well. Immediately after finishing, Dr. Harris said "That reminds me of a similar story which I have told you before."

John Toombs and Alexander Stephens were once the senators representing the State of Georgia. Toombs was a large six-footer and Stephens was a small runt of a fellow but he had a very powerful brain. In fact, he was the brains of the Confederacy and served as it's Secretary. If his health had been stronger he would have probably been its president. Anyway, big, double-jointed Toombs got raving mad at Stephens in a speech once and turned to him saying, "Why you little shrimp, I could eat you alive."

"If you did," replied Stephens calmly, "you'd have more brains in your belly than you ever had in your head."

Went to the Civil Aeronautical Authority class tonight to get a story for the Banner. Got the dope from Mr. Al Hutchinson and Dean Lewis. Dr. Slack was teaching the class. Rented Partee's car and went to see Mary Engle. She said, "Why don't you go with someone you're sure of?"

"Not a bad idea." I replied.

Friday, November 10, 1939 Gave Abrahams $5.00 for the Honor Committee key. In the library this evening I noticed that Susan was studying with Nello so I went in the other room. On one occasion, Susan came into the room, talked to Van Irwin and walked out. I noticed her as she passed but I did not look up from the book. She walked out of the room directly behind me. I didn't look up. She didn't say anything. I studied for another hour. Finally, she came back into the room. This time she said "you seem to be working mighty hard." I invited her to sit down for a few minutes and we talked about sundry things. After finishing up my reading I went into the main reading rooms and sat with her for a few minutes. Wrote Mother a letter tonight. Heard Guy Lombardo play over the radio. I always like his medley of old favorites; "To You," was one of them tonight. I had a long telephone conversation with Jordan, and called Louise Sykes and asked her about a card that she sent me from California. Made a date with Damaris Witherspoon for the gym dance tomorrow night. She said that she didn't want to accept because she "confided" in me that she didn't have a date. Heard "Pigskin Parade" honoring the Sewanee spirit. It goes out over a national hookup.

Saturday, November 11, 1939 Henry Clay spoke on Sparticus' speech and quoted part of it. Along towards the end of the class he said, "Let Austin speak." It was quite a compliment. Yesterday he said in a joking way, I don't see why a talker like you can't do better with Susan." I confessed my bashfulness. Mr. Will, from St. Louis came and ate lunch with us at the house today. Bill Shumaker and I went by the Theta House for Susan this evening. Had a talk with Henrietta Hickman, Ann Shaw and others of the alumni. Sewanee and Vanderbilt locked horns at two on Dudley field. Vandy won by a score of 25–7. After the game we went by the Tally-ho for hot chocolate. I escorted Damaris Witherspoon to the dance tonight. Went with Merrill Stone, Jack Foley and Trimmier McCarley. Had a good time. Virginia Youmans saved the second no-break for me. I told her how much I thought of Bud Bray. She insisted that I tell her about my wrestling match with Bud when my knee was hurt. The case when Bud would not touch my knee. She liked it. Talked to Shirley Caldwell about a dinner date soon. Eason kept Susan out a long time after intermission, as usual. I danced the fourth with her. She said that piece is "I Get Along Without You Very Well," in "quotes."

"That means somebody else said it and it does not apply to us, am I right?" I said.

"Yes, that's it." she replied. I hope she means something by that statement. Henry Clay is peeved at Katie Heitzburg for seeing Joe Hutchinson so much. He says he never wants to see her again. He introduced me to Florence Cheek tonight. Florence had a date with Mac Dickinson. Susan told me about Bitsie Napier inviting us out to breakfast on the morning of Thanksgiving. Eleanor Richey talks more freely than Susan. I went out with her to get an orange drink during one of the fast pieces. She was telling me how she used to be able to whip Little John. She said that they used to have "knockdown and dragout" fights. I asked her if she could whip Susan. She said, "No." Susan just tells her to "shut up" and that is all there is to it.

Sunday, November 12, 1939 Uncle Ragan came by before I got up this morning. He told me to call Mr. Martin and talk to him about the

Lakemont property. I did so and Mr. Martin said he would swap. I called Uncle Ragan back and told him I would be free to drive to Lakemont with him next weekend if he wished to make the trip. Finished reading Pratt's, "The Heroic Years." The part about Andrew Jackson was the most interesting.

Monday, November 13, 1939 After Sanborn's class I sat with Susan in the library for an hour. Said she was going to study in the library this evening. We studied together awhile. I then went to my wrestling class. Had about ten or twelve new boys today. Went back to the library after eating. Jordan came by and talked to me. Susan came by after her sorority meeting. She was reading about marriage and the family for sociology. She read that in the town of Middleton one, out of every four, marriages ended in the divorce courts. She said, "Sounds discouraging." I told her that people have a hard time adjusting themselves to each other. I also pointed out that Mary Wallace and I are getting a practical course in sociology and adjustment. Jean McEwen was sitting with us. At ten o'clock Susan asked me if I wanted to ride home with her and Jean. I did. Their chauffeur followed her car to the Theta House, by 1909 20th, and on home. I called her a sissy for having them make a special trip to follow her home but I guess it pays to play safe. I was talking to Joe Davis in the library. He said, "Your doing a lot of courting lately. A person can see it in your face." I said, jokingly, "They haven't quoted me in the papers yet." Partee had in his column Sunday that a certain tennis star said "I'll admit I love the girl." In history class today a note was handed me from a girl two seats down from me. It read as follows:

"Just between us—I think you have the sweetest smile I have ever seen on a boy—"Tacky."
P.S. I don't want a nickel either."

"Tacky" (Mary Engles from Memphis) is a very good friend of mine, but I never expected anything like that. Shirley Caldwell told me that she could not go to dinner with Jordan and me tomorrow evening but she made me promise a "rain check." She has one of the most intriguing personalities of anyone I know.

Tuesday, November 14, 1939 Spent every available moment on my history readings, but didn't have enough to turn in the report today so I decided to wait until next time. Rode to town with Jean Stephenson this evening to get my Zipper model from Mr. Snodgrass. He had not finished it so I rode back to the gym with Tom Cummings. Ate dinner with Bill Jordan at the Brass Rail. Both of us were below par physically. Went to the library to study. Susan was studying, Money, Credit and Banking with two boys. I did not bother her but sat across the table. She put on her glasses. They are flesh colored, horn-rimmed spectacles. It is the first time that I have ever seen her in them. They do not detract from her appearance very much. She looks okay. Mary Wallace told me that she put them on the other evening after I left the library. I went by for Jordan at ten and we went to the Warner Drug Company for refreshments.

Wednesday, November 15, 1939 I was dead tired so I slept through my first class. Did not go to school until eleven o'clock. Saw Susan in the library. She was studying with Damaris Witherspoon and Nello Andrews. I ate lunch at the Deke House and then went back to the library until four. Susan came up at two and told me that she had just been playing tennis with Mary Wallace. Said she forgot who won (modestly) Mary Wallace told me that she and Susan won every game. She also said that Susan pointed out to her some fine points of the game. In the library I asked Susan if she had an escort for the dances in Knoxville this weekend. If not I told her I would write my little brother there and get him to come to her rescue. She said that some boy had asked her to go to the game with him and also that she had to study while there. Uncle Walt came by tonight and gave me $15.00 for expenses. I discussed my dress suit plans with him and he said it was okay. Also mentioned my plans for a career. He suggested the year at Harvard, Columbia or California might prove a satisfactory way of starting off. I called Susan and asked her for a date for the second Deke dance. She said, "That will be fine." also she said I could have the first and third gym dance dates next term.

Thursday, November 16, 1939 Dr. Harris entertained us with quotations from Bob Ingersoll's and Edward Everett's famous lectures—"Had occasion a few weeks since to take an early train from Providence to Boston."

I was supposed to have a date with Virginia Youmans tonight but when I got there nobody was home. I came on back and called up Mary Engles and got a date with her. She is leaving for a vacation in New York tomorrow.

Friday, November 17, 1939 Virginia Youmans told me that she and her dad had a fuss and that he would not bring her home in time for the date at nine. They were out to dinner. Saw Susan just before she left for the game in Knoxville. After Dr. Binkley's class I went to town and paid the phone, gas and light bills. I had a headache this evening so I let Clark Giles conduct the wrestling class. Jordan came by and chatted with me for an hour or so tonight. Mary Wallace served sandwiches.

Saturday, November 18, 1939 I hurried home this evening to listen to the U.T.-Vandy game. I had a feeling that Ray Morrison was going to pull something "out of the bag." I was as nervous as if I had actually been in Knoxville. It was a great game. During the first half, Vanderbilt had made several first downs and Tennessee had not made one. Vanderbilt on one occasion came within two feet of a touchdown. On another occasion Vandy carried the ball to Tennessee's twelve. In the third period Tennessee scored on three passes and in the last few minutes of the game scored on an intercepted pass. Their yards rushing was minus 3. Neyland said after the game, that Vanderbilt should have won this time. "I don't see how Vanderbilt could possibly have lost six games." After the game, which ended 13–0 Jordan came by for me and we went to the Brass Rail, formerly Andrew Jackson's old stables. We talked awhile and then went to see "Dancing Coed." Jordan and I enjoyed this light musical starring Artie Shaw's band. After the show we took a drive around Nashville, through the Negro and red-light districts, up Church and stopped at Dominicks for a Coca Cola and chili. Drove some more, stopped at the Tally-ho and saw Alex Porter, Paul Clements, Harry Nelson (son of the President of the Nashville Trust Company) and then on home. We discussed human beings until two. In the "Short Subjects" at the show tonight we saw an interesting study of the Smithsonian Institute. Was particularly interested in William Austin Buck's model of the typewriter. It has been a very interesting day.

Sunday, November 19, 1939 I read the papers and then composed a questionnaire to determine how many students read the daily news papers and what interested them most. Read some philosophy in Webber and Perry. Hit on a good idea for a speech to be used in the Houston Oratorical Contest after Christmas. The basic idea is that people who have children do not die. The strand of life between mother and child is not broken from generation to generation. I am going to weave my speech around that thought. Jordan and I went to the Tally-ho for a frosted malted milk at ten.

Monday, November 20, 1939 I saw Susan for the first time since she came back from Knoxville. She seems to have held up well. Said she took in all the dances. She got back at three yesterday evening. I went to town this evening and bought a full dress suit (tails, white tie) It cost me $40.00, plus incidentals, at Petway-Reaves. I remembered hearing Mrs. Ruby Bible, years ago, refer to Little Jack's tux and I thought such a thing impossible for a Stevenson boy. I just couldn't believe her. What a difference a few years and a few dollars make. What a difference environment makes. I purchased those tails this evening with the nonchalance of a boulevardier; not half the thrill of wearing my first tux. Mrs. Mary Stahlman Douglas told me today that there is a crying need for a skirt and blouse that are fastened together by means of a Zipper. It would allow a number of different blouses to be used with the same skirt and vice versa. Phoned Susan at the sorority house and asked her to call me when she got home, where she had her date book. Said she had rather not call. I told her not to be so modest. She said she would bring her date book to school. There was nothing more I could say.

Tuesday, November 21, 1939 I jested with Dr. Pomfret this morning. Since I caught him in such an obvious trap last week he has been leery of arguing points with me. I asked him if the Greeks used the word 'paramesium." He bit, and I pointed out that the microscope was not invented at that time. He made a slighting remark today about the questions that the census takers take so I asked him if he thought the questions were important. "No, no I don't want to argue the point with you" he said, "my remark was merely pedagogical. Anyway, I didn't mean to set your great mind moving." The class roared with laughter. Talked to Susan for a few minutes this evening. She reminded me that we already have a date for the Deke entertainment this Saturday. Had a large wrestling class this evening. Jack McCullough and I worked out afterwards. He is pretty good. He ought to be a cinch for a position on the freshman team. Uncle Walt gave me a check for $50.00 this evening to pay for the dress suit. Since Susan's party is formal I am going to wear it Thursday evening.

Wednesday, November 22, 1939 Pictures of Joe Little, Trimmier McCarley and Bobby Pitts were sent to the Banner office this morning. They were tapped by O.D.K. members. I sat with Susan the period before chapel and she seemed interested in finding out who the new members were going to be. Went to Petway-Reaves for the dress suit this evening. Jordan went with me. After my gym class Jordan, Fleming and Simpson came by and we went to the Tally-ho for dinner. Dr. Mims was at one of the tables. As he left he came over to our table and said to me, "Austin, don't let these boys corrupt you." This is in reference to the fact that Dr. Mims knows that Jordan and Fleming are more atuned to the Ransom School of literary criticism than to his concept of merely enjoying poetry. At about nine Jordan came by my apartment and we talked until twelve. I told him of my suggestion to Mr. Max Benson, of the Quarterback Club, that they interest some of the younger members of the Vanderbilt family in Vanderbilt. We then discussed the possibility of turning next Homecoming Day into "Commodore Vanderbilt Day" and inviting every member of the family to Nashville. I called Mr. Hill Turner about it and he thinks it's a great idea. We are going to start working on the idea immediately. We are going to call in Fred Russell and Max Benson as a committee to work on it.

Thursday, November 23, 1939 Eleanor and Susan's dance at the Belle Meade Club is tonight. I put on my dress suit and Jordan came by for me at nine-thirty. We went by the Albemarle and saw the folks for a few minutes and then to the Ryman Auditorium and saw the last part of "Tobacco Road." After the last curtain we went back behind stage and saw Sheala Brent, the girl who played the part of the sensitive, hare-lipped girl. She was very nice looking when her grease paint was removed. Jordan had a date with her last summer. We got to the dance about eleven o'clock. Spoke to Mr. and Mrs. Cheek. Saw quite a few members of the Cheek family that I recognized: Florence, Joel, Jr., the Farrell girls and others. Henry Clay and Katie Heitzburg were there; met Paul Davis, who was dating Henrietta Hickman; broke on Governor Prentice Cooper when he was dancing with Martha Wade; Shirley Caldwell had on a stunning evening dress; she is a smooth dancer; Miriam McGaw said she could go on forever like this; Mac Dickinson was squiring Frances Carter, who was looking her best, and dancing beautifully with John Ransom; Bud Bray was with Virginia Youmans; Fleming did not show up; "Red" Anglin was a stag; I had a short talk with Mrs. Glenn. Saw Eason and Nello Andrews talking to her; also Arch Trimble. Damaris called me a sore thumb. I said, "No, every dog has his day." This is just not my day. Craig's orchestra played delightfully; numerous waltzes and slow pieces. The last time I danced with Susan and told her how much I enjoyed the dance she said "I am glad you came and it would not have been complete without you." Also she said, "I heard a nice compliment about you but its a long story and I won't attempt to tell you now." After the dance Jordan and I drove to Petrones and drank hot chocolate. Several of Bing Crosby's records were played. We relived together the experiences of the night. It is pleasant to dream. We departed for home at three o'clock.

Friday, November 24, 1939 As Susan and I walked up to the Student Center she told me the compliment she heard. Henry Clay had told her that he plans to pay tribute to me in a speech Saturday. She said he told her that I was one of the finest boys in Vanderbilt. He has won my heart if he does not say a thing Saturday. Susan is the one that really matters. I ate at the Deke House and she in the Student Center. We met in the library and studied together until three o'clock. Had dinner with Jordan at the Tally-ho.

Saturday, November 25, 1939 In my speech, I paid tribute to the Vanderbilt spirit as exemplified by Vanderbilt-Tennessee game last week and by Bud Bray when I wrestled him in the Intramural finals two years ago. Henry Clay paid me the tribute that Susan had told me about. Listened to part of the Notre Dame-USC game and then came home and cleaned up. Used Uncle Ragan's car to pick up Susan at five for the Deke party. Susan and I had planned to go to see "Ninotchka" at Loews but she said her throat was beginning to be sore. I ordered some cough drops for her and she consented to go on to the show. We parked and saw part of the Christmas parade and then went to the movie. Greta Garbo was great, as usual, and the humor in the production was new for Garbo. On one occasion a very young little baby was shown and I never saw Susan break down her reserve so completely as she did in expressing how cute she thought the baby was. We went home immediately after the show and then I went to the A.O.Π. dance. Was glad to see Jean Noland, Hardy, Frances Spain, and Alice Williamson (now Morris).

Sunday, November 26, 1939 Uncle Walt returned from Stevenson today. He had news that Dad and Rebecca are fat and that Henry D. fell and hurt his hip in the Georgia Tech track meet. Went to the Belmont to see Paderewski in "Moonlight Sonata." Catherine Anderson told me that she has seen it three or four times. She saw Susan and me at Loews last night. It was a treat to see, in a picture, the greatest living pianist. Saw John Caldwell at the dance last night and we discussed how Kappa Phi is getting along. He is President now. Finally he said, "Ben, you are the most levelheaded person that has ever attended our meetings." In reality my discussions with them were not superior to those of others who argued the question of going local. I merely employed one of the most fundamental of all principles for winning support from a group that is divided on an issue. I conceded every point possible to the opposition, showing them that I was not prejudiced, and went so far as to suggest helping them work out their plan. When we ran into insurmountable difficulty, as I knew we would, we had to fall back on a status quo compromise which I was in favor of all the time. Arguments from a prejudiced person have no weight.

Monday, November 27, 1939 Ran into Susan and Nello Andrews. Nello had to go over to Dr. Toms to get a malaria shot, as he left us he said, good-naturedly, "I am glad that she will be well escorted from the forks of the path to the library." Nello is not a bad sort of a fellow. Susan and I studied in the library and discussed flying to Chattanooga with Temple Chester. Susan said her dad would not let her fly. If she were going as far as California though she would like to travel by air. She and Mary Wallace were at gym together this evening. Someone took $9.00 out of Susan's purse and $4.00 out of another girl's. I went to the State Capitol library this evening and read from the July 1860 editions of the "Nashville Union and American" newspaper. I am writing a term paper on John Bell of Tennessee. Andy Bagwell and two or three others of Mary Wallace's classmates came to our apartment to study this evening. They reported a good time. Tonight I got a letter from Henry D. and one from Max Benson about the football books, and of the idea I suggested to him on the phone the other evening. Mr. Manville returned the raincoat. I composed a sales letter for the football book. I am going to put it into the hands of all members of the faculty and a great many students.

Tuesday, November 28, 1939 Today I had a very interesting conversation with Mr. Hill Turner. We discussed Jim Buford, Max Benson, and Ray Morrison, among other things. Candidly, according to Mr. Turner, Buford thinks he is going up too slowly. Benson is selfish and must see where he personally will benefit before he goes into a thing. He does not pay his alumni dues. I was surprised to hear confidentially that there is something to the Peabody feud. Little Bill Schwartz coached Roy Huggins, Heistand and Flannigan and occasionally tries to keep up with them. Morrison objects. Consequently the Peabody group does not function properly. This would make it so. Mr. Turner told me that he told Morrison that he ought to give the Peabody group full rope so that they would hang themselves. Men are pretty petty at times. Only once or twice in a lifetime do you run into men that are as big as Dr. Dyer. Dyer has personal faults but he is above reproach on the big issues. Even ex-Chancellor Kirkland was pretty susceptible to flattery, according to Mr. Turner. At the close of our discussion Dr. Pomfret came in. He and Mr. Turner are working on the plan to raise money for the university. At the house today, while we were eating lunch, Bill Hume said, "Austin, that invention of yours is the talk of the town. I was at a dinner last night where it was being discussed and one of the elderly ladies said that Mrs. Cheek pointed you out to her. The lady thought it incredible." Hume said he replied "Oh, yes, I am his fraternity brother. I was quite flattered that Mrs. Cheek should take an interest in it. After lunch I went to the history seminar and then to town to see Mr. Tyne. At the wrestling class today Henry Clay told me that he let Susan read his finished speech concerning me and then he asked her if she agreed. "Yes, I certainly do" he reported her as saying. To this I replied, "The class makes no difference to me, nor the general public, but showing the speech to her means everything." I invited Henry to dinner with me but he said he would some other time. Called Susan and made arrangements tonight for our date tomorrow evening. Also Mrs. Connoll, Society Editor of the Banner, to see that the date list was in. Invited Dean Sarratt to visit my wrestling class sometime next week.

Wednesday, November 29, 1939 The Theta dance tonight with Craig playing was good. I went by for Susan at nine. She had been in bed all day resting up so she could go to the dance. She has been sick with a headache and cold. I sent her an orchid and she looked beautiful in a light blue dress. I wore my full dress suit and was complimented by Homer Howell, the acrobatic instructor at the gym, and others. Saw Dr. Mayfield, Mrs. Glenn and Paul Davis in the chaperon's balcony. Danced the first with Susan, the second with Shirley C., and third and fourth with Damaris Witherspoon and Henrietta Hickman, respectively. The orchestra played a waltz for the fourth. Andrews and Eason had the second and third with Susan. She could not go to Ann Pope's breakfast with me so I went by myself after taking her home. We played a kissing game, spin the bottle, and I never saw a group of girls act so silly. Each was afraid of what the others would think. All would like to have entered whole-heartedly into it, if my guess is right. Only the hostess was sensible. Saw Val Hain, Alfred Estes and Eddie Morton at the dance. They are here for the game.

Thursday, November 30, 1939 Susan could not go to Bitsie Napier's breakfast with me so I went alone. Dick Henderson and Jim Tuck came for me. Mrs. Napier showed me her home, which was built a year before or after the Hermitage. The floors are made of pure red cedar. The kitchen has a large open fire. I was sitting alone at a side of the room and Shirley Caldwell came over and said, "I never saw you with a more blank expression. Why don't you come over and sit with us?" I did and it was a pleasure to talk to her, B. F. Byrd, and Ann Stegall. Eason came out with Witherspoon. Stegall sang, "Oh Johnny, Oh Johnny, How You Can Love" for us. Could not find my ticket for the game so I had to talk to Leo Dickinson. He said, "And you are in the Honor Council—okay, go ahead." I have never seen such a sorry game. Vanderbilt was never so listless. Alabama beat us 49–0. It was the worst defeat in twelve or fourteen years. Went by for Susan at nine to go to the Barney Rapp dance. We stopped by Dr. Taylor's for a Coke and I began telling her that she ought to loosen up and talk more freely; brag a little if necessary. She said, "Are you giving me a lecture?"

"No, I am pleading for a better understanding" I said. She said that our lack of freedom of discussion may be partly her fault but also that it is partly on my account. She intimated that she talks more freely with some other people. At the dance they had several intermissions and no-breaks and on almost every one of them Eason was dancing with her at the time and took her to the balcony for the duration of each one. I was never so jealous in all the days of my life. Merely looking at Eason made me burn. I guess it was because of my low physical condition. I was dead tired and the game this afternoon did everything but bolster my spirits. I was terribly morose all evening and I know

Susan was bored stiff. Especially since she herself is on the ailing side. Saw Mr. and Mrs. Bashinski. Also met Mr. and Mrs. Bray, parents of Bud Bray when I took Susan home, just before she went in I said, "I love you so much. This is the first time I have ever summed up enough courage to tell you." She smiled coyly.

Friday, December 1, 1939 I was sleepy in class today. I went to get Susan at nine for the Deke dance. Just before going after her Jordan came by and talked with me. I also looked up the words to several cheery songs that I have known so as to get into a light and gay mood. We stopped by the Tally-ho and talked. I drank a cup of coffee to further stimulate me. I was determined not to be low in spirits tonight. There were not too many people at the dance and plenty of room for dancing. Susan and I danced when we wanted to and rested otherwise. I got to dance three no-breaks with her including the Deke Special and we really enjoyed it. By my request, he played the Strauss waltz and his medley which includes "If You Were the Only Girl in the World" for the fourth no-break. Craig played a waltz medley of classical pieces including "O Sole Mio." I don't know when I have enjoyed a dance more. Susan on the way home, sang very low "Heaven Can Wait." I said, "How can it wait for you?"

She modestly assumed the literal interpretation. "Oh shortly after I die I hope."

"I don't think that song is a hymn." I said, later on in the evening I sang the Deke song to her, "When Day Is Done" and switched into "Oh Johnny, Oh Johnny, How You Can Love." The sudden change in mood amused her. I repeated "Skies were gray that April day we parted in the rain, was it tears that fell or was it rain?" As we stopped in front of her house I kissed the back of her hand and said: "You know what?" She smiled a smile of remembrance and then at the door I told her I appreciated her doing so much in order to be able to go to the dances with me this weekend.

Saturday, December 2, 1939 Dean John Pomfret is a smart teacher and a wonderful man, but is a little pompous at times. We have a nice bantering relationship with each other but I'm afraid I was a little rough on him this morning. In his lecture he was talking about John Calvin and made a slip. I asked him if it wasn't Martin Luther who tacked the 95 theses to the church door at Wittenberg.

"That's the one fact you remember about German history, isn't it Mr. Austin?" he said sarcastically.

"Yes, I'll have to admit that I find it easy to remember that incident," I said, in mock sarcasm, "It is the classic example of a little guy talking back to his mentors and getting away with it."

Sunday, December 3, 1939 I went to the Kappa Alpha Theta House this afternoon where our D.K.E. freshmen were being introduced. After eating sandwiches we went to the Ping-pong room on the third floor and, after singing several songs, each one of us was called on to perform. George Ed Wilson sang a few "hillbilly" songs. I did a timestep shuffle that the little colored boys in my hometown taught me years ago. I used to join them in dancing for the coins that would be thrown from the windows when the trains stopped for dinner at the local hotel. This was before Pullman diners were prevalent. Some people would eat in the dining hall and others would wait for the colored waiters to bring large trays of food to the train windows. Ann Pope and Damaris Witherspoon were charming hostesses. Susan was her sweet self.

Monday, December 4, 1939 I saw Susan at school for the first time in several days. We drank Coca Colas in the Student Center and chatted before going to library. She has lost a little weight but otherwise she seems to be okay. Went with Joe Davis and John Steele to see "Another Thin Man," starring Myrna Loy and William Powell at Loews. It was a pretty clever detective picture. For the first time in my life I guessed the name of the murderer right at the start of the picture. It is always the least suspected one of all. I had lots of fun wrestling with Rainey Frierson and Walter Robinson this evening. Charley Moss called this morning and asked me to see about getting a poster advertising Jennings Perry's speech at the Hillsboro Church Sunday before last (24th). He is trying to determine whether or not the speech had a "red" tinge. I have been unable to locate a poster but I have found some other interesting information. Henry Clay told me that Billy Eason really fixed him up with Katie at the Bachelor's Ball Saturday evening. Henry says he is a real talker. He took Katie off the floor and talked to her for nearly an hour. He told her that she was the one that was losing out; that she will never be as happy with anyone else.

Henry said that Joe Hutchinson was really burned. Henry said that Eason is really a fine fellow, after you know him; that he is smart and a slick talker. From what I have heard from other sources, he must be pretty loquacious.

Tuesday, December 5, 1939 Eleanor Reed Clay gave Henry a piece of advice. She said, "Never ask a girl to give up one of her boy friends. It will make her mad every time. Even though I loved Jack more than any other boy it would have made me mad if he had asked me to stop seeing another." Received an invitation from Mr. and Mrs. Richard Norvell to a dance in honor of their daughter Peggy at the Belle Meade Club on December 20th. I am to take Susan. I went to dinner with Simpson, Jordan and Mr. Jordan Monk, Bill's stepfather. We ate in the loft of the Brass Rail and enjoyed an old-fashioned joke session. Mr. Monk told the old one about the meaning of B.S, M.S and Phd ("piled high and dry.") I attended the last part of the Phi Beta Kappa meeting this evening. Susan and Shirley Caldwell were serving. They will perhaps be taken in next fall. I wrote my account of the affair from a copy of Dr. Benton's speech, which was given me. Afterwards I went to the Tally-ho with Jordan and he attempted to be nonchalant about the honor he had just received, but the nervousness and beads of perspiration on his brow gave him away. The Phi Beta Kappa key represents a certain achievement, even though, in Jordan's case, no great effort had to be exerted. As I have said to him so often, though, it would be unfair to the rest of us if he possessed drive and determination as well as brains.

Wednesday, December 6, 1939 I took the Phi Beta Kappa story to Mr. Duncan and came back to the library to start working on my term paper. I was sitting with Jean Ewen when Clark Hutton asked her what she plans on doing next year. She answered very frankly: "Begin looking for a man with a good job." Late in the afternoon I met several girls, including Ann Pope and Elizabeth Surles, and took pictures for the newspaper questionnaire layout.

Thursday, December 7, 1939 My speech in Dr. Harris' class this morning was not spectacular. It was not a subject that I was vitally interested in and therefore generated no spectacular interest in the audience. I ate lunch in the Kissam Hall cafeteria with Nello Andrews, Miriam McGaw and one of her boyfriends from out of town. I went to the library and studied with Susan until four o'clock, time for my wrestling class. She said she would like to go to "Petrified Forest" with me Saturday evening, before the gym dance. Henry Clay came home with me this evening. After cooking and eating T-bone steaks we read poems, looked at my scrap book and I gave him a demonstration of my invention. He likes it. He said, "Austin, you have more ideas than any one man I have ever seen. Tonight has been most constructive; I have learned more and enjoyed it more than any other day this year." He left at ten o'clock. A fire immediately behind us on Hillsboro made Mary Wallace excited. Wrote my story about the newspaper poll.

Friday, December 8, 1939 Saw Susan and gave her a cool greeting. Had a chat with Youmans at noon yesterday about her trip north. She told me about knowing Carl Rudder, whom she met on the train between here and Stevenson; also about the meals boys bought her between here and New York. We discussed the technique of getting acquainted on the train. She asked me how girls do it. The newspaper poll story made front page. Ate dinner with Jordan; lunch with Sykes and Stone. Nello invited me to the S.A.E. dance tonight but I did not feel like going since Susan and I plan to go to the play and gym dance tomorrow night.

Saturday, December 9, 1939 Virginia Youmans went to Public Speaking class with me today. Darned if I don't believe she is the most beautiful girl I have ever seen. I don't see how any man could ever deny her anything. But she is unpredectable and undependable. I guess with her dazzling beauty she can get away with it. Susan and I studied in the library this evening until four o'clock and then I rode home with Mickey Carmichael and Buddy Stone. Just as I got home, Mrs. Cheek called and said that Susan had come home sick and could not go to the dance with me tonight. I told Mrs. Cheek that I realize there must be a stopping place somewhere. I told her to tell Susan it was okay and not to worry about breaking our date. Mary Wallace had four members of her Sociology class out at the apartment this evening making a scrapbook. I sat by Joe Davis at the play "Petrified Forest." It was an enjoyable evening. At the gym dance I had the second no-break with Eleanor Richie Cheek and the fourth with Jean Wettereau. Damaris was in a strange mood. She said: "Ben, you know I have an urge to do crazy things sometimes!"

"I'm ready anytime you are." I said.

"You do what you want to," she said, "But you don't want to do the crazy things I do."

"How do you know I don't?" I replied.

"You don't have anything to do with people you don't like."

"You must, though," I said, "That is the price you have to pay for being a woman." Her remarks set me to thinking. I wonder what she meant by that. At some future date I am going to talk to her more and try to find out what she has on her mind. Later in the evening I noticed her looking at me. She would not give me a late date.

Sunday, December 10, 1939 Slept late, read Philosophy and finished my term paper. I enjoyed reading a story about William Randolph Hearst in Fortune magazine. He and Jordan remind me a little of each other; even in looks.

Monday, December 11, 1939 In Dr. Sanborn's Philosophy class we discussed the true and false in Plato and Aristotle; what to believe and what not to believe. In answering this question Dr. Sanborn told the story about the fellow who asked: "If we find that the seat of emotions rests in some organ other than the heart, what are we to do with our poetry?" For example, "Maid of Athens, 'er we part, please give me back my heart." To this someone said: "Maid of Athens, 'er we sever, please give me back my liver." At ten o'clock I sat opposite Miriam in the library. A little later Susan came in and sat at the table next to us. During the hour I glanced at her several times but I did not move over to where she was sitting or even talk with her. At the close of the hour she got up and walked out, glancing neither to the right or to the left. I could tell that her walk was a little different than usual.

Miriam and I are more relaxed with each other now that my whole life is not wrapped up in her. I went to Dr. Frank Owsley's class and participated in a lively discussion about the balance of power between the North and South being disturbed by the South acquiring more territory as a result of the Mexican War. The future Civil War generals were being trained in this war as members of General Winfield Scott's staff. Robert E. Lee was chief of staff for Scott, the greatest military scholar produced in America. After lunch with Sykes, McGaw, Stone and McCarley, I returned to the library and found Susan in the back room where we usually study. She said: "Let's sit at the other table with our backs to the light." I sat to her right instead of her left and noticed she had put on glasses. It is the first time she ever wore them while studying with me. Sensing, perhaps, my coolness this morning, and the fact that I was sitting near Miriam, Susan's conversation this afternoon was warm and affectionate. At three o'clock I left Susan and went to town to do some Christmas shopping. I have looked at a fine leather notebook for Susan.

Tuesday, December 12, 1939 I met Dean Pomfret's class for the last time. He and I disagree at times but he is a competent scholar and likeable. Talked to Dr. Eberling and Dr. Crouch in the bookstore. In spite of almost going to sleep in Dr. Binkley's class this evening I got a lot out of what he said. "It is not important what you remember in this class. If you have a better idea of what goes on behind the scenes in writing history, the problems facing the historian, and a general idea of what history writing is all about, you have achieved the main purpose. If you have developed a critical attitude you have nor spent your time in vain." I saw Mrs Cheek going to the library with Susan. I met them on the steps and said, "Well, Mrs. Cheek are you coming back to school?" She smiled and said, "Yes, for a little while anyway." Susan told me tonight that she was getting a book for John, Jr. Gave Damaris and Anne Pope some pictures that Frank Gunter took on the campus last week. I took a nap this evening and studied philosophy tonight. Jordan called for a chat.

Wednesday, December 13, 1939 Met Dr. Sanborn's class for the last time this term today. After reporting to Mr. Moss on my conversation with Dr. Eberling I went to the library and studied with Susan until eleven o'clock. She then went to women's chapel. She told me that her dad flew to Florida last Wednesday. Susan said, "He may let me fly now." Ate lunch with Damaris Witherspoon in the Student Center. Bill Simpson spent three hours with me this evening studying philosophy. It cleared up quite a few questions. Now it is merely a matter of memorizing the outline. Paul Grubb came by and got three Spanish verb wheels. Clark Gable is coming through Nashville tomorrow on his way to Atlanta

for the world premiere of Margaret Mitchell's "Gone with the Wind."
I had rather have written that book than any other novel by an American.
I never worked harder or concentrated any steadier than I did in memo-
rizing that philosophy.

Thursday, December 14, 1939 I studied until noon and then went
to the Philosophy exam. It was just what I expected and I did well on
the part that I memorized. Think I passed it. Just after finishing the
exam I was standing in front of Calhoun talking when Elizabeth Surles
passed. I spoke to her and asked her if she wanted to go to a show
with me. She said she couldn't go. Right behind her I saw Susan. I
was somewhat on the spot. I immediately asked her if she would go
to the show with me. She couldn't either so we went to the Student
Center and drank a Coca Cola. Her mother was to meet her at four.
As we parted she said, "I'm glad to have seen you." I believe it is the
first time she ever said that after a causal meeting on the campus. I
went to see "Elizabeth and Essex" at the Knickerbocker. Uncle Walt
called this morning and told me he was sending down the radio that I
talked to him about months ago. Aunt Nell also called and said he was
sending it. I don't know why the sudden change of mind. Listened to
the Maxwell House program tonight and then to Bing Crosby. After
that I heard Kay Kayser playing at the "Gone with the Wind" ball in
Atlanta. The world premiere of the picture takes place tomorrow night.
Senator George, the president of NBC and others spoke on the program.

Friday, December 15, 1939 Got up at eleven and went to the library
to study. Damaris Witherspoon was in the hall looking for Susan. They
had been studying together and Susan disappeared. I was sitting and
talking with Jean Ewen and I continued talking to her instead of going
into the other room where Susan might be. We discussed the debut
parties that are in style in Nashville these days. I told her I thought
they were useless. She said, "I can see your point but for some girls
who haven't anything else to do it is okay. It will be sad if some poor
boy marries any of them for their money though." Ate dinner with Aunt
Nell this evening. Got $25.00 from Uncle Walt. Drank a Coca Cola
and did not shut my eyes all night.

Saturday, December 16, 1939 On my way to the library I encountered
Virginia Richey. We were both getting checks cashed at the bank. Said
she was going home tomorrow so I asked her for a date tonight. "OK,"
she said, "I started to call you up but I thought you might be busy."
(I had asked her to call me anytime she wanted to go to a show or
something.) She seemed very enthusiastic over the prospect of our date.
I studied in the library until five-thirty and then came home and dressed.
We went to see Douglas Fairbanks, Jr. in "Rulers of the Sea." It is

the story of an old inventor who had quite a bit of trouble getting backers for a steam engine that would replace sails. At one place he said, "I have plenty of imagination but no money. Those who have money have no imagination." After the show we went out to LynnMeade lunchroom and danced. Saw Tom Blair Pierson. After dancing awhile we drove up on Hills Road and looked at the lights of the city. Both of us were in a fine mood. She had just finished her double-duty work in the library at W.B. and was in a carefree mood. She is very beautiful and sweet as anyone would want. I could go for her if I didn't hold myself in check. She and I talk very freely about our mutual troubles. She is understanding of mine and I of hers.

Sunday, December 17, 1939 Martha cleaned up the house today. At noon I went to Partee Fleming's Christmas dinner. Jordan and Simpson were the other two guests. We ate steaks at Nick Varallos. When I came home at two Joe Davis, Andromedia Bagwell and Henry Clay were waiting for me. Henry had shown them my invention and they were all down on the floor looking at my scrapbook. Henry was reading poems to them. We studied Public Speaking until six o'clock. Called Susan after they left. Haven't talked to her in several days. She seemed extra nice. Just before saying good-bye I told her to be rested up for Peggy Norvell's party, that I was looking forward to it. She said she would and that "exams will be over."

Monday, December 18, 1939 I went to town to get Susan's present. Coming back I saw Wilson Green and Joe Moss. Joe said, "Ben, somebody told me you single-handedly put a stop to the cheating at Vanderbilt; that you put the fear of God in their hearts."

"Hardly that," I said, "but we did work pretty hard to stop the wholesale cheating that was going on out there and I think the situation has improved." Then Joe told me that he was going to return the book that I loaned him several years ago. The Public Speaking exam was comparatively easy today. It was about what I expected, we covered it pretty thoroughly. After the exam I went to the library and studied until nine o'clock. Went by the Phi Delta Theta House and got Barney Ireland's book "The Slavery Controversy," by Lloyd. Got the Xmas cards that Tom Cummings left at the Deke House for me. Mr. Miles paid me $8.00 for a half-months' work at the gym. Mary W. told me that Jordan came out and studied in my room tonight. During the past few days I have been thinking more than usual about my life's work. I have read of many men who believed that they were placed in the world to do a certain thing; by God, if you will, and I have doubted their sincerity or perhaps their sanity . . . mental balance, to say the least. But more and more I find myself believing that I myself have a mission; that I am destined to do something in the world; to leave it better than I found it. The idea has perhaps grown from the success I have had in adding a new twist to common activities; the inventive instinct, if you will. By lining up teacher support in each session room at Hume-Fogg I was able to guarantee a larger printing of the school paper and thereby increased the circulation from three hundred to three thousand and to reduce the price from three cents to one. No R.O.T.C. company had ever gone through an entire term without any man getting a demerit. I challenged the company, which I commanded, with the idea that it was the company that got the fewest demerits that was best and that absolutely no demerits would make history. They accepted my challenge. Normally a line of marching men dress on the right guide. The right guide is taught the proper length step and cadence by practicing on a indexed pavement. I lined up an entire platoon or company on the right guide, while he was practicing, and the whole group got the benefit of the practice session. The results were phenomenal. The army uses the numbers system to teach the manual of arms. I borrowed the idea and applied it to teaching the fundamentals of wrestling. I broke down each hold into its component parts and used a number system which permitted me to teach fifty wrestlers in the same amount of time that it would normally take to teach one pair of wrestlers. In the Honor System fight, the thing that was different was that I went after the cheaters, rather than sitting back and waiting for reports which seldom if ever come in. I am constantly examining premises. Is this the best way to do this, or is there a better way? To find a better way and then to have the courage to explore the new course must be a God-given talent. One other ingredient is needed: the patience and fortitude to suffer the consequences when you are wrong.

Tuesday, December 19, 1939 Partee Fleming drove me home and we discussed tactics in handling women. He pointed out that women are animals just like men, only more so. They don't take as much exercise as men and therefore have more energy to expend along sexual lines. I interpolated that the problem is to make it easy for them to give in. It is strange how one goes along for years making the same mistakes and then, all of a sudden, a casual remark wakes one to reality. At different points along the line, things probably tried to right themselves, but you, in your stupidity, interfered. Partee said that some boys try to kiss a girl good night on her own front steps, in the bright lights, and wonders why the girl turns her head away. Girls want to be kissed, but they want it to be at the right place and at the right time. All these years what a fool I've been!

Wednesday, December 20, 1939 Alfred Lord Tennyson, in his poem "The Princess," gives another slant in dealing with women. He attributes it to advice his father gave him:

'Tut, you know not, the girls.
Boy, when I hear you prate I almost think
That idiot legend credible. Look you sir!
Man is hunter; woman is his game.
The sleek and shining creatures of the chase.
We hunt them for the beauty of their skins;
They love us for it, and we ride them down.
Wheedling and siding with them! Out! for shame!
Boy, there's no rose that's half so dear to them
As he that does the thing they dare not do,
Breathing and sounding beauteous battle, comes
With the air of trumpet round him, and leeps in
Among the women, snares them by the score
Flatter'd and fluster'd wins, tho dash with death
He reddens what he kisses.''

The article that Bitsy Napier wrote for "Pursuit," that I liked so much, told of her visit to Germany last summer. She told of going to the Sportsplatz to scoff at Hitler and his parading soldiers, but even she got caught up in the dynamism of the spectacle and found herself raising her arm in salute.

Thursday, December 21, 1939 Last night was a very special occasion. I dressed in white tie and tails and escorted Susan to Peggy Norvell's debut party. Mr. John Cheek met me at the door and told me about his flight to and from Florida. Said he enjoyed the flight but was a little shaky at first. I gave Susan the sealskin notebook and she gave me linen handkerchiefs. Francis Craig's orchestra was playing nice danceable pieces and champagne was flowing freely. Susan remarked about the $75.00 orchid corsage which Peggy was wearing. We both thought it was rather extravagant. Billy Eason had consumed several cocktails and was tipsy, or at least was acting that way. Susan did not appreciate it very much. He would break on her every few minutes and when someone else broke he would hang around and break again. Once she went out with him and stayed quite awhile. When she got back she could see that I did not like it very much so she said she was very tired and almost fainted. Once when I attempted to break Eason kept on dancing and Susan had to push away from him. I could see the expression of disgust on her face. Willie Cornelius also noticed his lack of dignity and mentioned it to me. After the last piece was played Eason continued talking with Susan. I waited around to give her plenty of time to become thoroughly disgusted with him. When I finally came up she said: "Oh, is the dance over?" It was an attempt to make the break-away easy. We chatted pleasantly on the way home and when I stopped in front of her home I parked in the shadows rather than the direct light. I kissed her cheek and almost her lips and made her promise to write on the very day that she gets a letter from me. Earlier in the evening I introduced Susan to Dr. and Mrs. Curruthers, who were chaperons. Mrs. Curruthers said: "I asked Tommy who he wanted to have Christmas dinner with and he said Ben Austin." She went on to say that I was Tommy's idol. Saying such nice things before Susan was especially appreciated.

Friday, December 22, 1939   Packed and caught the train at ten o'clock. Met a Williams boy from the Law school on the train. Got home about two o'clock. Wrote Susan and mailed forty-five Christmas cards. Played Chinese checkers with Dad and Anderson.

Saturday, December 23, 1939   I drove to the Sequatchie Valley this afternoon and visited the beautiful Sherman home. It is set back against the mountain as a backdrop. It is one of the most beautiful settings I have ever seen for a home. There is a lagoon between the house and the beautiful lawn which stretches several hundred yards in front. I started reading Henry Miller's "The Cosmological Ego." Miller has some quaint ideas. They are quite different, to say the least. In one place he tells of walking the streets of Paris "without food, without friends, and without a language." He says he took charge of himself and made himself into a god. Since he became a god he is supremely indifferent to the outside world. Anything that matters to him must come from within. Surprisingly, he says he does not want to inspire anyone. He says to have hope is to admit a weakness—that you are not what you would like to be—you are in a sense dead. Joe Rains, the former cobbler at Stevenson, came for a visit and told the brothers, who have been away, what a good athlete Wilson, our baby brother, is.

Sunday, December 24, 1939   Christmas in a large family is not, I suppose, like it is in smaller families where one or two children can be showered with gifts. Large families have each other. Once I remember having a memorial Christmas in which I was the only child of three families and I learned how the other half lives. Uncle Walt, my mother's brother, who lived in Nashville, had no children. Aunt Nell, my mother's sister, who married Uncle Ragan, lived in Nashville, also, in a large castle-like house on Hayes Street. The Skieles lived upstairs and they had no children either. Nellie Ben Ragan, whom I was named after, would borrow and keep me for weeks at a time in Nashville. On one of these perennial visits, when I was about two or three years old, it happened to be at Christmas time. I shall never forget the tremendous tree and the bags of toys under it. All of them were for me. Aunt Nell and Uncle Ragan kept the family entertained for years telling about my exploits with them. If they took me for a ride in their Maxwell touring car in the evening I would always say, on the way home, that I wanted to buy something, "I don't know what, but something." A story that always got a laugh was the one about their asking me before we got off the train in Nashville if I wanted to go to the bathroom. I said "No" and as we were standing on the median in front of Union station, waiting for a street car, Uncle Ragan said he looked around and noticed that the ladies were jumping back and holding up their skirts, and there I was in the middle of a large circle all by myself.

Monday, December 25, 1939 This is not only Christmas day but the 29th wedding anniversary of Mother and Dad. They were married in the home of Dr. George A. Loftin in Nashville in 1910. Dad's sisters, Aunt Belle and Aunt Fannie, and Aunt Edwina, Uncle Bill's wife, and her family—Bill, Virginia, Dan and Bob—came over for Christmas. Tonight I went up to Clyde and Lulu Woodall's dance. As a courtesy I danced with all the girls. Got stuck a couple of times but enjoyed the evening. Freda and Walter Bogart had been to a dance in Scottsboro before coming to this dance. Freda has developed into a smooth dancer. When I danced with her she said: "The last time I danced with you was last March, wasn't it? Why so long?" I explained that I have not been to Stevenson since then. I made a date with her for next Wednesday. "Are you still seeing Miriam?" she asked.

"Occasionally," I said, "But she doesn't thrill me as much as she once did."

"Yes, it sometimes happens that way," she said, with a slight suggestion of wistfulness in her voice.

Tuesday, December 26, 1939 Anderson, Dad, "Fatty" Johnson and his father, Mr. Frank, left this morning for a deer hunt in South Alabama. A letter from Susan was brought to me in bed this morning. She told about the numerous parties that were taking place in Nashville over the holidays. She said she had fixed their family tree and that my notebook would be one of the first presents to be put under it. I called Susan long-distance tonight and asked for a date Friday night for the Kappa Phi dance. She said she had a date until ten o'clock and after that she was supposed to take her date to the skating party that was being given by Bill Oliver. I told her we would go to that if she wished. It was raining hard in Nashville. It was hailing here.

Wednesday, December 27, 1939 I wrote letters to "Flip" Timberlake, Mr. Crouch and to Frank Jones. I wrote a book review of Pfeiffer's "Science in Your Life" and sent it to Mrs. Mary Stahlman Douglas. The Saturday Evening Post came out today with Fred Russell's article on Major Bob Neyland, "Touchdown Engineer." It is estimated that 9,000,000 people will read the article. Henry D. went to see Mary Elizabeth Talley and I went to see Freda this evening. We drove to South Pittsburg and saw Mickey Rooney and Judy Garland in "Babes in Arms." In New York this summer I saw them do in person the same songs and dances. In a short subjects feature I saw and heard the author of "Yearning," "Carolina Moon," "You Started Me Dreaming," "Baby Face," and "Margie," sing parts of each of his song hits. Charles Simpson asked us to ride home with us. We stopped by the "Eastern Star" dance but the stench of whisky and vomit was so strong we went across the street to "Kate's Kitchen" and got hamburgers and coffee. Dropped Charley off at his home and then drove out the rough road to Bass. I enjoyed reminiscing with Freda. She was my first love. Miriam was my second and now Susan is my third. I will always have a warm spot in my heart for the pretty little redheaded girl who once dominated my dreams and aspirations.

Thursday, December 28, 1939 Percy Armstrong is one of those personalities that dominates whatever scene he happens to occupy, whether it be in a city or a small town. I do not mean by any force except pure personality. His mother was a fine woman who once taught me in Sunday school. His father was a loudmouthed roustabout. Percy and his brother Jimmy, a prominent dentist in Miami, inherited the best from both sides. I did not know the other brother, Fulmer, too well. I met Percy on the street today and had my usual delightful chat with him and his wife, Alice, who is no slouch, as a personality, in her own right. I continued reading Henry Miller. He is pretty pithy in places. I sometimes wonder about the motivation for writing literature of questionable taste. Here is a paragraph from Henry Miller:

> *"The face of the American woman is the index of the life of the American male. Sex either from the neck up or from the neck down. No American phallus ever reached the vital center. And, so we get the gorgeous burlesque queen with the divinely beautiful body of a goddess and the mentality of an eight year old child, or less. In every burlesque stage a bevy of gorgeous nymphomaniacs, sexing and desexing at will; they writhe and squirm before an audience of mental masturbators. In all the world there are no bodies like these nothing which for sheer physical beauty and perfection can compare with them. But if only they were decapitated! The addition of the head, of the sweet virginal face, is heartbreaking. Their faces are like new coins that have never been put into circulation. Each day a fresh batch from the mint. They pile up. They choke the treasury vaults. While outside the treasury stands a hungry mob. The whole world has been ransacked, every piece of gold melted down to make these gleaming new coins—but nobody knows how to put them into circulation. There she is, the American woman, buried*

*in treasury vaults. The men have created her in their image. She's worth
her weight in gold—but nobody can get at her. She lies in a mint of gleaming
faces and her pure gold substance goes to waste."*

Charles Simpson was telling us the other night that he went to see
the show "The Women" in which even the dogs were female. Charles
said "I never wanted to see a man so much in all my life."

Friday, December 29, 1939 I had a wonderful breakfast—orange juice,
delicious ham, eggs and hot biscuits. Anderson drove Rebecca and me
to Nashville. Dad went by the Southern Trust Company to get the interest
on a loan cut from 6 percent to 4½. I saw Howard Ball in their offices
looking very much the part of an executive. Dad told me that Frank
Johnson was drinking on the way to South Alabama and was a "Keeley
Cure" within himself. Anderson went with Susan and me to the skating
party given by Dr. Oren A. Oliver for his son Bill. It seemed that almost
everyone from Vanderbilt was there: Miriam McGaw, Virginia Youmans,
Damaris Witherspoon, Virginia McClellan, Mac Dickinson, Jim Reed and
Henry Clay. Anderson did real well on skates. Susan and I were pretty
shaky at times but we did not fall. After the party we took Anderson
by the Deke House, where he had parked his car, and I took Susan
home. Anderson and I talked until the early hours. He tried on my
tails but they are a little small for him. He is about six feet three and
one half inches tall and weighs well over two hundred pounds. He is
a tremendously large man with long flexible muscles from swimming.

Saturday, December 30, 1939 I ate breakfast with the Ragans. Anderson and Dad departed for Stevenson. Tonight I used Uncle's car in
dating B. Kemsey.

Sunday, December 31, 1939 Another year is at an end. Now that
the course, as far as school is concerned, is about run, I am relaxing
and taking, for the first time, courses that I like, rather than what's
good for me, and my grades reflect the difference. For instance I made
the only "A" in the Public Speaking class. I made "B" in Philosophy,
"B" in Sectional Controversy and "C" in Colonial History. Could I
do it over would I change my curriculum? "No!"

Monday, January 1, 1940 I spent the day writing letters and the
speech I hope to give in the Houston Oratorical Contest. It is five-
thirty. I have finished my work and I find myself at loose ends; just a
little bit lonesome. Lonesomeness is perhaps the most devastating of
all human emotions. Men make slaves of themselves at their jobs so
they will not have time to be lonesome. Women dedicate their lives to
making themselves attractive so men will pay attention to them and
they will not be alone. The reason peer pressure is so great is that
the alternative is ostracism; loneliness. Add to loneliness the inner pres-

sure of a nagging sexual drive, which is second only to self-preservation in the hierarchy of God-inflicted values and no pressure in human experience exceeds it. The dilemma of maturing youth is a problem that has plagued every civilization since the beginning of time and none has ever come up with a completely satisfactory solution; least of all our complex modern society. Susan is the one I want to call but I don't feel I should, after she forgot that I had a date with her for the first gym dance. Even the supposedly "funny" Jack Benny show tonight was sad. Jack had told his company what a good time he was going to have on his date tonight; New Year's Eve. At the last minute his girl called and said she could not fill the date. Rochester said: "What this world needs is less people who are making less people unhappy." John Shumaker called and asked if I would like to go to a little celebration party he had planned. That saved my day. They came by for me at eight. Theresa Howley was John's date and Ed Reeves, the boy who was in the wreck with Joe Moss the other evening, was there. At the "Gingerbread" we ran into a group from the Community Playhouse, including Fred Coe, who is in the Yale School of Fine Arts. Fred is my prep. school fraternity brother and I have attended many Kappa Phi meetings and dances with him. He is such an intense fellow. There are no halfway measures with him. It is all or nothing, always. Alice Elizabeth Griggs, Henry Evans, an editorial writer for the New York Times, Louis King, head teller at the third National Bank, and his date Eleanor Bailey, one of the nicest people I know, were there. Matt Pratt, the highly intellectual student at Vanderbilt, who edited the "Masquerader," and left school to become a motorcycle patrolman, was there in his uniform. My shirt collar was a little tight and my head was aching as the old year came to an end.

Tuesday, January 2, 1940 President Roosevelt has gone on record as favoring Cordell Hull as his successor. I think Hull will be acceptable to the people and will make a good president, in spite of the fact that many years ago he was largely responsible for Congress passing the graduated income tax; the soak the rich scheme which soaks everybody else but the rich. Tennessee was beaten by Southern California by a score of 14–0. Georgia Tech. won their game by a score of 21–7 and Texas A & M eked out a victory over Tulane in the Sugar Bowl. Anderson drove William Simpson and Mary Wallace to Nashville from Stevenson. Bill Stern, who announced the Rose Bowl game, told why Tennessee is called the "Volunteer" state. During the Spanish American War the President called for 2,300 soldiers from Tennessee and overnight 20,000 volunteered. The Trojans of U.S.C. were too big and too husky for the Tennessee team and mercilessly overpowered them, as they are accustomed to doing to West Coast teams; but Bob Suffridge, whom I played against one bleak October afternoon, when we were both in high school, played in the California backfield all afternoon. During the last few days feeling a touch of melancholia, I have missed Bill Jordan. It is strange how you get in the habit of seeing and talking with certain people and then wake up all of a sudden and find you miss them more than you thought. Jordan drops in on me at all hours and the ideas he generates are so refreshing and stimulating that I feel a letdown when his influence is no longer present.

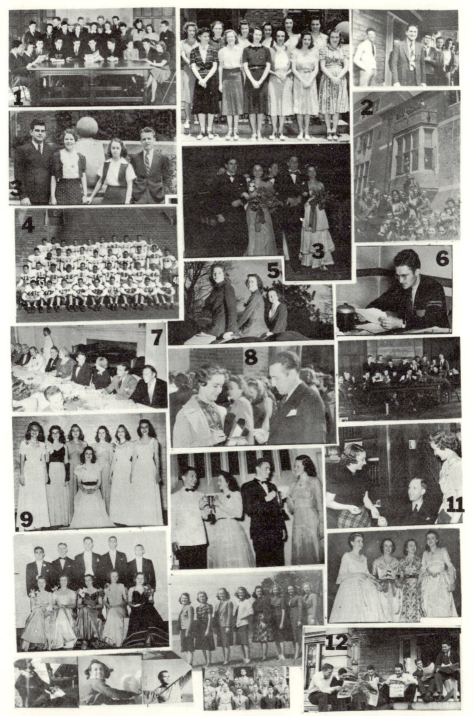

1. Pursuit staff. 2. Students looking out the windows of Alumni Hall at the running of the Turtle Trudge. 3. Billy Sanderson, Annie Lee Crowell and Ovid Collins. 4. Vanderbilt University football team. 5. Katie Heitzburg's younger sister, Martha Wood and Elizabeth Zerfoss. 6. Scott George. 7. Student Union banquet. 8. Miriam McGaw and Dean Sarratt. 9. Virginia Youmans and her court. 11. Ann Carolyn Gillespie and Dot Evans sell a ticket to Mayor Tom Cummings, Sr. 12. Sunday morning at the Deke house.

1. From Left to Right, Ann Carolyn Gillespie, John Millikan, Ann Trimble, Mickey Carmichael, Virginia Youmans, Conway Hall, "Pee Wee" and Francis Craig. 2. Third from the left is my little red headed sweetheart, Freda Atwood. Henry D. and Mary Wallace Austin are to her left. Aileen Lloyd is on her right. 3. Front Row, Left to Right—Susan Scoggins, Betty Blackman, Katsy Aycock, Mamie Edwards and Virginia Youmans. Back Row, Louise Sykes, Tempe Chester and Bess Sorrels. 4. A picture taken of my father 40 years before 40 years ago, while he attended Vanderbilt Dental School. 5. Colonial costumes at the Owl Club George Washington Ball. Left to Right—Shirley Caldwell, Susan Cheek, Andromedia Bagwell and Alice Beasley. 6. My mother, Mary Louise Anderson Austin, when she attended George Peabody College for Teachers.

WINTER
1940

Wednesday, January 3, 1940 Reported for classes today. I saw Susan coming from the library and talked with her for a few minutes. I did not mention the tea that Mary Wallace is planning for Sunday, to which Susan is invited. I attended Professor Robison's class for the first time. He had to call Elliott Trimble and me down for talking. Virginia Youmans was "down in the dumps," when I saw her in the library this afternoon, and I attempted to cheer her. We went into the Social Studies reading room where there was more privacy. She was feeling so bad she cried. I invited her to come out to the apartment with me where I let her read poems from my scrapbook. That cheered her because inspirational poems comprise most of the ones I have collected. We read them until four o'clock when I had to go to my wrestling class. I worked out with Rainey Frierson and it discouraged him that he can never throw me. Later, the giant of a man, Leonard Anglin came to the class and I worked out with him. Later Rainey said: "I feel better now, after seeing you hold Anglin."

Thursday, January 4, 1940 I saw Susan in the library this morning and did not talk to her. I was sitting at a table with Sara Worley. Susan came in and sat at the table just across from me. I did not get up and go talk to her, or even speak to her, for that matter. When she passed our table Sara placed her hand on me as if to hold me. "Take it easy" she said. This evening I was sitting in the Social Science Reading Room with Katherine Simpson, when Susan came in she took the first seat which was on the other side of "Simpe." I did not look up but kept on reading. Susan came over and asked me if I knew where Dr. Mims would be at this time. I told her I did not. She went on back to her seat and I continued studying. In about an hour Catherine left, leaving a vacant seat. Susan then came over and asked my opinion on writing a note to the administrative committee asking permission for the McMurray girl, who is recovering from an appendectomy, to be allowed to take her exams early so that she can be initiated with her class. After talking a few minutes she moved her books and established herself in the seat by me. Instead of answering questions I just wrote out a petition as I would write it. She liked it and said, "I see now why people are always coming to you to get you to help them write speeches." When the petition was completed we took it down to Dean Sarratt and then we went to the Student Center for Coca Colas. When we resumed our studying in the library I noticed Susan was using the notebook I gave her for Christmas. She said she liked it. Jordan returned home tonight and called me immediately. The radiator in his car had frozen so he had to take a taxi to my apartment. We went to the Tally-ho for a bite to eat. Jane Roborg, his lab partner, and a Phi Beta Kappa, came by and sat with us. She and her girl friend took us home. In our discussion of dates Jane said: "Men are like goats." I agreed with that as a sound observation. My book review came out in the Banner this evening (Science in Your Life.) Katherine Anderson called and said she had read it. Bill said he read it on the train somewhere in Arkansas. I gave the book hell in a nice sort of way.

Friday, January 5, 1940 I took a bad fall on the way to school yesterday. The streets are covered with ice and snow. I made my first speech in Mrs. Hart's Public Speaking class. The class critic said it was the best speech of the day. I nominated Bert Marshall for the honorary office of Bachelor of Ugliness. The critic got a laugh from the class when he said I was a little "mixed up" in my politics. (Bert is not in the Senate, my political organization.) I spoke loudly and energetically. I told them that Burt resigned from the Presidency of the Student Council rather than to take credit for work he does not do. He has a job outside of school and does not have the time to do the council work. I also said that he did not want his name put up for B.U. because it would deprive his fraternity of other offices. I pointed out that "It takes a big man to do either of these things." I invited Susan to eat lunch with me but she could not. I ate with McGaw and Sykes. Susan saw me go into Kissam with them and made it a point to be in her regular place in the library when I came there after lunch. She said she got her business in town attended to sooner than she had expected. She mentioned about being invited to tea at my apartment and that I could come by for her at four Sunday afternoon. Stopped by Jordan's room on my way to wrestling class and he gave me a pretty tie as a Christmas present. We had a very good wrestling class but my head was aching. When I got home I drank a large glass of sauerkraut juice and slept for an hour and then I felt better. Marion Long called and asked me to come to the fraternity house for the hazing part of the initiation ceremonies. For the past two years I have asked the blindfolded freshmen embarrassing questions and have told them horror stories while they ate raw oysters with strings on them. We particularly enjoyed the responses of Andrew Sweat and George Ed Wilson. Dr. Henry Nelson, an alumnus, was at the house. Roy Huggins told me that after talking with my brother Anderson last summer he is ready to sign with the Naval Flying Service. I rode home with Merrill Stone and Bill Shumaker.

Saturday, January 6, 1940 I went to the Banner office and wrote a story about Dr. Weatherford's book being placed in the Oglethorpe University crypt in Atlanta and it will be sealed in with several other artifacts of our civilization until the year 8133 A.D. In Dr. Walker's History class I asked him why it is that the Northern hemisphere is always placed at the upper part of a globe and the Southern hemisphere at the bottom. "Is there any relationship in outer space that demands one hemisphere being represented as up and the other as down?" He turned the globe upside down, looked at it and laughed.

"I like the idea," he said, "I never thought about it that way before."

While I was sitting in the back room with Susan, a stranger came up to me and said: "Do you know M. W. Austin?"

"No, I don't believe I do," I said, scratching my head and turning over in my mind all the possible combinations of names represented by the letters M and W. "Sorry I can't help you." The stranger left and about the time he reached the door it dawned on me that it was my sister Mary Wallace that he was looking for. Susan and I laughed for five minutes over that incident. When I relayed the item to Jordan later he said: "If I were you I would not tell that story to anyone but close friends who love you anyway." After helping Mary Wallace clean the apartment I took a bath and prepared for my date with Virginia Youmans. I met her mother and sister. Her dad was working on some book so we did not go in the living room. We drove to the Stork Club and she ordered a gin rickey and they informed her that they did not have any alcoholic beverages and that we would have to drive down to one of the neighboring places to buy the alcohol. We bought a pint of gin and she ordered her drink. I ordered a cup of coffee and as usual she felt badly that she had ordered a mixed drink by herself. They always feel embarrassed when their escort fails to drink with them and I've never met one yet that would order the second drink under such circumstances. We danced for awhile and then came by my apartment to see Mary Wallace. Bill Jordan was at the apartment visiting and he and Mary Wallace were snacking on Roquefort cheese. Virginia wanted to read what I said about her in my diary when I had a date with her two years ago. The early volumes of my diary were stored in the basement in one of my uncle's apartment houses, the Wallace on 17th Avenue. We drove there and had the janitor, George Delk, haul the trunk from the basement to the first floor. We got the diaries and spent the next few hours poring over them. We found the date and I had said she was pretty. I also quoted her as saying that she always falls in love with someone who does not love her. She got a kick out of that and also the items about my love bouts with Miriam McGaw. It is fun to look back over those old times. Virginia told me she loved Billy Kennon, son of Dr. Kennon, who is an Ear, Nose, and Throat specialist in Nashville. She said he loved her too. She hopes she can hold him four or five more years. Emmy Leake used to go with him and she and Youmans have a characteristic hatred for each other. Virginia says she fell in love with Billy when D. Y. Proctor deliberately took her to the Stork Club where he knew Billy and Emmy were. That night Emmy put her arms around him, messed up his hair, and engaged in other acts designed to make Virginia jealous. This summer at the Vanderbilt Hospital they saw each other every day. They took long strolls together. Said she just lived from one day to the next so that she could see him. That day, last week when she was blue was the day that he left for school. He is studying to be a doctor. Took her home at one o'clock and her father was still up reading. She says he sits up that late every evening.

Sunday, January 7, 1940 Marie Smith came over early and helped Mary Wallace prepare the sandwiches. At three-thirty I went to school to get Susan and then we drove by for Andromedia. Andy told Susan that I was the only person to make "A" in Public Speaking. Also that Henry Clay thought lots of me. When we arrived at 4:20, Bill Jordan, Bill Scott and Russ Dorn had already arrived and were in the midst of a confab. We all gathered around and joined the conversation. Mary Wallace and Marie excused themselves and finished fixing the food and the rest of us began playing games. "Stinky Pinky" and "Culture." Bill Scott, Andy, Susan and I sat at the card table in the front room and Mary Wallace and the others ate in the kitchen. The chicken salad sandwiches were splendid. The tomatoes, the pineapple and the cottage and Philadelphia Cream cheese sandwiches were also good. I did not particularly care for the spiced tea but all else was good. The icebox pudding was the best dessert I have ever tasted. When the boys were getting their coats to leave and Susan and Andy were the only two persons in the room, Andy asked, "Where is that picture of Susan?" I got it out of the drawer for her and she put it on the radio and said, "Now that looks better." I put it away again though before the crowd came in again so that Susan would not be teased. I drove Andy home first and then Susan. Susan said she had a fine time and she thought Mary Wallace was mighty smart. I thanked her and came on home to find Jordan, Uncle Ragan, Aunt Nell, Frances and Mary Wallace in a discussion. Mary Wallace looked pretty. She had her hair fixed just right and her black silk dress was very becoming. At eight o'clock Jordan and I drove by for Frances, Jordan and Bill Simpson. We came out to the apartment, ate again and danced for awhile. Jordan stayed with us until ten. This made Simpson mad because he wanted to be alone with Mary Wallace. Frances seemed to have a splendid time. Took all of them home at eleven.

Monday, January 8, 1940   After Dr. Sanborn's class I went to the library and studied with Susan until eleven o'clock. She asked me about Tom Manchester but would not tell me why. Owsley conducted another interesting class. Willie Cornelius and I got into a discussion over grades by writing notes back and forth. I maintained that grades are not the important thing in a course. Willie was mad because he did not get an "A." I ate lunch with Sykes and Elizabeth Surles. Met Susan in the regular place at one o'clock and we studied together until four. I was still reading the life of "Alcibiades." I read her several passages from it. That Alcibiades was a fascinating character; one of the most interesting people I ever read about. I had an extra large class in wrestling today. There were forty or fifty people there. Clark Giles rejoined us today. He is a big help. We work together perfectly. He is a darned good wrestler too. Tonight I went to the first home basketball game with Jordan. We sat by Dean and Mrs. Lewis. Dick Henderson came up later. It was a very close and thrilling game. Vandy won from Cumberland by a score of 54 to 43, I believe it was. "Pinky" Lipscomb was the high score man, as usual. They say "as Lipscomb goes, so goes Vanderbilt." John Milliken also did some brilliant stealing of the ball. Joe Little is a wonderful stabilizing force for the team. He's a coolheaded athlete. Team captain. Ross Hanna did well. Maurice Holdgraf played a little rough once and the other side got a little huffy. Nothing came of it though.

Tuesday, January 9, 1940   Henry Clay was giving my wrestling class their exercises when I showed up at 4:15 o'clock. He always says and does the right things, but he can't keep a boxing class because he can't resist the temptation to hit when an opponent drops his guard. It is almost an instinct. I talked with Lucille Johnson about a case of cheating

and in Dr. Sarratt's office I learned of another case of stealing from
the lockers at the gym. Turned in my paper on Alcibiades to Dr. Harris.
I wrote a story about the Bachelor Maids installing Mortar Boards at
Vanderbilt.

Wednesday, January 10, 1940   Between classes I saw Nello Andrews
and Susan walking to the library. I went on to the Banner office to
turn in my story. Had a nice chat with Fred Russell. He accepted an
invitation to dine with Mr. Hill Turner, Mr. Cecil Sims, Jordan and
me next Wednesday evening. We are going to discuss ways and means
of establishing a closer relationship between Vanderbilt University and
the Vanderbilt family. I heard one of the best speeches ever in chapel
today. Henry M. Schneider, President of Wofford College was the
speaker. Dr. Mims gave him a very flattering introduction and pointed
out that he is President of the late Dr. Kirkland's Alma Mater. When
he got up to speak he said, "Dr. Mim's introduction was very flattering.
It was very good. I am sorry he stopped—but then he ought to be
good because I taught him." His subject was "Chapel Talks—are they
worth anything anyway?" In speaking of a Dr. Caldwell he said, "In
the first place he was a Republican and it was thirty years before I
could get over the idea that a respectable, good citizen could be a Republican. I'm still having trouble in that direction." "When I was at Vanderbilt, the faculty, almost to a man, covered as much of their countenances
as they could with beards and looking around me today I am not so
sure that the old custom ought not to be revived," (applause) He said
that many of his students come back to him and say "I have been associating with men and books, That sentence always sounds good," he commented, "you ought to use it sometime." He quoted Henry James' advice
to a group of young ladies, "Young ladies, know a good man when
you see one." Quoted one sentence from Billy Phelp's autobiography
"A Puritan saint with the charm of a sinner." Told the story of a Puritan
picture that appeared in the old "Life" magazine. Three girls were sitting
on a fence without being sufficiently clothed for the weather and sang
as they strummed on their ukulele—"Oh Puritan father, which shall it
be, Onward Christian Soldiers, or Abide with Me?" "Attach yourself
to a great idea" was his key sentence. Scott George bought my "Gone
with the Wind" tickets for Sunday night January 23. Planned to meet
Susan in the library but my trip to town made me late. Saw Francis
Craig at the Hermitage Hotel and talked over with him the idea of a
waltz period at the Deke dance on January 19th. Craig liked the idea
and suggested a fifteen minute period of Viennese waltzes and later a
fifteen minutes of American waltzes. Came back to the library and Susan
returned from gym. I told her about my talk with Craig and also about
the G.W.T.W. tickets. She had to go up to the law library to brief a

case. She managed to get back a few minutes before four in order to tell me good-bye for the day. Was it because of courtesy, or was it a sign of her affection? That is the biggest question in my life at the present—"Does Susan love me?" Got a nice letter from Buster Birdsong. He told me how his bride-to-be walked out on him just a few days before the planned wedding. He concluded that it was best though. He had returned to his plan, with a new zest, to become a doctor.

Thursday, January 11, 1940 In Public Speaking I spoke on the Honor System. It was the first time I have spoken on that subject. Henry Clay remarked to me that it was the best speech I have made and the best speech that he has ever heard in a Public Speaking class. The class critic—Crifshire—ignored the good points of the speech and picked out a few minor mistakes. Andy, Henry and others expressed their resentment to me over the report. Susan went to lunch with me. We sat with Miriam, Bill Braden, Nello Andrews, Henry Clay and Mac Dickinson. Susan had a long list of figures to add so we walked over to the Bus. Ad. room and used their adding machine. I called out the figures to her and she operated the machine. I got a kick out of working with her. She and Susan Scoggins worked problems from three until four. At nine this evening Jordan and I drove by Ward-Belmont and picked up Virginia Richey and May Vanderen. We went to the Tally-ho for Cokes. We had an unexpectedly good time so we stopped by the Sugar Bowl for a few dances. They invited us to come back to see them next week. We played the game "Stinky-Pinky." Saw Merrill Stone, and Mickey Carmichael.

Friday, January 12, 1940 After Dr. Sanborn's Philosophy class I went to the library with Susan and I could not help noticing how beautiful her hair was. I asked her how she kept is so glossy. "Brushing it, I guess," she said. She went on to say that she likes the way Mary W. fixes her hair now—straight back and curly only at the ends. I agreed with her. After Owsley's class I ate with Susan, Surles, Sykes, and Stone.

After finishing our exercises in the wrestling, I worked out with McCullough. I managed to throw him. I am glad that I can do it because it will keep him from becoming conceited over his wrestling ability. Some people seem to think that he has a tendency to be conceited over his good looks. Henry Clay and I went up to the "Y" and scouted the Castle Heights "Y" teams. The Heights boys won by a score of 18–6. I met both coaches. I believe the Heights coach is named Stores. I told him I knew Jim Homes and Hozier, who are now associated with Castle Heights. When I returned home I called Susan and found that she had gone to the "Taming of the Shrew" at the Ryman. Lunt and Fontanne were superb I hear. I guess I should have asked Susan to go to the Ryman instead of to the wrestling meet with me. Her grandmother went with her. Mary Wallace told me something funny that happened to Susan this evening. Susan had just been to town to make a purchase of gloves and underclothing and someone stole the latter (six pairs) out of her car and she was furious over it. Damaris Witherspoon kidded her saying that she must have been threadbare. This, of course, embarrassed her.

Saturday, January 13, 1940 Jordan came by from the play saying that he had been locked out. He proofread the article on amateur wrestling that I had written for "Pursuit" and then we went to bed. He said the play was the best he had seen. We slept late and Mary Wallace fixed breakfast for us. It was very nice. I was the critic in Public Speaking class today. Rainey Frierson, Nell Edward, Henry Clay, Rush Dozier and Crifshire spoke. I started out by saying that I wasn't interested in picking flaws but in looking at the speech as a whole and attempting to suggest some avenue of improvement. I pointed out the sincerity of Frierson's speeches (he spoke on the Honor System). In discussing Nell's speech I said, "Women are naturally better speakers than men— at close range." I would suggest "more contrast—rise to greater emotional heights and vice versa." I said Henry made his best speech. He was free and relaxed. We did not worry over his forgetting his speech nor did we struggle with him for the right word of description. When Rush is speaking I can never quite forget that he is making a speech. I can't quite lose myself in the subject. I would suggest more peppy descriptions, stories and jokes. Crifshire is a good speaker, seems to have a natural flair for it; moves easily and freely on the stage, but he is just a bit oratorical and sounds like a preacher. He seems to overlook his audience, however, in addressing his remarks to the teacher. After that report Andy came up to me and asked if I would not be the critic on Thursday some week when her section of the class was speaking. Ate at the house today and then went to see "Raffles" at Loews. It is the story of a high society crook, on the order of a Robin Hood. He called himself the "Amateur Crooksman." It was cleverly done. We came by the Banner office and Hoffman told us a joke or two. I introduced Henry Clay to Fred Russell. I escorted Virginia Richey to her first Vanderbilt gym dance. The music was good but humidity was great and the floor was crowded. Virginia did not know many people and even though I introduced her to several she still got stuck with dancing several selections with the same person. It hurt her pride. She felt so badly about it that after the dance she cried. I told her in the most soothing terms that I knew that it was not important and that I had enjoyed being with her. After her cry she felt better and she began to smile and laugh. We drove down to Nick Vorallas, ate a bite and then came home. I did not dance very much with Susan. She was pretty, as usual, and I danced with her once while they were playing a waltz and again while they were playing the Deke song. She asked me to ask Eleanor Richey for a no-break but she had already been asked for all of them. She said Eleanor was worried about the dance. Susan asked me if I had studied in the library this evening. I told her "no." It flattered me that she seemed interested in my studying there—expecting her— and her not showing up. I had to stand Susan up on the fourth no-break as I was with Virginia Richey. Jordan was supposed to have it with Virginia but he was dancing with Shirley Caldwell at the time and could not make it. I saw Henry Clay with Susan.

Sunday, January 14, 1940 Jordan came by and we went to the Tally-ho for dinner. After eating we drove out to Damaris Witherspoon's to see if she wanted to take a ride with us. Instead of riding we just sat and talked to her. She is very interesting. Coming out of a street into Hillsboro, we pulled in the path of a car that was coming faster than we figured. The man driving the other car was Dr. Neel and he drove up behind us and blew his horn several times as he passed. He gave us a "dirty" look and yelled what sounded to be several invectives at us. We did not reply but followed very closely behind him for several blocks. When he turned we would turn. Finally stopping in front of his house so we pulled up beside him and also stopped. Jordan turned the switch off and got out, walked in the direction of the doctor and his wife. I know what thoughts must have turned over in their minds as Jordan, who looks as big as a grizzly bear, approached their car. He did not say a word until he reached the driver's side and then he said, "I wish to apologize for pulling out in front of you. I am not a very good judge of the speed of automobiles." I never saw such an expression of relief come over a man's face. He could not accept the apology fast enough. He was all smiles as he introduced himself and his wife. I think I'll write this incident up as a short, short story. Tonight Jordan and I went up town to a meeting of a group which is sponsoring a creative writing magazine. Ruth Denson and Tony Denson, a Mrs. Potter and two other people were present.

Monday, January 15, 1940 Susan was beautiful in a yellowish-cream colored blouse. I don't know when I have seen her look as pretty as she was this morning. Miriam sat directly across from us and I noticed her casting eyes in Susan's direction occasionally. After lunch we returned to the library and Susan let me take one of her psychology examinations to determine if I am an introvert or an extravert. My leanings are to the gregarious or social side. Willie Cornelius came and talked with us for awhile. I think he invited Susan to the Miami Triad on March 2nd. Willie likes Susan and tries to win her favor by being a tease. I don't think that approach appeals to her though. Arranged our no-break for the Deke dance. I am going to get the first and third with her and the second with Eleanor Richey. Partee came down and worked out with the class today. Anglin was too much for him, in the condition Partee is in now. I worked out with Bob Whitnell and got plenty tired. After the class I went up to Partee's room and talked to him and Jordan. Instead of going downtown we decided to buy some groceries, including a large steak and go to my apartment to cook it. I have never eaten such a meal. It was a WOW! We had shrimp cocktails, grapefruit, pork and beans, hot tamales and two quarts of milk. After eating our fill we called up Virginia Richey and invited her down to help eat the dessert. We met May Noi on the way so we brought her down too. We had Coca Colas, ice cream and cake. Virginia Richey liked the assortment of cheeses. We had a nice lengthy chat and then drove to the Rustic Tavern for dancing. Virginia was as smooth as usual and May Noi is a good dancer too. I danced two pieces with her. Earlier in the evening Fleming told me of a conversation that he and another boy had yesterday. He said they picked me out as the boy at Vanderbilt most likely to succeed. I didn't mind that statement but I resented a reference to Susan, in that connection.

Tuesday, January 16, 1940 While eating along with Susan at Kissam Hall cafeteria today I told her how pretty I thought she was yesterday in that yellow blouse. Dr. Mims is one of my favorite teachers, but he can be dogmatic at times. I spoke to him about our plan for bringing about a closer relationship between the Vanderbilt family and the university and he dismissed the idea with a wave of the hand. "Everything that can be done to bring this about has been done!" That pompous statement is foolishly narrow on the face of it. It is disappointing sometimes to see the feet of clay of those you are accustomed to holding in high esteem. I wrote and sent to Anderson another speech for students at T. M. I. When, on a burst of inspiration, one does something well, it is extremely difficult, and even precarious to try to follow up, but life can't stop because of one success. One must keep on, even if he "can't recapture the first fine careless rapture." This second speech for Anderson is perhaps not as spectacular as the first, but it has some good points. Here it is:

LIVING UP TO A REPUTATION

One of the strangest quirks of human nature is that some people spend a great part of their lives living up to a reputation that may have been made in three or four unthinking minutes. That reputation, in many instances, may have been based on some particular set of circumstances, which may have been present at that one time and never again. As a result, a person may be noted for something entirely foreign to his nature and personality; it may be a completely false reputation.

Abraham Lincoln, as a farm boy in Illinois, got a reputation as a teller of funny stories. This reputation followed him throughout his life. Even when he was President, people would not be satisfied with one of his speeches unless it had a funny story in it.

Lincoln's Gettysburg Address was considered a flop by the people who heard it. Several theories have been advanced to explain why this literary masterpiece did not go over well with the audience. Mine is that when Abe Lincoln took the podium people expected humor and, since he did not supply it in this speech, the people were disappointed. They could not forgive him for failing to tell a funny story, even in a speech commemorating "those who gave their last full measure of devotion."

About 47 years ago a fellow by the name of John L. Sullivan got a reputation as a fighter. His reputation grew to the extent that almost every man, woman and child in America knew something about the "Boston Strong Boy." Sullivan believed, as did the rest of the United States, that there was not a living man who could lick him. One day, however, there appeared on the scene a man by the name of Corbett, "Gentleman Jim" Corbett, and he accepted Sullivan's open challenge.

On that fateful night of September 7, 1892, in a dimly lit arena in New Orleans, Jim Corbett, after 21 rounds of skillful boxing, knocked out the mighty Sullivan and blasted his reputation as America's invincible hero.

On September 11th this account appeared in the New York "World."

> *"He (Corbett) has robbed a country of a very striking individuality. If he had gone to Switzerland with a shovel and dug away Mont Blanc he could not have hurt the feelings of the Swiss more than he damaged the feelings of hundreds of thousands of Americans . . . It is unquestionably true that he is a very gentlemanly young man and a remarkably gentleman fighter, but then we do not want a gentlemanly fighter. We want a fighter to be nothing at all on this earth but a fighter."*

The same might be said of Jack Dempsey. Dempsey's reputation was even more powerful than the defeat at the hands of Gene Tunney.

Buried deep in our history books is an account of the battle of Waterloo. The account says that Wellington won, but the only name that most of us remember is Napoleon Bonaparte. "The Little Corporal's" reputation was so great that even the disaster at Waterloo could not dim it.

Reputations are powerful things, and once started, they will sometimes lead you further than you may want to go. It is essential, therefore, that the processes of making reputations be guarded carefully, lest we be taken in directions in which we cannot be proud.

Some boys get a bad reputation early in life and make desperate attempts to live up even to this kind. If you get a reputation as a boy who pays no attention to the rules; as a boy who is willing to take part in all kinds of mischief, the minute any other boy thinks up a prank, he will head straight for your room to work out the details. It is hard to put your foot down once a bad reputation is abroad.

The person who has a reputation for always doing the right thing will not be bothered by temptations of this kind. Neither will he be suspected by the authorities once the job is done.

You boys know as well as I that in your dealing with the fairer sex you will never try any of your high pressure salesmanship on girls with spotless reputations. It is only with those whose reputations are shady that you become a Don Juan.

The same principle applies to your school work. If you want to make "A's" then you must make a reputation as an "A" student right from the start. Even if you change teachers the reputation as a good student will follow you. The teacher naturally looks for good points in a good student's paper and for the mistakes, which she expects, in the bad student's examinations. The good student is given the benefit of the doubt; the poor student never.

"To him that hath, it shall be given. To him that hath not, it shall be taken away, even that which he hath."

Wednesday, January 17, 1940   While studying with Susan in the library I read Avery Craven's "Edmund Ruffin—Southerner." Dean Sarratt and Jim Buford came over to the gym to see my wrestling class work out today. They complimented the technique of teaching holds by the numbers. I can teach a large number at once by this technique. Had dinner this evening in Kissam Hall with Jordan, Turner, Alumni Secretary, and Fred Russell, Sports Editor of the Nashville Banner. We made plans to have members of the Vanderbilt family sit in a box at the Vandy-Princeton game. In 1941 we plan to have them come to Nashville.

Thursday, January 18, 1940   Dr. Owsley said that in the early days of our nation many people were as scared of Thomas Jefferson as we are of Kuhn and Browder, Hitler and Stalin's representatives today.

He was considered a revolutionary. He was also considered the tool of Napoleon. Napoleon had annexed Holland, Spain, Italy, Belgium and then Russia annexed him. It is interesting to note, however, that wherever Napoleon went he overthrew autocracy and established equality before the law; the Roman system. He gave these countries a system of laws superior to their neighbors. Sectionalism in the United States was a contest for control of the Federal government. Following the war of 1812 the Chocktaws, Chickasaws, and Creek Indians were driven out of Alabama, Georgia and Mississippi and settlers rushed in and grabbed the land. Excessive borrowing of money for land speculation led to the panic of 1819. Slavery was not profitable (because of the growing ratio of household help to field hands) and recognized as an evil long before Missouri asked to be admitted to the Union as a slave state. As Jefferson said, this came as a "fireball" and upset the delicate balance between North and South. The Missouri Compromise soothed feelings from about 1821 to 1850, but when California entered the Union, and there was talk of building a transcontinental railroad, competition among different sections for the site of the roadway developed and any one state entering the Union as "Free" or "Slave" would upset the fearful balance of power. Moral arguments were injected into the Sectional Controversy and the dogs of war were loosed.

Friday, January 19, 1940 Pop J. Jamison, director of Dixie Camps, called early this morning from Tom Keeling's house. He had just arrived in town. Webb Follin and I went out to see him this afternoon. Webb camp is not going to operate this year so Webb wants a job. Later we went to Dr. Carruther's home and then to Protestant Hospital to see Bob Foote. On the walls of the hospital waiting room I saw pictures of Joel and Leslie Cheek, Mr. L. A. Bowers and Dr. Blanton, the late President of Ward-Belmont. At six-thirty I went by to get Susan to go to the banquet and dance at the club. Eleanor and Tom Manchester had left thrity minutes earlier. When I told Susan about seeing her grandfather's picture at the hospital she told about the trouble they once had getting her father into the hospital. At the banquet Tuck made a few remarks about not having speeches. He said Trimble and Austin would speak if called on, but that Austin gets enough publicity since he runs the Nashville Banner, with a little help from publisher Jimmy Stahlman. The two waltz periods that I had requested from Francis Craig were the hit of the ball. It is amazing what a different tone these waltz periods gave to the dance; elevated it to the status of a grand ball. I believe it was the best dance I have ever attended. It was perfect, in spite of the fact that Eason was there. Merrill Stone said he invited him. Eason had been out trying to sell his sister insurance. Met Mrs. Pickens and Mrs. Hutton, the chaperons.

Saturday, January 20, 1940 Made my cornerstone laying speech this morning, but before doing so I prefaced my remarks with some comments about the waltzes at the Deke dance. The audience agreed with me. After history class I rode to town with Ted Feinblatt and went to the Brass Rail to dine with Pop J., Mr. Keeling and Mrs. Connoll, Society Editor of the Banner. They had already become acquainted when I got there and were talking about newspaper work. We stopped by the telephone plant to see the new dial system that was recently installed and then to the Carruther's home where we showed camp movies to ten boys. Dr. Beverly Douglas, Mrs. Scruggs, Mrs. Martin (of McKesson-Berry-Martin, wholesale drug firm), Mr. Louis Davis Sr., Mr. Keeling, Dr. Carruthers and Mrs. Connoll were also there for the showing. I invited the kids to the gym some afternoon to see my freshmen wrestlers perform. They were enthusiastic about it. The mothers asked if I could keep them all afternoon. I believe we accomplished something at the meeting. This evening I called Virginia Richey and ask her if she would like for me to come to see her late tonight. She agreed so we went to a show and drove around for awhile. She objected to our stopping because it was so cold. I stopped by a fruit stand to buy her some bananas and then drove her home.

Sunday, January 21, 1940 Aunt Ethel, Katherine Anderson's mother was operated on for goiter yesterday. She was not put to sleep. Jordan, Fleming and I went to the Brass Rail for dinner and afterwards engaged in a round table criticism of each other. We agreed that I laugh too much and am not as tolerant as I might be. Fleming said I made enemies from the Honor System battle last year. We agreed that Fleming makes a pig of himself eating and is not as "couth" as he might be. Jordan, of course, as brilliant as he is, and as strong in opinion, is too weak to break the apron strings. He also needs to develop a little muscle to go along with the blubber. It is amazing how the three of us can be so bluntly critical of each other and still be friends. It is perhaps because each knows that the other two respects him as an individual and admires the strong points of the others, which is largely insatiable intellectual curiosities.

Monday, January 22, 1940 I was studying in the library this evening with Susan when Eason came in. He talked for a few minutes and then asked her to go to town with him. She turned to me and said: "Well, I guess I go home and study now." They went off together. Mary Wallace told me that Dr. Gus Dyer talked for thirty minutes about the Cheek family in class today. He said they are the richest family in Nashville and that H. G. Hill is second. He quoted the former at $10 million and the latter at $4. Some of the boys in the class took issue with him for citing the Cheek family as benefactors of the community. Dr. Dyer said they are the biggest tax payers in the city and they always contribute freely to the community chest and other civic enterprises. Intramural wrestling started today. I refereed in one ring and Clark Giles in the other. I was booed by the Sigma Chi's for one call, but that's to be expected.

Tuesday, January 23, 1940 Four inches of snow fell last night and practically all traffic was stopped. I phoned my wrestling story to Dudley "Waxo" Green instead of taking it down. Susan was sitting with her back to the door in the library and when she told me she was studying for an examination I left her alone and went to the bookstore to take some pictures of Pat Sturman and Damaris Witherspoon playing in the snow. They will be used in the Society Section of the Banner. In talking with us individually this evening Dr. Walker said to me: "You have a mind that takes such an interesting slant on things . . . at first I wasn't sure you had one, but I found out you have . . . very definitely." I was talking with Libby Zerfoss, Bitsie Napier and Virginia Youmans when I decided to talk to Virginia personally about the danger of spending too much time with a married man, Pierce Winningham. She did not take offense because she knows I like her very much as a close personal friend. As Virginia and I were going into the graduate room for our private discussion we saw Susan there and immediately stopped and went into another room. Damaris Witherspoon looked at me strangely. I then sat with Susan until time for gym. She told me that Andy Bagwell had told her about my speech on the dance Friday and also about my critics report. I officiated at the wrestling matches again today and then worked out with Clark Hutton, Jack McCullough and Homer Howell. A letter to Uncle Ragan from George L. says he is being graduated from Randolph field and is going to Kelly. I am proud of his progress because I know it is what he wants to do.

Wednesday, January 24, 1940 Dr. Sanborn gave us a cut today so I did not have a class all day. Sat with Susan from ten until twelve and Susan Scoggins was attempting to read palms. She told Susan that if she missed marrying at 23 she would not marry until she was 28. Susan and I ate lunch at the Tri Delta House today. The coach of the Castle Heights wrestling team came by to see me at the gym today to discuss the possibility of changing the date of our meet to Saturday. In refereeing one match today I had to disqualify a wrestler because he was too rough. The crowd applauded. Willie Cornelius said: "You should have disqualified him sooner." It was Whit La Fon's roommate. I had to rush to get out to Susan's for my date. The moon was full and the snow on the magnificent lawn at Oak Hill, with the huge white columns in front of the house, made a veritable Christmas card setting. At the Community Playhouse we saw "What a Life," a play depicting the hardship of Henry

Aldrich, a troublesome schoolboy. As we were going home she hummed the tune "Music Maestro Please" and said she liked the part which said, "He danced divinely." I joined her in the part that says: "He used to like waltzes." She wrote with her finger on the frost covered window: "Ben is a nice boy." I told her it reminded me of "Love Letters in the Sand." When we stopped in front of her home I told her: "Look at me . . . I love you." She just blushed and we went in. Earlier in the evening she told me about Owsley Cheek, her cousin, having to make a forced landing in Stevenson and that my brother Wilson had asked him and Rufus Pardue Jr. to spend the night with my family. She said my folks were very hospitable to them. A letter from mother confirmed the story. Since there are no hotels in Stevenson, two linemen are occupying the front room so mother gave the boys her bedroom. It's an interesting coincidence that Susan's cousin should get lost on the way to Birmingham and make a forced landing in Stevenson. I suppose mother asked Owsley if he were kin to Susan, otherwise how would Susan have known about the incident.

Thursday, January 25, 1940   In my speech today I eulogized Ted Timberlake. I attempted to speak very freely and to move about at will. I even stepped down from the stage when I told of the accident in which Ted was killed. After the climax I stepped back on the stage and finished by quoting: "Green grows the grass above him, friend of my better days, None knew him but to love him, None spoke but to praise." When I sat down Henry Clay said I had as much poise as the teacher. What a wonderful friend Henry is. He always knows the exact thing to say, and he does not do it as flattery. He sees his friends as they ought to be. Ate lunch with Shirley Caldwell, another person of rare charm and beauty. Add to this circle Louise Sykes, Elizabeth Surles, Andromedia Bagwell, Miriam, Susan, Jordan, Fleming, Willie Cornelius and practically a whole campus of wonderful people . . . how lucky can one guy be? Rode to town this evening with Frank "Frosty" Dority and met Mr. Devereau Lake. I showed him my invention and he told me about his company, the "Sandusky Foundry and Machine Company" of Sandusky, Ohio. He said he owes much to Vanderbilt and he is anxious to bring a Vanderbilt man into his company. He said: "I am almost tempted to tell you to come next week and take the job." I explained that I would not get out of school until June. He needs a man immediately. I told him of my plan to contact the Talon Company soon for job possibilities. He invited me to see him next summer. He gave me the names of several people who might help me in the way of giving advice: Greer Marechool, Dayton, Ohio. He is Mr. Lake's patent attorney. E. E. Berry, Beloit Iron Works, Beloit, Wisconsin. He said that Berry has the same kind of mind that I have and that he is an able inventor.

He also told me about a friend of his in Mobile, Alabama, Mr. Lake's hometown, who for fourteen years was Edison's Chief Engineer, Miller Reese Hutchinson, Mobile, Alabama. Hutchinson worked especially on electrical devices. Tonight I told Susan about my talk with Mr. Lake and the Sandusky proposition. She asked me what kind of a job it would be and she seemed very interested. She said her father once worked in a steel mill in Sandusky. If I had brains, or courage, I would ask her to marry me now and go to Sandusky. How much better start can a young man make than as a protégé of the boss?

Friday, January 26, 1940   Met one of the most interesting persons I have ever encountered this evening. Jordan came by the gym for me and we went out to the Caldwells for Shirley and met her mother. Mrs. Caldwell was sitting by the fire smoking a cigarette. She did not get up when Shirley took us in for the introductions but sat there in a broken-down chair, unruffled by our entrance. We shook hands as if we had been lifelong friends and she and Jordan began to talk about a mutual friend they knew at Webb School. They both agreed that Sawney Webb's son cannot hold a candle to the old man. "His son is mortal, Sawney was immortal," they agreed. I ventured the observation that the son rarely lives up to the standards of an illustrous father. I stood silently by the fire, listening and warming for another few minutes and did not get into the conversation until they got on the subject of politics and Roosevelt. Mrs. Caldwell said that the President's mind is afflicted. It is always the case with cripples she said. I reminded them that Roosevelt's crippleness came late in life after his character and personality had become somewhat settled. At this point the direction of the conversation was focused on me and Mrs. Caldwell turned squarely to me and said: "If you are so damn smart, as Shirley says you are, let me hear you say something." Immediately I made the point that practically every great accomplishment in the world came about as the result of some person trying to overcome a physical handicap. I cited the case of Demosthenes and Benjamin Brewster. I called their attention to the fact that the poet Pope was a hunchback and that Glenn Cunningham once had his legs burned to the extent that his doctors were fearful lest he could ever walk again. He over came this, not only does he walk but today he runs the mile faster than any living man. When Mrs. Caldwell spoke of me as being smart, Jordan wilted like a lily. He is not used to other people being referred to as being smart, when he is around. In a few minutes I suggested that we had better go to town and eat lest all the eating places put away their supper menus. Mrs. Caldwell invited us out to eat sometime. Shirley said we would perhaps not like hash. We then drove to the Brass Rail and ordered steaks. We talked of the artists duty to write about the whole of life—a là Henry Miller—

and then about religion. Before the evening was over I told them of a letter that I had received from an old friend of mine, Louise Leming, from Decherd, Tennessee. Louise married several years ago, but evidently she has gotten a divorce. She said in her letter that she is just a little bit older but that she is as spry as ever. Says she is coming to Nashville soon and wants to tell me about her "small troubles." She said she mentioned to her mother "I wonder what has become of happy-go-lucky Ben and she suggested that I write you." After leaving the Brass Rail we went to the Student Center for a few minutes and Shirley and Bill continued on home and I stayed for the Tri Delta dance. Willie Cornelius was with Elizabeth Surles. I see them together quite a bit of late. What a gal she is! Miriam was there and Frances Carter. The Carters were there admiring their daughter's antics. Shirley made the remark that she sat in the library this evening and watched Frances acting even when no one was watching her. In a later conversation with Jordan he pointed out to me why the Carters and Caldwells are not so thick now. He had just read "Caldwell and Company" which pointed out that Mr. Carter was once Rogers Caldwell's most trusted confidante and that Carter turned state's evidence when the Caldwell financial house was investigated by the courts.

Saturday, January 27, 1940 Spent the night with Jordan and we talked until two. We drank bouillon and Ovaltine before retiring. At two P.M. eighteen people connected with the freshmen wrestling team left for Lebanon to wrestle the Castle Heights team. They won by a close score of 18–16 but it was a good meet. I am proud of the fine spirit every member of the team is showing. At the Tally-ho for dinner we saw Billy Wade and Jimmy Love, who used to go to the University of Tennessee. Love said he used to run on the cross-country track team with Henry D. and that "Henry has the spirit that it takes to be a winner." I took one of the volumes of my diary to the restaurant with me and read a few selections to Jordan. He said: "Austin, be careful to keep a record of what I say. My biographer may want to refer to your records. I'll leave a note saying 'See Austin's diary.' "

Sunday, January 28, 1940 I spent the whole day resting and looking forward to seeing "Gone with the Wind" with Susan tonight. We left her home at seven thirty after a short conversation with her father. The snow was still thick on the roads so we had to drive slowly all the way. Clark Hutton and his family were there. Saw Ann Stahlman and her mother in box seats. There was an introduction of music preceding the picture and it got everyone in the mood. The color photography was exquisite and the stage settings were as elaborate as I have ever seen. The characters, when silhouetted against the sky, were the most impressive pictures of all. Jean Ewing had told me that it was a three handkerchief picture but I did not shed a tear. I did feel a little choked up at times, however. Susan cried a little but not as much as I expected. She was moved most deeply when the baby was killed and when Scarlett came out of Melanie's room and wept on Ashley's shoulder instead of Rhett's. Rhett stormed out of the room and did not come back. He never showed any more affection for Scarlett. One of the spiciest scenes in the picture was the morning after Rhett was drunk and carried Scarlett upstairs in his arms and to bed. It showed Scarlett there in bed snuggling between the covers and smilingly recalling the events that had taken place that night. According to the book, this was the first time that the fires of married love had been kindled in Scarlett. The picture was toned down just a little bit. The movie version left some hope that Rhett and Scarlett might be reunited. The ending was the most disturbing part of the book because of the uncertainty it left in the mind of the reader. Death would have been easier to cope with. I suppose that was the intention of the author; to leave the audience dangling; for dramatic effect. Seeing this grand picture was an emotional experience for both Susan and me. As I told her going home, I would not have enjoyed it half so much had I not seen it with her. I gave her the souvenir book and kissed her cheek as I said good night.

Monday, January 29, 1940 Susan and I ate in Kissam Hall with Miriam McGaw, Louise Sykes, Buddy Stone and Bill Braden. In discussing the Junior Prom someone asked who Maurice Holdgraf, President of the Junior class, planned on taking. The girl he would liked to have taken already had a date. Stone said "Looks like she would break the date to get to lead the Prom. Remembering that Miriam did that to me last year I remarked that I did not think that would be right. Miriam and Louise snickered. Susan and the others laughed too, but I don't think they realized what the snickering was about. George Bentley came by for me after the tournament this evening and we had a steak dinner. George is one of my very special friends. When I was a freshman, he and I used to work together in the library and while dusting books, or returning them to the shelves, we would have long talks. We got to know each other pretty well. He is tall and thin and when he dances with a girl he bends down and envelops her shoulders in his arms. The lower parts of the bodies are far apart. He is considered one of the best dancers at Vanderbilt. His interests are wide and he is smart, but down-to-earth. After George left I had to sit up and write a paper on John Wesley, founder of the Methodist Church. It is called Methodist because the founder was so methodical. He kept not just a diary but an hourly account of what he did each day. He would send copies to his family instead of writing separate letters.

Tuesday, January 30, 1940 McLaughlin fought a wonderful fight this evening and, in an overtime period, defeated Bill Northern, pride of the Sigma Chi's. Clark Hutton threw David Patterson, another Sigma Chi hopeful. John Shumaker called me about arousing some interest in the "Seventeen" contest on the campus. He suggested a talk in Chapel. Tom Manchester, so Mary Wallace says, called two or three times before I came home this evening. When I called him he said that his grandmother had just eaten dinner with them and that she could not go home until she got her Zipper unjammed. Her slip was caught in the side of the dress. Tom asked me if I knew anything about Zippers and I told him that I had worked on them some. He said how do you get one unjammed. He finally said that he would bring the dress and slip over to me. He and his dad came over at nine. I spread the clip, separated the two garments and fixed the thing like new. It pleased them. They said the grandmother had to spend the night on account of this jam.

Wednesday, January 31, 1940   This morning after hearing Dr. Kate Zerfoss speak to the girls in Women's Chapel I made an announcement concerning the "Seventeen" contest in which some girl might win a free trip to Hollywood. When I got through I asked them how many would bring books and practically all of the girls held up their hands. Dr. Kate came over and spoke to me complimenting my speech. Damaris Witherspoon came by and said "Ben, you are a hot boy." I was standing in the hall talking to Virginia Blair and Lucille Johnson when the lady dean came and said, "Ben, you tell Mr. Duncan that I could not refuse you or him anything." Saw Susan in the library and she said, "It was a nice speech you made in chapel." At two she left her books and went to the gym. She did not come back at three. At a quarter of four I met her as I was leaving the library. She said she had to go by the Theta House for something. I ate dinner at the house this evening and the boys were "hot" about the late announcement of the change in scoring. Under the one point for each match system the Dekes had the tournament sewed up at the semifinals. The only way the Sigma Chi's could win would be by increasing the points to 3 for the semifinals and to 5 points for the finals. This Wilson Ward did. Tonight I had a private conference with Mr. Jim Buford and presented the Deke's side of the argument and asked him to do something about it. He talked as if he would attempt some adjustment. At seven-thirty we met the Y. M. C. A. wrestling team. My freshmen won by a score of 21 to 9½. I was especially proud of Rainey Frierson who wrestled to a draw with Howard Ball. McLaughlin lost but he put up a game fight. Whitnell and Alder won decisions. McCullough wrestled a beautifully built man and won. After the meet several people came around and congratulated the team. Dr. Tom Zerfoss was full of praise for them. Mr. Jim Buford said it was nice work. Clark Giles was sick and could not be with us.

After the meet we drove by the Tally-ho and had another of those elaborate banquets. Each of the boys came to me and said how much he enjoyed it.

Thursday, February 1, 1940 Partee had a story yesterday quoting me as saying "X marks the spot where we'll slay the Y mob." He quoted Buck Allison as tersely replying "Austin's funny predictions slay me." Of course neither of us made such statements. Today's paper said, "Benjamin Franklin Delano Austin's pachyderms downed Buck Allisons "Y" team etc." Made a campaign speech in Public Speaking.

Friday, February 2, 1940 Dean Sarratt told me at noon: "I have been watching your activities in connection with the Intramural tournament and think you are doing a fine job. It is particularly pleasing when the kind of leadership you are showing, comes from a student." I picked up my sweater, with the Varsity letter, at Loew-Campbell. Willie Cornelius has been kidding me, in front of Susan, about talking with other girls. He said: "The other day he made a speech in Women's Chapel. That's the only way he can corner all of them." The Hustler carried the "Seventeen" story and Walter Park's commented: "The Banner's Ben Austin presented the plan in Women's Chapel and got plenty of responses." Came home this evening and took a nap. Frank Gunter, the Banner photographer, came by for me at ten and we went to the Miami Triad dance. The Triad is composed of fraternities that were founded at Miami University in Ohio. They are Phi Delta Theta, Beta Theta Phi and Sigma Chi. We got some excellent pictures. I danced with Virginia Youmans, Damaris Witherspoon, Elizabeth Surles and had a no-break with Susan. Levi Wade was her date. Damned if Eason wasn't dancing with her every time I looked in her direction. He was sticking to her like a leech. I think I'll cut down on the number of times I dance with her from now on. There is no reason why I should make a fool of myself, just because he does. At times I hate it that I do not have more control in regard to feelings toward women. In Locksley Hall Tennyson wrote:

> "Shall it not be scorn to me to harp
> On such a moldered string.
> I am shamed through all my nature
> To have loved so slight a thing."

Saturday, February 3, 1940 Bill Shumaker and I picked up 100 books at the Deke House alone for the "Seventeen" program. At three o'clock we went to the Old Gymnasium for the Intramural Wrestling Finals. Jim Buford, Wilson Ward and I officiated. I was surprised that John Hutton, Billy Swiggart and Tom Manchester lost. Clark Hutton won from Herbert Carmichael. I asked Mr. Buford not to announce the final fraternity winner until we had checked and rechecked the figures. I also asked that the point in question about changes in the scoring system be submitted to an impartial jury. Mr. Buford agreed. Dean Lewis, Dean Sarratt, Dr. Eberling, Dr. Tom Zerfoss and Dr. Fishel will be the judges. I ate dinner with Jordan and Fleming and we rehashed the whole case. Later we went to the last half of the basketball game. I am feeling terrible. I must be coming down with the flu.

Sunday, February 4, 1940 I stayed in bed all day. Jordan and Simpson came by to see me. Later on Jordan and I went out to dinner and then to the Belmont theatre to see "Intermezzo." Leslie Howard was the star.

Monday, February 5, 1940 The committee decided to award two cups—one to the Dekes and the other to the Sigma Chis as cochampions. Saw Susan for a few minutes this morning and asked her how she made out over the weekend. She said she was going to do only the things she wanted to do from now on. I told her I was surprised at her making a statement like that but that I didn't blame her. "I see no reason why people should not do what they want to—within certain bounds," I said. Went to the Banner office with Jordan and at three o'clock I went to the library. Susan was there and Nello Andrews was sitting between my chair and hers. I continued studying and so did she. At four o'clock Susan had walked out into the reading room. As I went out I met her and we talked for awhile. I gave her several pictures of her sorority sisters for their scrapbook. I worked out with the Varsity this evening. Started reading Lincoln Steffen's autobiography tonight. I was interested in the statement that "Charlie Pradger was the only man, except my father and Colonel Carter, who kept his word with me, when I was a child." That story has a parallel in my own life. Charley Grider, a good-looking traveling salesman in our town, once promised me his old Model-T Ford. I really believed him and I never did forgive him for lying to me.

Tuesday, February 6, 1940 Saw Susan at noon and spoke to her. She looked pretty tired and sleepy. I thought about her remark about doing as she pleases, regardless of sleep and rest. Jordan and I took the books that we had collected down to the lobby of the Paramount theatre. I never saw such a collection of books. I collected my salary from Mr. Moss and discussed the book contest with Mrs. Mary Stahlman Douglas. Mary Brock withdrew in favor of another candidate. "Tiger Joe" Thompson helped us deliver the books. My freshmen have been working out against the varsity and it has given both teams some good practice. I went in to use the Lady Dean's telephone this afternoon and Dean Sarratt came in. "What are you doing here?" he asked, jestingly.

"Don't tell him!" interjected the Lady Dean.

"Oh, yes, I know" said Sarratt smilingly, "You are teaching her to wrestle." He then went on to tell her what a fine job I had done with the freshman wrestling team.

"He's just a fine boy." said the Lady Dean.

"Oh, I wouldn't go quite that far." said Sarratt. Jim Buford told me this evening that it was Dean Sarratt who suggested the solution to the fraternity squabble by giving two trophies to cochampions.

"Just leave it to Sarratt!" said Mr. Buford admiringly. I went to see Virginia Youmans for a few minutes this evening but she has a History exam tomorrow so I cut the visit short. Stopped by and said "hello" to Virginia Richey. I got another letter from Louise Leming.

Wednesday, February 7, 1940 Nello Andrews was sitting with Susan when I went to the library this afternoon. He seems to have taken a new lease on life. I wonder why? Dr. Tom Zerfoss and his daughter "Libby" came over and sat with me at lunch. The good doctor and I talked about wrestling. I saw Eason wandering about the campus this afternoon. I could not imagine who he was looking for.

Thursday, February 8, 1940 Today I am 23 years old. Mother remembered. To my surprise I got a card and letter from "Flip" Timberlake. I served as Chairman in Public Speaking class today. All of the introductions were run-of-the-mill until I got to Henry Clay and then I said: "And now, my friends, the main address of the day—the one for which we have all been waiting—an address by the President of S. A. E., that glamour boy of the prize ring; that distinguished son of the South, Henry Clay!" Henry got up and delivered his oration in the same spirit as the introduction. The class enjoyed the banter. I asked Professor Dan Robison, of the History department, to let me wait a day or so to take the midterm examination, since I had lost his book. He flatly refused. The book was returned to him today. He was very nasty in his remarks. He said: "Anybody who tries to get by without buying a textbook does not deserve any consideration." Later, persisting in his nastiness, he said. "I thought I counted nine in the class before Austin came in and there are nine now—your presence must not count much." He smiled derisively.

"Professor Robison," I said, using the same smile and tone of voice, "How much a man counts for depends on the situation. I, myself, for instance, will be teaching a class in wrestling this afternoon at Wesley Hall gymnasium and if you would care to come down and find out how much *you, yourself,* are worth in *that* situation, I will personally conduct the examination."

Friday, February 9, 1940 Rush Dozier outweighs me by about 20 pounds, but I wrestled him, anyway, this afternoon. It was a savage workout. I finally got him off his feet and rode him three or four minutes. He said when we finished: "That was the best workout I've had all season." Jordan came by and said: "I have a new place to dine." The old Cheek home, just off Elliston Place, has been converted into a dining club. We took Duncan Brown and Leroy Leatherman with us. Brown is quite an interesting chap who is preparing to study medicine. He is old beyond his years. He hails from Baltimore, where he says his father is on the Board of Admissions of Johns Hopkins. He went to L. S. U. for awhile and has studied music for years. He is a protégé of George Marion O'Donnell. In social conversation he is a negativist. It appears to me that he tries to impress his listeners by employing the opposite of flattery. He runs down, or minimizes, his own position and winks at the third party present. He sides with new members of a party. I resent people who side with people rather than with issues involved. Somehow or other I can't accept him at face value. Maybe later I'll change my mind—maybe. I was worried this afternoon for fear I had lost my wallet with $30.00 cash. I finally located it. In our freshman wrestling match with Castle Heights this afternoon, our first four men, Burns, Anderson, O'Neal and Robinson lost. Two of them were pinned. They were suckers for the wing, where you hook your opponent's elbow and flip him over your back. Our last four Frierson, McCullough, Whitnell and Alder, won by decisions. The final score was 16 to 12 in their favor. It was a good meet though and we lost to a better team. In the Varsity matches Clark Hutton, Rush Dozier, John Pellett and Dewitt Smith's had outstanding bouts. Pellett worked for a pin consistently and Hutton executed the most nearly perfect switch I have ever seen. On congratulating him later he said: "Look who taught me." He was, of course, referring to the fact that I started him off as a freshman. The Varsity won the meet and we all went to the Tally-ho for refreshments. As we went in the Joe Louis-Arturo Godoy fight was in the fourteenth round. I had a talk with Joselin and he told me that Henry D. is one of the best track prospects at the University of Tennessee. Bob Demas a friend of Henry D.'s, told me of seeing my kid brother Wilson and, because of his red hair, asked him if he weren't an Austin.

Saturday, February 10, 1940 I acted as Chairman for Public Speaking and Rush Dozier paid me a nice compliment. After speaking for several minutes on the need for honest, courageous men in politics, he closed by proposing my name as the type of man needed. He said, "He is a leader in every field that he enters and is the type of man needed." At the close of his speech I said, "Forgetting the personal reference, I would like to say that Rush has made a good point in saying that we should interest our best men in politics. If they don't come from the colleges where are they coming from?" Went to the Banner office to make definite plans for the Prom pictures. Jordan and I then went to the Tally-ho and discussed men and books. The day was dark and rainy. The melancholy atmosphere was stimulating. I took a nap from four until six and went to the Albemarle Apartments where Aunt Nell showed me a book which allegedly exposed the scandle of President Harding's illegitimate daughter, Anne. I picked up Susan at seven-thirty and we went to the basketball game. We sat in front of Slim Porter, one of my high school football coaches, Elizabeth Zerfoss and Frances Carter. The Vandy team, weakened by the loss of "Pinky" Lipscomb and others, lost by a score of 39 to 57. Red O'Donnell, the Nashville Tennessean daily columnist, passed and yelled "Benjamin Delano." At Candyland, where we went for refreshments Susan asked me my favorite poem. I told her I like "The Man Flammonde," "Gray's Elegy in a Country Churchyard" and so many others that I can hardly pick one above all others. She likes "Ode to a Nightingale." It starts out: "My heart aches, and a drowsy numbness pains my sense, as though of hemlock I had drunk . . ." Keat's poetry is beautiful, but the sentiment is a melancholy wish for self-destruction; a wish to escape from the real world into one of poetic fancy. I was surprised that she should name this poem. It seems the opposite of her nature. She is first, last and always a realist. Like most women, she is a pragmatist. It is the men who dream. After leaving Candyland we drove to the H. G. Hill road and stopped. Susan said: "Don't you think we had better go, someone might pass?"

"I never get to talk with you alone. We are always dancing or socializing with friends."

"We can talk at home." she said.

"I can never feel completely free there." I said. She did not demand that we go immediately so we sat and talked for awhile. She refused as gracefully as she could to let me kiss her properly. A peck on the cheek and neck was unavoidable. She shivered when I touched her neck. Her reason for refusing was the same as always.

"I do not love anyone and I don't think its right unless it really means something." I explained that it means something to me, and I asked her if she cared anything at all for me. She said very emphatically that she did. She also promised to tell me if she ever reached the stage that she could not love me. I told her that she is perhaps expecting too much from a would-be lover.

"Maybe you're expecting a storybook affair, where the knight dashes up on a white horse." I asked her if she wanted to fall in love.

"Not just yet." she replied. When we got to her home Eleanor Richey was entertaining Charles Plaxico, Helen McMurray and a few other friends. We went to the dining room and danced several pieces to her portable radio. I was tempted to ask her where she got it; as if I didn't know.

Sunday, February 11, 1940 Around noon Jordan came in, as I was reading the paper, and we went to the Tally-ho for dinner. Afterwards we drove out the Hillsboro pike and up Tyne lane just past Susan's house. We passed an old house sitting back on a hill so we got out and walked up to it. The ground is soft from the recent freeze and rainy spell. It was a typical early spring day. On my return I called Susan and made certain of our no-breaks for the Proms, and asked her if she would care to take a ride with us next Sunday afternoon. She said she would enjoy it. Tuesday evening we are going to see "The Hunchback of Notre Dame." When she said she liked scary pictures because her mother would not let her see them when she was young, I said, "You like to give vent to your emotions through that harmless medium, don't you?" I told her that I had been thinking of our conversation last night and that I had much to discuss with her. Jordan and I saw Mr. and Mrs. Irby Hudson in the Tally-ho. I was surprised that Mrs. Hudson called me by my first name. We talked for a few minutes. Bud Beasley came in at this time. They knew him of course. He is President of the Union.

Monday, February 12, 1940 I continued reading Lincoln Steffen's autobiography tonight. I like his style of writing the climax—surprise ending of each chapter. Just finished the one about the prince and the cowboy. The prince, as a boy, wanted to be a cowboy so he gave up the luxuries of court for the life of a cow puncher only to find it "not what it's cracked up to be." Steffens imagined he was a prince and longed for it to become a reality. In this connection I think of Scarlett O'Hara wanting Ashley Wilkes until she got him. In the library this morning Susan came and sat by me. She was not feeling well. The condition of the breath is usually a good indication of one's state of health. For the first time since I have known her I was aware of a slight unsweetness (as Shakespeare would put it) of breath. At one point she turned to me and said, "Have you been keeping up with what the Youth Congress is doing in Washington? It is backed by the C.I.O. Its Communistic tendencies are dangerous." Her dad must have been talking about it at the breakfast table. I started to ask her jokingly if she were not alarmed as an "Economic Royalist." She believes in the capitalistic system. Its funny how people's views are determined by the side of the fence that they are on. This noon I ate with George Marion O'Donnell, Mrs. Brainard Cheney, and Harry Coles. O'Donnell is a character. I don't know of anyone I had rather hear talk. He is teaching a survey course in English. Took pictures of Bitsie Napier, Jim Tuck, George Ed Wilson, Walter Parkes, Madelaine Bidwell, Blair Batson, Helen

McMurray, Virginia Youmans, John Hutton, Bud Beasley, Carolyn Campbell and Elizabeth Surles this evening. Wrestled Dick Norvell, McLough-
lin and Jack McCullough in the class. Mac tried to pull me down from
a standing position once and I sat down right in his midsection and
cracked the breath out of him. Mary Wallace told me tonight about
two girls that are crazy about Ray Dempsey: Jean Burke and Ann Carolyn
Gillespie.

Tuesday, February 13, 1940 It was raining when I left for school.
At noon I went over to Kissam to attend the luncheon at which Mr.
Robert Mackie spoke on behalf of students who are suffering in the
war stricken areas of Europe and the Orient. Miriam McGaw was chairman of the group and Willie Cornelius was, more or less, campaign
manager. The Lady Dean invited me to eat at her table. Susan, Andy
and others sat at the next table with Dean Sarratt. In the course of
the conversation, Dean Stapleton said to me, "You have not come in
and discussed with me your reaction to my resigning as Dean of Women."
I have not, I said, because when I saw the reports I did not believe
them. Susan made a motion to the effect that a representative from
each of the schools represented be selected to take the message back
to their schools. It passed. I later suggested that the first thing to do
in any campaign is to set a goal. I then asked Mr. Mackie to tell us
what other schools are doing so that we might have some idea of what
to expect from our group. I walked in the rain with Susan and Lucille
Johnson, to the car and then to Dr. Walker's History class. After the
class I went to the library and studied for awhile. Susan, after going
to the beauty parlor came to the library and sat with me until three
o'clock, at which time she went to Alumni Hall for a picture for the
colonial tea. Injured my knee in wrestling this evening. It is the same
type of injury I had last year. The knee was out of joint for a few minutes.
It is not very painful but weak and sore. Uncle Walt came by at six
and we went to the Ragans for half an hour. Saw David Hall and Mildred
and their two children. I then went on out for Susan. The rain had
turned to snow and was very pretty. I brought her a box of candy,
since this is the eve of Valentine's Day. Said she had been wanting
some candy. We then went to the Belmont and saw a very clever picture,
"Daytime Wife." It was the story of a girl who wanted to learn what
secretaries had that wives don't have. The plot became very tangled
when one business executive dated his secretary who was, unknowingly
to him, the wife of one of his business associates who was also dating
a secretary. They all came together at a blind date party and finally
became untangled. When I took Susan home I asked her to promise
that sometime real soon she would let me kiss her good night properly.
She said, "Perhaps—sometime." Called Jordan and he told me about

taking a ride this evening with Virginia Richey. He said that she paid
me a compliment. She said, "He has more gusto than any boy I know."
I don't know exactly what she meant by "gusto."

Wednesday, February 14, 1940 This St. Valentine's Day things are
as usual. Went to a hot political meeting tonight to help straighten
out the Pi Phi plan. There is no earthly reason for taking them in and
the feeling on both sides had grown pretty hot. I made a short speech
to the group saying, that one party was basing it's stand on petty,
personal feeling rather than on issues; that both sides were wrong; that
the Sigma Chis were mistaken because we don't need the Pi Phi's and
that the Tri Delts and AOPI's were wrong in that their opposition was
based on petty jealousies." The vote had perhaps already been fixed
but the motion failed and the Pi Phi's were not taken in. I consider
this the wise course of action. I am sorry that I had to say anything
that would put Walter King who dates a Pi Phi in a bad light. Tonight
Jordan, Fleming, and I got together and discussed the National Youth
Congress and we regretted that we could not have been there and complained about the issues that were railroaded over some of the unsuspect-
ing delegates. We agreed that the Youth Congress was not representative
of the youth of the land.

Thursday, February 15, 1940 I rode to school this morning with Dr.
Sanborn. He told me about an uncle of his who fought in the Civil
War. He lived somewhere in Alabama. I did not go to the Public Speaking
Class this morning. Three people spoke. Clay, they say, did best. At
noon today I wrote a letter for the Hustler condemning the N.Y.C.
"Red" Anglin was telling about hearing of a "tiff" that Pierce Winningham and I had last night. He said that he wouldn't have taken ten dollars
for that incident. At one o'clock Anne Stahlman, Henry Clay, Susan,
Katherine Simpson and Marguerite Wallace met me in the Student Center for pictures. We took pictures of Clay and Elaine Haile practicing
a dance step and then went to the "Town and Country Shoppe" to
take pictures of Susan and Anne Stahlman looking at evening dresses.
Susan tried on the prettiest dress I have seen in a long time. She really
was beautiful. Did not dress for wrestling this evening on account of
my injured knee.

Friday, February 16, 1940 When I saw Susan this morning she had
just been to see a doctor. Her right eye was red and inflamed. The
doctor prescribed "Arjarol" as an eye wash. Told me she was going
to the Lady Dean's tea this evening. My letter to the Hustler editor
was published today. Several people endorsed the sentiment. I said that
the National Youth Congress does not truly represent American youth.
Went to the Banner office this evening and saw the rest of the pictures
and elaborate layout that R. A. Gotto was working on for the front

page of the Society Section for next Wednesday. It is spectacular. I did not dress again today for wrestling. Called Susan and made dates for the first and fourth gym dances next term. She says the fourth will be the senior farewell. I asked her for an earlier one than the fourth but she said her mother didn't want her to make too many dates with the same person. "What does your mother want you to grow up to be—a bigamist?" If I had thought of it soon enough I would have said it, but repartee is better never than late. Mary Wallace went to a Peabody dance tonight with Harry T. Moore, I think Marie Smith and her date drove them. I asked Dr. Owsley to answer one of the questions that I was asked on the exam the other day and he, to my surprise, said pertly, "I answered it once before—borrow someone's notes."

Saturday, February 17, 1940 I was afraid to get up this morning to give my oration. It was a pretty complicated speech—one which required accurateness of expression. I stopped after the first paragraph or two and told them I wanted to read it to them. Rush Dozier was the chairman. After Public Speaking I went to Prof. Robison's class; had my new book. Uncle Walt came by and left his car so I went on out to Tommy Carruther's house where all of the kids had collected. Those present were Billy Rose, John Lee, Charles Green, Frank Turner, Charles Turner, Bernard and Nordie Elam, Scobey Rogers drove out with me and we took them first by the Tally-ho for a frozen malted milk and then on to the gym where I showed them some wrestling and then took them in to see the basketball game between the Phi Delta Theta's and the Dekes. The Phis won. The kids had the time of their lives in the gym. They climbed the rope, scaled the walls, ran around the track and scuffled to their heart's content on the mats. We sat together at the wrestling match. Joe Hutton, Clark and Johns's little brother and Charles Robinson, Walter's kid brother, joined us. When each Vanderbilt wrestler came on the mat we would give him a yell and each time the wrestler would bow and smile at the kids. After the match was over the kids shot some goals in the big gym, scuffled some more and then Scobey and I took them home. Dr. Tom Zerfoss came to me and said there ought to be 200 of the kids at the wrestling events. Mr. Hutton was at the matches and saw both Clark and John win their bouts. He told me his heart would not stand many more like John's match. He seems to be such a nice fellow. That Joe is really a case. Jim Reed sat by me and seemed to enjoy the show. When he goes in for a sport he really works hard at it until he learns everything he can about it. Libby Zerfoss sat close to us. Martha Wade was there pulling for John Pellett. Mr. Giles called me aside and told me about Clark telling him that I had persuaded Horace to do some wrestling. He seemed to appreciate it very much. He told me about Horace having an inferiority complex. He said "he

is so much like I was at his age that it hurts me to think about it."
Horace does have an inferiority complex and I have been trying to interest him in wrestling. Dr. Fishel was there with his usual amount of enthusiasm. Partee Fleming was conversing as big as you please with Jim
Buford and Ward. Captain Bud Bray lost a tough decision. I felt so
sorry for him. In the dressing room he said, "I'm just not a wrestler—
I've made a sorry captain." I assured him that there is more to being
captain than just winning points. He is a fine captain because he is a
fine boy. He is one of the finest I have ever met. I went up to the
Albemarle tonight and ate with Aunt Nell and Uncle Ragan. Katherine
Anderson was there and we had a fine discussion on Communism and
the National Youth Congress. Mary Wallace said she went to the dance
at Peabody last night and met several people who knew me. One girl
said, "Are you Miss Austin? Yes, I know your brother. I am in his history
class under Professor Robison and the best part of it is getting your
brothers point of view as compared to that of Elliott Trimble's. He may
not know me," she said, "but everybody knows Ben." That's laying it
on pretty thick.

Sunday, February 18, 1940 Jordan told me about his long drive and
conversation with Virginia Richey yesterday. They left Nashville at noon
and drove to Murfreesboro and then to Bell Buckle, where the famous
Webb School is located. I kidded him into thinking I had a date with
her that night. He gets a kick out of cutting in on someone else's girl.
I think it is the competition rather than the biological urge. My term
paper for Prof. Robison is going to be on wartime propaganda so Bill
and I went to the library and checked out books on the subject. Partee
joined us in order to go eat with us. I am going to call him "Wimpy"
from now on. We ate at the Brass Rail and then went to the Hillsboro
Presbyterian Church to hear Allen Early, Harry Burks and others report
on the National Youth Congress, recently held in Washington, D.C.
All of the reports were favorable to the proceedings there except one.
The Dale girl said she disapproved. I am glad someone spoke up for
the other side. Late in the meeting I asked if booing the President of
the United States indicates the best kind of citizenship. Is it a wise policy,
in fighting for the continuance of the National Youth Administration
(the program which provides financial aid for students) to turn against
the man who started it in the first place? Jordan and Fleming stayed
only a few minutes, but I was there on assignment. I spoke to Mrs.
Hart and Dr. Kerr, the minister, after the meeting. Next week the general
subject will be "Will Finland prove to be another Belgium?"

Monday, February 19, 1940 I sat up until two o'clock last night writing
my article for the Banner so I slept through my nine o'clock class this
morning. Went to the Banner office and turned in my story and also a

couple of cartoon ideas. In connection with the N. Y. C. I suggested that two little kids be shown behind the barn experimenting with cigarettes and cigars and that the smoke be entitled "C.I.O." or "Communism." For the other I suggested that the old man, John L. Lewis be shown eloping with the innocent young thing, the N. Y. C. In talking with Susan in the library this afternoon she asked if I had heard that John Steele and the Rye girl eloped. I felt like telling her "No, but that might not be a bad idea for you and me." She was tired but looked so frail and pretty. I felt like taking her in my arms and soothing her. I was flattered, but could only sympathize with the girl who looked me up to tell that someone had stolen her ring which she left in the washroom. "This stealing at Vanderbilt must stop." she said.

Tuesday, February 20, 1940 Dr. Harris spent the morning talking about his hero, Daniel Webster. A kinsman of Ralph Waldo Emerson, as a newspaper man, followed Webster around and reported on his speeches. He quoted Emerson as saying that Webster was thicker from his shirt stud to his backbone than any man he had ever seen and that his shoulders were a yard wide if they were an inch. He wore a number eleven hat. Dr. Harris thinks Webster was the greatest orator this country has produced, even greater than William Jennings Bryan. Joe Davis and Willie Cornelius came out to my apartment tonight. Joe showed me his line of clothing and Willie looked at my scrapbook. When he saw the piece about Anderson's 85 mile swim down the Tennessee river he said he was in South Pittsburg, Tennessee at the time and the swim was all he heard about. Jordan came by after his date with Virginia Richey and said that his motive for going with her is that she stimulates him. Also, he thinks she needs the stimulation he can give. Perhaps he's right. A little female stimulation will certainly do him good and as for her . . . maybe. I told him though that his ethics are like those of a fisherman who casts his bait into someone else's basket instead of into the open stream.

Wednesday, February 21, 1940 The picture layout that I worked up for the Prom. came out on the front page of the Society Section of the Banner today. Mr. Moss, the managing editor, called and congratulated Miss Kate Talbot while I was there. It was a beautiful panorama of pictures and story and I showed it to Susan before the papers hit the streets. At lunch time today Chancellor Carmichael stopped by my table in Kissam Hall and said "Austin, I read your letter in the Hustler about the Youth Congress and I think you have summed it up about right. Congratulations on the letter." The article about the speeches at the Presbyterian Church also appeared. The article indicated that editors are not too careful to delete editorial opinion from news stories; especially when they agree with it. I was particularly proud of Winston

Tipton in throwing Howard Ball in our Y.M.C.A. matches tonight. Jordan called and told me about "Katsy" Aycock calling him and arranging dates for the Junior Prom.

Thursday, February 22, 1940 Joe Davis delivered a wonderful speech in Public Speaking today. He drew a word picture of life as he would like for it to be and contrasted it with life as it would be if we went to war. Richard Hart gave a report on the economic reasons behind our possible entrance into the war. After eating with Susan at Kissam Hall she said she had to go to Calhoun to get a book list. She was gone about an hour. In the meantime Eason came in and talked with me. When I returned to the library from a Coke break at the Student Center, Susan was sitting with her feet propped up on the chair she was saving for me. I told her it took her a long time to get a book list. She was looking pretty, though, and it showed that she had combed her hair. Dr. Mayhew stopped by and chatted with us for a few minutes. He told us about his invention of a monkeywrench. In the middle of the afternoon Susan turned to me and said: "Ben, I would like for you to have the second no-break with me at the Theta dance."

"The second!" I said, in amazement.

"Yes, the second," she said, "I'm letting Nello Andrews take me."

"I would be delighted," I said, "And I don't feel badly about your asking Nello to take you. I know he has been nice to you."

"Yes, he has," she said, "And I do like him." In a few minutes Eason came back, pulled up a chair and talked to Susan. He asked her to take a ride with him and she meekly refused. We studied until four when I walked her to the parking lot and I went to the gym. My wrestling class was waiting for me. Jack McCullough was elected Captain and Rainey Frierson was elected alternate. I attended the Houston oratorical contest and saw Frank Clement win the $50.00 prize. I thought Frank's first cousin, Jimmy Weems, should have won it and I told him so. He said he appreciated my telling him that more than from anyone he talked with. Later I called Susan and told her it was all right to change our no-break from the fourth to the third. She said Henry Clay had asked her to change his from the third to the fourth.

Friday, February 23, 1940 Took some stories to the Banner, attended Dr. Owsley's history class, worked out in the gym and took a short nap at home before getting dressed for the Prom tonight. Jordan came by for me and we then got "Katsy" Aycock. The very beginning moments of a dance, like the first puffs of a cigar, are always the best. I don't know whether the orchestra is actually better, or if it is just the beginning realization of a long anticipated event, that makes it so much better, but it always is. Later on, or the second time around, the thrill is not the same as the "first fine careless rapture." In any event I enjoyed just standing and listening to Hal Kemp's band play their famous piece: "Got a date with an angel, got to meet her at seven . . ." Ed Finch used to play this record at the fraternity house and mimic the orchestra leader and go crazy when the tripple, tounging trumpeters were featured. I used to sing this song so much that Miriam McGaw thought it was written in her honor. His theme song "How I miss you, when the summer is gone" drips with the honey of nostalgia. For the second no-break, which I had with Susan, he played a Strauss waltz. Just as the third no-break was announced, Eason rushed in and attempted to break. I turned to him and said: "This is the third no-break."

He turned to her and said: "Don't I have it?"

Susan blushed and said: "But you said you weren't coming." I thought about her telling me that it was Henry Clay that had the third with her. Eason turned on his heels and we did not see him anymore all evening. I had a talk with Kemp after the dance and showed him the newspaper layout we used in promoting the dance. He seemed like a nice sort of fellow. While we were out for snacks "Katsy" ask why I was opposed to the Pi Phi's getting in the Senate. I explained to her that it was not a matter of likes or dislikes, but that the basic principle of a political combination is to have as few organizations in it as possible to win. In that way more offices are available to each fraternity. She accepted the explanation. We then got off into a discussion of the Honor System and Bill could hardly get in a word. Saw Mr. E. B. Stahlman in the balcony watching Ann dance. Once when I was dancing with her Joe Little came up and said, "Oh yes, dancing with the boss's daughter."

"You ought to know about such things," I said. People call Joe "Little Chief" because he goes with Sara Goodpasture, daughter of the dean of the medical school, where Joe hopes to go next year. It was at my request that Kemp played the waltz for the third no-break and I heard several people say they were pleased with the selection. Somebody mentioned it to Susan, as we were leaving, and she responded: "My date was responsible for his playing it."

Saturday, February 24, 1940 Slept until eleven o'clock and then dressed for the tea dance. Picked up Susan at two-thirty. Eason was at the dance and broke on Susan at every opportunity. When a good piece was playing he would get someone to break on me and then he would break right back. I have to restrain myself sometimes to keep from socking him on the nose. I danced the third no-break with Miriam and Eason had it with Susan. After the tea dance we went to the Deke House for a Dutch supper. Saw Louise Sykes, Leo Bashinski, Bill Hume and his girl from Illinois and, of course, all the brothers. Jack Perry was dating Bill Hume's sister. I dressed in my white tie and tails for the final dance this evening. The dance was not crowded and I really enjoyed it more than the others. There were not many stags and Susan and I got to dance together quite a bit. I was afraid she was uneasy about getting stuck so I attempted to set her mind at ease by telling her that I would be delighted to dance all the time with her. This was the beginning of a long an intimate discussion. We continued the conversation at intermission and I told her that I think of her every time I hear a love song. I told her this was my way of saying: "I love you." Back at the dance Kemp was playing fast pieces so we got our coats and left. We drove slowly down Broad Street and out 8th Avenue to the Franklin Pike. She sat close to me and I held her hand firmly and expressed the thrill of just that. We discussed happiness and how dependent we are on others for our own happiness. I told her how lonesome and homesick for Nashville I was on New Year's Eve. We discussed love and how one can tell when it is the real thing. I suggested that perhaps, if all other things are equal, such as drinking or gambling and the like, then it is just the person you think about the most and the person you enjoy being with the most, and look forward, with the greatest anticipation, to seeing.

"But all things are not equal!" she said most emphatically. I don't know exactly what she meant by that. It may be that there is a drinking problem in her family, as there is in most, and because I do not drink, and have discouraged drinking among the freshmen in my fraternity, she may think I am too straightlaced to discuss it with me. Could that possibly be a bar between us . . . I wonder? If I should lose the person I love more than anyone else in the world because of such a notion I would feel like jumping off a cliff. When we arrived at her home I leaned over to kiss her good night and she turned her face away. I argued, but to no avail. I asked if it were a matter of pride. She said no, it was a matter of principle. I kissed her hand and cheek and let it go at that. Earlier in the evening I asked her if she were too warm and she replied: "No, I never get hot."

"Maybe you should, sometime." I replied, jokingly.

Sunday, February 25, 1940 Dr. Owsley quoted some interesting statistics from Common's "Documentary History" and Shannon's "Economic History of the United States Before the Civil War." While Northern writers were going through the South, just before the Civil War, writing inflamatory articles about slavery, 15,000 women were working in New England shoe factories for 8¢ a day. Two fifths of the women were less than 16 years of age and working 16 hours a day. One third of the laboring population of New York were sleeping in cellars. On an earlier period he said that Jackson was accused of dispatching Sam Houston and David Crockett (whom he hated) to foment revolution in Texas

against Mexico. There is no evidence to back up such a claim. Stephen
F. Austin certainly had no idea of revolt, but was forced to it. Peonage
in Mexico was a form of slavery. If a person owed you money he was
your slave, yet the owner had no responsibility for the slave. Santayana
led a group of Mexican half-breeds against the Alamo and every man,
including Crockett, was killed. Later Sam Houston retreated and the
Mexicans followed. Houston's troops turned and in the battle of San
Jacinto, mutilated the enemy. Texas entered the Union as five slave
states.

Monday, February 26, 1940 Just heard my favorite dance orchestra,
Guy Lombardo play "Music Maestro Please." I am so tired of "jitterbug"
that Lombardo's music is like a gentle breeze after a storm. The piece
just mentioned has a double attraction for me. In the first place it became
popular two summers ago when I was spending a very pleasant summer
at a boys camp in the mountains of North Georgia and occasionally
enjoying the company of a pretty little girl by the name of Lucia Bellinger.
We spent many pleasant evenings watching the moon rise above the
lake at the Bellinger home "Persimmon Point." She used to sing "Music
Maestro." Going home from a dance, not so long ago, Susan hummed
the piece and said she liked the part about, "He used to like waltzes,
so please don't play a waltz. He danced divinely and I love him so,
but there I go." Went to lunch with Susan and asked for a date for
the Deke barn dance on April 5th. Merrill Stone and Louise Sykes joined
us. Wrestled Clark Hutton. Refereed Leonard Anglin's match with Fleming. Anglin threw and almost pinned Partee. Wrote Mr. Devereau Lake
and sent a sympathy card to Rousseau Duncan, City Editor of the Banner,
who was operated for appendicitis.

Tuesday, February 27, 1940 I have just returned from a meeting in
which the girl's literary organization, Chi Delta Phi, entertained the men's
organization, the Calumet Club. Martha Haynie is President and Jesse
Clay Orr is Program Chairman. Others attending were Susan Cheek,
Shirley Caldwell, Elizabeth Surles and Ann Carolyn Gillespie. The Calumet Club members attending were Bill Jordan, Partee Fleming, Willie
Cornelius, Bill Booth, Watson McGee, Harris Abrahams and myself.
Dr. George R. Mayfield showed some old Calumet Club pictures. Susan
had on a beautiful blue dress. It's the first time I have seen her in
blue. After eating lunch with Sykes, Surles and Clay we spent the rainy
afternoon studying in the library. When I am with Susan it is much
more than merely studying in the library. At lunch we discussed tempers
and agreed that about the only time we show our tempers is to our
home folks. I have often said that if I had but one wish I think it would
be never to speak harshly to those I love and those who love me. Tonight
I finished my paper on Daniel Webster for Dr. Harris.

Wednesday, February 28, 1940 Since Jordan and I eat so frequently at the Brass Rail, I am reminded of something Dr. Owsley said about Andrew Jackson. His mother told him never to settle personal differences in court, especially when personal honor is at stake. Many people believed it was cowardly to settle such disputes in court. I guess that is why Jackson had so many duels. I remember hearing my uncle tell the story that Jackson was asked, on his death bed, if he had any regrets: "Yes, one," replied Jackson, "That I did not shoot John C. Calhoun." Jackson, of course, was a strong Union man and Calhoun was the spiritual leader of "States Rights." Daniel Webster's 7th of March speech, in which he said "Union, now and forever, one and inseparable," saved the Union for ten years, thereby saving the Union.

Thursday, February 29, 1940 This is Leap Year. Mr. Jack Harris, Program Director for W S M radio station, put on an interesting show in the Student Center. He got four couples on the stage and sought to determine which could propose better, boys or girls. Virginia Youmans, Elaine Haile and Ann Wright did fine for the girls. Barney Ireland and B. B. Carr represented the boys. Asked Susan to eat with me today. She refused saying she did not like to eat in Kissam. When I asked her if she planned to study in the library she said she didn't think so. When I asked her "Why" she said, "You are too inquisitive." Perhaps I am. I'll correct that flaw by ignoring her for a few days.

Friday, March 1, 1940 Mr. Moss, Managing Editor of the Banner, called this morning and asked me to get pictures of Dave Hinkle, Clyde Sharp and J. B. Sherrill. They were driving home from the Pi Kappa Alpha dance last night and Hinkle, Sharp and two girls were killed. I hate to think about the possible causes of such a catastrophe, but I do know that Hinkle, my predecessor as President of the Calumet Club, did a little drinking. There was a vacant seat opposite Susan in the library this morning, but I did not take it. Instead I sat at the opposite end of the library. She turned her head slightly so I could see who she was but I ignored her and left soon. Rode to town with Bobby Oliver to attend to some errands and returned to the campus for the wrestling banquet tonight. Nearly all of my freshmen were there, but Bud Bray, John Pellett and Jim Buford were absent. Dr. Tom Zerfoss was Master of Ceremonies and he called on me to speak first. I said: "Since Captain Bud is not here to 'Bray' for himself, I will attempt to speak for him by telling a story of one of my experiences with him. But before I do let me congratulate the varsity and your splendid record. You have made a good record in wins, but even more important you have been good sports. I told my freshmen on the first day of practice that I did not care how many meets we won, nor am I primarily interested in developing expert wrestlers. We can't hope to do that in one year.

I do hope to increase your interest in the sport so that you will enjoy participating for many years to come. The presence of so many freshmen here tonight is an indication of your interest." Then I told the story of how Bud, when we were wrestling for the Intramural championship, refused to touch my injured knee during the whole of the match and I won. Good sportsmanship meant more to him than winning. I closed by asking the freshmen to work with the varsity next year, and to bring others into the sport. I said they are to be congratulated on selecting Jack McCullough as Captain. McCullough then spoke, expressing, on behalf of the team, thanks to Clark Giles and me. Clark Hutton was elected Captain of next year's Varsity. Professor Robins and Dr. Fishel also had a few words to say. Willie Cornelius came by and offered a ride to the Theta dance but I wasn't ready so I leisurely dressed and walked over. I danced with practically everyone on the floor before I danced with Susan. I broke on her only once. During the second no-break she said, "Ben, I am sorry I was so mean to you yesterday at noon. I had not gotten much sleep for several nights and was tired and nervous. Everything seemed to fret me." I told her that I accepted her apology but that her unkindness did hurt me. Ann Pope saw me dancing the second no-break with Susan and she winked at me. Later on when I danced with her she said: "You look so nice in a tux that you ought to wear one to school every day. Either that, or after you make your fortune, take a certain person with you to New York and just live in the night clubs." I told her that I thought she and Joe made a fine couple too and I am pulling as much for you two as you are for Susan and me.

Saturday, March 2, 1940 I heard, on the radio, William Green, President of the American Federation of Labor, make a speech at a great mass meeting in Atlanta. They are attempting to unionize the South. He is a powerful speaker. After hearing him, I can understand why he is their leader. When I took my monthly string to the Banner Mr. Moss, the Managing Editor, asked me to turn in a story on the C.I.O. movie that will be shown in town tomorrow. The Kappa Alpha Theta basketball team beat the Gamma Phis and the Independents beat the Tri Deltas. I saw my sister Mary Wallace play for the first time, with the Independents. She was the best guard on the floor and her teammate Marguerite Wallace was the best forward. Both girls were brought up in families of boys. I saw Susan sitting directly across the gym from me. I wanted to go over to sit with her but restrained myself. Eason, who was sitting a few seats from me, did, and after the game he left with her. I rode home with Marguerite Wallace and Mary Wallace and stopped by Western Union to send a telegram to Susan. I wrote the following message:

Dear Susan:

I hope this telegram does not scare you. It's message is not important but I have carried in my mind for a whole year a particular date so that I could send congratulations, not on being born 21 years ago, but for all the things you are today.

Ben Austin

Sunday, March 3, 1940   In reading Walter L. Fleming's "The Sequel To Appomattox" I learned that two things were settled by the Civil War: (1). The Negro was to be free. (2). The Union was to be perpetuated. Two billion dollars invested in slaves had been wiped out. Southern capital had vanished in worthless stocks and bonds. Factories were confiscated. Land owners lacked labor, seed and livestock. Northern creditors, having sustained heavy losses, were slow about lending again. In Alabama, Mississippi and Georgia in 1865 it was estimated that 500,000 white people were without the necessities of life. Some aid was sent from the North, particularly from border states. The condition lasted until 1867. Susan's birthday. I suppose she got my congratulatory telegram at noon today. Horace Hornberger took her to the gym dance last night. I danced with her several times and told her I saw her at the basketball game, yesterday evening. Said she didn't see me or else she would have spoken. She is very nearsighted. At three o'clock today I went to a C.I.O. meeting at 417½ Church Street. Mr. Moss, Managing Editor of the Banner, asked me to cover it for him. About 200 people were there and a picture of the newspaper strike in Chicago was shown. This is the fifteenth month of the strike against Hearst in New York and the fellow who was commenting on the film was a former reporter for the Chicago American. The speaker referred to Jimmy Stahlman, Publisher of the Banner, as an "Arch" enemy and said he was in Chicago and took part in the events which led up to the strike. I saw several people there that I knew. A few of them were from the college community and attended the N.Y.C. in Washington. Allen Early, Harry Burks, Miss Eulalia---- and others. Also saw Harold Katz and Walter Parks of the Hustler and Charles Houk, Hillsboro Presbyterian Church. Made a report to Mr. Moss tonight. Denny Ray called this evening and told me that Bob Bell, one of the most handsome and best liked boys at Vanderbilt, shot himself at the Sigma Chi house this evening. Danny says that Bob had just returned from his home in Springfield where he had asked his parents for permission to get married. They probably objected so Bob came back to the Sigma Chi House, got his roommate's pistol and shot himself. Jack Faust and Swan Burrus were the only boys at the house. They rushed in on hearing the shot and tried to stop the blood which was squirting about ten feet. Bob died before they could get him to the hospital. I saw him at the Kappa Alpha Theta dance Friday night with Polly Ann Billington. He had been drinking at the time. He played end on the football team and was well liked by everyone. He was an honor graduate from St. Johns Military Academy. Attending that meeting of the Union this evening impressed on my mind the futility of mass meetings, also the fact that people are continually fighting for money and more money. The mistake that these people are making, as I see it, is that instead of trying to get more money by means of organizing a union, they ought to organize their own talents in a field where they can make more money. As my Mother once told Dad, "You shouldn't have wasted your life's blood trying to bring business and money to the little town of Stevenson, you should have set up where the money and business already are." In other words, "don't try to bring the money to you, go where it is." An individual is much more mobile than established businesses.

Monday, March 4, 1940 One year ago tonight, after taking Susan home from the A.T.O. dance I kissed her for the first time. I never will forget it. I was not sure of myself so I did not dare to take her in my arms. I merely leaned forward as I said good night and kissed the left corner of her mouth gently and then almost ran to the car I was so excited. Never before had I been so thrilled. Yesterday was her birthday anniversary. Today is an anniversary for me. I carried my report of the C.I.O. meeting to Mr. Moss this morning. Also, my story of Bob Bell's death. After leaving Mr. Moss, Fred Russell showed me the proof of a story that Ray Morrison had resigned to take a job with Temple University at an alleged salary of $12,000. Fred is in favor of Red Sanders of L.S.U. and he asked me to seek out campus opinion on Morrison's actions and also the feeling about Red Sanders as a possible successor. I talked to Hill Turner, Dr. Gus Dyer, Prof. Robins, Dean Sarratt and many students. Sarratt said: "I'd like to see a young man get the coaching job here!"

At ten I went to the library and sat with Susan. After a while I was handed a note from Susan. It said, "I appreciated the telegram yesterday. It made me enjoy my birthday much better." When she handed me the note I stuck it in my book and started reading. She insisted that I give it back to her. I then wrote an answer to her epistle and asked her why she blushed so when I wanted to keep the note. Ate lunch with Henry Clay today. We saw Susan there with a group of girls in a meeting. Bob Bell's death is quite the gossip of the campus. At two o'clock Susan came and sat with me in the library. When she came in I told her I was just thinking about her. "Speak of the devil," she said. We studied until four o'clock and then Joe Davis and I went to town to look for a suit. We rode home on the street car. Marguerite Wallace

and her mother came by for Mary W. and me at seven-thirty. I sat
with Mrs. Guy Wallace at the game. Dr. Harris's wife and his daughter
Mrs. Bob Schmidt sat by us. Sara Cecil sat on the other side. The Independents won by a score of 31 to 19. It was as fast as a boys game.
Mary Wallace played a bang-up game at guard. Several people told
me she was the best guard in school. I was really proud of her and
would have announced to the audience, "That's my sister." One of
the Theta's said to me jokingly this evening, "Ben, can't you put some
poison in your sister's food tonight so the Thetas can win."

I saw Susan and Billy Eason sitting directly across from me again.
The Thetas were pretty quiet because they did not have much reason
for being enthusiastic. Coming on home I had Marguerite stop at the
drugstore and I bought them ice cream cones, Mary W. and Bill Simpson
went to the Belmont Theatre to see "Henry VIII." Bill Jordan dropped
in on his way to see Virginia Richey. He had just returned from Pine
Bluff. He is coming by after leaving her. I am going to invite her to
go to the Community play house to see "Our Town" Wednesday night.

Tuesday, March 5, 1940 Dr. Harris lectured on William Jennings
Bryan today. He told of Bryan's visit to Nashville and his lecture in
the Ryman Auditorium "Is the Bible True?" He imitated Bryan in giving
the account of his being attacked by a local newspaper. In Bryan's speech
he read the part of the article which said "Bryan should stay out of
the field of science, where he does not know whereof he speaks." Bryan
then told of his education A.B., M.A. law degree and seventeen honorary
degrees. "I have never used those," he said; merely a card, William
Jennings Bryan, attorney-at-law. But if these attacks don't stop I am
going to have a card printed listing seventeen degrees after my name
and go out to this university on the hill (pointing with his thumb) and
ask one of those sons of an ape to match it." Dr. Harris said that pande-
monium reigned for ten solid minutes. He also told of the wrong thing
that Bryan once said. He yelled, in one of his speeches, "They can't
make a monkey out of me." Somebody yelled from the balcony, "No,
the Lord beat them to it." At the end of the period, as he was giving
back the Webster papers, he said, "The best paper that was turned in
was Ben's. It has a literary flavor that surpassed the rest, although several
others were good." I thought he was spoofing when he told me about
it at first. "The reason I am not turning it back is because I am having
it copied for our files." Ate with Clay and Whit La Fon. Drank a cup
of coffee and felt wonderful all evening. I felt so good that I wrote
several pages of my Honor System oration. At three o'clock Susan came
in and studied with me. She went home today for lunch and came back
to gym. We studied together until a quarter of four and then went to
the student center for the milk shake which I won from her on the

Independent-Theta game. She paid off cheerfully. In discussing Bob Bell's death I told her about Bob being to blame for hurting his mother. She objected violently and said she blamed the family for bringing him up like that and for not letting them get married. After leaving Susan I went to the Banner office where they kidded me about putting in my story that the blood squirted ten feet out of his head. I asked Mrs. Douglas to let me review the new book about Atticus Green Haygood. It so happens that the author had just brought the book to her and she agreed to let me have it. Haygood was the man that I have heard Dr. Sutton speak of so often in his speeches at camp. Mary Wallace's team, the Juniors beat the frosh team tonight. She told me that Andy Bagwell put her in charge of the team and insisted that she play the whole game. Gray Moore was the only other person who played the whole game. She also said that my strategy of having her spread her legs in guarding the little short forward, Ruth Threlkeld worked. Ruth fouled her three times in the first period.

Wednesday, March 6, 1940 After Dr. Sanborn's class I went to the library. Saw Susan in the hall and talked to her for a few minutes. I asked her for a no-break at the S.A.E. dance next Friday evening. We made arrangements for the second. Studied until twelve and then went to Kissam Hall to hear Dr. Green, one of the most popular teachers at Princeton talk to a group of students. He is preparing a report on the Humanities and is traveling around the country holding forums with students. Bill Jordan, Fred Mullen, Walter Parks, Scott George, Martha Hoke, Mickey Carmichael, and others were present. It was almost like a history seminar. We discussed why we are in college, the place of the humanities (History, English, Philosophy, etc.). In closing he said if you could give one sentence of advice to a younger brother on morals, what would it be. I suggested the golden rule and someone else said maintain your self-respect. We ended with a religious note. At the close I told Dean Pomfret that he ought to sign up Green for a return engagement; if not that to bring more people here like him. Green reminded me of the benevolent priest in "The Magnificent Obsession" or "Green Light." I forget which. I noted also that Dr. Green is crippled. We got through at three. At four o'clock I took Jordan down to see "Mice and Men" by John Steinbeck. It was one of the most powerful dramas I have ever seen in the movies. Jordan said it was the best picture he could recall. It was the story of a bright young fellow who took it on himself to look after a great big moron cousin. Lon Cheney Jr. was the moron cousin and he was really a likeable sort of fellow who was always getting into trouble. Finally his friend Lennie had to shoot him. The buildup showed the shooting of an old dog which was a faithful pet of its old keeper. The symbolism in the picture was splendid.

Thursday, March 7, 1940 Continued our radio speaking today. Andromedia Bagwell spoke on religion—her little niece died today after an operation for a brain tumor. Took a picture of the Independents and All Star basketball team today. This was my day to read my term paper and to conduct the open forum in Dr. Robison's class so I did it with much gusto. I read it as if I were reading a speech in which I was enthusiastic. I spliced in an account of the Zipper story to illustrate how gullible people are to believe cock-and-bull stories. I finished at exactly twelve o'clock. After the class was dismissed Elliott Trimble came up to me and said, "They really listened to you, and that is more than you can say for some of the others. I looked around and saw everyone paying the closest attention." I took the very dangerous subject "Propaganda." Ate lunch with Trimble, Bill Jordan, Louise Sykes, Miriam McGaw, Elizabeth Surles, Martha Hanie, Andromedia Bagwell, Madelaine Bidwell, and Henry Clay. Susan did not come to the library until four and we went to the student center for ice cream cones. I know she comes to the library to study but she perhaps would not sit with me so consistently unless she cared a little for me. It started raining this evening, and large snowflakes fell for awhile. A letter from home said Mrs. Spivey had committed suicide; hung herself in a closet. Poor soul. A letter from Anderson tells that he is on his way to the naval training school in Florida where he will learn to fly. I got an invitation to Ann and Mildred Stahlman's open house Sunday evening. Saw Ann this evening and told her I would be on hand. Mrs. Alder, of Hume-Fogg, called tonight and asked me to judge an oratorical contest at two tomorrow evening. Said she called Mrs. Henry Hart and asked the names of some advanced students. My name was given. I forgot my twenty class when I accepted. I'll cut it though. I think I can profit just as much at the contest. Then too I'll enjoy visiting my old Alma Mater again.

Friday, March 8, 1940 After Philosophy class I went to the library and sat at the front table. Susan came in after a few minutes. Nello was with her. Instead of sitting at the vacant chair she sat two seats from me. Poor Nello had to sit at the next table. That was as close as he could get. I continued studying as if I did not see her and I did not nod or say a single word the whole time we were sitting there at the same table. She left at eleven o'clock. At two I went to the oratorical contest at Hume-Fogg. Art Dealy won first place in my division and Peggy McComas came second. Went up to the Ragans for a cup of coffee and then to see, "Our Town," at the community playhouse. After the play I came home and put on my tails for the S.A.E. dance. My head was splitting so I took a couple of aspirin. Got to the dance in plenty of time for the second no-break with Susan. While I was dancing with her she told about going to see "Our Town" the other night. She said, "I had an early date and instead of going home and studying I decided to go to the play."

"I'm glad you told me," I said. I danced the third with Eleanor Reed Clay. Jack is really in love with her. I left the dance immediately after the third because I was so sick I was about to pass out. When I danced with Youmans she said I've got a compliment for you, "Someone said that you would really make something of yourself because you really have what it takes." She never told me who said it. When I got home Bill Simpson was still here. At one I told him he would have to go because I had to go to bed.

Saturday, March 9, 1940 I was up late but felt pretty good this morning. I was surprised. Mrs. Hart would not let me finish reading my "Arm Chair Adventure" script this morning. It was too different. Dr. Robison put me back on the stand this morning and questioned me about some of the statements in my paper. Ate lunch with George Marion O'Donnell, Coles, Jordan, and Miss Howell. We discussed marriage and courtship. Miss Howell said she once had a crush on Dan Robison just after he came back from the war. Said he went with one girl for a long time and then she turned him down. I then went to the library. I sat at the very front and Nello sat two tables back. Susan came in with two other girls and she sat at my right. The other girls went elsewhere. Nello passed several times but never did come up and sit with us. We studied real hard until four-thirty and then went to the Belmont to see "Geronimo." She at first had to call home. As we went to get in her car she said, "Would you like to drive my little car?"

"I'd be delighted," I said, so I drove us to the theatre. We bought a couple of bags of popcorn and enjoyed the comedy tremendously and serial with the kids who made up the audience. We got out at six and it was too dark for her to drive home by herself so she had to call up her mother and get someone to drive down for her. Her family had already started eating and she felt badly about having to make them come at such an inopportune time. I apologized for insisting that she go to the show with me. She said she really shouldn't have gone but that she hated to say "no" because I might not understand. Mrs. Glenn and the chauffeur, Leslie, came after her. She brought me home first. Jordan dropped by and we went to the Tally-ho for refreshments.

Sunday, March 10, 1940 Slept late got up and read the papers and at two went to the library to study. Susan was back in graduate room, as usual. She had on a light blue woolen dress with alligator skin buttons and belt. Her hair was back in windblown fashion and very lustrous. I don't believe I ever saw her when she looked prettier. We studied until five o'clock then I went by the biology building for Jordan. We ate at the new place across from the Vanderbilt hospital and then went to Aunt Nells. I heard Jack Benny on the radio doing a wonderful take off on "Mr. Smith Goes to Washington." Used Uncle's car to go to Ann and Mildred Stahlman's open house. Saw many high school and Vanderbilt people there. Afterwards I went to see Mary Engles for a few minutes. Mr. Jones, of the family with whom she lives, had just finished reading four volumes of "Robert E. Lee" and was starting on "Grant's Memoirs." We had a very lively discussion of the Civil War.

Monday, March 11, 1940 Today is the fifth anniversary of the founding of the Fogg Horn. What a wonderful feeling to know that something you have done, or something you started, lives after you. Never will I forget the skepticism Mr. Kirkpatrick, principal of Hume-Fogg, had for my enthusiasm for starting the paper, and the dramatic stratagem I had to use to get his permission to go ahead. Later, I'm told, the paper became his favorite of all student projects. Saw Susan in back of Calhoun Hall but did not stop and invite her to lunch. Instead I went with Henry Clay. Mary Wallace's picture was in the newspaper this afternoon as a member of the All Star basketball team. Jordan took Virginia Richey to Puryear Mims' art exhibit at the Centennial Club.

Tuesday, March 12, 1940 Studied with Susan from nine until ten and then read my goodwill speech over the public address system in Public Speaking. After lunch with "Buckshot" Gene Flowers, Tom Shea and Henry Clay I called Katie Heitzburg and talked for nearly an hour about Henry Clay. Bought some medicine for Jordan so he can study all night. After reading philosophy for several hours tonight I concluded that a good definition of a philosopher's work is "A contest to see who can state, in the most superlative way, the incomprehensibility of God."

Wednesday, March 13, 1940 My new suit from Petway-Reavis arrived. Called Susan and thought she might be tired and impatient, with exams coming up, but on the contrary, she was pleasant and talkative. She gave me a date on the 29th, which she usually would not have done because it is so far away. She said Mrs. Craig, Mrs. Carter and several other ladies on Franklin Pike are having a historical pagent on that night at Robertson Academy, but she would be in it only a few minutes. Dr. Harris, after copying my paper on Daniel Webster for his files, handed back the original. It's a very good paper. The first few paragraphs were as follows:

THE IMMORTAL DANIEL WEBSTER

Daniel Webster is one of those strange individuals that even a Boswell could not have sufficiently preserved for posterity. You can search the cold records of his times and find very little the man did to merit the exalted position he holds in history. He loses prestige when submitted to the microscopical analysis of the historian.

Yet, perhaps no man who ever lived had a firmer hold upon his fellow man. When he sat on a platform no one else could be seen. When he walked down the streets of London people stepped to the curb and paused, as in reverence, to the man who looked like God. When he rose to speak, every man, woman and child sat motionless and that magnificent voice rolled out like thunder from Mt. Sinai.

John Milton's description of Beelzebub, in "Paradise Lost," comes closer to giving an apt description of the compelling stage presence of a great statesman, such as Webster, as we can find in the English language. Webster, himself, often quoted it:

> —"With grave
> Aspect he rose, and in his rising seemed
> A pillar of state. Deep on his front engraven
> Deliberation sat, and public care;
> And princely counsel in his face yet shone,
> Majestic, though in ruin. Sage he stood,
> With Atlantean shoulders, fit to bear
> The weight of mightiest monarchies; his look
> Drew audience and attention still as night
> Or summer's noontide air, while thus he spoke:"

"The dignity of his solid figure, the rich and varied music of his voice, above all the penetrating splendor of his eyes, gave his spoken words a glory which we cannot recover, effective as his speeches often are in print."

Thursday, March 14, 1940 Took the Public Speaking examination this morning and philosophy this evening. I never, in all my life, wrote such a scatterbrained paper as I did on the philosophy questions. I could not remember a systematic account of each philosopher so I just scribbled ideas at random, hither and yon. I knew most about Spinoza. If I had it to do over I would spend three hours with Bill Simpson, as I did before the exam last quarter. I don't need it for graduation, though, so I am not particularly concerned. I read about a hundred pages of Dr. Owsley's book "States Rights in the Confederacy." The book was published in 1925 and gives an interesting account of how the governors of the various states withdrew and withheld troops from the central command, in order to protect their own states. Lee was never able to mass the entire strength of the southern forces at any one time or place.

This was the primary cause of the South losing the war; not the blockade, which was only partially effective; not the North's superior manufacturing facilities, because the South was able to get manufactured goods from England and elsewhere, but when Lee's men were barefooted, during the later stages of the war, the Governor of South Carolina had enough shoes in his warehouses to equip the entire army. The South was a victim of it's own philosophy of "States Rights."

Friday, March 15, 1940 Took the Sectional Controversy exam. and did rather well on everything but the question on the Penninsular Campaign. After the exam. I strolled about the campus for a few minutes, talking with Dr. Mims and others that I happened to pass. I went to the library and found Billy Eason talking with Susan. Every now and then I would hear Susan tell Billy to be quiet and leave her alone so she could read the reserved book which she had out of the stacks. An hour passed and he was still jabbering. He stayed until it got dark and when Susan got up to go he followed her. I once had an idea for a poem called: "My Rival." It would go something like this: "His grotesqueness I did not see, 'til he became a rival to me."

Saturday, March 16, 1940 Took the Robison examination and think I did pretty well on it. Saw Susan a few minutes after twelve and we went to town to see Charles Laughton and Vivian Leigh in "The Streets of London." The acting of Charles Laughton is always superb. I enjoy so much the expressions on his face and the beautiful way he reads lines. I think he is my favorite actor of all time. Vivian Leigh is beautiful but a hellcat at times, just like the Scarlett O'Hara part in "Gone with the Wind." We stopped by Candyland for refreshments before going back to her car on campus. Later in the evening I drove around town with Fleming and Jordan. We went to the Tally-ho and the Sugar Bowl, where we saw Doug Handly, George Appelby and Ray Beasley. Rip Blackmer was with Josephine, the very beautiful girl who used to work in the Vanderbilt bookstore. I understand she has three or four children.

Sunday, March 17, 1940 Aunt Nell called this morning and told me about seeing in the paper that Ann Pope, one of my very dearest friends, shot herself last night. I then read about it in the papers. She left notes saying that all her life she had attempted to live up to certain ideals but that now she felt she was not living up to them. She left instructions to give her clothes to a poor girl. She also wanted the little girls that she had been taking to Sunday School looked after. She had been studying so hard so that she could be initiated into the sorority and it looked as if she were not going to make it this time. She was not a good student, but she had the most sympathetic and understanding nature I have ever encountered. I remarked to Joe Davis last week that she came nearer to having all of the feminine qualities that I admire in women than any girl I know; my own girl, Susan, excepted, of course. She had the knack for making everybody's problem her own and she was the type of person you could go to and be sure of getting the soothing and encouraging words which are so helpful and strengthening in times of despondency. I never had a date with her, but we talked many times and I visited the Pope home. I never shall forget how cute she and her mother were when they were once hostesses for the Theta breakfast. They served country sausage and both of them were all for the good old small town game called "spin the bottle." Some of the more citified girls, with a show of sophistication, turned up their noses. I was amused. Once or twice I had asked Ann for dates, but always she had previous engagements or previously scheduled activity. Every time she saw Susan and me together, in the library, or dancing a no-break, she would give me a knowing smile and later tell me what a nice couple she thought we were. I had told her on numerous occasions that I thought she and Joe Davis were two of the nicest people I know and that I thought they too are an ideal couple. I really thought so. Tonight, when I went to see her for the last time, I saw Joe, who had been there all day. He accompanied me to the upstairs, but would not go inside. He waited outside the room. There she lay, as pretty and as sweet as ever, almost as if she were asleep. I thought of the line: "One more unfortunate, weary of breath, rashly importunate, gone to her death." When I came out I asked Joe when he last saw or talked to her. "I called Thursday," he said, and tears began to come to his eyes, "And fussed at her for not taking her examination." I told him that he must not feel that way. None of us know what is going on in another person's mind. I will miss her sorely; as much as anybody at Vanderbilt, and yet I only saw and talked with her every now and then. But always, on these occasions, her interest was in my problems rather than her own. It was the same with others who knew her. When people die it is natural to think only of the good points in his or her life, but I did not have to wait for Ann to die to realize her sterling characteristics. I have spoken many times, to many different people, how fine a person I thought she was. I know Susan is upset over her death. Susan was the pledge trainer and Ann's failure to qualify for the Theta initiation was, without a doubt, an important factor in the catastrophe. That was more than likely the "ideal" that the note referred to. The ideal seems to have been what was expected of her as a Theta pledge. The sorority, of course, is not to blame. Their expectations were reasonable. The fault is in the system itself and in the individual. The importance of fraternity and sorority relationships is unduly exalted. New students are given a distorted view of their value. It is not until one gets through this period that he realizes how unimportant it all is. Nothing, even school itself, is important if it impairs one's health. Self-preservation is still the first law. We are treading on dangerous ground when we allow anything to become more important in our minds. A quotation on Miss Adelaide Lyon's bulletin board at Hume-Fogg read as follows: "Learn to put first things first." She was such a delightful lady that I have always been amazed some man did not recognize her charm. Jordan got sick, came by my room, and I took him home and put him to bed. His mother called and was worried to death. She made me promise to call the doctor and to awaken Mrs. Mayfield. Had a pleasant talk with Dr. Tom Zerfoss when he came. I slept in Bill Anderton's room.

Monday, March 18, 1940 Got up early and intended to go to the funeral but it was raining. Mrs. Mayfield insisted that I eat breakfast before leaving. Mrs. Mayfield is not a pretty woman, but what a wonderful personality she has. Women of her nature are really appreciated during times of illness. They revel in administering to the sick and helpless. This is their glory. They are a fine institution. At the Banner office I showed Mr. Duncan and Mr. Moss the letter I had from Mr. James E. West, National Executive of the Boy Scouts, disclaiming any relationship with the American Youth Congress. Talked to Dean Pomfret about the need for a closer personal contact between students and faculty and a decentralization of fraternity and sorority influences on the campus. He quoted Dean Sarratt as saying that $15,000.00 is sent by fraternities and sororities each year to their national headquarters. He liked my idea of a trophy case in College Hall or the Student Center for the Independents. He also said he agreed with the idea of sending a letter to freshmen explaining that it is not necessary to join a social organization at Vanderbilt. Pomfret said: "Austin, I find that our ideas have been more in agreement lately than awhile back. Either you are growing more mature or my ideas are changing. There is a lot of merit in the things you have been saying lately." I answered that it is probably due to the fact that I am in a little better position this year to stand away from the battle lines and to look down on them with a better perspective. At lunch in Kissam I ate with Miriam McGaw, Louise Sykes, Dr. and Mrs. Harris and their daughter, Mrs. Schmidt. After they left Dr. D. P. Fleming, one of the best informed men in the nation on foreign affairs, came in and sat with me. He said that because of the popularity of the International Relations Club, which he sponsors, some members apply for their younger brothers and sisters. Later in the library I discussed, with Jean Ewing and Shirley Caldwell, the tragic death of Ann Pope and what can be done to prevent such tragedies in the future.

Tuesday, March 19, 1940 I rode with Willie Cornelius and his mother to Bill Jordan's room. Willie fussed at his mother for the way she drove. Jordan read aloud the first chapter of Ecclesiastes. We both marveled at the lyrical beauty of the passage: "Vanity vanity, all is vanity." These words are repeated just at the right time, like a Beethoven symphony. Seeing Dot King, from Tullahoma, recently reminded me of the days just before I entered Vanderbilt. To paraphrase Shakespeare, "This is the stuff that memories are made of." Three years ago, just before entering college, I took a drive with a boy from Decatur, Alabama, to Sweetwater, Tennessee, where he was enrolled in Tennessee Military Institute. The song "I'm in the Mood for Love" had just come out and we heard it played several times as we drove through the beautiful countryside northeast of Chattanooga. The leaves were beginning to turn and the landscape was a panorama of bright colors. I never hear that song that I don't think of that most exciting period of life, when I was about to go away to college. I believe it was Wordsworth who wrote: "There was a time, when meadows, groves and streams, the earth and every common sight, to me did seem appareled in celestial light, the glory and the freshness of a dream."

Wednesday, March 20, 1940 I packed my bags and caught the train at one-thirty for Easter vacation in Stevenson. The ride was long and tedious and the weight of recent events in my love life were hanging heavily over me. I was feeling low when I arrived at my planned overnight stopover with Louise Leming's family in Decherd. Louise was waiting for me when I got off the train at four o'clock. We drove out to her home, which is a beautiful castle-like residence in a small country town. Her mother prepared a splendid supper of steak, gravy, hot rolls, peas, corn and the best home-canned peaches I have ever tasted for dessert. I slept in a big feather bed.

Thursday, March 21, 1940 Boy, oh boy, did I get a good night's sleep! The cackling of the guineas added to the charm of the country atmosphere. I awoke at eight quite rested and refreshed. A hot steaming breakfast awaited me and we drove over to Winchester to visit her grandmother. Their names are Taylors and the grandfather, on the mother's side was minister of one of the local churches. I met Ray Buchanan, a bank clerk, Katherine Summers, who works in a grocery store, Inez Meadors, a beauty parlor operator, Willene Finney, whose brother is a dental technician with B. F. Moore in Nashville and Roscoe Sisk, who is cashier at the cafe. Went by and spoke to Dr. Anderton, the dentist, who is the father of Bill Anderton, who lives with Dr. Mayfield at Vanderbilt. I attempted to catch the Dixie Flyer but it does not stop at Stevenson. As I started to enter the train I saw Margaret Noland and Helen McMurray get off. They had come to spend Easter with Bill Anderton. Helen seemed very surprised to see me. I had to wait for a four o'clock train so Louise and I went first to her home and then on to Winchester. At the cafe we danced awhile and we heard Bing Crosby sing "Pack Your Troubles in Dreams (and Dream Your Troubles Away.)" It make me feel better. I played it two or three times—I remember a line or two. "When skies are cloudy and gray—they are only gray for a day—so pack your troubles in dreams and dream your troubles away—remember you were king for a day—castles may crumble and all fade away—life is funny that way" and so forth. Funny how music can lift you up when you are blue. Got in the car and drove to the Decherd graveyard and spent an hour just walking around in the crisp spring atmosphere looking at the graves. At four o'clock I caught the train and saw William Simpson, Jim Frank, and Maizie Rudder going home. Arrived in Stevenson at five o'clock. Ate the best steak for supper I have ever eaten. After talking to the family for awhile and to coach Hodges who visited us, I went down to Jack Bible's drugstore to pick up the gossip. Talked to Mr. Percy Armstrong, Mr. Barrie, Mr. Robert Rudder and to Mr. George Fellows. Most of the people talked very intelligently about the war situation and about politics. Mr. Percy told a good one on Judge Jim Benson. He said Mr. Benson stopped him on the street the other day and solicited his vote. "Now look here, Jim" Mr. Percy said, "You told me two years ago that you only wanted this office for one term and then you would be willing to give it up."

"Yes," said Mr. Benson, "I did tell you that and at that time I was perfectly honest in making the statement. But you know I got in there and got a taste of it and I liked it."

Percy laughed and said, "You can't beat a man like that. He's at least honest about it." Finally the conversation got around to National politics. I was surprised at so many of them favoring Roosevelt for a third term. I voiced the opinion that with out a doubt Roosevelt is the ablest man in the country and has done lots of good but that I don't want to see any man break the third term precedent. "It is our last citadel of democracy." I am worried over the state of our people who will, for expediency, give up so valuable a precedent.

Friday, March 22, 1940 I went to Dad's office to have my teeth cleaned and one tooth filled. I still hate that drilling, although Dad is replacing a lot of it by scraping the cavaties with instruments. Rebecca came in this evening very enthusiastic about the perfect conduct of her little children at the Easter egg hunt which she and Miss Bessie Sanders had put on for them. Rebecca is taking on weight and is really enjoying her work. Tonight I went to see Freda. Patti was at home and W. J. Talley had brought four boys from Tulane with him. We listened to the radio, danced and played rummy with two boys who had come from Scottsboro. After I got home Henry D. drove in with Dewey Jones from the University of Tennessee. We talked for awhile and then went to bed.

Saturday, March 23, 1940   After breakfast I went to town to type a letter for Henry D. to Pop Jamison accepting the offer of a job this summer. Robert Graham, of the bank, let me use his typewriter. Mr. Gus McMahon came in and said: "I have told Doc many times that when you boys were youngsters you got into more mischief than any other boys in town but that you have all grown up to make fine young men." I also talked with Judge Bogart and Clyde Woodall, of the bank. Read an interesting article in the Saturday Evening Post about James R. Cromwell, husband of Doris Duke, the richest woman in the world. He is Ambassador to Canada and is in hot water because of an anti-Nazi speech he made. Ronald Trice dated Mary Wallace tonight. J. Selly McGriff was here last evening.

Sunday, March 24, 1940   Flagged the Dixie Flyer at three thirty and Frances Jordan, a Reed girl from Scottsboro and I boarded it for Nashville. Elizabeth Surles was in a different car and Bill Anderton and Helen McMurray got on at Winchester. We read poems and discussed our philosophies of life. Aunt Nell told me this evening that my name was in the paper in connection with the historical play at Robertson Academy next Friday. Katie Heitzburg's picture was in the paper with the announcement of her engagement to Joe Hutchinson. I have never seen a prettier picture, but then there are not many prettier girls than Katie. My heart bleeds for Henry Clay. He loved her so.

SPRING
1940

Monday, March 25, 1940 I rode to school this morning with Dr. Sanborn. He lectured on Immanuel Kant, one of the great minds of all time. In discussing him, Sanborn cites Kant as saying: Perceiving is a time and space relationship. Space and time are not concepts but intuitions. The image of unit is one moment of time. The unit is called "schema." Image of "affirmation" is filled time. Image of "negation" is empty time. The schema of substance is "duration." "Cause and effect" are two ways of looking at the same "time." Whew! Sanborn said Kant believed theology to be "heuristic" fiction; false, but useful at times. Of art Sanborn said that art is concerned with form, not content. Beauty is a symbol of absolute morality. You never find perfect beauty in art, but it is in the artist's mind. Art is not knowledge; it is a field of its own. Music is the most perfectly formed art. It is mathematical.

As I was walking towards Calhoun Hall Susan and Andromedia Bagwell were directly behind. I walked a good distance without turning around. Susan was talking pretty loudly so I would hear her. I knew she was there all the time and finally I turned around and spoke and walked the rest of the way with her. I did not say good-bye to her as I usually do. We just finished our conversation and she went to her class and I went to mine. Ate lunch with Henry Clay, who had just returned from a stay in Florida and was tan and healthy looking. He is holding up well under the ordeal of losing Katie; outwardly, that is. We discussed, with compassion, Ann Pope's death. Saw Susan but did not even stop to talk to her. In the library Jim Reed said to me: "I wonder what Ben Austin's explanation would be if I were to commit suicide?" I went along with the gag and said that I would know that he had a big insurance policy to do such a thing. Received a wire from Jordan: "Will be there Tuesday night—be at home. Love and kisses—Bill." Talked to Virginia Richey on the phone and she said she would like to hear the Philharmonic Orchestra in Chattanooga. She laughed when she said it. As much as to say: "I don't give a darn about the company." Women are like that, sometimes, I guess.

Tuesday, March 26, 1940 Today in Public Speaking Mrs. Hart assigned ten minute speeches and Dr. Harris told us we would devote the term to reading before the class. He read us the story of "Molly Bird's Christmas Dinner," and he gave us a poem to commit to memory. After finishing his reading he told us he used to take his daughter and another little girl on his knee and tell them the same story night after night. They would make him repeat the same story every time and if he used the wrong word they would correct him. He said that until you experience the thrill of taking your own child on your knee you have not completely lived. He is a fine old gentleman. I had rather my wife had been brought up by him than anyone I know, outside my own family. W. T. Adams, Homer Howell and Walter King came into our class under Professor Robison today. "Chippy" Chapman is going to buy a half interest in my book. Rode to town with Mrs. Hart on the street car today and she told me about her married son and daughter. I told her that if a person intends to go to school for a long period of time, unrequited love is a blessing in disguise.

"I never heard anyone express such an optimistic philosophy," she said, "But I guess you are right." I told her about my scrapbook and diary and she said, "I guess that is why you write so well. There is nothing like daily practice for acquiring skill." After leaving her I decided to speak on "My Philosophy of Life" for my opening address next Thursday. I thought about it all evening and jotted down notes every time I stopped in my itinerary about town. As I was walking towards the Doctor's Building I noticed Susan directly in front of me. I walked close by as if I did not see her. I was so near it scared her. She turned toward me, all of a sudden, and her eyes were full of fear. She laughed when she saw who it was. She was on her way to the dentist. In talking to her about the elections in her sorority, in which she won an office, I told her that I did not know the elections had been held. I thought she was predicting. She tried to appear peeved, "Why Ben Austin, I don't know you," she said. I went on down the street laughing. A wire from Jordan asked me to get his car and meet him at the station at eight. I did and we reported to each other about our respective trips.

He says he has sown the seeds for breaking the grip that his mother has on him. He wants me to go to his home and help him make the fight. I told him that I was willing to advise but that I knew better than to get mixed up in a family affair that is none of my business. He says he is determined to develop his body in proportion to his mind. It is a matter of pride with him. Says he is not willing to perpetuate deceit. He realizes that his body is not as strong as it looks. With me, I told him it is just the reverse. My opponents often say: "But you don't look strong." Jim Buford handed me a check for $50.00 that he has been carrying for three weeks. He said I was the first person who ever worked for him who did not ask about money. Dean Sarratt was eating with him and heard the conversation. He said: "I have seen Austin work with the freshmen wrestlers and I knew he was having too much fun to think about the money."

Wednesday, March 27, 1940   In describing the South at the end of the Civil War, Dr. Owsley said that the Negroes were freed but there was no government to enforce law and order. By January 1866 the Negroes began to realize that the U.S. government was not going to support them the rest of their lives. The system of peonage; coercion to make the Negroes stay where they got their groceries, started at this time. W. L. Fleming's "Sequel to Appomattox" is one of the best treatments of this period. Thaddeus Stevens, the Radical Republican leader of the Senate, was one of the smartest men of his time. Owsley said: "I don't doubt that he was as smart as Hitler." He wanted to treat the South as a "conquered province." In explaining the childlikeness of many of the Negroes he said humorously: "Many of them came to the polls with sacks to get their franchise." Susan came to the library and studied with me about five minutes and got up and left. She seems undecided these days what she wants to do. Went to the gym and wrestled Roy Elam.

Thursday, March 28, 1940   I was the first speaker of the new term and I talked about my "Philosophy of Life." I pointed out the limitations of friendship, of love of a girl, religion and the usual things that people turn to in times of distress. Music, books and hobbies are good, but the thing I turn to is poetry; not just poetry at random, but specialized poetry to meet specific needs. Often it is committed to memory and brought out in times of stress, exactly as one would call up Red Cross Life Saving knowledge when it is needed, or fire drill training. "Stone walls do not a prison make," for instance or "If you can wait, and not be tired of waiting." Many members of the class liked the quote: "When you get to the end of your rope, tie a knot and hang on." Paid $90.00 tuition. At nine I heard Thomas E. Dewey speak on the radio from Chicago. He does not have the charm, perhaps, to ever be President, but the courage he exhibited in fighting the racketeers in New York, has never been surpassed.

Friday, March 29, 1940 Dr. Willis A. Sutton, Superintendant of the Atlanta Schools, was conducting some seminars at Peabody Demonstration School, so Bill Jordan and I went over to discuss with him the possibility of speaking at Vanderbilt on May 1st. I have known Dr. Sutton for many years, because of his chapel talks at Dixie Camps, and I know him to be one of the most sought after speakers in the country. Gus Dyer, the Economics Professor at Vanderbilt, is getting old now, but he has been rated one of the ten best speakers in the country. What a natural if we could get these two nationally known speakers to debate. What better subject than to have a leader of secondary schools, and a college professor, debate: "Resolved That Education Is a Failure?" Jordan and I later went to the Knickerbocker Theatre to see Edward G. Robinson in "The Magic Bullet." It was the story of Dr. Ehrlick's "606" experiments in the search for a cure of syphillis. We had to rush in order for me to get to Susan's for the play at Robertson Academy. I represented Captain Anderson, in a tableau with Susan, Sue Craig and Walton Stamps.

Saturday, March 30, 1940 In Public Speaking today Dr. Harris said that Edmund's work has been excellent, but "Ben turned in the best paper I have received this year." "Flip" Timberlake and Mary Fisher came from Decatur, Alabama, and Ernestine Mann came from Stevenson. We drove out to see Catherine Timberlake, who lives in with the Harry Burk family, owners of Chayburks Fur Store, and sits with their daughter occasionally. Had to leave them temporarily in order to take Susan to the gym dance. She and I usually have the fourth no-break, but tonight when I went to dance it with her, she had given it to Eason. She said: "But this is a new term." I did not bother about dancing with her again.

Sunday, March 31, 1940 Jordan came by and we took my house guests to the Hermitage, home of Andrew Jackson. It is one of the most beautiful and most peaceful of all the homes of past presidents. A magnificent line of cedars leads to the front of the house, where one enters through large colonial columns. The furnishings are pretty much as they were when Jackson built the house for his wife Rachael. He played the role of a ruffian in challenging a duel to anyone who made slighting remarks about his pipe smoking wife, but the Hermitage has the charm and elegance of a French provincial home during the reign of Louis XIV. Jackson was rough hewn but had a nobility of spirit.

Monday, April 1, 1940 I went to town with Jordan and got the sign from Loews. It was really a good sign. Even though it is conspicuous I took it to class with me and set it up front. Everyone laughed when they saw it. I guess I shouldn't have done it. Lunched with Jim Reed,

Elizabeth Surles, Clay and Louise Sykes. Going in to the cafeteria Henry and I saw Susan in front of us. He yelled at her and she waited for us. As we were walking towards Kissam he told her to hold up her shoulders. She went to the Dean's council. I studied in the library until four and then went to town with Jordan to see "Rebecca." The plot of this picture was one of the most carefully contrived that I have ever seen. "The House Manderley" is one I shall never forget. Went up to the Andrew Jackson for dinner. It so happened that Jim Farley, Postmaster General and presidential candidate was there speaking. We sat around the lobby for a few minutes and saw him come out of the meeting. He walked in an impatient trot just like Pop J. does. He reminded me very much of Pop J. His eyes were small and squinty and his face was flushed. As he got into the awaiting car he waved good-bye several times and called to several people by their first names. He is noted for that trick. After eating dinner Jordan and I discussed the ways and means by which people climb to greatness in political fields. Jordan said, "Austin, it is inevitable that you and I eventually take part in something where we work with people. With me it will probably be in connection with the impending fight over socialized medicine. I predict that it will be one of the foremost issues before the country in a very few years." We agreed that someday we would perhaps work side by side in some field. It may be research. I told him that if we were both lawyers fighting a case I had rather have him on my side than any man I know. He retaliated by saying that in a fight he had rather have me on his side than against him. We agreed that the way for a man to get anywhere in politics, or in any other activity, for that matter, is to have someone you trust and can confide in, pulling for you. In school elections, for example, you can't nominate yourself, but what if you have a pact with a buddy? I never actually did this, but it makes sense. Neither one of us mentioned it, or even thought about it until we had completed our schooling, but Harris Abrahams followed along in my footsteps, not only in high school, but college, holding the same offices. Farley was here for Mule Day in Columbia, Tennessee.

Tuesday, April 2, 1940 I read an article on how Hitler used propaganda to rise to power. The people grew tired of numerous elections and failures of democracy and were ready for a man to assume the responsibilities of government and do their thinking for them. After a long and bitter period of hoplessness Hitler offered hope. He sold the German people a bill of goods; that they could get something for nothing. If they had colonies like the Dutch they wouldn't have to work so hard. He surrounded himself with the best propaganda machine the world has ever seen. At first they took pictures of crowds of people and superimposed Hitler's picture speaking. This gave the impression of early and wide acceptance. When Hitler took chances, such as sending troops into the Rhineland, and did not meet resistance from the rest of the world, then the crowds became real. He was a winner. Even though he is our enemy and millions of Americans may have to risk their lives fighting him, his showmanship entrances us, even as it does his own people. Heard Jim Farley speak on the radio before a college group in Missouri. His voice sounds somewhat like that of John L. Hill, who is famous for his speeches before the men's class at First Baptist Church in Nashville. Farley, a planner behind F.D.R.'s campaigns, is somewhat of a showman himself, but not in the same league with Hitler's crew. As great a public speaker as Roosevelt is, Hitler may be even better. Churchill may be better than both of them; mainly because he writes better speeches than either, and is not dependent on style and delivery alone. But what an experience, living at a time when three of the great orators of all time are on center stage of the world simultaneously.

Wednesday, April 3, 1940 Jordan and Martin Lichterman helped prepare for the Turtle Trudge today. We put up ropes and marked off the track. Whit La Fon also helped. Bobby Cook got together a small band and played while the crowd was assembling. Henry Clay and Martin Lichterman served as bookies and received the registrations. Twenty-five turtles were entered. John Shumaker and Frank Gunter came out from the Banner. The girls had to go to Chapel but they looked out the windows of Alumni Hall. There were several hundred people crowding around the track sides. Capt. Taylor was on hand to keep order. Cook, called the turtles to their post and at my signal Marty lifted the lamp shade, covering the turtles and they were off. The crowd surged in. "Dog" Young picked the winner and Hartwell Weaver picked no "2" and "3." The Pi Phi turtle "Ferdinand" won and the Beta's "Scrappy" came second. On the Lady of the Bracelet story I guessed wrong. I had picked Sara Goodpasture and she was the first to be eliminated. Virginia Blair won over Lucille Johnson by a vote of 107 to 101. We did not have a picture of her nor did we have time to make one. I had to phone in the story and then take a picture for the sports edition. It was a very good picture. Bought a cute little cup for the Pi Phis from Loew-Campbell. I am having it engraved. Ate lunch with Rousseau Duncan, Mr. Hilliard Wood, John Shumaker at the Canary Inn. They have a very cute waitress there by the name of Virginia who is a big flirt. She is very attractive, though. Came home and took a nap. Jordan and Fred Wolfe, a PH.D. from Harvard came by and talked to me for a while. We drove to town for dinner.

Thursday, April, 4, 1940 We did not have to go to Public Speaking class today so I did not go to school at all. Instead I went over to Wallace School and taught a class for Partee Fleming. I taught a freshman

English Class. "Ducky" Henry, O'Neill Clayton, Bryan and several other boys whom I already knew, were in the class. They were studying Scott's, "Lady of the Lake." I had forgotten all I ever knew about the poem but I gave them a lecture on the value of poetry in general then let them read for themselves. I enjoyed my time with them. Jordan came at the end of the hour. I studied in the library and then rode to Hillsboro with Jordan. At the drugstore we again ran into Rabbi Marx and I talked to him a few minutes about camp for his son. Tonight Mary Engles and I went to see "Berkeley Square" at the Community Playhouse and then came home and listened to the radio for awhile. She was prettier and sweeter than usual tonight. Mary Wallace went to Knoxville today with the Sociology Department at Vanderbilt.

Friday, April 5, 1940 A new Lady Dean was announced today—Dr. Blanche Henry Clark, formerly of Ward-Belmont. Jordan and I went to town after lunch and shipped the turtle to Detroit, heard Gibby Blake's birthday recording to his girl, heard Orson Welles interpretation of "Julius Caesar," and then came on home. At twelve thirty today I saw Susan and asked her about the dinner invitation at the Theta House. Susan said no other boys were going to be there and that it would be best at another time. I said O.K. Her attitude made Henry Clay mad. He said, "I have tried to be nice to Susan and to like her but of late I have come to the conclusion that she is a phony. She's not pretty. I don't see what you go with her for." I told him I thought she is very pretty, sweet and nice, but at times I, too, am a little skeptical of her. At nine John Shumaker came by to take me to the Tri Delta dance. It had been going on an hour when I arrived. I had the second no-break with Susan and did not dance with her until that time. The orchestra played a very pretty medley including the waltz—"Beautiful Ohio," "I Love You Truly," and "Let Me Call You Sweetheart." I danced with her two or three times after that but not often. She told me that she had not really started studying yet and that she was going to have to start coming to the library. Nello Andrews was complaining to me because of the number of times that Billy Eason was breaking on him. He told me I wasn't doing my part in carrying on the good work. Miriam was beautiful tonight. She is leaving for Atlantic City and New York Monday. I had the third no-break with Elizabeth Surles and Eason danced Susan near the orchestra where Susan could see us, or where we could see them, I don't know which. Anyway Susan walked back to the other end as soon as the no-break was over. Went out for intermission with Billy Wade and rode home with Buddy Stone. This evening I went again to Wallace School to help Jordan teach the senior History class. He was asking them questions and they were pretty noisy. I approached them quite differently and told them an interesting account of why the

South lost the war. They were as quiet as lambs and one or two of them came up after class and told me how much they enjoyed the story. After it was all over Jordan said, "Austin, you really know how to handle kids. I was using the wrong technique." The truth of the matter is that he has not had as much experience in dealing with kids as I have. Kids of all ages love stories. I really felt good over this minor success. I can understand how teaching inflates the ego.

Saturday, April 6, 1940 After Robison's class I met Jordan and, after a chat with Dr. Morrell of the math department, he and I drove to the airport to meet C. P. Lee, the young author and Rhodes Scholar who is going to spend the weekend with him. The plane was an hour late so we went over to look at the new airplane factory. They are putting in the work benches now. Tom Cummings Jr. was there trying to get a job. I think he is going to work there instead of going to law school. I think he will be making a mistake not to go ahead and finish his schooling. We took C. P. down to the Hermitage grill room for a sandwich. He told us about his various experiences in England and Mexico. At six o'clock we picked up Dr. Frank Owsley and George Marion O'Donnell and went to Mrs. Brown's for dinner. I saw Henry Colton at one table and Dr. Mims and his party at another. The meal was fine. The peas were dripping with butter, beans were cooked in meat and splendidly seasoned; corn bread, biscuit cakes and chicken were delicious. It was really an old-fashioned cooked meal and I surely did enjoy it. Owsley told me about the Austin clan down in Wetumpka, Alabama. He said that they are honest but that they are always getting into shooting scrapes. Said that a couple of years ago he was in Washington and saw Will Austin, head of the Census Department and thought he was the Will he knew at home. We discussed at length the new poem-play about Huey Long. At nine they brought me by Uncle Walt's. Uncle had left the car down at 1909 20th. I was so late getting by for Susan that I would not take time out to put on a costume. She had a very cute costume with a big bow in her hair. My head was splitting and she said hers was too when we went to the dance. The noise was tremendous and it was hot and the dust pretty bad. I began to feel better, though, later on in the evening. I never saw Virginia Youmans so pretty. She's got a beautiful figure too. I told her so. I took Susan home immediately after the dance. The most interesting part of the dance was that the crowd made our bodies collide on numerous occasions. Susan tries to be so darned modest. I met Bill Jordan, C. P., and Carpenter at the Tally-ho at twelve. We talked for awhile and then went to the Mayfield's and spent the night.

Sunday, April 7, 1940 C. P. Lee, Bill Jordan and I ate a leisurely breakfast and drove to Franklin, Tennessee, to visit the site of the famous

Battle of Franklin of the Civil War. The most famous spot is the Colonial mansion in which five Confederate Generals lay side by side with mortal wounds. Tennessee was a border state and there was much sentiment for preserving the Union. Uncle Walt Anderson's father-in-law was Judge Edward H. East, wartime Governor Andrew Johnson's Secretary of State. Later Judge East, who was General Counsel of the L. and N. railroad, helped select the site, in a cornfield, for Vanderbuilt University.

Monday, April 8, 1940   Owsley was good today. He told about the problems that faced Andrew Johnson when he became President after Lincoln was killed. Johnson was drunk, they say, when he was inaugurated President. He was not a drunkard, but he was drunk on two unfortunate occasions. The race riots in Memphis and New Orleans were the immediate causes of Johnson's impeachment. It failed by one vote. If Johnson had been removed from office, Ben Wade, a roughneck would have been elevated from the vice-presidency. Wade was a suicide dueller. He duelled with shot guns at three paces and with Bowie knives with legs tied together. The only thing that saved Johnson was the fact that most congressmen did not want Wade to serve as President.

Tuesday, April 9, 1940   Walter Parks and I were standing talking today and a girl came up and said I have a compliment for both of you. The Lady Dean was presenting a plan to the girls and said, "Talk this over with the campus leaders such as Walter Parks and Ben Austin." We thanked her. We verified our date with Gus Dyer for the big debate on May 1st. Dyer is one of the great ones of our time. He says he accepts a lot of high school speaking engagements because it is good for Vanderbilt to keep in touch with them. Henry Clay is worried about his mental attitude. Says he is turning into a dreamer, and a wisher, instead of a realist. I reminded him that his outlook was different when he and Katie were clicking. I heard him say once that a man could do anything, with a girl like that behind him. Took a picture of the sorority presidents at four o'clock. Susan looked pretty, but she is always shy and self-conscious. I saw Dave Barringer, who works at the drugstore, and he brought me home. He knows Oscar Wright, Jack Perry at Vanderbilt. He graduated from Central in 1936 and did not go to college. He showed just a slight touch of an inferiority complex when we discussed college. That is one of the main reasons I was determined to go to college. I wanted to burn all bridges behind me; to never be able to excuse myself for inferior performance with the excuse that I never went to college. A lot of college superiority is bunk, but you never know that until you actually experience it.

Wednesday, April 10, 1940   I recited the first stanza of Edward Everett's famous address, "The Glories of the Morning," which starts out: "I had occasion, a few weeks since, to take an early train from Providence

to Boston, and for that purpose rose at four o'clock in the morning
. . ." I did it about as well as anybody else, but Dr. Harris said he
never heard so many excused from one class on a single assignment.
Jordan and I went to see Spencer Tracy and Hedy Lamar in "I Take
This Woman." There was one good line in the movie: "Time wounds
all heels." After the Owsley class tonight I had a date with Jane Davis.
We danced awhile at the Rustic Tavern and then went sparking on the
Hettie Ray road.

Thursday, April 11, 1940 Today's newspapers report an intensifica-
tion of the European war. The Nazis have marched into Denmark and
have already taken Oslo. What a fateful time in world history! My generation was born at the end of World War I and we were brought up in
the depression years of the early thirties. Roosevelt is about the only
President we have known, since we have been old enough to know of
things in the outside world. He won the hearts of our parents by his
masterful voicing of such phrases as "The only thing we have to fear
is fear itself," and he now tells us he hates war and that we will not
be called on to fight in a foreign war, but those of us who are of military
age know better. President Woodrow Wilson told our fathers the same
thing and maybe . . . just maybe, if William Jennings Byran, a greater
peace fanatic than Wilson, would have kept us out, had he been nominated and elected President. Who knows? Maybe, if we had stayed out
of that one, a local European war would not have developed into a
great world war . . . and a continuation of that war would not be facing
us today. The thought of millions of young bodies being torn by shrapnel
and high explosives is too horrible to contemplate, and yet we are part
of our great country. We have accepted the best that it has to offer
. . . and it has been good . . . and now we may be called on to show
that we have been worthy of the best. We have not achieved this measure
of freedom without someone paying a price and I am under no illusions
about the price for preserving it. I don't want to die young. Nobody
does. I have merely tasted, but not savoured enough of life. I shall
not personally challenge fate, but will go when called. I shall do what
is expected of me.

Friday, April 12, 1940 At eleven o'clock I passed Susan as she was
entering the Student Center, but I did not stop to talk to her. I merely
spoke. While I was in the library in the afternoon Susan came in. She
made a move as if she were going to sit across the table from me.
Instead of sitting, she noticed a girl friend at the next table and spent
a few minutes talking with her. When she finished her conversation
she came around the table and bashfully made a move in the direction
of the chair two down from me. At this point I spoke and made it
easy for her to sit next to me. This is the first time in two weeks that

we has been to the library sitting together. I said: "You are going to flunk out if you don't start studying." She smiled and said, "That's true." I went to the Calumet Club meeting and laid before the membership the plan for bringing Dr. Sutton to the campus to speak with Dr. Dyer. They accepted enthusiastically. Willie Cornelius was beside himself. My book review on Atticus Green Haygood, Bishop of the Methodist Church and founder of Emory University, came out in the Banner this afternoon. Dr. Sutton had looked it over when he was in town and offered corrections. It was through Sutton's speeches at camp that I first heard about Haygood.

Saturday, April 13, 1940 Dawson Frierson made a "Cracker Jack" of a speech yesterday. It was a religious speech, much on the order of a sermon. I have made a few religious references in my speeches, but have never gone this far. It took courage to give it, but it went over well. I went to see the Davis family and signed Louis for a return to camp. The family wants him to go in for boxing, wrestling, horseback riding and the manly sports. I told them I would get my brother Henry D. to take him under his wing. After leaving the Davis' last night I went by the Hermitage Hotel for the last part of the dance. Susan seemed glad to see me. Will Dunn Smith was her date. I had told her in the library that I probably would not be there. The Hustler, campus newspaper came out Friday with a nice front page story and pictures of Dr. Sutton and Dr. Dyer. They gave Richard Donaldson a "by-line" for the story I wrote. Ate lunch today with Clay and he was telling me how it used to be in the good old days when he and Katie were so much in love. Finally I said to him: "Henry, you took her too fast. You worked yourself out of a job." He laughed and agreed that I might be right. In a discussion with Susan in the library I suggested that the chief difference between us is that she is a conformist and that I am a nonconformist. She said: "I don't think you are a nonconformist," but she did not explain what she meant. I called Virginia Richey tonight and asked if the Ward-Belmont library had a particular book. She said they did have it but when I got there I found that they didn't. We borrowed Uncle Walt's car and went on a date anyway. She was tired and fatigued in mind and body and needed relaxation. We drank Cokes at Candyland and drove up on Flagpole Hill to watch a crescent moon set. We were sitting and talking when a car with bright headlights came down the hill. Instead of just sitting, as we should have done, we both ducked to avoid the headlights. The lights got closer and stopped beside us. A spotlight was thrown in our faces . . . a man jumped out of the car . . . who should it be but cops! They asked us what we were doing, looked over and around the car, told us we ought to go out in the country if we wished to park. They said nearly every car that parks

here is from Vanderbilt. What an experience! I would not have minded
the Peeping Tom mentality of the cops, but it is embarrassing to the
girl.

Sunday, April 14, 1940 When Jordan and I went to town yesterday
to get the tickets for the Sutton-Dyer debate we stopped by the Banner
office and Mrs. Jessup told me the author of the book I reviewed for
last Wednesday's paper came by personally to thank all of them for
the splendid review. He was so impressed with it that he is going to
get the type and run off more copies. Jordan and I got the tickets and
then stopped by the Clarkston Hotel to visit with my old friend and
French tutor Mr. E. E. Daugherty. He is an architect who spent seven
years in Paris and graduated from the Beaux Arts. During the depression
he taught French as an income supplement. The main thing I learned
from him was to appreciate the rhythm of French. I also enjoyed his
French parables. He has two sons who are getting out a fashionable
magagazine in Washington called "Beau." One is art director and the
other is treasurer. Mary Wallace and I went to Dr. Carruther's home
for dinner. We thought we were going to be the only persons there
but we found about ten other guests: William Kingsbury, feature editor
of the Nashville Tennessean, Tommy's Sunday School teacher; Miss
Elizabeth Ann Chitwood, a French teacher at Ward-Belmont. Her father
is a historian and she is a high spirited, New England type, school mistress. Ann Walker from Beaumont, Texas, knows Homer Howell and
John McReynolds. Betty Ewell is from Huntington, West Virginia. A
Huff boy from Decatur, Alabama, knows Clarence K. "Flip" Timberlake.
Helen Hilton is Tommy's teacher from Palmer School. Dixon Johnson
is City Editor of the Times. I went by the Albemarle and saw Uncle
Osgood Anderson, Aunt Ethel, Katherine and Osgood Jr. Back at the
library I found Susan sitting in our regular place. Nello Andrews was
with her. At home tonight I was lonesome and a large Persian cat came
to the door and I let her in. She spent several minutes looking over
the room and then climbed up on the chair for me to pet her. I was
amused at how affectionate she was. I guess all animals, including the
human ones, are pretty much alike.

Monday, April 15, 1940 I went to see Chancellor Carmichael and
suggested that he get Mr. Knudsen, President of General Motors, to
speak at Vanderbilt when he comes to Nashville next Thursday. Said
he would look into it. Andy Bagwell told me about her recent trip to
New Orleans. Shirley Caldwell went to Kissam with me to eat with Sykes
and Surles. I told bachelor Al Hutchinson, who teaches in the engineering school, about the charming Miss Chitwood, whom I met yesterday,
and suggested that he get in touch with her. Partee Fleming and I went
over to the football field to see a scrimmage. Mr. and Mrs. Fred Russell

and Mr. and Mrs. Bob McGaw were there. I spoke to them. My brother Anderson came up to Nashville to buy a tuxedo he plans on wearing to a wedding. Mother came with him.

Tuesday, April 16, 1940 Dr. Sanborn says of sculpturing that it is a realistic presentation of the body and is limited in scope. It can present only a small degree of shade; cannot present the human soul. Painting is a step higher in that it gives an infinite variety of colors. Music transcends objective presentation; comes closest to reality. Hegel goes a step further and says that poetry is higher than music; the highest art form. Goethe once said of art, "It is not the what, but the how." In other words, it is not the subject, but how it is handled.

Wednesday, April 17, 1940 Sold Mr. Turner three tickets this morning. I placed 200 in the bookstore. The new football coaches, "Red" Sanders, "Bear" Bryant and assistants Alley and Scoggins were introduced in chapel this morning. After they made short speeches I made an announcement about the Sutton-Dyer debate. Phoned in the election results and studied in the graduate room while Nello and Susan sat in the main reading room. Susan made an excuse to come back to the room where I was studying to say "Hello." Jordan and I picked up Katherine Timberlake from Art School. She got something in her eye and we had fun trying to get it out.

Thursday, April 18, 1940 Darn it! I slept through a class this morning that I really wanted to meet. I had a ten minute speech prepared. It rained all night and all morning. As I was coming out of History class I saw Susan standing in a doorway and invited her to eat lunch with me at Kissam. I am not as free with her, however, as I am with the regular crowd, and she is not as free with me. I don't know whether that is a good or bad sign. We walked through the rain to the library and studied all afternoon. I moved over so Lucille Johnson could sit between us and study Business Administration problems with Susan. Mary Engles and I went to see "Grapes of Wrath," the story about the bad treatment a poor family received on their way to California and then we drove to the top of Hill road and listened to the pitter-patter of the rain on the roof of the car.

Friday, April 19, 1940 At lunch today Henry Clay and I discussed Joe Davis' speech. Henry says he gave the professors hell. Professor Hayes refused to give him the Sociology scrapbook that Ann Pope made before she died. He repeated his remarks in an impromptu speech at the oratorical tryouts last night. Eugene Flowers was cussing out ODK for their poor selections. Went to see W. C. Fields and Mae West in "My Little Chickadee" and then to see Wilson Austin and Dinkey Rudder who had driven from Stevenson.

Saturday, April 20, 1940 Frierson told how a tobacco crop is grown and Edmunds spoke on the European war. I was amused at Henry Clay telling me what Bill Jordan had done since coming to Vanderbilt and said he ought to be ODK if anybody is. I had made the identical remarks to Flowers yesterday and Flowers had relayed them to Henry. Immediately after eating this evening I settled in a chair in my room and started studying. After reading a few pages I found my mind wandering to the girls of my acquaintance and wondering what they are doing. I was tempted to call Susan and break a month old resolution that I would not call so frequently; to keep it from appearing so obvious that I am completely dependent on her for spiritual comfort. I miss my frequent phone conversations with her and our weekly dates. I am going to ask her for a another soon, but will do it casually.

Sunday, April 21, 1940 Jordan and Dot Reinke came by at noon and we drove to Rawlings for dinner. We discussed our respective plights. We are both burned out on our present life styles and are anxious to get away from Nashville and Vanderbilt, and into the main stream of life. We feel we are stagnating and we are ready for a change. He is going to the Harvard Medical School and I hope to work for Talon Inc. After Jordan took me home I began to feel lonesome again. Started reading William N. Brigance's "Classified Speech Models" and was particularly interested in Clarence Darrow's closing speech to the jury in the "Leopold and Loeb" trial. I have never read a more compelling piece of persuasive literature. In a brilliant sleight of hand maneuver he shifted the jury's attention from the case at hand to a philosophical consideration of the moral question of capital punishment.

Monday, April 22, 1940 Owsley read from Walter Fleming's "Sequel to Appomattox" and I told him after class about reading Henry Ward Beecher's speech, which was delivered in Liverpool during the Civil War. Walked over to Kissam with Susan to hear Dr. Odum, of the University of North Carolina. Susan and I made arrangements to meet later in the library. I was talking with Miriam when she came in. After finishing that conversation I told Susan that it had been a month since I had a date with her and that it seemed like two. "Yes," she said, "The last date was the Deke dance." I reminded her that in about a month and a half school would be over and that I wanted the last weeks to be as pleasant as possible. She agreed and said that if I would call her at home, where she has her date book, we could make our plans for the remainder of the term. She left for town and I studied with Bill Booth and Jim Penrod. Maynard Thompson helped me put up some Dyer-Sutton posters. I went by the Phi Delta Theta House and gave Willie Cornelius instructions for completing our advertising arrangements. He is efficient and dependable. Discussed the possibility of getting Jesse L. Laske, the Hollywood producer who is here getting material for the

Alvin York story, to speak to the Calumet Club. After making the dates with Susan this evening by phone, perhaps I won't be as lonesome as before. I will, at least, have something to look forward to.

Tuesday, April 23, 1940 Dr. Owsley said that the Union League was the instrumentality of propaganda through which Negroes were changed from amicable people to savages. The Ku Klux Klan was a direct answer. The Negroes could be taught to hate in the abstract, but seldom in the particular. When they decided to burn Florence, South Carolina, almost in front of every gate some Negro would say: "These are my white folks, let's not burn their homes." About the only thing burned was the female academy.

Wednesday, April 24, 1940 The picture of Elizabeth Carey appeared. The junior college elected Joe Davis, Nell Edwards and Robert Lord to offices. I took pictures of them to the Banner office. Tonight Partee Fleming and I went to the old Hippodrome to see Jack Dempsey referee the wrestling matches. Partee got us in. Met Mrs. Rentrop at the door. She is a very interesting woman. Says she has been watching wrestling matches all her life. Her son Charles took us back to the dressing room and called out his dad, who introduced us to Dempsey. He was sitting there on the table playing a two-handed game of cards. He looked up, shook hands with us and continued his card game. His hands were as thick and as big as any I have ever felt. He is about my height and about what I had expected. If anything he does not look as tough as one might think. He is not scarred badly. When we asked him questions he would look up and answer very interestedly and he would refer to you by your name if he had caught it. Leonard was interviewing him for the Banner. Fleming persuaded Campbell Blye to take our picture with him, so when Rentrop asked the favor of Dempsey, he responded quickly and put his arms around the two that were closest to him. Well do I remember listening to his last two fights with Tunney. I, at that time, never dreamed that I would ever be in the same dressing room with him with the opportunity of talking as freely as I wished. I merely stood and gazed. After leaving the Hippodrome I went by W.B. and got Virginia Richey. We drove out the Memphis road and talked. She was very determined to have her own way and wanted to go home. I took her after twenty or thirty minutes of quarreling and then I went out to the S.A.D. dance at the club. Jack Teagarden's band was pretty good. Especially I liked his Strauss Waltz. Did not get home until three o'clock.

Thursday, April 25, 1940 I had a test in history this morning. I had forgotten that we were to have it. Studied all evening in the library with Jean Ewing and Shirley Caldwell. Both are very interesting people and we had a good time. Had a date with Susan to see "By Request."

We got there near eight-thirty and there was standing room only. Susan had been playing tennis all evening with Harriet Williams and was too tired to even think of waiting on seats or standing up so we decided to go to a movie. Went to the Paramount to see "Free, Blonde, and 21." It was the story of two doctors who were in love with two types of girls, one was deserving and the other not so deserving. The deserving one won out. Susan gaily talked and laughed as we were going home. Our relationship was purely platonic even in thought. I did not hestitate for a pretty speech when at the door. Looking back over the evening, after arriving at home, I concluded that I had had a delightful time. As I was walking late this evening Eason passed me going in the opposite direction. He turned around, came back, picked me up and drove me home. He was telling me about his business. "I would like to hear more about it sometime," I said.

"Well," he replied, "When we get you out of school and to work I will tell you about insurance."

Friday, April 26, 1940 I had a test under Owsley today. It was not so difficult. Ate lunch with Surles and Clay. Clay was telling Surles all about Katie. This evening after looking at "Life" and "Time" I went by for Jordan, we picked up Martha Wood and went to the tennis matches. Joe Davis beat Bobbett Russell of Ga. Tech in a very close and thrilling match. Jordan, Wood and I then went to town to see Clark Gable, and Joan Crawford in "Strange Cargo." We enjoyed it. After taking Martha home we went by for Dot Reinke and Pat Warren and went to the carnival. The rides made me dizzy. After leaving the carnival we went by the "Slide Rule" dance for a few minutes and then rode around before taking the girls home. Pat was real nice looking and sweet. Her dad runs the Warren paint store. Patricia is a senior in the high school at Ward-Belmont.

Saturday, April 27, 1940 I made a speech on Zippers today in Public Speaking class. I spoke for 17 minutes. They listened intently when I told them how I happened to hit on the idea that made my idea practical. Robison gave me only 79 on my history paper. He told a joke, after class about "service." He said that he did not know exactly what people meant when they spoke of service. He remembered, however, when he was a boy he noticed that one of their cows started acting funny in the pasture. His father instructed him to take her down to the neighbors and get her "serviced." After seeing that he said he knew what service meant. Clay went to the Deke House to eat lunch with me today. We both ate far too much. Jordan came by for me and I took the book review "Five and Ten," a biography of Frank W. Woolworth, to the Banner office. I sat up until three o'clock last night writing and typing it. I got in one crack that I was proud of. After telling about Barbara

Hutton and Jimmy Donahue spending the "5 and 10" fortune I said, "But when a man's shadow lengthens beyond his grave, it is always the man and not his shadows that deserves our attention."

Yesterday I got a letter from Mr. Kelley stating that he had turned my letter over to the employment agency of the Talon Co. with his recommendation based on our talk last summer. He closed his letter by saying, "I hope you hear from the personnel department soon but in any event, I don't think it a bad idea for you to drop by the Talon Company in your travels this summer." I showed my letter to Mr. Turner and he thought it sounded pretty good. He asked me if I intended going to New York this summer and when I told him I might, he asked me if I would like to go by and talk with the personnel people at the House of Morgan. Their President, Mr. Henry Alexander who is on the Board of Trustees at Vanderbilt, told Mr. Turner that he would be receptive to having a young Vanderbilt graduate come up and look around for a year or so to see if he fits in with their programs. It would be a good contact whether I wanted to go into banking or not. Tom Cummings Jr., the mayor's son, came by for me this evening and we went to the community playhouse to see "By Request." The satire on the city administration, Jimmy Stahlman, and other city leaders was very clever. There was one crack about a large house of our town being built by the drippings of the fluid which is "good to the last drop." At the gym dance later I noticed that Marvin Holderness was breaking on Florence Cheek almost as often as Eason breaks on Susan. I asked Florence, when dancing with her, if they had already played the third no-break. "I already have it," she said.

"I wasn't asking you for it, I merely asked if it had been played."

She smiled and said: "I am quite conceited, am I not?" She told me about her schooling at Peabody and in Florida. She is going to the finals at Princeton next Wednesday.

Sunday, April 28, 1940 Jack Harris, program director for W S M told me last night at the play that he was the one who put on the Dyer-Eberling debate a few years ago. The "Cap and Bells" was the official sponsor. I gave him tickets and some publicity information about the Dyer-Sutton affair. Also sent tickets to Jimmy Stahlman. Read an article in Fortune magazine about Jesse Jones of the Reconstruction Finance Corporation. Willie Cornelius went to town with me to patch up some signs. He can almost "out-enthusiasm" me. They tell me he has about twice as many points as are needed to get into O.D.K.

Monday, April 29, 1940 Susan invited me to the Kappa Alpha Theta House for lunch Friday and to take her to the Sigma Kappa prep. school sorority dance on the third of May. Bought a good standard typewriter from Partee for $11.00. Got a card from Dad, who is in Washington on a business trip. Brother George L. Jr. graduates from Kelly Field May 10th.

Tuesday, April 30, 1940 Read about a hundred pages of President Roosevelt's speeches. They are masterpieces of political appeal. Had lunch with Charley Moss and Rousseau Duncan, Managing Editor and City Editor of the Banner and Dick Battle, a feature writer. They were kidding around with a pretty waitress and joked about a possible wrestling match between Battle and me. Asked Dr. Owsley to let me out early to hear a lecture on "Criminality" by a Mr. Hebran, but heard part of Owsley's discussion of Thomas Nelson Page, who set the style of writing about the South. He idealized plantation life and his romantic writing completely changed the Northern opinion of the South. Joel Chandler Harris, realist that he was, did the same when writing about plantation life. He told the story of a Negro in the legislature who had just sold his vote, was asked by a white constituent why he was laughing: "Well, Suh," he said, "I'se been sold eleven times in mah lifetime, but this is the first time that I, myself, ever got the money."

Wednesday, May 1, 1940 Jordan came by for me at five o'clock this evening, and we went to the Hermitage and met Dr. Gus Dyer and Dr. George Mayfield in the lobby. Dr. Willis A. Sutton and his wife had just come in and had taken a room. When Dr. Sutton finished dressing he came down and we ate in the main dining room of Hermitage. We discussed the various phases of problems facing Vanderbilt students and adjourned for the Student Center at seven o'clock. Bill had not arranged for an organist, as we had planned, so the people had no music to amuse them until everyone arrived. The crowd came early and by eight o'clock there were over 500 hundred people in the auditorium. Jordan introduced me as the man who sold the Calumet Club on the idea. I got up and said; Mr. Chairman, members of the Public Speaking class (I meant to say members of the Calumet Club), the audience broke into an uproar. I hestitated a moment—laughed with them and said "unconscious wit." I called attention to the fact that the speakers did not wear tuxedoes—that the affair was informal and that we are here to have a good time. Then I explained the procedure of the night and told this story. A man once left his home in California to go to Alaska in search of gold. When he arrived in Alaska he found that the nuggets that the men were searching for were the same as those that he had been kicking around in his own backyard. The situation is quite different here at Vanderbilt—we have a gold nugget here in Dr. Dyer (laughter) and we recognize it as 24 carats."

Dr. Dyer got up and said, "I am glad he didn't say nut." From here he went on into one of the best speeches I have ever listened to. He told his story about the educational system needing criticism but that nobody in or out of the system could afford to criticize it. One of his biggest joke hits was the one where the fat man would not let another fellow sit down by him on the ground, that the fellow standing was drunk. Finally, the fellow said—"Yes, I'm drunk but I'll be all right in the morning, but you're a hog and you'll be that way all your life." He went on to say that schools were in many cases, contrary to nature. Nature says go out into the open sunshine—schools say sit still. A child is inquisitive—can master any language by the time he is six years old. He pointed out that a large number of children are incapable of getting a high school education. He said that mind was above body, spirit was above mind. He closed by reading a letter to Dorothy Dix. There was a laugh in every line. Dr. Dyer spoke for one hour. About a dozen people left between the speakers. I noticed that Mr. and Mrs. Cheek were sitting on the back row. They left, and took Susan, after Dyer finished. Before introducing Sutton, I called attention to the fact that Willie Cornelius was the only other person in school as enthusiastic as I was about the speaking and that Dr. Dyer's remarks had exceeded even what I (I forgot the word anticipated) expected. Afterwards I introduced Miss Mary Louise Goodwin to the audience and then proceeded to the introduction of Dr. Sutton. I felt sorry for Dr. Sutton having to speak right after the splendid address of Dyer, but Sutton soon hit his stride and well accounted for himself. He dwelled on three points. He said we are hemmed in by time, space, and the mechanics of education. He hit at the idea of units, diplomas and the grading system. While Sutton was speaking Dyer lighted a cigarette and smoked right there on the stage. Dr. Sutton also spoke for an hour, closed with a very delicately put argument for a preservation of the Honor system at Vanderbilt. It was a wonderful speech. After he finished I rose and said— There is only one thing I can say at this time and that is "Amen, Brother Dyer" and "Amen, Brother Sutton." Out time is up and we won't have time for the questions but if any of you have a question you may come up to the front of the auditorium and I am sure the speakers will be glad to see and talk with you. That is all for now so good night." Dr. Mims came up, put his arms around Dr. Sutton and congratulated him. Then he turned to me and said, "I am surprised at such a splendid program." Mrs. Goodwin came up and was introduced to Dr. Sutton. Dozens of people crowded around. Jordan introduced Uncle Ragan, Aunt Nell and Frances. Dr. Mayfield and Mrs. Mayfield said the program was a grand success. Willie and I counted the money, paid Dr. Sutton $25.00 and took him to town for a glass of orange juice. He told us that he was so sick last night that he started to wire us that he could not come. He said that while Dr. Gus was speaking he felt badly. "I'll bet you feel better now," I said. He admitted that he felt good. "It shows the predominance of mind over body, I said. Drove Willie home. I was so tired tonight that I could not go to sleep for an hour or so. I had a tremendous let down after the excitement was all over.

Thursday, May 2, 1940 Every person I saw today was talking about the wonderful speeches last night. The Tennessean carried good pictures of both speakers and a nice story. Dr. Sharp, of the Biology department, said: "Ben, that was a fine program you boys put on last night. The only hope I see for us is that there are a few other men scattered about with ideas similar to those of Dr. Sutton. Several people said they wish they had copies of the speeches. So do I. Fred Wolfe said: "Dyer could convince me of almost anything." Henry Clay said: "Those are two of the greatest hours I have ever spent in my life. The thing that makes me mad is that every person in Vanderbilt did not hear those speeches." Miss Mary Louise Goodwin, who is generally regarded as the best English teacher ever to teach in the Nashville city schools, came up to me and said: "Mary Wallace has not changed much, but you have. You have grown more dignified." Miriam McGaw came up to me and said: "I hear you almost stole the show last night with your remark about the Public Speaking Class." At lunch today Henry Clay told me that Flowers used to think I was dumb, because of the questions I asked in History class, but last night at the program Henry said he pointed toward the rostrum and said: "There are two of the smartest boys in school up there with those two speakers." Dr. Dyer said to his class today: "I greatly admire Dr. Sutton for making the remarks he did last night, especially when you consider the position he holds." I agree with Henry Clay, I don't ever remember being so exhilarated by public speakers and it was not because I was involved in the program. The speeches were that good. Because of the controversial subject "Education Is a Failure, I am sure some professors came to scoff, but they stayed to ring the rafters with their cheers at the conclusion of a program in which two great educators poured out their hearts. Frances Scruggs told me that the Chancellor and Mrs. Carmichael were a little skittish about the subject, but I have heard nothing but praise from everyone. There was not a single complaint. Dawson Frierson came by my apartment tonight to revel in the memory of such memorial oratory. Dr. Harris, head of the Public Speaking department, was beside himself in his praise. So was Mrs. Hart. It will be a long time before any student group tops that program.

Friday, May 3, 1940 Susan had invited me to eat lunch with her at the Theta House today so we met at noon and went over to the house. Dr. Harris was the only other man there. The Lady Dean came in a few minutes after we arrived and she ate with us. Susan drove us back to school at one. Talked to Dyer for a few minutes and he said: "I was surprised at the number of students that turned out last night to hear a discussion of education. You may have started something. Maybe others will turn a critical eye on our educational system." Went by for Susan at nine and we went to the Sigma Kappa dance. We stayed until twelve and then went to the Theta Phi dance. As we were going on out I said, "We have a date for the last two dances of the finals don't we?"

"Why no!" she said, "you did not ask me for them," I assured her that I had and that I had a record of it in my book. She insisted that I had not asked her. After a few minutes of blank silence I told her I did not care whether we had the dates or not. Finally I told her that I don't know why I ever brought up such a subject because it ruined my evening. When we arrived at the club, Jim Reed, who is always teasing Susan, began to cut up when he saw us. He came over and gave Susan a chair, and, in his usual manner, put his arms around her in a playful manner. I was in no mood for horseplay so I told him very bluntly to scram. He did and then we sat down quietly. I did not see Reed anymore. We stayed at the dance until two. When I got home I looked in my engagement book and found that I had the dates and no-breaks listed but they were for the finals last year. I had made the mistake of thinking they were for this year and that I had already talked to her about them. What a heck of a blunder to make.

Saturday, May 4, 1940 King gave his report in History class today. Saw Susan shortly after twelve and she was looking for a meeting that she was supposed to attend. They had not told her where it was to be held. I went over to Kissam and Dr. Tom Zerfoss asked me to eat with the boys who are here for the Southeastern tennis tournament for prep. schools. After Joe Davis, Tommy Tart Brown and the coaches present had spoken I was called on. Dr. Tom told them that I was coach of the freshman wrestling team and liked to talk. I stressed the small classes and close relationships between faculty and students at Vanderbilt. I closed by telling about Dr. Tom. I quoted Dr. Mims in saying that Dr. Tom as a student, was able to properly combine scholarship and athletics and that as school doctor he was one of the best friends that students have had. I also said that I wished that my stay at Vanderbilt could have been the next few years rather than the past few. "I am expecting great things from Dr. Tom's regime as head of the athletic board," I said. After leaving the luncheon I saw Susan and Shirley Caldwell and talked to them. Susan and I went to the tennis courts and saw Johnny Hyden win the no. two spot on the team from Tommy Tart Brown, and then we saw Joe Davis defeat Frank Guernsey who is national inter-collegiate champion, from Rice Institute. I had to leave at four o'clock for the picnic. Marie Smith and Mary W. drove me home. Randolph

Cate escorted Annette Robertson. Simpson was with Mary W. We went to Edwin Warner Park. After the picnic, which was a honey, Annette and I had a little date all our own. We drove out and looked over Radnor Lake.

Sunday, May 5, 1940 Today is Mary Wallace's birthday. Got up at six o'clock and drove to Stevenson with the Ragans. We got there about ten o'clock. I went to town and talked to Mr. Frank Timberlake, Doug Timberlake, Bill Lindsay, and Mr. Jack Bible while Dad worked on Uncle Ragan's tooth. These men are down on England for not aiding Norway against Germany's aggression. Had a fine dinner and then went down to see the farm. We took a motor boat ride on the lake. We left for Nashville about four o'clock. I drove all the way home. As we were eating a sandwich in Murfreesboro I saw a very beautiful girl that looks a lot like Damaris Witherspoon. We got home about nine o'clock and Charles McMurry, who dates Susan occasionally, came by to see me for a few minutes. When I saw Susan today I apologized for insisting I had made dates with her for the finals. I admitted that it was a mistaken idea in my own mind. I said I was glad I did not fly "off the handle" and say things I would have regretted. "I knew you were mad, but you didn't say anything out of the way. I think it is better to get mad and fight rather than keeping anger to yourself." I agreed with her that suppressed anger is perhaps more dangerous than when it is expressed. I told her that I make so many dumb mistakes that I hesitate to blow off steam until I am absolutely sure that it was not I, myself, who was wrong in the first place, and by this time I am usually calmed down and have no desire to express anger.

Monday, May 6, 1940 Found out today that I only have to make seven more quality points to graduate and five of them will come from my 20 courses if I make as much as a "C." Also found out that I do not have to make up that Philosophy. Ate lunch with Catherine Harris Schmidt, Louise Sykes, Miriam McGaw, Henry Clay and Jim Reed, five of the nicest people on campus. Took my string to Mr. Rousseau Duncan and discussed with him my successor. From two until four I collected material for my term paper on the New Deal. At four I went to the gym and wrestled Parker. Don't know when I have enjoyed an afternoon so much. Lydel Sims is now married.

Tuesday, May 7, 1940 Learned from Owsley that the Ku Klux Klan was started in Pulaski, Tennessee, more or less as a prank, but seeing the effectiveness of its policies, it was siezed on as a means of controlling the Negroes. Where the Klan operated effectively, the Union League disappeared. General Nathan Bedford Forrest was asked, on a witness stand, what he knew about the Klan. Forrest said: "I have heard of it." Polk Young gave a very interesting speech on coeds today. He says the reason they are pampered is that there are so many more boys than girls on campus. He says that next year Ward-Belmont girls are going to be allowed to date much the same way that Vanderbilt co-eds do. Too bad I am not going back to school next year. Bill Chapman reported in History today on the Reorganization Bill of President Roosevelt. At lunch today with Henry Clay and Elizabeth Surles, Surles was telling about a job interview at the National Life and Accident Insurance Company. They asked her if she could type or take shorthand. She could do neither. They made considerable fun of her mere sheepskin as qualification for a job. Clay and I went to see Mickey Rooney in "Young Edison." The troubles he was always getting in, as a result of tinkering, reminded me very much of my own childhood. They tell me that about the time I was beginning to walk I broke the glass of the speedometer on my Dad's new car to see how it worked. Clocks, watches, radios, typewriters and all mechanical gadgets were irresistibly appealing to me. As a very young boy I bought old typewriters, repaired them, and sold them at a profit. I bought a radio for the family about fifteen years ago, when radios were scarce. It was an Atwater-Kent and had an amazing number of knobs and dials. I remember sitting up many nights, until the wee hours, listening to radio KDKA in Pittsburgh, WLS in Chicago and WSM in Nashville. Uncle Dave Macon, the banjo, picking singer was a featured performer on the Saturday night program out of Nashville called, by "The Solemn Old Judge," Hay, "The Grand Ole Opry." The "Big Rock Candy Mountain" was a current song hit. In order to hear their names on the radio, the local people would call long distance and make song requests. Static was bad and the sound would come and go like ocean waves. It was especially irritating, when listening to an important event, such as the Dempsey-Tunney fight in 1927, to have the sound go out. We would water the ground wire and tighten the aerial connections, but nothing helped.

Wednesday, May 8, 1940 Today was "Undignified Day" at Vanderbilt and I have never seen the likes of such quaint costumes. I had a business appointment in Belle Meade at three so I did not dress or go barefooted, as so many others did. Andy Bagwell was the first person I saw on campus and she proceeded to remove my tie. In a few minutes a bunch of Deke freshmen took off my shoes and sox. In a few more minutes the real fun came. Shirley Caldwell and Mary Helen Henry decided to take my shirt off. They grabbed me and began to unbutton it. I let them get it about half off and then I grabbed both of them, one arm around each of their waists, and set them very delicately on the ground. I sat on one while I unbuttoned the blouse of the other. They took the defensive immediately. I took both of their skirts and blouses about half off before letting them go. They seemed to enjoy the scuffle. When we finished I told Mary Helen that I had not realized before that she was so attractive. Shirley and I went to the Student Center to get refreshments. This evening I put on my summer tux and went to the All-university sing before taking Susan to the Kappa Phi dance. It was fun, but the Sigma Chis won for the boys and the Alpha Omega Pis for the girls. The Sylvester orchestra was good. Susan and I enjoyed the first part of the dance, but realizing she would not know many people she said: "Mama told me I have to be in by twelve." It gripes me to hear her say her Mama told her so and so. I know she does pretty much as she pleases, but she knows there will be no argument when she puts the blame on her mother. In discussing our future Susan said: "We are going to miss you at Vanderbilt." I told her that there are a great many dissimilarities in our hopes and plans, but that compromises are a part of life. I want to do exciting things in business; she prefers the quiet normal life in Nashville. I want to accomplish something, to be of service to mankind; she wants to maintain the status quo. I suppose if I were catered to in Nashville, as she is, for something my grandfather achieved, I too might be content to rest on family laurels, but fortunately, or unfortunately, as the case may be, I am not in that position. I think, down the road towards the end of life, if someone asks: "What have you done with your allotted time?" I don't know that it is critical what you actually achieved, but it will be of utmost importance that you have tried. There is no tragedy so great, I think, as reaching the end of life and wondering what you might have done if you had dared to try. When we stopped in front of her house at one o'clock I asked her for a good night kiss. She refused, saying something to this effect: "You live in a dream world; the storybook kind, and you want the end to be a kiss so that you can write it up in your diary."

"I'm glad you said that," I replied, "I have suspected for some time that the reason you would not let me kiss you was because of your fear I would write it up in my diary. You can't bear the thought of having it written down, in black and white, that someone kissed Susan Cheek." What a tremendous blunder it was that I once showed her a volume of my diary! How could I have been so stupid? That one fatal blunder probably robbed me of any chance that Susan would fall in love with me. If she had let me kiss her she might have fallen in love. That is perhaps the usual way it happens. There is, first, association, or proximity, then attraction, but not until the animal instincts and passions are aroused, is there real love. Except for this one small incident, my dreams might have been fulfilled. Now I know what the poet who composed "Maude Müller" meant when he wrote: "Of all sad words of tongue or pen, the saddest of these, it might have been."

Thursday, May 9, 1940 Dr. Owsley told about the disastrous friendships of President Grant. Among them were Jay Gould and Jim Fiske. When the Congress voted themselves pay raises and back salaries, it was called "Black Friday." The Union Pacific was granted huge tracts of land and loaned $120,000,000.00. Oakes Ames distributed stocks of the "Credit Mobilier" among high government officials; Grant, Garfield, Blaine and 40 others. John D. Rockefeller was even getting rebates on oil shipped by other companies. In Public Speaking I spoke on the New Deal.

Friday, May 10, 1940 Mary Wallace gave a dinner for Jim Arnold, Keith Broyles and Marie Smith. Don Linton came by to see me and we reviewed old times. Uncle Walt came by later and we listened to President Roosevelt's Pan-American Scientific Conference speech. Roosevelt's enunciation is so careful that interpreters from foreign countries have little trouble translating. We sent two congratulatory telegrams to brother George who is graduating from Kelly Field.

Saturday, May 11, 1940 Today I read my paper, or as much as the teacher would permit, in class. Dan Robison, who is an ardent New Dealer, got so mad that I don't belicve he heard a word I said, after the first few paragraphs, concerning the New Deal spending program. After about thirty minutes he stopped me and we had one of the most heated arguments I have ever had with any teacher. The class sat there scared stiff. The subject of the paper was: "Has The New Deal Carried Out the Party Platform?" They haven't, of course. The platform promised to cut spending by 25%. Spending was increased by 50%. I dealt with the features I considered important. He accused me of picking out a few items at random and building up unfair criticism of the New Deal. I finally told him I would say what I pleased in the paper, because I signed my name to it; the by-line indicates that I accept full responsibility. He said I could not say what I wanted in his class. After about thirty minutes of heated argument, when the professor had lost his composure and dignity completely, I finally told him that the only control he had over the paper was to grade it and that if I did not like the grade I would take the whole matter to the Chancellor. I was so furious after class that I could not study. Jordan and I went to town to see Jack Benny in "Buck Benny Rides Again." When Uncle Walt brought his car to me this evening and I told him of my tiff with Professor Robison, he said it was the greatest happening since I came to Vanderbilt. The thing I see about it is this, I told him: "It shows the tendency of classroom dictators to regiment the thoughts of their students. I doubt that any other student at Vanderbilt would have stood up and fought the issue as I did, because my graduation was in the balance but he was so wrong to let his emotions become involved in an academic matter, that I had no choice but to fight. The tendency is to agree and humor the man who holds the whip handle of grades. Colleges, as I have said so many times before, have a tendency to beat down the individualism of students."

Sunday, May 12, 1940 Annette R. and I went to the "Grand Ole Opry" at the War Memorial Building last night and then drove up on Hill Road for a look at the moon. She told me about the Peabody girl who is afraid the war will take all the young men and leave her an old maid. Jordan, Jane Raborg and I went out to the airport late this afternoon and took a ride in a plane for one dollar. It was the first ride I have had in a long time and I really did enjoy it, especially when he banked sharply. I believe I could fly a plane without much trouble. It is a thrill to look out at the landscape from a thousand feet up. I thought about the war and how easy it would be to bomb houses and farms from up in the air. But when I thought of the antiaircraft guns it was not so pleasant.

Monday, May 13, 1940 Jean Stephenson and Henry Clay reported in History today. Margaret Noland was a new member of our luncheon party. Sykes, Surles, Clay and Maddox were the regulars. Miriam left the Dean's Council to come to sit with us. Susan was at the Council table. She passed by our table once and looked the other way. She is so formal and self-conscious that it strains relations between her and almost everyone with whom she comes in contact. I wish she'd break down and be natural and normal . . . and sociable. Went by to see Dr. Owsley at two o'clock and read him part of the paper on the New Deal. He seemed to like it. At least he is not as narrow and as prejudiced as Professor Robison. I am getting ready to leave this section of the country. Just before going to bed, I sat for a few minutes gazing about my room: the desk, typewriter, books, radio, easy chair and thought what a nice place this is and how much I am going to miss it next year. I will miss Mary Wallace, the Ragans and Andersons and all of my Nashville friends. Most of all I will miss Susan. How helpless we sometimes are when our happiness depends on another person; worst of all, a fragile little girl.

Tuesday, May 14, 1940 I had to catch a taxi to school in order to get there in time for my Public Speaking class nomination of Bert Marshall for Bachelor of Ugliness. Professor Robison was in a good mood today. I suspect, after thinking it over, he realized how far out of line he was the other day in letting his political prejudices show. "Led" Adams reported on the T. V. A. Saw Susan at twelve and she accepted my invitation to eat in Kissam with Henry Clay, Margaret Noland and me. She was very pretty today. Catherine Harris spoke of having a compliment for me but would not tell me before Susan. Susan and I went to the library and studied until four. Shirley Caldwell and Virginia Youmans sat directly across from us. Frank Witherspoon told me about seeing my brother, Henry D., win the mile in the state meet. He said there was not a man within 25 yards of him. His time was 4:38, only one second off the record. At four Susan and I went to the Knickerbocker theatre to see Joel McCrea and Ginger Rogers in "The Primrose Path." It was the story of a girl who came from a red-light district family and the difficulties it caused her when she married. We both thoroughly enjoyed it. I drove her car to town and afterwards to the Toddle House for hamburgers and coffee. It was one of the nicest evenings I have ever spent with her. She looked very chic in her glasses at the show. We studied in the library until ten o'clock and William Cornelius drove me home. A letter from Pop J. commented on the recent Dyer-Sutton affair. "Dr. Sutton spoke most enthusiastically of the meeting with the Vanderbilt crowd. He said it was about the best promoted gathering he had ever seen and that you deserved a lot of credit for the way you had worked it up."

Wednesday, May 15, 1940 The war talk is buzzing. Holland is split and Italy is expected to enter the war on the side of the Germans. The jokesters have already written off Italy. One wag said it didn't make any difference which side Italy joined. If they're against us we'll have to send a division down to defeat them. If they are with us we'll have to send a division to protect them. There is really nothing funny about the war situation and each passing day seems to draw us closer into the vortex. The O.D.K. and Mortar Board tapping ceremonies took place in chapel today. I saw Susan and Shirley Caldwell tapped for Mortar Board. The twelve O.D.K. pictures were in the Banner this evening. Cathering Harris Schmidt told me the compliment she had promised. She said her father said: "Ben is healthy, intelligent, good-looking and interested in girls. He will make some girl a good husband. He is the type of person I would want for a son."

"That's a strange coincident," I said, "Just the other day I commented I had rather my wife had been brought up by Dr. Harris than any man I know." After lunch with Sykes and Surles at the Tri Delta House I went to my comprehensive with Dr. Binkley. It was pretty much as I had expected. Passed by the West End Methodist Church and saw Elizabeth Craig and the Weaver boy exit from their wedding. I saw Katherine Anderson, my first cousin, and congratulated her on getting her PhD. in Pathology.

Thursday, May 16, 1940 I made a speech this morning on war time propaganda. I really put some feeling into it. The class particularly liked the epigram: "When war is declared, truth is the first casualty." Andy Bagwell thought it was the best speech I have ever given. Ate lunch with Andy, Louise Sykes, Miriam McGaw, Libby Zerfoss and Cecile Hyman, who has just returned from New York where she has been studying in a dramatic school. She was telling us about the Nashville people who are in New York. Mr. Jim Buford, the basketball coach, sat with us for awhile. He has the unfortunate ability of making people feel ill at ease around him. It is because he, himself, is so self-conscious. Studied until five and then went to the Hermitage tap room for coffee and conversation with Jordan. He is such a brilliant guy that my conversations with him over the past few years have been almost as valuable as lectures by the professors. For me he has made Vanderbilt into an Oxford. Stopped by the Wesley gym on the way home and talked with Henry Clay. He said he told Jack about my comment when he did not make O.D.K. "There is one thing better than achieving a certain honor and that is deserving it."

Friday, May 17, 1940 Took my English History exam under Dr. Walker today. It was really rough. Came home, took a nap and went out to Susan's for my weekend date. Her grandmother, Mrs. Glenn, met me at the door and as usual we had a good conversation. Her age makes it easier for her to talk freely and she says what she pleases. It is a relief to hear a word, or two, of bragging every now and then. It adds a human element to ones personality. She told me about "Little John" making the highest grades in Castle Heights and how proud his mother is of him. Mrs. Glenn's comment was: "I wish there was some member of the family who would just take it easy and just get by." She said Mrs. Cheek wants Susan to go to school just to have a good time. It tickles me the way she uses "ain't" and "don't" in the wrong place. Susan and I went to Loews to see "My Son, My Son." It is the story of a father who did too much for his son. A woman came between them. Finally the no-good son repents and dies a hero in the war. We sat down in the show two rows in front of Henry Clay and Billy Eason. She didn't notice who it was with Henry so she asked me: "Who's with Henry?" She was a little embarrassed when I told her. I was feeling fine tonight and enjoyed the date tremendously. Susan's hair was fixed prettily and she had on a beautiful dress. She cried several times; especially when the son would not tell his father good-bye. After the show we went to Candyland and discussed the philosophy expressed in the picture. She said it was sad for parents to do too much for their children. I told her what I heard my father say when asked what he intended to make out of his five boys. "I am not going to make anything out of them. I'll give them the advantages I can afford and if they want to make something of themselves, that is up to them." I also told her that my father often said: "If you ever get in jail, don't come to me." Susan said she would certainly hate to go to her father to get out of jail.

Saturday, May 18, 1940 Received a telegram today which read as follows: "WOULD LIKE SEE YOU MONDAY NETHERLAND PLAZA CINCINNATI OUR EXPENSE." E. F. Anderson, Talon, Inc. I went out to Uncle Walt's and then to town to get a weekend bag. Wired Mr. Anderson via night letter that I would meet him in Cincinnati at ten o'clock. Showed Dr. Owsley the telegram and he said it would be OK to miss his class on that day. Saw Mr. and Mrs. Frank Gunter, Tommy Hale, Henrietta Hickman and Jean Ewing in the Hermitage tap room.

Sunday, May 18, 1940 The train pulled out of Nashville's Union station at eight-thirty-five in the evening. I retired to the sleeper shortly thereafter. I enjoy the atmosphere of riding on a Pullman and the expectation of excitement in Cincinnati tomorrow heightened the experience. I could not sleep well, but under such conditions I am never too anxious to get to sleep anyway. I love to lie on the Pullman bunk, propped up on pillows, and watch the moon come up across the fields and then be blocked out by the buildings and stations of small towns we pass through. I love the night sounds of the train as it stops for the loading of mail or freight; the voices in the night. There will probably never be a more colorful era in America than when the railroads were in their heyday. The deluxe breakfasts and dinners in the dining cars were experiences to long remember. Strong black coffee served in heavy silver pitchers, with pure cream to enrich it, and flaky crusted apple pie, with a heeping scoop of vanilla ice cream on top, will never be surpassed as the finishing touch of an exquisite meal. It is difficult to pack more romance into a single event than dinner in the diner.

Monday, May 19, 1940 Along towards morning I raised the shade and watched the daylight break through a dark gray mist. I thought of a hauntingly beautiful poem by a hobo poet by the name of W. H. Davis, called "Early Morn." One stanza said: "It seemed as if I had surprised and trespassed in a world of gold, that should have passed while men slept." I arrived in Cincinnati at seven o'clock and ate breakfast in their very beautiful terminal. Coming out of the station I met a fellow from Chattanooga by the name of Charley Smith who works at the Lunkin Airport. He was at the station to meet a fellow who was there to get an airplane he had bought. Went immediately to the Netherland Plaza Hotel where I got a shave. It was the first shave I had ever had in a barber shop and it was actually painful. My father was shaved by a barber almost every day of his working life. I don't see how he stood it. My first shave, in a commercial place, was certainly no luxury. At ten c'clock I called room 722 and then went there to talk with Ed Anderson and Mr. Morgan, who is local representative for the Talon company in the Cincinnati district. Mr. Anderson looks a lot like R. A. Gotto. He asked me why I did not make good grades on the subjects I did not like. I explained that my mind ran like a racehorse on some subjects, but balked like a mule on others. I pointed out that I participated in a lot of extracurricular activities, which I consider important, such as, writing for the newspaper, coaching wrestling, and campaigning for stricter observance of the Honor Code. Some people have a knack for making good grades; others do not. "If you could go into any branch of the company, which would you choose?" I knew they were from sales but I answered without hesitation, "Research." We talked for about thirty minutes and then we adjourned for lunch. Mr. Anderson said he thought I had a brilliant mind but that he agreed that I should be in the scientific end of the business. He said that I had very definite ideas about things and that if he could give me a job with sufficiant responsibility to dominate my thinking, he would readily do it, under the present circumstances I ought to contact Mr. E. A. Bessom, of the Research department. I went to a theatre to see Bing Crosby in "If I Had My Way" and caught the train at six and arrived at home at two in the morning. Sat with a group of girls on the train who do demonstration work for the A & P company.

Tuesday, May 21, 1940 In chapel today Chancellor Carmichael made his first speech to the senior class. He is an excellent public speaker. He said the university invested $1,000.00 in every student over a four year period. "We have an interest and an investment in you and we want you to maintain an interest in the university." Hill Turner presented the Living Endownment plan and Jim Tuck spoke for the class of 1940. In a talk with Mr. Turner later he pointed out the difficulties of independent marketing of an invention. Henrietta Hickman came in before we finished. At the Calumet Club banquet tonight Drs. Mims, Mayfield and Davidson made good speeches and Castellano, Manchester and George Marion O'Donnell rolled 'em in the aisles with their jokes. Jordan had Willie Cornelius introduce Fleming and me as two of the best speakers in the country. Willie was elected President for next year. Jordan and I entered the Founder's Day oratorical contest by proxy. Think I'll speak on "A Return to Fundamentals."

Thursday, May 23, 1940 At four o'clock I picked up Susan for the Deke picnic. She asked about my trip and my plans for the future. She said she was never so surprised as when she recognized my handwriting on a letter from Cincinnati. "If you were to work for Talon as a salesman, would you be on the road all the time?" she asked.

"No," I would establish a residence and make periodical trips from there." I also mentioned the possibility of getting on with the J. P. Morgan Company of New York and she perked up. Later in the evening she told me about an interesting poem she had just read. The keynote of it was that a boy can win back his love after a breakup. This was perhaps my cue. She gave me an opening and I should have moved in with firmness and insisted that she marry me and start a plan for the future. To paraphrase Shakespeare: "Me love too much! Love makes cowards of us all. There is a tide in the affairs of men, which taken at the flood, leads on to victory. Omitted, all the voyages of their lives are hemmed in by narrow shallows." How sadly true! It might also be quoted that "Pride goeth before a fall." I am probably too proud to stay around and play the role of a Heathcliffe, and yet to play it otherwise is to lose my only chance at winning true love. If I only knew what the odds were!

Friday, May 24, 1940 The days are growing short. It is almost as if the world is coming to an end and I have foreknowledge of the impending date. The consuming passion of my life hangs in the balance. It is to be or not to be. The world is at war, and we are on the verge of becoming involved. Not only is love at stake, but life itself. It is suggestive of Goethe's German mysticism; the interlocking of love and death. Is it any wonder that suicide is an avocation of the young?

Saturday, May 25, 1940 Dr. Owsley gave me my 450 comprehensive questions yesterday and I spent the evening taking the examination. Practiced my oration before Dr. Harris and forgot it in two places. Henry Clay went to the apartment with me to write his speech and I spent my time trying to memorize mine. I have such a hard time committing something to memory that when I once get it I remember it forever. At five we took naps and then had shrimp cocktails and T-bone steaks for dinner.

Sunday, May 26, 1940 President Roosevelt gave one of his Fireside Chats tonight. Hitler is on the verge of invading England. Edward R. Murrow reported on the war directly from London. Jordan called at eleven and we went to the Tally-ho to discuss and evaluate the world situation. Our discussions are as intellectually stimulating, perhaps, as those that used to take place in the coffee houses of London or the beer halls of Heidelberg. Gene Tunney was a guest on "Information Please" tonight with Clifton Fadiman and Oscar Levant and did very well. Eddie Cantor, Bob Hope, Edgar Bergen and Charley McCarthy appeared on a program for the Red Cross. Judy Garland sang "Over the Rainbow."

Monday, May 27, 1940 Bert Marshall won the B. U. election by a vote of 508 to 222 for Bud Beasley. Ray Andrus withdrew from the race. Tom Cummings Jr. had his dad, the mayor, send out a motorcycle escort and a big parade was staged. Harris Abrahams was at the microphone on a sound truck and, naturally, was in his glory. Mortimer Trull, Hilliard Wood and I got pictures and a story about Marshall's win. The party was at the Sigma Alpha Epsilon House. Got my expense check for my trip to Cincinnati from Talon. It was $20.65. At the Founder's Day Oratorical Contest tonight Tom Cummings Jr. spoke first, I was second, Jimmy Weems third and Henry Clay fourth. I thought all the speeches were good and since I did not win I am glad Jimmy did. He has lost three contests this year on the same speech. It probably meant more to him than it did to me. My fun came in getting some things off my chest. This was my swan song.

Tuesday, May 28, 1940 The Glenn Gray dance last night was excellent. Glenn, himself, is a big six feet two or three inch tall individual with broad shoulders. He is like what I picture Rhett Butler as being. He introduced Gene Austin, of "My Blue Heaven" fame, and he also acknowledged the presence of Francis Craig in the audience. Susan looked nice in a blue evening dress and the only thing wrong was that her escort was Billy Eason. I spotted Catherine Harris Schmidt in the balcony and motioned for her to come down for a dance. I told her that it is a good thing school is over shortly because I like her better every time I see her.

Wednesday, May 29, 1940 Read an article in the Saturday Evening Post on the newspaper columnist Dorothy Thompson. She and Sinclair Lewis are living apart now. It is hard enough for amateur critics to live together, much less professionals. Harold L. Ickes article attempts to exonerate Ballinger, who was Secretary of the Interior in the William Howard Taft administration, from misconduct in office. He accuses Gifford Pinchot of conspiring to frame him. At lunch today Henry Clay told about the love affair he had in Atlanta before he met Katie. I don't suppose mine is the only love that does not run smoothly. Shirley Caldwell sat with me in the library this afternoon. Susan came in and sat at a table just across an aisle. We sat thusly for several hours without nodding to one another. Jordan and I were sitting at a table in the bookstore when Dan Robison passed. Jordan called to him: "Say, Professor Robison, I understand you are suppressing freedom of discussion in your classes." He came back, sat down, and entered into an argument about that and other subjects. The war is mainly on the minds of all of us. John Caldwell joined us and said he is ready to go to war. I was surprised at his stand. It interested me to see Jordan and Caldwell tangle wits. Jordan soon overawed both Caldwell and Robison. It is most amusing to see people, who think they are clever, lock horns with Jordan. George Marion O'Donnell is the only man I know who can make Jordan seek cover. George does it by shifting the scene of discussion to his own particular specialty which is poetry and literature. Herman Lusky accosted me today and said: "I don't know whether I have mentioned it or not, but I think it was kind of you to pay the tribute you did to Miss Mary Louise Goodwin at the Dyer-Sutton debate." Mary

Wallace told me that Dr. Hayes heard Dr. Sutton Monday night at the commencement ceremonies at Watkins Institute and is more than ever sold on him.

Thursday, May 30, 1940 As I came out of class today Susan called to me and said that she found out that someone else had made a date with her for the Senior Farewell dance and that she wanted to tell me so I could make a date with someone else.

"Who," I asked.

"Billy Eason," was her reply.

"Well, as I have said before, anytime you want to break a date with me you can." I was never so surprised. Wonder what prompted her to do a thing like that. I felt badly when I got up this morning. Now I feel worse. A drive around the countryside with Jordan made me feel a little better. We stopped by Dr. Morrel's, the Physics professor's home. He told us about an invention to determine how much gasoline is in a tank. He pumps air in and by raising the atmospheric pressure a certain amount he can set up a ratio which will accurately indicate the capacity for more gasoline.

Friday, May 31, 1940 Saw Mr. Robert Cheek coming out of the Kissam cafeteria with Chancellor Carmichael yesterday afternoon. I had not realized how much he looks like Dr. Gus Dyer. He was much neater, of course. Henry Clay says he is a whiz at Chineese checkers. Met Annette Robinson's father tonight. She and I had planned on going to the Community Playhouse production of "First Lady" but there was standing room only so we drove out to the beautiful hill overlooking the Franklin Pike and watched the lights of the cars go by. It is a beautiful vista which Jordan showed me. Elizabeth Surles asked me if she could bring her brother to my tea on Thursday so he could meet the gang.

Saturday, June 1, 1940 Went to town and bought wedding presents for Mr. and Mrs. Bill Kammerer (Marcella Driskill), Katie Heitzburg and Joe Hutchinson. Jordan and I went to see "Abe Lincoln of Illinois." I saw the stage play in New York last summer, but did not associate it with Susan and me at that time. Today I was impressed by the similarity of the problems presented. Mary Todd was ambitious and goaded Lincoln into a full realization of himself. She chose Lincoln over Douglas because she discerned in him the qualities of greatness. Lincoln was presented as a man with little ambition. He was a peace, loving man who just wanted to be "let alone." One sentence of Miss Todd struck me. "Lincoln may split rails for other people, but he will never build a fence around himself." Lincoln failed to go through with the marriage at first. He went away for awhile. He visited the scene where he had met and loved Ann Rutledge. She died. After returning from New Salem he decided he had done an injustice to Mary Todd and he went ahead and married her. Returning to New Salem, which was now a mere desert, Lincoln's statement reminded me much of one that Susan had once made. She said: "A person can never completely cast off the halo around his old hometown, or the scenes of his childhood, until he has been away for a good many years and then returns." Dr. Mims puts it, "The good old days that never were." I went to the Hermitage tap room this afternoon for a cup of coffee with Jordan. Francis Craig's orchestra was playing. It dawned on me that Craig's music will be one of the things I will miss when I leave Nashville. We went to Zibarts and Mills bookstores and bought copies of Adolf Hitler's "Mein Kampf" and John K. Winkler's "Morgan the Magnificent." I want to know all I can about them before I interview them this summer. I also want the book about Morgan which was written by his son-in-law Herbert L. Saterlee. In Lincoln's farewell address to the people of Springfield, as he left for Washington, he used lines something like this: "A ruler of the East once commanded his wise men to give him lines that would fit any occasion and they were these: 'Even this shall pass away.' "

Sunday, June 2, 1940   Talked with Dr. Sharp yesterday about how we might go about arousing more interest, among members of the Vanderbilt family, in the University. I don't know whether he was joking or not, but Jordan said that last night some burglars were trying to get into his car so he yelled down to them: "Don't you want the keys?"

"No," one burglar yelled back, "I'm having more fun this way."

Monday, June 3, 1940   Took the final exam on Dr. Owsley's course and did well on it I think. I have enjoyed Owsley's irreverence. He is no stuffed shirt when dealing with historical figures. Saw Susan at the library desk and she was looking pale and wan. Maybe she is studying too much. I have been studying hard for Professor Robison's Recent American History because we have not been getting along very well lately I don't know what to expect from him.

Tuesday, June 4, 1940   I thought Robison's exam was this evening so I leisurely got up at nine o'clock. At ten I got a call from Walter King asking if I had forgotten the examination. I was never so shocked; on my last examination, forgetting it. I rushed to school and got through with the exam. at noon. Robison told me that he said to the class: "If Austin is as slow working on Zippers as he is in getting to class, he is in pretty bad shape." Ate lunch with Sykes, Surles and Kay Schmidt. Besides being such a good-looking woman I have finally decided what gives Kay that extra something; she is a good listener, hanging on every word as if she can't wait to hear the next. I would like my wife to be like she is. The only other woman I have ever said that about is Mrs. Evelyn Connoll, Society Editor of the Banner. Both are charmingly attractive and full of life.

Wednesday, June 5, 1940 Called Mrs. Hart tonight and she said I did not have to give a final speech as an examination tomorrow. I am exempt. I told her how much I had enjoyed her course this term. She is a good teacher. Andy Bagwell and Joe Davis came by my apartment tonight to get me to help them write their speeches for the examination tomorrow. Joe was telling me that he felt he had not done anything worthwhile in life. When I reminded him of being one of the top eight tennis players in the nation he said: "But what is that?" I argued that being the best in any field requires dedication and work and it signified achievement, even though it is only in sports. He said he wished he knew as many quotations as I do. I answered that if he had as much interest in poetry and prose as I do he would probably know more.

Thursday, June 6, 1940 Got up early today and cleaned the apartment for the tea this evening. Cousin Frances Ragan helped me make the sandwiches. At four o'clock Miriam McGaw, Louise Sykes, Elizabeth Surles and her brother Ed arrived. Jim Reed came a little later and we went by Wesley Hall for Henry Clay. We had an enjoyable time just sitting around talking. At eight-thirty I went out to get my date, Shirley Caldwell, for the Proms. Talked to her father, Meredith, and her sister Allison, and then to her very charming mother. I have not smoked for several months, but when she offered a cigarette, I could not resist. She said to me: "Shirley tells me you are one of the smartest boys at Vanderbilt. Let me hear you say something smart." I laughed and told her about the thrilling prospects of going to work on my first real job, but that I am having difficulties in my love life. She knew what I was talking about. She said: "I have known Susan for twelve years and I still don't know her." Dick Jurgens played for dancing, not for the spectators, and I thoroughly enjoyed the dance. Shirley is a smooth, flowing dancer and we danced most of the evening together because there are very few stags at the Proms. On the Ace/Owl Club Special we were not supposed to dance it but they played the "Missouri Waltz" and we could not sit still. We marched in the Senior Prom for the second time. We called it our second anniversary. At the intermission Nancy Houghland and her date went to Candyland with us. After the dance we went to a restaurant downtown and talked until four o'clock.

Friday, June 7, 1940 At three o'clock I went to the tea dance. Danced the second no-break with Surles who had just been notified that she had been given a job with the National Life and Accident Insurance Company. Danced the third with Virginia Youmans, one of the most beautiful women in the world. She was Prom. Queen last night. Danced a special with Susan. I came home after the tea dance, took a nap, and went back at ten for the final dance. I asked Henry Clay if he would mind if I asked his date, Margarete Holman, from Texarkana, Texas, if she would go to the breakfast with me at Rawlins. He said he would be delighted for her to go with me and she agreed. She is a very attractive girl and full of life. She likes Henry. At the farewell Deke breakfast, Homer Howell, the new Deke President, called on me to make the last speech. I told them that if I were to give advice I would give it to the graduating class because they are the ones who will be facing the crisis. The undergraduates will get along; they always have. "If war should come," I said, "We should be willing to bear the responsibility of it because we are the fortunate ones. We have had the best advantages that the richest nation in the world affords. Whether in peace or war, let us conduct ourselves in the future so that we will be a credit to our fraternity, school, and to our nation." Margaret and I then drove home. It was broad daylight.

Saturday, June 8, 1940 Packed my clothes and by afternoon had the apartment ready for the other people to move in. At eight thirty I picked up Eugene Flowers, Will King and Henry Clay and we went to see Spencer Tracy in "Edison the Man." It started out showing the elderly Edison being honored at a banquet. Tracy looked like the pictures of Edison and admirably caught the spirit of the brilliant, but hard of hearing genius. I was glad that, early in life Edison did not take the $300.00 per month job, which offered security, but would take him away from his real interests. In later life he refused a hundred-thousand dollar loan when it would give the lender a voice in the policies at Menlo Park.

Sunday, June 9, 1940 Went with Uncle Walt to the Commencement ceremonies at Vanderbilt to hear one of his classmates deliver the main address. We liked Dr. Edmonds, but were a little disappointed in his sermon, which he read instead of giving. Katherine Anderson went with us. There was one interesting observation attributed to Einstein. When Nazism threatened Germany, the free institutions were looked to for leadership, but they were silent. The press, which had cried out so loudly before the crisis came, was also silent. Only the church stood up and fought. Cousin Katherine, who got her PhD., and I were guests of honor at a splendid steak dinner at the Ragans tonight. Later I went to the Hermitage tap room with Jordan where we reviewed the year's activities. It has been an eventful experience at Vanderbilt. The school is large enough and prestigeous enough to command respect, but small enough to know most of the professors and students. There is a comradeship and family spirit that would be lost if the school were much larger. It epitomizes the best of the good life associated with a high class university.

Monday, June 10, 1940 Finished packing and put on my summer tux and went to the Senior Farewell Dance. Did not dance with Susan until real late in the evening. Had the Special with her at the end of the dance. Eason was her date. Met a very pretty girl from Franklin by the name of Martha Williams. She got my name and address to invite me to the Franklin Cotillion Club dance on the 21st of June.

Tuesday, June 11, 1940   Had a disagreement with Uncle Walt and Aunt Nell this evening over nothing. I am glad to be finishing my schooling so I can have a semblance of independence. The timing is pretty good. I am getting out on my own about the same time that I have become completely fed up with my dependence on others.

Wednesday, June 12, 1940   I got my Bachelor of Arts degree today. Dr. Dave Hennen Morris, husband of Commodore Vanderbilt's granddaughter, delivered the baccalaureate address. His voice did not carry very well, but the address was good. Dean Leathers, of the Medical School, said that Katherine Anderson's PhD. thesis is the best he has ever read. After the services Dad and Mother got around quite a bit. Dad talked to Dr. McGill, his old Chemistry teacher and friend. I introduced Susan to the family. When I introduced Dr. Mims to Mother he said: "Your son has certainly been an important part of the university. He has run Vanderbilt for a couple of years." Dr. Harris paid the nicest compliment of all. He said: "Ben has been a joy to me. He has been a tremendous help to my classes. The university owes him a great deal." I am glad to have finished the course because I vowed to myself long ago that no matter how many setbacks, or how long it would take, I would graduate from Vanderbilt. As far as the diploma itself is concerned, however, I feel about it pretty much the same way Daniel Webster did when he struck a match to his. Dr. Dyer said to Dad: "Your son Ben and I see eye to eye on this diploma business. This morning when I told Dyer the story about Jim Benson "getting a taste of public office and liking it," he came back with this one. A politician once asked a particular man for his vote. The man replied: "I'd vote for the devil first."

"Well," replied the politician, "Since your man isn't running I wish you would give me your support." This evening Bill Jordan and I had our farewell dinner together. After visiting the Ragans, Dr. Reinke and Jane Raborg, went to a restaurant. There have been Damon and Pythias, David and Jonathan, and other close friendships in history. My friendship with Jordan has not been one of complete immersion, as have so many of the others, but strictly one of mutual intellectual stimulation. What better could you ask from anyone? It was a fortunate chance meeting in time and space.

Thursday, June 13, 1940   Called Susan tonight in order to arrange a parting date. She was busy in the evenings but said I could come out some afternoon, perhaps Monday. She said she had something to talk with me about that she had rather discuss face-to-face.

Friday, June 14, 1940   Signed up Billy Rose for camp today and had a long talk with his very interesting family. I went to town and settled all of my accounts with local stores.

Saturday, June 15, 1940 Paris has been entered by the German army. The French have declared it an "Open City" in order to save it. The French government has retreated to Southern France. Hitler said in an interview in the morning papers that the Monroe Doctrine should work both ways. It is just as essential that it keep America out of Europe as it does Europeans out of the Americas. He put it: "Europe for Europeans and America for Americans." I partially agree with his interpretation of the famous doctrine, but friendly colonizing is one thing, but open aggression against established peoples is quite another. Hitler is overrunning smaller governments and on that ground there is some excuse for giving material aid to the Allies. If we were to attack Mexico or South America, their getting aid from foreign powers would be legitimate. In seeing and hearing about the bombing of Paris in the newsreels today, I learned that the German planes rose some thirty thousand feet, completely out of sight, to drop their bombs. Anti-aircraft guns are ineffective at that height. The die is really already cast. If we don't want Hitler as a neighbor, the United States is going to have to bear the brunt of defeating him. Nobody else can. On my way to town today I saw Elizabeth Surles and we went to a movie to see Margaret Sullivan in "The Mortal Storm." Margaret was charming in her boyish German costume and husky voice. The story was about the effect of the Hitler regime on a Jewish scientist, teacher and his family. It was pure propaganda, of the inflammatory sort, but not false propaganda. It's purpose is to excite, but not to mislead, and is therefore acceptable. A patriotic flag making short completed the program. Surles and I discussed what a girl must do to win her man. We agree that she must be interested and enthusiastic about his plans and interests. She must give undivided attention to him when they are out together. She asked me if she should tell a boy she likes him. I told her "Yes" by all means, when he indicates an interest.

Sunday, June 16, 1940 Marshall Petain, the 84 year old soldier, who said at Verdun in World War I, "They shall not pass," replaced Renaud as Premier of France. What a difference a few years make. The same man who was at the helm when France was saved in 1918, has now taken over when France is in defeat. I remember reading, just a few years ago, that France had the most modern army in the world and that the Maginot Line was impregnable. It appears now that vulnerability, or invulnerability, of a nation is not a matter of weapons or defenses, but of the will of the people.

Monday, June 17, 1940 Today Marshall Petain sued for peace. Hitler is now master of the continent of Europe. Only England stands between him and complete domination. Whether we agree with Hitler, or not, we must recognize that he is perhaps the most powerful individual in the world today. Hitler is alone. He has no family tie or ambitions for future heirs. He can be ruthless because he has no one to answer to. A less courageous, or perhaps wiser individual, would have turned back long ago. Even though he started out timidly in occupying the Rhineland, the lack of courage by other leaders to confront him, has enabled him to pile victory upon victory, and now his daring knows no bounds. Where it will all stop nobody knows. Jimmy Stahlman, Publisher of the Banner, returned from vacation today and started his column again, "From The Shoulder." His strong voice will be a welcome addition during these troubled times. I went to Susan's this afternoon at four and we went out of doors and stood by the stone fence and talked. Mrs. Cheek was out directing the pruning of trees. Mr. John was just standing around admiring his property. John Jr., was in the back yard shooting his 22 calibre target pistol. Susan told me about the new Buick convertible that the family had given John Jr. The lawn was freshly manicured and beautiful. I don't believe I have ever seen a more lovely setting than Oak Hill was this day. We started discussing our future plans but did not finish our conversation. We'll meet again.

Tuesday, June 18, 1940 The Honorable Winston Churchill, Prime Minister of Great Britain, addressed Parliament today. In the whole history of the world there has probably never been a more dramatic set of circumstances. A tyrant has overrun Europe and threatens the safety of the entire free world. Country after country has given in to him, starting with the sacrifice of Czechoslovakia and followed by the Scandanavian countries, Poland, and now France. The little island of Great Britain stands alone between Hitler and complete domination of Europe and perhaps the whole world. As so often happens in history, a strong man arises to fill the void. In this case it is Winston Churchill, whose voice calling for preparedness against the threat of Hitler, has been repudiated time and again. Only in the eleventh hour was he called to leadership. But what a leader! Today he stood up in Parliament and, in majestic language, perhaps not equaled in our mother tongue, threw the challenge back into Hitler's teeth. On June 4th he spoke to Parliament as follows:

> *"We shall go to the end. We shall fight in France, we shall fight in the seas and oceans, we shall fight with growing confidence and growing strength in the air; we shall defend our island, whatever the cost may be. We shall fight on the beaches, we shall fight on the landing-grounds, we shall fight in the fields and in the streets, we shall fight in the hills; we shall never surrender."*

Today he said:

> *"But if we fail, then the whole world, including the United States, including all that we have known and cared for, will sink into the abyss of a New Dark Age, made more sinister, and perhaps more protracted by the light of perverted science. Let us therefore brace ourselves to our duties, and so bear ourselves that, if the British Empire and its Commonwealth last a thousand years, men will say, 'This was their finest hour.'"*

Wednesday, June 19, 1940 If ever in my life I felt like giving up the ghost it was tonight after my date with Susan. For some three years my hopes and aspirations, my dreams of the future, and the air castles that I have built have centered around her, and tonight in a single sentence, she knocked the props from under my dream structure and it fell on me with a resounding blow. I was left flat. One who has never been in love; one who has never made his universe turn around a single person; one who has never made his every thought and action point in one direction, can never know what it means to have that guiding light suddenly go out. On my last date with her I suggested that we discuss her plans for the future. We went back to one of the small rooms and listened to the radio and sat before the fire and danced and talked. At about nine we began to talk seriously. She said that she had been elected President of the sorority next year and that her mother wants her to take a course in interior decorating next year. I told her my plan to work for a small company, perhaps Talon, and then one day set up a southern branch for them, or for myself. Finally I said, "Susan, we have been going together long enough for you to have some idea as to how you feel about me. You know how I feel about you."

"Do you really want me to tell you," she said. I told her to go ahead and she said she did not love me.

"Is it because of someone else?" I asked.

"No," she said, "I just don't love anyone." She went on to say though that she hoped to get married when she finds the right man. I asked her if she wanted to break our scheduled dates.

"No." she said, "Unless you do." I told her I appreciated her honesty and frankness and that I respected her right to like whom she pleases.

"It is your duty," I said, "To find the right person." After leaving her I went down to the station and talked to Jordan before he got on the Pullman for home. I told him of my conversation and suggested that however bitter the pill to swallow it is probably for the best. God works in mysterious ways, I suppose. I believe that our destinies are guided by an unseen hand for our benefit and protection, but it's sometimes hard to keep the faith. Until tonight I have dreaded the thought of leaving Nashville, but Susan has made it easy for me to go. I held up well when I was talking to her. I was fine in spirits when I talked to Jordan. But when I got back to my room, and the full impact of her statement began to dawn on me, I felt miserable. I would have been better off if I had had someone to talk to at length. I felt so alone. As I so often do in times of trouble, I sat down and began to write. I wrote her a six-page letter. At three o'clock when I finished it I was feeling a little better. I had gotten it off my chest. I went to bed and it was not long until I was asleep.

Thursday, June 20, 1940 I woke up at the crack of dawn, even though it was four o'clock this morning before I went to sleep. At six, realizing I could sleep no more, I got up, slipped on my coveralls and took an early drive in the country. Jordan dressed at my apartment last night and left his car for me to take to Dr. Mayfield's today. I drove around town for a few minutes and then, as if by instinct, headed for Franklin pike. The early morning air was invigorating and with the rising of the sun I felt a new day was dawning for me. No, it would not be the day I had hoped for, but a new day anyway. I drove out by Susan's home to get a last glimpse of the place where she lay sleeping. I drove up to a slight rise where I could see the giant oaks on the lawn and the great white pillars in front of her house. Streaks of sunlight were beginning to break though the haze and glisten on the dew wet grass. I pictured in my mind the entrance hall and the library, which I knew so well. Then my mind wandered up the circular stairway, where I had never been before, to some unknown bedroom at the end of a hallway. I could see her sleeping peacefully there, on a fluffy white pillow. She was undisturbed, but I was stricken with the cold chill of reality. I felt a tightening of the chest and throat and I began to breath with difficulty. I could feel the cooling effect of perspiration on my brow and a clammi-ness in the palms of my hands. As if by magic, the picture faded. I could not see her anymore. I could not reach out and hold her there. She was gone; and so was the beautiful world I had built with such loving hands. The picture of love and youth can never change, as long as imagination and reveries live, but they cannot diminish the bitterness of her no longer being there . . . but maybe she never was.

The End

EPILOGUE

This is the first of a multivolume series that will include the business world, just after leaving the class rooms, the life of a draftee and later a foot soldier's blow-by-blow account of the war in Europe, from the invasion at Omaha Beach to V.E. Day.

I had been in the army less than a year when I received a letter from Francis E. Williams, a PhD. at Vanderbilt, who was facing the prospect of being a "ripe involvee" in the great war. He asked for advice.

In answering the letter I gave a nutshell view of what I, as a young man involved in the war, thought of the sacrifices all of us were being called on to make. Two of my brothers were killed in the war. I am proud of having written such a letter, when I might have said with the poet, Harold E. Fey, "We who are about to die salute . . ."

In retrospect, almost 40 years later, after seeing several other generations face the same problems, and seeing some react quite differently, I subscribe to the same basic theme and commend it to future generations.

Ben Austin

VANDERBILT UNIVERSITY
Nashville, Tennessee

November 13, 1941

Dear Ben:
I was talking with Miriam McGaw today and she mentioned hearing from you at Fortress Monroe. Naturally, we were discussing the draft

situation, and as I am a ripe involvee, I was interested in the work you are doing, etc . . ."

Francis E. Williams

PRIVATE BEN AUSTIN
Fortress Monroe, Va.

November 20, 1941

Dear Francis:

I hardly know how to answer your letter and what course to advise but I am glad you wrote. Any person whose Alma Mater is Vanderbilt is a friend of mine and I'll always do what I can for him, even though the request is nothing more than advice.

I have been in the army over eight months and I don't hesitate to say that they have been enjoyable months. I have worked pretty darned hard. I have made some sacrifices and have had some disappointments, but the same was true in civilian life. I have profited from my stay in the army. I thought I understood people less fortunate than myself, but I really didn't. Perhaps I don't know now, but I certainly have a better idea about them. For instance, my experience of teaching in the illiterate school gave me a sense of humility that I had never before approached. I have learned how simply people can live; how unimportant money can be; how much excess baggage people gather about themselves in civilian life; and how happy a person can be with merely food, clothing, shelter and interesting work. Intellectual work can make free time extremely short and worthwhile.

Since you are working on your doctorate I know you hate to interrupt your work. I had a good position with the Talon Company, in the Research Division. I don't hesitate to say the future looked bright. I was in love with my work. The war altered my picture, as it is about to do yours, and I accepted it philosophically, as you must do. When a person meets necessity in the road there is only one thing to do . . . bow to it. The sensible person bows gracefully and determines to make the best of the new conditions.

Besides being a college graduate, I had had three years of military training and had attained the rank of Cadet Captain, commanding a rookie company. When I came into the army I must admit that it was quite trying to have to listen to non-coms slaughter the English language and to take orders from officers when I, myself, because of previous experience, could give the commands better than my officers. Such conditions are continually met by young people, however, in every walk of life, and learning to bide one's time is part of the game.

If you come into the army as a draftee, you will have to put up with much that will go against your grain. If you volunteer, the same is true, but being able to select your branch of the service may be an advantage. I don't know because I let nature take its course. The trouble with volunteering is that you don't know enough about the army to know what branch you are best fitted for. They assigned me to Coast Artillery, AntiAircraft, consequently I like that best. Personally I think Fortress Monroe is the best army post in the United States. There may be better ones, but I don't know about them. I do, however, know of worse ones. Sometimes it is best just to gamble with fate. Let it do its worst, and you do your best.

I once heard what I consider to be a very wise saying: "Happiness is not in doing what you like, but in liking what you do."

I would conservatively estimate that eight out of ten of the men drafted into the army don't like it. If their talk is any indication, this is true. I feel I paid as big a price as any of them, and much bigger than most, and yet I like it. Honestly and sincerely I like it. Why? Because I realized, from the beginning, that my stay in the army would be a pleasure, or misery, and I chose the former. I disciplined my mind to the extent that I even enjoyed those KP duties that I used to catch periodically. If education does not train a man to adapt himself gracefully to almost any and every condition of life, I think it has been a failure.

Therefore, I think the most important advice I can give any man who is about to become involved in the army is to develop a good philosophy; not just to accept it passively, but to enter into it with the same enthusiasm that he would in a chosen profession. I have done that and I am proud to say there has not been a happier man in the army.

Your being an English major and a man of poetic nature, as you no doubt are, I should think you would relish the idea of starting off as an enlisted man. What a marvelous opportunity to study your fellow human beings. When you get into the officer class you run into much of the sham that clutters civilian life. You would have your dignity to think of, your artificially established rank, and your social obligations. Working for a commission is desirable, I think, but you will miss a great deal if you don't start as a private.

Sorry I can't give more implicit advice, but it is every man's own problem, and he must make the decisions for himself. Frankly, there is not much to choose from. There is good and bad in all of it. If the stuff is in you you will do well in any branch of the service, if it is not, you're in for a hard time. Go in with the right attitude and I'm sure you will be a credit to yourself, your school and your country.

Sincerely yours,
Ben Austin

POSTSCRIPT

In most instances many years of drudgery and struggle go into the writing of a good book. Why does an author expend this much of himself? Very few books make money. Fame is illusory. Ask the author why and he will usually be as unknowing as the reader.

I have read about salmon swimming upstream against unthinkable odds to get to their spawning grounds. I have read of elephant grave-yards. I suppose man, like other animals, is driven by his God-given instincts, but different in one respect, he is conscious of his short time on earth and has a yearning to give a good account of himself . . . to stretch his personality beyond his given years . . . immortality.

Most authors die without knowing what impact they may have had on their fellow man; if they have succeeded in broadening understanding, or the extent of giving pleasure to others. They usually have only the limited judgment of professional critics.

What a wonderful blessing it would be if a reader of this, or any other work, would take a few minutes to write the author a short note stating his feelings about the book. Good or bad, such would be appreciated. The effort would be small compared to the author's, but the collective impact of knowing what the readers think would have a tremendous effect on the nature of literature. Many an author would write better and die happier.

Send your review to The Kilmarnock Press, Post Office Box 1302, South Pasadena, California, 91030.

INDEX